CHAINSAW

CHAI

SAW

THE NOTORIOUS CAREER OF AL DUNLAP IN THE ERA OF PROFIT-AT-ANY-PRICE

JOHN A. BYRNE

HarperBusiness
A Division of HarperCollins*Publishers*

HarperCollins books may be purchased for educational, business, or sales promotional use. For information please write: Special Markets Department, HarperCollins Publishers, Inc., 10 East 53rd Street, New York, NY 10022.

FIRST EDITION
Designed by Joseph Rutt

Library of Congress Cataloging-in-Publication Data
   Byrne, John A.
        Chainsaw : the notorious career of Al Dunlap in the era of profit-at-any-
   price / John A. Byrne.
            p.   cm.
        Includes index
        ISBN 0-06-661980-7
        1. Wall Street—History—20th century. 2. Dunlap, Albert J. (Albert
   John), 1937– . 3. Speculation—United States—History—20th century 4.
   Investments—United States—History—20th century 5. Sunbeam
   Corporation—History.
   I. Title.
   HG4572.B97   1999
   332.64'273—dc21   99-34634

99 00 01 02 03 ❖/RRD 10 9 8 7 6 5 4 3 2

For my father
John J. Byrne
a true working-class
hero from New Jersey

All ambitions are lawful except those which climb upward on the miseries or credulities of mankind.

Joseph Conrad

CONTENTS

THE PRINCIPAL PLAYERS

The Big Investors

    Michael Price, Mutual Series Fund

    Michael Steinhardt, Steinhardt Partners

    Ronald Perelman, chairman of MacAndrews & Forbes Inc.

The Wall Street Analysts

    Andrew Shore, PaineWebber

    Nicholas P. Heymann, Prudential Securities

    Elisabeth Fontenelli, Goldman Sachs

    William Steele, Buckingham Research

    Constance M. Maneaty, Bear, Stearns

    Deepak Raj, Merrill Lynch

    R. Scott Graham, CIBC Oppenheimer

The Chief Executives

    Paul Kazarian, 1991–1993

    Roger Schipke, 1993–1996

    Albert Dunlap, 1996–1998

    Jerry Levin, 1998-

The Management Team

Under Albert Dunlap

    Russell A. Kersh, vice chairman and chief financial officer

    David Fannin, chief legal officer

    Lee Griffith, president, household products group

    Frank Feraco, president, outdoor leisure group

    Robert Gluck, controller

    Donald R. Uzzi, senior vice president

    Rich Goudis, vice president, investor relations

James Wilson, vice president, human resources

Gary Mask, vice president, human resources

Dixon Thayer, vice president, international

Newt White, executive vice president, consumer products

Ronald Newcomb, vice president, manufacturing

Kevin McBride, vice president, marketing

Paula Etchison, director, new business

The Outside Advisers

Donald Burnett, Coopers & Lybrand

Philip Harlow, Arthur Andersen

Mark C. Davis, Chase Securities

William Strong, Morgan Stanley Dean Witter

Blaine "Finn" Fogg, Skadden, Arps, Slate, Meagher & Flom

The Board of Directors

Peter Langerman, Mutual Series Fund

Howard Kristol, Reboul, MacMurray, Hewitt, Maynard & Kristol

Charles Elson, Stetson University law professor

Faith Whittlesey, president, American Swiss Foundation

William T. Rutter, senior vice president, First Union National Bank

Shimon Topor, Steinhardt Partners

PROLOGUE

ALBERT J. DUNLAP, the mercurial chief executive of Sunbeam Corp., settled into his first-class seat aboard a Northwest Airlines jet. The Detroit-bound plane leveled to cruising altitude when Dunlap's traveling companion, Donald R. Uzzi, flipped down his food tray and pulled a sheaf of financial documents out of his leather briefcase.

Uzzi, Sunbeam's top operating executive, planned to make an unusual appeal to his boss on this wintry day in January, 1997. He was going to ask Dunlap, widely known as Chainsaw Al for his brutal cutbacks of people and plants, to reconsider a decision to close down a small factory in Bay Springs, Mississippi. The plant employed only 125 people, but Uzzi and his fellow executives believed it made no economic sense to lay off the skilled laborers at the facility.

Indeed, when the details of the decision crossed Uzzi's desk, the long-time marketing executive wondered if Dunlap or his chief financial officer, Russell Kersh, were trying to test his financial competence. To save less than $200,000 a year in transportation costs, the company would have to spend up to $10 million to close the plant and consolidate it with another forty miles away. The appliance maker wouldn't see a payback on the closure for decades, if ever.

"I thought it had to be some sort of trick," recalled Uzzi. "I thought Russ or Al was trying to see if I knew what I was doing."

As Uzzi and others later discovered, it was hardly a test or a prank. Dunlap, who had built his career on draconian downsizings, understood that Wall Street handsomely rewarded companies that shuttered plants and laid off workers. The more people a company fired, the more Wall Street seemed to applaud, sending a company's stock price higher and higher. In the 1990s, when corporate downsizing seemed almost trendy, Dunlap had emerged as one of the most celebrated executives on the Street.

After heading up the Scott Paper Co. for 18 months as its chief executive, Dunlap drove the stock price up by 225%, increasing the company's market value by $6.3 billion. At Scott, the self-styled turnaround artist fired 11,000 employees, cut all corporate philanthropy, slashed expenditures on plant improvements and research, and then sold the company to a major rival. Wall Street cheered as Scott became the sixth consecutive company that was sold or dismembered by Dunlap since 1983.

He was recruited to troubled Sunbeam by two of Wall Street's most powerful and savvy investors, mutual fund maven Michael Price and hedge fund superstar Michael Steinhardt. Within days of taking over the company in mid–1996, Dunlap promised a dramatic restructuring. The Bay Springs closure was part of his plan to rid Sunbeam of half its 12,000 employees and eighteen of its twenty-six plants.

So when Uzzi tried to bring Dunlap's attention to the financial documents to make his appeal, his boss quickly rebuffed him. Dunlap already was livid that the mayor of Bay Springs had become an outspoken critic of him. Dunlap had previously told Uzzi and other executives that he would not reconsider the decision, in part, because he wanted to show that the mayor of a small backwoods town could not oppose him and win.

"Forget it!" growled Dunlap, as Uzzi attempted to make his case on the airplane.

The startled executive tried to bring up the subject several times during the flight, but it was futile. Dunlap had made his decision, and he was obviously sticking to it. Uzzi, as aptly surnamed an executive as one could find in a Dunlap company, shoved the papers back into his briefcase and ordered a drink.

Dunlap had become the leading champion of a new management philosophy, "shareholder value creation." Like investor Michael Price, he decried the more traditional view of the firm that said that corporations have many constituencies: stockholders, customers, employees and the communities in which they do business. To Dunlap, the only people who really mattered were those who put their money on the line, people like Price and Steinhardt, the investors. "Stakeholders are total rubbish," insisted Dunlap. "It's the shareholders who own the company."

In the 1980s and 1990s, the growing acceptance of that powerful idea helped to transform the economic landscape. To enhance profits and boost stock prices, American corporations shed millions of employees and thousands of plants. The massive cutbacks, though assailed by many Europeans as "jungle capitalism," led to huge gains in productivity and wealth, the longest bull market on the stock exchange, and the largest peacetime expansion of economic growth in U.S. history. For a while, at least, it also led to Wall Street's canonization of Dunlap.

But when shareholder value creation becomes not merely the highest goal, but the only goal, something else happens as well: organizations become committed to maximize short-term performance and to satisfy only short-term investors. Downsizing is taken to its illogical extreme, increasingly divorced from reality and economic sense, and increasingly informed by personal animus, ego and greed. The story of Dunlap's rise and fall is emblematic of its costly downside.

1

MEAN BUSINESS (THE NONFICTION VERSION)

ONE BY ONE, they briskly walked into the penthouse boardroom of the Sun-Sentinel building in Fort Lauderdale, Florida. It was the only truly exquisite space at Sunbeam Corp. headquarters. Perched atop the modern glass-and-concrete structure in a dome, twenty-one floors up from the ground, it offered stunning views of the Atlantic Ocean. Through the vast tinted windows on three walls, visitors could see the sun glisten off the ocean's surface, watch the rolling waves of incoming storms, and glimpse the sea gulls gliding on the salty air.

The men, restive and fidgety, took their places in the dark green leather chairs around the mahogany table.

James J. Clegg, the towering chief operating officer, had canceled his family vacation in the Caribbean to be there. He had flown in from Chicago's O'Hare Airport the night before with Richard L. Boynton, Jr., the feisty and volatile president of the household products division. Rob Johnson, the acting head of outdoor products, had come from Nashville, where he was based.

1

Corporate staff were there already, waiting for the man who would soon decide their fates. David Fannin, an earnest Kentucky lawyer who had been the company's chief counsel, had hammered out an employment contract for Dunlap's longtime sidekick Russell Kersh so that Kersh could be at Dunlap's side on his very first day of work. Paul O'Hara, the lanky chief financial officer, and James Wilson, the thin-as-a-rail head of human resources, didn't know what to expect.

At precisely 9 A.M., on this Monday, July 22, Albert J. Dunlap marched into the room without introduction, without issuing a single greeting to any of the anxious men around the table. He looked exactly as he appeared in many of the photographs that accompanied the various articles the men had read that weekend. He wore his pinstripes like a military uniform, meticulously pressed, without a single wrinkle or a stray thread, and perfectly fitted to his stocky frame. A white handkerchief peeked out of the chest pocket on his dark blue suit jacket. On his left hand, he sported a chunky West Point class ring above his gold wedding band.

The silver-haired Dunlap also wore a severe look on his face. His hard blue eyes, hidden by dark glasses, canvassed the room, fixing on each one of them. Only Spencer J. Volk, the baritone-voiced international president, was missing. Just moments before Dunlap's entrance, he had gone out to the men's room. And when he returned, no more than a minute past the appointed start time, Dunlap attacked him with vigor.

"Who are you?" he shouted as the man gingerly tiptoed to his seat.

"I'm Spencer Volk, sir. I'm head of international business," he said in a voice as smooth as a network television anchor's.

"Why are you late?" barked Dunlap.

"I was in the men's room," Volk nearly whispered.

"When I say we have a meeting at 9 o'clock," bellowed Dunlap, "it starts at 9! Gentlemen, look at your watches. Your lives will never be the same from this moment onward."

Like George C. Scott in the movie *Patton*, Dunlap began by delivering a spellbinding, if sometimes disjointed, monologue on himself and the company.

"The old Sunbeam is over today!" he proclaimed. "Let's get one thing clear: By God, I'm not Schipke. And I'm not Kazarian," he said, referring to the company's two previous chief executives, Roger Schipke and Paul Kazarian.

"You guys are responsible for the demise of Sunbeam!" Dunlap roared, tossing his glasses onto the table. "You are the ones who have played this political, bullshit game with Michael Price and Michael Steinhardt. You are the guys responsible for this crap, and I'm here to tell you that things have changed. The old Sunbeam is over today. It's over!"

Glaring fiercely, Dunlap kept repeating the phrase, again and again, saliva sputtering from his lips. His chest was puffed out and his face flushed a bright red. The men stared in silence, incredulous at this outrageous performance, almost expecting Dunlap, like Patton, to slap someone out of frustration. Dunlap's bluster and mad grin, his oversized gleaming teeth too big for his face, seemed to fill the room.

"This is the best day of your life if you are good at what you do and willing to accept change," continued Dunlap, through his clenched teeth. "And it's the worst day of your life if you're not."

Virtually every executive there already believed that his survival would be merely a matter of chance. What they knew about the business or what they had achieved in the past was irrelevant. Survivors, they would soon understand, had to humbly accept blame for failure, and had to swear allegiance to Al and to Russ. Little else mattered.

Because on this day, the first day of the Dunlap era, they were a bunch of duds. They were losers and washouts, directly responsible for the company's failures. Dunlap wanted them to know that's all they were: corporate trash. P. Newton White, who had worked with Dunlap at Scott Paper and would soon join the team at Sunbeam, thought that Dunlap's management skills came right out of the military. "Yeah, Al, I understand," he would say, "piss all over them and then we'll build them back up." Except that some didn't want to be reconstructed by an Albert Dunlap. Some of them already wanted out. At least then they could take their severance pay and walk away from what was surely going to be a living hell, working for an impulsive and abusive loudmouth.

Dunlap tossed off questions and remarks as if they were hand grenades, waiting for an explosion to occur. After noting that Sunbeam had missed five consecutive quarters of profit and revenue estimates, he turned to Paul O'Hara, the company's chief financial officer, who sat next to him, and said: "And you delivered these numbers. How could you in good conscience have done that? How could you have supported these forecasts?" O'Hara could not answer the question, nor did he dare to provide a response.

Michael Price and Michael Steinhardt could not have picked a more extreme opposite of Sunbeam's previous boss. Roger Schipke was a quiet, unassuming man with refined and subtle tastes. He was an executive of integrity and honor, his business judgment informed by his decades at General Electric Co., the academy of Corporate America. He was soft-spoken, well-reasoned, extraordinarily good-hearted, and eminently likable because he seemed so pleasant and agreeable. Unfortunately, though, these were the attributes that contributed to his downfall.

Their new boss, on the other hand, sat at the table like an imperial demagogue. He cheered his own past accomplishments, reminding the men that he had done eight turnarounds on three continents and Sunbeam would be his ninth. He even urged them to buy his forthcoming book, *Mean Business: How I Save Bad Companies and Make Good Companies Great*, so they would know exactly what he expected from them.

After a ten-minute harangue, Dunlap seemed ready to hear the presentations the men had prepared.

"All right," he said, "let's get started."

Clegg, the president and chief operating officer, was first. He had long coveted the job that was now Dunlap's. He had campaigned for it, had been told he was a legitimate candidate by Peter Langerman, who was Michael Price's top lieutenant and representative on the board. Clegg believed that he deserved the chance to lead the company. He had joined Sunbeam when it was in bankruptcy in December 1988 and had been instrumental in the company's turnaround under Schipke and Kazarian. A strapping ex-basketball jock, he had proven himself a master salesman and had more support in the company than any other executive.

What Clegg didn't know was that he was walking into an ambush. Before his arrival, Dunlap had conferred with longtime director Charles Thayer, who had told him that Clegg was not a keeper. He had undermined Schipke, tried to get his boss fired, and was just as responsible for the missed numbers as Schipke himself.

"Okay," said Dunlap, "let's talk about competitors. What do you know?"

Clegg began to give a lengthy and detailed answer to Dunlap, who simply wanted a quick rundown of the major competitors and their market shares. Frustrated by the detail in Clegg's response, Dunlap cut him off and accused him of not knowing the details of his business.

"That's enough," Dunlap said. "That's enough."

"He actually thought I didn't know this stuff," recalled Clegg. "I had been to every housewares show in the past eight years. I not only knew the competition, I knew where their factories were located and what each one made. I knew all the people in the business. But it was not an exercise to find anything out. It was an exercise to see if he could humiliate me."

Though some had spent hours preparing elaborate presentations, most were forced to keep their remarks short. It was rare for anyone to get more than fifteen or twenty words out before Dunlap broke in with a pointed question. When anyone hesitated, even momentarily, Dunlap would snap: "I expect you to know these things." "It was like a dog barking at you for hours," Boynton later said. "He just yelled, ranted, and raved. He was condescending, belligerent, and disrespectful." Recalled attorney Fannin: "It was a very, very hostile environment. Everything was a confrontation and a put-down."

Indeed, the men noticed something especially bizarre about their new boss: It was as if he were a fighter in a ring, as he had been at West Point, carefully pacing himself, delivering words as if they were blows. "He would get going and then kind of calm down, and then say something to himself that would drive him off again," said James Wilson, the head of human resources. "The guy had an incredible capacity for elevating his voice and keeping it up there for hours and hours."

Dunlap cut the day up into pieces, rarely sitting still for more than fifteen minutes at a time. He would simply get up, pace the floor or leave the room to take or return a phone call from a reporter or a Wall Street analyst. Sometimes he would walk out with Kersh and Thayer, from whom he would solicit opinions of the men in the boardroom. Based on the presentation, Dunlap believed Boynton came across confident and authoritative. Dunlap told colleagues he thought he might keep him. Clegg, on the other hand, was a goner.

Back inside the meeting, after yet another break, Dunlap asked O'Hara for his presentation.

"Well," O'Hara opined, "the reason you're here is because we weren't able to do a number of things. Here's some of the things we need to do." O'Hara then went through a long list of suggested items, culled from a memo written a month earlier by Rich Goudis, a young, enterprising financial analyst at the company. O'Hara urged Dunlap to close down several facilities and consolidate them into the new Hattiesburg, Mississippi, plant, and to ditch dozens of unprofitable products the company still produced. "We've got to reduce costs," said O'Hara.

This was exactly what Dunlap, who had made a career out of cutting back on everything from plants and products to people and research, wanted to hear. As the chief financial officer went through a laundry list of cuts, Dunlap began taking copious notes for the first time.

"Are these your ideas?" asked Dunlap, his voice finally softening.

"Well, yes, I'm putting them forward," replied O'Hara.

Clegg smirked. A month earlier, he had required that O'Hara provide this information. Now, O'Hara was posturing, as if the list of money-losers was something new.

"Do you think any of this is funny?" barked Dunlap.

"No," muttered Clegg.

"Then, what's that look on your face," he snapped.

"Al, it's been a long time since I've sat and listened to this much bullshit."

"God, it can be dangerous in here," Dunlap countered, apparently enjoying the dissension he had encouraged. "A person could lose an eye."

Rich Boynton, Clegg's longtime friend, quietly steamed. At the first break after the exchange, he called his office in Schaumberg, Illinois, and told his lieutenants: "O'Hara is dead. Cut him off. Don't even talk to him." Today, Boynton says "He was *et tu Brute*. He stabbed Clegg right in the back. I had never seen anything like it."

Back in the boardroom later, Dunlap was off again, into a rage of questions for which only Schipke had answers.

"Why do we have so many headquarters?" Dunlap demanded. "It doesn't make sense."

No one could advance a reason—because the company did not have the six separate headquarters Dunlap claimed. The offices outside of Fort Lauderdale were simply branches.

"Either somebody is bullshitting me, or they just don't understand business. Which is it?" There really was no answer.

Dunlap's day-long attack stunned the men. "I don't think there had ever been a meeting in my life where I stared at the top of my shoes for that long," said Wilson, head of human resources. "He screamed at us all morning. It had to last three to three and one-half hours. He went after each one of us individually. He was so intimidating that when he finished, we didn't know which end was up."

No less stunning was that Dunlap then expected the battered group to join him for a private dinner at the Chart House, a restaurant a couple of blocks from headquarters. He had arranged for a private room upstairs where everyone could sit around a single table. It simply prolonged an excruciating day. Most of them sat quietly, listening to Dunlap tell stories that flattered only himself and his confidant Russell Kersh, whom he praised as one of the finest executives in America. "We didn't know what subjects to bring up or what to chat about," said Rob Johnson. "You could feel the tension in the room." Nearly everyone at the restaurant wished the entree had been dessert.

IT DID NOT TAKE very long for Dunlap to claim his first victim. During a break in the presentations on the second day, he had huddled again in his office with Kersh and Fannin.

"It's obvious that Jim Clegg can't work for us," Dunlap told them. "We've got to get rid of him, and there will probably be some others, but I want to do this right now. You do the paperwork to get rid of him," he told Fannin.

The lawyer knew Clegg would be the first to go, but he had no idea it would be so quickly. Like the others holed up in the boardroom, Fannin had listened in horror to Dunlap's verbal assault on Clegg. "You had to feel sorry for him," said Fannin later. "You knew he was going to get killed. It was like in England where they used to make the condemned ride to the scaffolds on their own coffins. You're forced to go through this humiliation, only to be fired."

Wasting no time, Dunlap sent Schipke's administrative assistant, Sharon Grussing, to get Clegg. She stuck her head inside the boardroom door where he was waiting with the other executives and asked if he had a minute to meet with Dunlap. He walked down the hall and into Schipke's old office where Dunlap sat behind his desk, with Kersh, Fannin, and Thayer seated around the room.

"You know," Dunlap said, "you're just not going to fit into the team."

Clegg looked at Dunlap blankly, with a mixture of relief and resignation.

"I understand," he said softly, his eyes moist.

"It's better we part ways now. Go with David Fannin and he'll have you sign the papers. We'll honor your contract."

Clegg slowly walked Fannin back to his office in the southeast corner of the building. There, the general counsel sadly handed him a standard release form that spelled out his severance and confidentiality agreement, giving him a year's salary, his already vested stock options, and only a month's worth of medical benefits.

"Jim," said Fannin, "on a personal level, I'm very sorry it came to this. But you may turn out to be luckier than the rest of us."

Clegg asked a few brief questions about exercising his stock options on more than 140,000 Sunbeam shares, many of them accumulated from the days he had worked for Kazarian, some of which were priced as low as $5 a share. They were worth millions of dollars, enough to cushion the financial, if not emotional, blow from the loss of this job. Then he left. Less than fifteen minutes after leaving the boardroom, he returned to pack his briefcase. "I'm out," he said to his shocked colleagues. He strolled to the elevator banks and once down caught a taxi to his hotel, where he called his wife, Cynthia, to tell her the news. "It was shocking and it hurt," she remembered. "Because it was Dunlap who did it, it seemed to dig a little deeper."

Not content to simply fire him, Dunlap wanted to publicly humiliate Clegg as well. He insisted on issuing a press release to trumpet the news that he had fired Clegg and to blame him for many of the company's problems. Fannin hoped to convince Dunlap not to do it. "Look, we don't want to be sued because of a press release," he told Dunlap.

That did not deter his new boss, who wanted the outside world to see how quickly he could draw first blood. He insisted that the news get out. Fannin later drafted a short release that failed to completely satisfy Dunlap, who badly wanted to put out something that would sting more. "Anybody who knows anything knows that this says the guy was fired—and this is as bad as it needs to be," recalled Fannin. Kersh agreed that the announcement should be as short as possible and to the point.

The very next day, July 24, Sunbeam announced that the company's second-quarter earnings fell 36 percent on sales that were 12 percent higher, and that Clegg was gone.

"As reflected in our quarterly earnings release earlier today, the poor performance of Sunbeam obviously will require a massive restructuring," Dunlap said in the statement. "To accomplish this, we will be recruiting an executive to run the operations of the company on a global basis. I expect to announce this appointment quickly. Other organizational changes will be forthcoming as well.

"Consistent with this decision, Jim Clegg, formerly chief operating officer, North America, is no longer with the company, effective immediately."

The juxtaposition of the two sentences made it clear that Clegg was taking the fall for Sunbeam's poor performance. Only Fannin's pleadings made this a bit less pointed. That same day, Dunlap announced that Kersh would be executive vice president of finance and administration.

The most unusual part of Clegg's firing wasn't the fact that it was done arbitrarily or capriciously, within two days of Dunlap's ascension to power—and before any new executive could legitimately assess whether Clegg could have helped him. It also wasn't the fact that Dunlap rushed to announce the firing. The most extraordinary part of it was that Dunlap did the firing himself. For although he had laid off tens of thousands of employees over the course of his career, Dunlap had rarely fired anyone on his own.

The Dunlap era had officially begun at Sunbeam.

2

"I SO LOVE THEM"

THE DAY AFTER Sunbeam announced that Albert Dunlap would be its new chief executive, Andrew Shore could not take his eyes off the computer screen on his cluttered desk. The PaineWebber Inc. analyst was bewildered by the constantly changing numbers blinking in front of him. Throughout that day, July 19, Sunbeam's stock price soared higher and higher. It had opened at $12.50 a share and was approaching the $20 mark.

Whenever Shore gets jittery, which is often, he paces the floor in his stocking feet and a blue oxford shirt. His well-shined black shoes are tucked under his desk, while his blue-pinstriped jacket hangs behind the door of his midtown New York City office. Shore's shiny swept-back hair and rapid-fire speech make him look and sound like a slick salesman. His voice rises and falls as quickly as a roller-coaster, nearly matching the intensity in his eyes.

In the 1990s securities analysts like Shore had become the new, powerful stars of Wall Street. Their recommendations moved billions of dollars in and out of stocks every day. Their connections often led to mergers and acquisitions that brought brokerage houses millions of dollars in investment banking fees and trading commissions.

Not all that long ago, they were, as one observer put it, "the mole-like civil servants of the brokerage world." Their bland and lengthy reports on the strengths and weaknesses of publicly traded companies were snail-mailed to clients who then decided whether to buy or sell the stocks. Then personal computers and the Internet effectively put a stock ticker into every household that has spare cash to invest in the market. It also lent analyst recommendations, which now traveled over the Internet, sometimes dangerous speed and power. For every analyst, the stakes had moved appreciably higher as had the need to act quickly, if not impulsively, on every shred of news or rumor and every new financial number that spilled into the marketplace.

So on July 19, as Sunbeam stock powered ahead, Shore felt unsettled. Sometimes picking a stock is like running with the bulls in Pamplona. You jump in for a moment, then skip out of the way fast, before you get gored. Shore wondered if he should run with the crazy bulls on this one. Was he missing something big and exciting? Several of Shore's rivals at other brokerage houses jumped on the news, and were heartened by Dunlap's appointment. "This is like the Lakers signing Shaquille O'Neal," declared Scott Graham, an analyst at Oppenheimer & Co. Nicholas P. Heymann of NatWest Securities instantly slapped a buy rating on the stock. So did Dean Witter Reynolds' upbeat William H. Steele, who soon would maintain that Sunbeam had become "a more disciplined company" from the day Dunlap was hired.

The intense Shore, however, did not share the instantaneous enthusiasm of his Wall Street brethren. He had been an analyst long enough to know that the stock market could certainly act irrationally. This run-up in Sunbeam's shares made no sense to him at all. On a typical day, fewer than 200,000 Sunbeam shares were traded. On July 19, well over 7 million shares changed hands. By day's end, the stock had shot up nearly 60 percent, to $18.63, the largest jump in the exchange's history.

Shore simply didn't believe the appointment of a new CEO was all that big a deal. He even refused to heed the advice of an esteemed PaineWebber colleague, Richard Schneider, that he change his "neutral" rating on Sunbeam. The day before, when the news moved over the ticker and the exchange halted trading in the stock, Schneider had urged him to put out an "immediate" buy. "He's going to make big money," he advised. "He's great at cutting costs."

Schneider, who covered paper and forest-product companies, knew full well the magic of Dunlap's name on Wall Street. Schneider had become the industry's leading analyst thanks to Dunlap. Schneider had been visiting Scott's Philadelphia headquarters the day Dunlap's predecessor, Philip E. Lippincott, announced his resignation. He felt sure that the board would seek a more decisive successor and began recommending the stock a full five months before Dunlap arrived.

Investors who followed his advice and were patient enough to hang on made a killing: Schneider tapped the stock at $38 a share and it ran up to $120. Lauded by his clients for the timely stock pick, he won enough votes from them to become the industry's number-one analyst in *Institutional Investor*'s rankings of Wall Street's best both in 1995 and 1996. For Schneider, that meant more than mere prestige. It meant big money, because the top analysts also garnered the highest pay. A number-one ranking in the business magazine was worth between $1.5 million and $2 million a year in pay.

Shore, too, had won his share of accolades and compensation. He had been trained by the legendary Perrin Long, a well-regarded analyst who long covered the brokerage businesss. The pipe-smoking analyst taught Shore the value of hard work and skepticism in the early 1980s, shortly after Shore entered the world of Wall Street in 1982. Now, at the age of thirty-five, he was pulling down more than $1 million a year for a job he considered "the greatest in the world." "Where else can you get paid what I am paid, besides selling drugs, doing pornography, or being an athlete!" he later quipped. Year after year, his investing clients heaped praise on him for the quality of his research reports, but he had never taken home the winner's trophy in the industries he watched over, cosmetics and household products. The best Shore had done was place second in 1995. Holding cautious on Sunbeam while its stock was skyrocketing wasn't going to help him gain any ground.

Even worse, a day earlier, the outspoken Shore had said some rather unflattering things about Dunlap to a *Wall Street Journal* reporter. Shore was articulate and eager to give his opinions, shouting into the receiver that "Al Dunlap is the perfect announcement to give the Street, because the Street wants to believe he can do with Sunbeam what he did with Scott Paper. But his history is as a cost-cutter and not a brand-builder—and Sunbeam's problems are more sales-related."

SOON AFTER getting up at 5:30 A.M. at his Boca Raton home, Dunlap rushed to pick up Friday's *Journal* to read its treatment of the announcement. When he got to Shore's remarks in the story's fourth paragraph, he was incensed. It made him even angrier to think that a *Journal* reporter would quote this Shore character before himself. Though Dunlap eagerly courted the media and greatly enjoyed reading stories about himself, he easily became enraged over the slightest negative reference.

He understood that analysts could move the stock up or down with a single comment. As institutional investors, from pension funds to mutual funds like Price's, have come to dominate the markets, analysts like Shore have become more powerful than ever. If Shore could convince a major client to buy a sizable chunk of stock in a recommended company, it's possible to move the market with a single sale. So winning over the analysts is crucial to getting the largest institutional investors to invest tens of millions of dollars in your company. None of this was lost on Dunlap, whose book includes a chapter entitled "Impressing the Analysts."

At Scott, Dunlap spent an inordinate amount of time romancing the people who followed the paper industry, and he was a master of it. Dunlap also realized that when he enlisted the support of an analyst, he also gained an advocate to help broadcast his own message. TV shows devoted to business news and financial magazines had a voracious appetite for material, and analysts were happy to satisfy it. At Scott, it paid off handsomely. Friendly analysts, who came to view Dunlap as the perfect profit-maximizer, gushed that Chainsaw was everything from a "hero" to "a gift from heaven."

Aside from Shore's doubts, the positive "buzz" was already working at Sunbeam. Dunlap had used the first tense boardroom sessions with the company's management team to prep himself for an upcoming telephone conference call with several hundred analysts, investors and business reporters. Dunlap had been on the job only two days, but he wanted to show everyone how quickly he could move. So on Wednesday, July 24, he got on the phone in his office and began talking away as if he had all the company's problems diagnosed and was ready to prescribe a treatment. Dunlap told the analysts that, if he were a Sunbeam shareholder, he would have "hung" former management. He pledged a "massive and swift restructuring" to turn the company around in less than a year. "We've got too many people, too many products, too many facilities, and too many headquarters," Dunlap proclaimed.

Shore wasn't impressed. Hearing Dunlap's high-volume voice for the first time, he thought the man was all bombastic bluster. When the *Journal* called Shore again for a comment, he wasn't very favorable. "Costs are not the company's biggest problem right now," he told the *Journal*. "The real issue is growth. But Al will continue to do what he does best—and that's cut costs." During the call, Dunlap also announced that the company's net income fell by 37 percent in the second quarter. Still, to Shore's chagrin, the stock kept rising, up 75 cents that day, to $19 a share.

Shore, who follows fifteen companies ranging from Procter & Gamble to Colgate-Palmolive, takes his analysis personally. When he sits on the sidelines of a stock or downgrades another, he quietly roots against the companies. When he advocates a buy, he becomes a gleeful cheerleader. "The greatest thing in the world about this job is that it gives you almost instant gratification," he said. "When Gillette is down three points, that feels good in a perverse way if you don't like Gillette." So it bugged him, in a way, that Sunbeam was doing so well while he continued to sit on his neutral rating—especially when many of the other analysts were touting the stock.

But Shore held firm. By the end of July, when he issued his first research report under Dunlap, he even began to sound a wee bit defensive over his stance. "We have never upgraded a stock based upon the appointment of a new CEO," he wrote. "Until Mr. Dunlap formulates a growth plan, we remain undecided on the Sunbeam story and do not believe his designation was worth $500 million in additional market capital in one day. Cutting costs is the easy task; growing sales will be the real challenge and the market will have to wait for that outcome."

DUNLAP DIDN'T SUFFER fools gladly, and he told his Sunbeam team he was certain that Shore was a fool. Angry over his report and his quotations in the *Journal*, he derisively called the analyst "a peanut at a gourmet dinner." He told some associates he was angry as hell at Shore for his critical comments. "Andrew immediately became public enemy number one," said James Wilson, vice president of human resources. By late September, Wall Street's analysts began their pilgrimage to Sunbeam's headquarters in Fort Lauderdale to hear what Sunbeam's new boss had to say. One by one, Dunlap met with the small fraternity of about a dozen analysts who followed the company. He wasn't going to lock out Shore.

On October 3, with Sunbeam's stock now up 92 percent, to $23.50 a share, the PaineWebber analyst and one of his two research associates boarded a plane at La Guardia Airport to meet Dunlap for the first time. To prepare for the session, Shore had spent two nights reading the 287 pages of Dunlap's just-published book. In it Dunlap boasted that he was "a superstar in my field, much like Michael Jordan in basketball or Bruce Springsteen in rock 'n' roll."

Like many, Shore was put off by the self-congratulatory tone of the text as well as its superficiality. "It was as if my fifteen-month-old had written it," Shore joked. And he wondered why the memoir contained more about Dunlap's dogs than his only son. Shore and Hari Chandra, his Indian-born associate, had assembled five pages of questions they hoped would help them discern Dunlap's strategy for turning the company around.

Shore had no idea what to expect. Less than a week before his first visit with Dunlap, he had heaped still more criticism on the chieftain in yet another *Wall Street Journal* story published on September 27, 1996. Under the headline "Is It Time Yet to Cash Out of Sunbeam," the newspaper reported that Michael Steinhardt had distributed his hedge fund's 21 percent stake in Sunbeam to his investors and partners. Steinhardt had been winding down his fund, and the Sunbeam stock was the last investment his fund still owned. Rather than sell and hand the proceeds back to investors, he decided simply to do a distribution.

In the story, Shore noted that Sunbeam stock was trading about twenty-two times its expected earnings of $1.07 a share for 1997, a higher multiple than enjoyed by Procter & Gamble, which was selling at twenty-one times projected earnings. "There's at least $5 of takeover froth" in Sunbeam's price, said Shore. "My guess is that the company also has been shopped for some time and there were no buyers." If Sunbeam doesn't earn much more than $1 a share next year, the analyst added, "then on a fundamental basis, it's one of the most overvalued stocks in the market."

Dunlap, already angry because he feared Wall Street might interpret Steinhardt's decision as a signal to take profits and sell the stock, threw a tantrum when he heard what Shore had told the *Journal*. He called the analyst "really totally out of step" with other, more bullish observers on the street. The stock price, Dunlap said, was still $4 below its 1994 high of $26, a level achieved "by the same management that I just fired" at a company that was "a doormat, an absolute basket case for years."

This latest salvo, Shore knew, would not help to endear him to the new Sunbeam chief. Besides, no one could ever predict Dunlap's behavior.

The anecdotes Shore had heard about the man from other analysts were plentiful and memorable. Nearly every Wall Street analyst had a favorite Dunlap story to tell, because while at Scott, he quickly won a reputation as an unconventional executive with a flair for the theatrical. After meeting with potential investors at the New York offices of Brown Brothers Harriman & Co. in 1994, Dunlap had ventured into the men's room to wash his hands. To his dismay, he discovered that the Scott Paper towel dispensers failed to contain his company's paper products. Furious, Dunlap began pulling out all the paper towels in the dispensers. Then he scurried into each of the stalls to rip out the toilet paper. Once through, he pushed open the door of the men's room and tossed all the offending tissue onto the hallway floor. Dunlap immediately searched for the Wall Street analyst who invited him to the meeting and proceeded to deliver a stern lecture. "I make toilet paper," he shouted, "and you people buy lousy toilet paper! For God's sake, look at the amount of money your shareholders have made on my stock, and you have crummy toilet paper! I want to see you buying better toilet paper."

So when Shore and his associate arrived in Fort Lauderdale and entered Dunlap's office, the analyst was already on edge. The chief executive immediately gave him good reason to feel that way. A glaring Dunlap stood as still and icy as a statue, his hands tucked under his armpits. Three other Sunbeam executives, including Kersh and Fannin, were standing just as Dunlap with arms folded across their chests. After he only reluctantly shook Shore's hand, Dunlap's face began to turn an angry shade of red.

"How dare you give a quote to the *Journal* before you even talked to us?" he bellowed. "You're completely off base."

"Look," retorted a tense Shore, "now that I'm here you can get me back on base."

"I'd rather teach you about the facts of life," Dunlap shot back.

"That's okay," Shore replied, "my father has done a pretty good job of that."

Even before they took their seats, Shore was drenched in sweat, his shirt soaked through with perspiration. The way this is going, he thought, would make it the shortest meeting he ever attended. But he wasn't about to be bullied out of the office. Shore was cocky enough to believe that he knew more about Sunbeam than Dunlap. Shore had been tracking the household products and cosmetics industries for a decade. He had kept a keen eye on Sunbeam since 1992, when PaineWebber was one of four brokerage houses that helped bring the company public. Almost to the day four years earlier, he had gone to a management review session at Merrill Lynch to hear Paul Kazarian and his executive team talk through the appliance company's history and financial numbers.

Without giving Shore an opening, Dunlap launched into a speech, telling him that Sunbeam was going to be his ninth turnaround in a row.

"Have you read chapter three of my book?" he asked, taking out *Mean Business* and opening to a page to read a few sentences aloud.

"Well, if you read chapter two, you'll see what I did at Scott."

"Al," Shore finally said, "I'm not here for your book tour. I read your book. I have a bunch of serious questions about the company."

Shore opened his black leather notebook to begin asking questions and taking notes when a picture of Magoo, his golden retriever, slipped out and onto the floor.

"Ahhhhhh," said Dunlap, peeking over his desk, "is that your dog?"

Suddenly, for the first time in the meeting, Dunlap's personality seemed to change. Previously aloof and condescending, he now seemed instantly warm and charming. Dunlap grabbed the two pictures of his German shepherds, Cadet III and Brit, and proudly showed them to Shore as if they were his children.

In truth, they were. At night the dogs retired to the master bedroom of Dunlap's home, where they sprawled out on twin bean bag beds not far from Dunlap and his wife, Judy. When he and Judy moved to a luxurious suite at the Philadelphia Four Seasons after Dunlap assumed the job at Scott Paper, the dogs had their own suite at the same posh hotel for seven weeks at the company's expense. In his will, Dunlap left detailed instructions for the care of his beloved dogs should he and his wife die. His bodyguard would be given custody of the pets and $1 million for each dog to insure that they could live in the lifestyle to which they had become accustomed.

"I so love them," Dunlap said, handing Shore the photographs. "You know, if you want a friend, you get a dog. I have two, to hedge my bets."

Shore had heard the exact same line before, in one of the many articles he had read about Dunlap. But he laughed, and the continuing banter about the dogs put Sunbeam's new chief into a more cooperative mood. Dunlap told him that Sunbeam was in worse shape than Scott Paper. The old Sunbeam, he said, claimed costs were okay, missed sales projections, had no substantive new product ideas, had abysmal purchasing, no vision, and indecisive decision making. Dunlap said he would change all that, but he was vague on specifics. An army of consultants from Coopers & Lybrand was dissecting the company's operations and would deliver the results to him by the end of the month. By mid-November, Dunlap said, he would be ready to detail the findings and discuss his strategy.

Their two-hour session ended with Dunlap convinced he had won over the skeptical Shore. But over lunch with Dunlap's investor relations manager John DeSimone, Shore was digging to get more information on exactly what Dunlap planned to do. Failing to gain much more insight, he asked: "How come Al's son is only mentioned once in the book? If that was my book, I would mention my family and friends more than anything else."

"I don't really know the nature of their relationship," DeSimone replied. What the men did not know was that Dunlap's slight mention of his son hid a darker part of his life.

The lunch over, Shore and his colleague hailed a cab back to the airport. While waiting for the plane to depart, Shore turned to his assistant and finally said: "Hari, we probably should upgrade the stock. I don't necessarily like him or trust him, but I think our clients can make money off him. We only have to be smart enough to get out at the right time."

The very next day, having missed nearly 100 percent of the stock's appreciation, Shore upgraded his rating from neutral to attractive and revised his estimates of Sunbeam's 1997 earnings to $1.40, up from a buck a share. "We believe there is plenty of upside left in Sunbeam's stock price," he wrote in a report that followed on October 11. "There is potential for a major turnaround and we believe Mr. Dunlap is the right man for the job . . . Mr. Dunlap is a man on a mission and will waste no time implementing his agenda."

Dunlap was right. He had won Shore over to his side, at least for now.

3

"STRIP ME NAKED!"

THE BEWITCHING POWER that Al Dunlap exercised over Wall Street came from an embellished track record as a corporate tough guy. Throughout his career, he almost always found himself in troubled companies that needed painfully tough medicine to survive and prosper. Dunlap, his record showed, did not shy from either conflict or adversity. He didn't agonize over difficult decisions that often paralyzed other executives, and he didn't allow emotion to prevent him from hacking away at costs and people. If Wall Street could have invented an executive that perfectly suited its style and its preferences, it would have created Al Dunlap. In a way, it did.

From the start, he worked long and hard hours, bringing a swaggering confidence and brutal toughness to every task. His very first job, in 1963, after he served his mandatory three years of military service upon graduation from West Point, was as a $650-a-month trainee at Kimberly-Clark Corp., the maker of Kleenex tissues. He proved a diligent employee, eager to take on any assignment thrown to him. It did not take long for the mere trainee to gain a promotion to a shift superintendent for a Kimberly-Clark factory in Neenah, Wisconsin. Dunlap worked all the odd hours, the "blue-collar shifts," as he called them. During those long nights, he tried out nearly every job in the factory, tending to the vast paper and converting machines and gaining the hands-on education he was convinced would further his career.

After four years with Kimberly-Clark, Dunlap was ready for a new challenge. He got it from Ely Meyer, the seventy-five-year-old owner of a private label tissue maker that sometimes turned over its additional production capacity to Kimberly-Clark. Meyer's Sterling Pulp & Paper Co. in Eau Claire was in trouble. The company had borrowed heavily to buy modern paper and pulp machines, but could not get the more sophisticated equipment to work well. To get more comfortable with Dunlap, Meyer invited him to his winter home in Tampa, Florida, for three consecutive weekends. Finally, in 1967 he offered the twenty-nine-year-old the job of general manager at an annual salary of $25,000.

If Dunlap learned about managing at Kimberly-Clark, as he says, he became a manager at Sterling—at least one who learned the power of cutting costs and of the anger that streamlining caused. Dunlap's first layoffs at the 1,000-employee company brought physical threats of violence, anonymous calls and letters threatening to blow up his car or shoot him. While it made him something of a pariah in the community, however, his work also also formed the basis for a father-son relationship between the young manager and the older owner.

Meyer grew fond of Dunlap. It did not trouble him that Dunlap had a stormy relationship with his son-in-law who served as Sterling's president. Meyer accepted him for both his talents and his failings, as a father would accept a son. Meyer was self-made, hard-working, tough, and a bit eccentric, a man who carried his will in his briefcase so he could change it at any time. Seven years after Dunlap began at Sterling, Meyer was hospitalized. Dunlap made a habit of visiting him on the way home every night, sitting by his bedside to fill him in on the details of the day's business. When Meyer died in 1975 at the age of eighty-two, Dunlap said "it was like losing a parent."

The family estate soon sold the paper plant to the New York–based conglomerate Gulf & Western, and Dunlap moved back east to take on a new role at American Can Co.'s corporate headquarters in Greenwich, Connecticut. Over the next seven years, Dunlap created enough enemies to last a typical executive a lifetime. As a general manager of two different divisions, he attacked costs as if he were on the front line and they were menacing adversaries. He closed plants, laid off employees, slashed investment, and ditched assets. Profits jumped, just as they did at Sterling.

The executives and managers whom Dunlap befriended spoke highly of him. Those who lost their jobs or inherited his businesses were often shocked by what he got away with. "He cut off nearly all research-and-development just when key patents were running out," groused one former American Can executive. "He refused to add production capacity when the plants were running full out and we had leading market share." Those short-term tricks helped to cut costs and inflate profits in the brief periods that Dunlap headed up a division. But he was greatly resented by the managers who had to reinvest and rebuild the businesses that he had squeezed for every last ounce of profit.

Even so, his superiors were unhappy to see him go. He relished messy situations that demanded tough, decisive actions. He not only brought competence to the job, they believed, he also brought courage. Frankly, he didn't care what others thought of him. He didn't care whom he offended or why. He didn't worry about making decisions that other men, perhaps with more conscience or different values, would refuse to make. Though he was brash, bold and irreverent, he also was completely committed. For him, work was an addiction or a disease without a cure or an antidote. He had few, if any, real friends—only business associates. "You always feel you have to prove something, like you have to do it," he once told a reporter. "And whatever success you have, you don't believe it. You think that if you don't keep doing it, it is all going to evaporate, anyhow."

He cast himself in the role of itinerant troubleshooter, moving to asbestos maker Manville Corp. in 1982, and then, when Manville became embroiled in asbestos litigation and his boss lost out in what he termed a corporate power struggle, on to disposable-cup-and-plate producer Lily-Tulip Inc. only nine months later. Lily, a company acquired by investment banking firm Kohlberg, Kravis, Roberts & Co. in a leveraged buyout, represented his first opportunity to be a CEO. Dunlap did not disappoint his investors. He got rid of 20 percent of Lily's staff, 40 percent of its suppliers, and half of its management. In three years, he fired eleven of the company's top thirteen executives. After a $10.8 million loss in 1982, Lily earned $8.3 million in 1983 and $22.6 million in 1984.

His success at Lily brought him his first taste of fame and fortune. He attracted some media attention as a hard-nosed operator who reveled in the nasty work of laying off people. The positive press brought him to the attention of the Anglo-French financier and corporate raider Sir James Goldsmith, a celebrated figure himself who soon became Dunlap's most influential mentor. In 1986, Goldsmith put him in charge of a troubled San Francisco–based timberlands company, Crown-Zellerbach, which he had recently acquired. Dunlap proved a faithful and effective hatchet man, cutting and slashing his way to success at Crown-Zellerbach and Diamond International, another Goldsmith company. And when Goldsmith launched his unsuccessful hostile takeover raids on Goodyear Tire & Rubber Co. and the British conglomerate BAT Industries, Dunlap stood behind him doing much of the legwork.

On the surface, their friendship seemed bizarre. Goldsmith was a polished Old Etonian, a Renaissance man and intellectual. Dunlap, whose New Jersey accent never really wore off, was a single-minded and simple man. Yet both were outsiders of the business establishment. They made their money the hard way: on their own. Goldsmith strongly believed that the very best executives come from modest beginnings and retain an inner hunger for continued success. "Al Dunlap is the epitome of that," he told associates. "My dear boy," Goldsmith sometimes quipped to his protégé, "you and I have an enormous respect for money because we had to make it. We had to live by our wits." Dunlap expressed it differently: "Strip me naked," he said. "Put me out on the street, and I'm going to survive."

They also shared an intense dislike for the corporate mainstream, and they were staunch anti-communists. Goldsmith, an avid champion of British Prime Minister Margaret Thatcher, had predicted the collapse of the Soviet Empire two years before it occurred. Dunlap, a conservative Republican, was an enthusiastic supporter of President Reagan. Goldsmith admired men who, as he put it, not only changed the places at the table, but turned the table upside down. Dunlap, never having had a network of friends rooted in the mainstream, took great pleasure in upsetting the order of things.

The glue to their enduring bond, however, was trust and loyalty. Goldsmith knew Dunlap was a lone ranger. He had the absolute loyalty that only a soldier would have to his commanding officer. In the cutthroat world of high finance and hostile takeovers, that deep commitment was essential. "Al was a soldier for Jimmy and he liked that," said a Goldsmith friend. "Al never really figured out how to fit in. That, in fact, endeared him to Jimmy as well. He liked people who were not accepted by the establishment. And because of Al's rough edges, Jimmy knew he could not be seduced away so easily."

Of Goldsmith, Dunlap would say that he had never met a more intelligent human being. "Jimmy could probably talk on any topic with equal intellect," Dunlap said before the death of his friend in 1996. "He is perhaps the most honest human being I have ever met . . . honest to a fault. I would have gone to my death working for Goldsmith."

It was only with Goldsmith's consent that Dunlap went to work for one of his friends, the Australian billionaire Kerry Packer. Goldsmith sat on Packer's board and urged his eccentric friend to hire Dunlap and give him free rein. His TV and magazine empire, Consolidated Press Holdings Inc., was in deep financial trouble. Packer's widely disparate operations were losing $25 million a year and badly needed the kind of makeover for which Dunlap had already became famous. In 1991 Dunlap moved to Australia to sort through the mess. Packer, however, was every bit as brusque and brash as Dunlap, and the two clashed mightily. The heavy-handed American slashed Packer's portfolio to core media companies, laid off thousands of employees, and fired the tycoon's friends and family members. Only two years into his five-year contract, Dunlap returned to the States. He claimed his job was complete, that he had turned the operating loss into a $623 million profit. But his premature departure suggested otherwise. Goldsmith said he kept "Kerry out of Al's hair until the business was healthy and eventually the two of them had an almighty row."

DUNLAP RETURNED from Australia in May 1993, some $40 million richer for his efforts, and spent eleven months in retirement before being recruited for the job that would transform him from a relatively unknown executive into a celebrated hero and Wall Street icon. His path to fame came at Scott Paper Co., an old-line, Philadelphia-based concern. Like Sunbeam, Scott Paper Co. was as American as McDonald's golden arches. Just as it was virtually certain that a Sunbeam blender could be found in almost every kitchen in America, it was virtually guaranteed that most homes contained Scott paper products. Founded in Philadelphia by brothers Irvin and Clarence Scott in 1879, the company was the first to market rolls of tissue for toilet paper and the first to pro-duce paper towels for the home. Over the years, Scott became the world's largest supplier of toilet tissue, paper napkins, and paper towels. Sales grew to $5.4 billion in some twenty countries by 1990.

But tough competition from rivals such as Procter & Gamble Co. began to erode profit margins as early as the 1960s, and like so many old-line American companies, Scott became a moribund bureaucracy. Chairman and CEO Philip E. Lippincott, a Quaker with an aversion to conflict and confrontation, was a plodding leader who managed by consensus. He had diversified into businesses he knew little about. He allowed Scott's payroll to become bloated. He put up with underper-forming divisions for years, and he failed to take aggressive, decisive action to halt the decline. The company had lost market share for four years in a row and posted a loss of $277 million in 1993.

Dunlap seemed perfectly suited for the job. He had been weaned on the paper business. He was tough where Lippincott was soft. And unlike one candidate, who turned the job down because he said he "lacked the stomach" for it, Dunlap was a man who certainly boasted a stomach lined with steel. After interviewing Dunlap in a lounge at Philadelphia Airport, Scott director Richard K. Lockridge believed he was "exactly right" for Scott. "He was a hard-driving guy who was down-to-earth and blunt. He had done his homework, and he had good ideas." Dunlap told Lockridge that he believed Scott was a vic-tim of years of what he called "custodial management." Not only did Dunlap feel certain that he could fix the company, but he told Lockridge and other directors that if he couldn't double the stock price within three years he would be ashamed of himself.

The only caution, strangely enough, came from the headhunting firm that had presented Dunlap in the first place. "Our only hesitation surrounds whether he might be too quick and bold for the Scott Paper situation," wrote Thomas Hardy, the search consultant with SpencerStuart, who helped to recruit Dunlap. "Previous turnarounds have been with operations in very, very serious trouble, often with heavy leverage and immediate cash flow needs, often with a dominant single shareholder, or pair of shareholders, and with very big earn-outs." For throughout his career, the companies he worked for tended to disappear after he left. In almost every case in which Dunlap occu-pied a leadership position, the companies were sold or liquidated.

Though some members of the Scott Paper board expressed reservations, Dunlap was unanimously voted the new CEO, the first to head the paper maker from outside the company. After years of working for private companies or in the shadow of others, Dunlap finally got his opportunity to become the chief executive of a major public corporation when he walked through the doors of Scott's opulent headquarters on fifty-five acres in Philadelphia on April 19, 1994.

Within two months of his arrival, Dunlap had written a brutal prescription for Scott. There would be major changes in management, a restructuring that would eliminate 35 percent of the employees, outright sales of units unrelated to Scott's core tissue business, and a new strategy for the future. Dunlap laid off 11,200 people, including 71 percent of the headquarters' staff, 50 percent of the management, and 20 percent of the hourly employees. "And guess what?" he said. "It was all fat, blubber. We didn't even tickle a muscle and there we are."

Scott executives, however, soon found something remarkably odd about the man. Almost everything Dunlap did, he did to exaggeration. Dunlap claimed to reporters he was at Scott only one week when he took his ax to the company's lethargic eleven-person executive committee. "I got rid of nine of the eleven, and the other two I gave more responsibility," he said. How did he know so fast whom to fire? "I've done enough of these before. Each time you do one, you get a little smarter. And after a while, it's almost predictable."

In fact, Dunlap didn't fire any of the eleven in the first week. Three had already announced plans to retire before he arrived. Another three were simply taken off the committee but remained employed at Scott. Four others, including two senior vice presidents, the general counsel, and the vice president for human resources, were ousted on May 26, five weeks after Dunlap came aboard. Another was let go a month later. Laughed one former member of the committee: "It was a fish story that got better with each telling."

Still, his impact on the organization was immediate. "Even if you didn't have face time with him, that guy affected your life and everyone knew it," said William J. Kirkpatrick, a Scott Paper executive who put in twenty-six years at the company. "Everyone talked about him. He put the fear of God into a lot of people. When he was in the building, people knew he was there. His presence was palpable."

While Dunlap's cuts at the company went far and deep, he originally told employees that his goal was to reinvest in the business and fashion a clear vision for the future. But many survivors said it soon became clear he was only interested in selling out. "At the employee meetings, he spoke about building the company," recalled a former marketing executive. "But by the end of 1994, it just became a volume-driven plan to pretty up the place for sale." The marketing department began weekly volume forecasts, up from monthly reports. "We're talking about a whole new definition of short term," said the executive. Dunlap slashed the company's research-and-development budget in half, to about $35 million, and eliminated 60 percent of the staffers in R&D. He put off all major plant and equipment maintenance for the 1995 year, a move that saved as much as $20 million and added another $5 million. The $40 million in savings on those two cutbacks alone dropped straight to the bottom line. "What he did was borrow a year, maybe two, from the future," said Jerry Ballas, Scott's head of manufacturing and technology worldwide. "At some point, you have to pay it back. If you wait too long, you'll pay it back double because the plants will operate inefficiently and the machines will begin to break down. We strung it out as far as we could without getting into unsafe conditions."

The cost cutters didn't go after just R&D and maintenance. Dunlap also forbade managers from being involved in community activities because that would take away from business duties. He banned memberships in industry organizations that allowed managers to network with competitors. Before moving Scott's world headquarters to Boca Raton, Florida—just after buying a $1.8 million home there—Dunlap eliminated all corporate gifts to charities, even reneging on the final $50,000 payment of a $250,000 pledge to the Philadelphia Museum of Art. He also scrapped a yearly event at which Scott met with its leading suppliers to improve relationships and get better prices for goods. Dunlap viewed the meeting as "nonsense," a waste of time and money.

The meeting dated from a major reengineering of the function that had begun in late 1991. Scott winnowed some 20,000 suppliers to about 1,000, knocked off more than $100 million in annual purchasing costs, and wrote up plans for a 75 percent reduction in the 200-employee department—all before Dunlap arrived. "The numbers were showing up just as Dunlap came through the door," said Theodore R. Ramstad, former director of worldwide procurement.

Dunlap ran Scott's factories and drove people as if the company were going out of business. As Ballas, who had spent thirty-three years working for Scott, put it: "You don't allow factory shutdowns. You do no training whatsoever. You don't hire anybody. You buy nothing unless you needed it today. And you try to sell everything you make. We were down to the bare bones. People were working unbelievable hours doing unbelievable stuff. We could not have continued to run the business the way we were for the future."

To push more product into the marketplace, the company's consumer sales force gave huge discounts to customers that were earned only when the product sold through at retail. The result was that Scott's finance staff could book the sale and profit at standard rates and only had to provide the discount in the future when retailers applied for the credit. That way, the paper company could show dramatic increases in sales without an immediate erosion in profit margins. Typically, such trade promotion discounts ran at 10 percent to 20 percent of revenue. To drive volume at Scott, especially in the final months before the company was sold, the discounts were doubled.

The lavish stock-option packages Dunlap generously gave to his senior executives kept them in the game, working slavishly on his and their own behalf. The grants directly linked their pay to the company's rising stock price, but only a third of the options vested annually. All of them could immediately be cashed in only if the company were to be sold or taken over. "We knew the game was change of control because the options all vested then," said a top Scott executive. "That was the carrot. Quarter-to-quarter earnings were critical. You had to deliver the earnings at all costs because you couldn't miss a number. You could lose all the [option] money you had. The question was what could you endure? If it challenged your values and your ethics, you would have to pack it in and give up. It came close a number of times."

THE HUMAN SACRIFICES were heavy and substantial. Among the first to feel the impact of Dunlap's chainsaw were hundreds of employees at Scott's expansive Mobile, Alabama, paper complex nestled alongside the Mobile River. For decades the facility churned out millions of rolls of towels, napkins, tissues, and toilet paper. At its peak, the plant and pulp mill employed 3,600 people and played a vital role in the local economy. Dunlap's layoffs reduced the workforce to some 1,400 people.

Emory Michael Cole, a gregarious and energetic man, had worked in the plant since 1958, following his dad's footsteps by joining Scott's general labor pool for $1.72 an hour. The oldest of seven boys in the Cole family, Mike was one of four who had worked in the plant at one time or another. He started after serving four years in the Navy, on November 17, 1958, at the age of twenty-one, working as a pipefitter and a welder. Over thirty-seven years, Cole worked himself up to a supervisory job as a shift team leader with nearly thirty people reporting to him and a $72,000-a-year salary.

Over those years, he had been a loyal and diligent employee. Cole crossed two union picket lines for Scott, walking past his own father, cousins, uncles, and friends, to work twelve-hour days to keep the plant humming in 1980 and 1986. By then he was a salaried employee, a supervisor, and his only choice was to work or to lose his job. "They wanted to kill me when I walked through those picket lines," he recalled. "There were hundreds of us who went in past husbands, brothers, and wives. It was horrible. Lippincott came down and told us how valued we were and how the company would take care of us. He could not believe the sacrifices we made to run the machines."

Soon after Dunlap took over, he made a pilgrimage to the complex, a stop that insiders facetiously dubbed the "Chainsaw Massacre tour." Some executives even made up T-shirts emblazoned with the phrase and the names of all the plants and facilities Dunlap had visited. He arrived at the complex in Mobile in a helicopter with two bodyguards. Dunlap showed his impatience with old-fashioned notions of corporate behavior. Touring the plant, Dunlap asked a friend of Cole's how long he had worked there. The worker proudly replied that he was a thirty-year veteran. "Why would you stay with a company for thirty years?" asked Dunlap incredulously.

"It was like the king came in and everyone was supposed to bow down to him," recalled Cole, startled by the contrast between Lippincott's earlier visit to a strike-torn plant in which he pledged loyalty and commitment to workers who kept the place open and Dunlap's expression of surprise that anyone would want to work anywhere for three decades.

On August 16, 1994, that contrast became all too real for Cole: he was called in from his vacation and fired, at the age of fifty-eight. "Loyalty didn't matter anymore," he said sadly. "They didn't care if you were there thirty years or three weeks. My wife almost had a heart attack when I told her I was fired. I wanted to work four or five more years to get my full retirement, nearly $4,000 a month. It's not fair. Dunlap worked for less than two years at Scott and made $100 million. I worked thirty-seven years and got $2,670 a month in retirement. I was there when the paper machines were built."

Jerry Michael Chambless, whose father had worked with Cole's dad at the same plant, was axed the same day from his $60,000-a-year job as a factory supervisor. The forty-nine-year-old had been active in the community as a tee-ball coach, a Boy Scout leader at the local church, and a foster parent. After the layoff, he looked for a job without success for nearly eight months, then suffered a massive stroke that confined him to a wheelchair. Though Chambless had had high blood pressure for seven years, he had kept it well controlled with medication and led an active life. He and his wife, Marty, began living on Social Security payments of $12,000 a year. Finally, she divorced him. Chambless now lives with his sister and mother. "He will never be able to do anything again," said his ex-wife, Marty, who blames Dunlap for her husband's illness. "I know Dunlap has the furthest corner in hell waiting for him."

Dunlap insisted that he was not insensitive to the pain his measures inflicted. "People say I've made a lot of money off the backs of people by cutting all these jobs," he said. "I find that personally offensive. I come from a working-class family. If I have to get rid of 35 percent of the people to save 65 percent, that's what I am going to do. It was me or Dr. Kevorkian."

LINES LIKE THOSE, delivered with the timing of a Henny Youngman, along with an aggressive public relations campaign designed to give Dunlap maximum exposure, worked to hype Scott's stock and Dunlap's image.

During his twenty-month stay at Scott, Dunlap generated more self-celebrating publicity than any other business executive in the world, with the possible exception of Microsoft's Bill Gates. He captivated the media and Wall Street because he seemed refreshingly candid and honest. His witty one-liners, collected and rehearsed and repeated over and over again, nevertheless seemed original and fresh.

Dunlap was good copy and great TV, and it was rare when you couldn't reach him in time to meet a pressing deadline.

Dunlap not only welcomed the attention, he courted the media in a way that shocked some of Scott's directors. He launched a media blitz, in short order becoming the Lee Iacocca of the 1990s. Though almost every journalist wrote of his layoffs, the stories about Dunlap were largely favorable if not adulatory. He frequently appeared on television, from NBC's *Dateline* to CNN and CNBC. He wrote opinion pieces for *USA Today* and the *Wall Street Journal. Fortune, Forbes,* and the *New York Times* portrayed Dunlap as a master manager, with articles that dispensed his advice and wisdom on management, executive pay, corporate governance, and the economy.

It was not as if Dunlap's veteran public relations agent, Peter Judice of Burson-Marsteller, had to work very hard to get him media attention. On behalf of Dunlap, he churned out more press releases in a month than most companies issue in a year. But more often than not, reporters' calls just flew in. Dunlap, unlike most chief executives whose eyes are fixed more firmly on their businesses, was anxious and willing to take the calls. When ABC's *Nightline* sought a CEO to debate Labor Secretary Robert B. Reich, Dunlap rushed to the challenge. When *Newsweek* asked more than fifty chief executives to discuss corporate restructuring for a cover story in 1995, only one CEO agreed to an interview: Al Dunlap.

Even as Scott's stock rose higher and higher, some board members who had brought him into the company began wondering if they had made the right decision. "For the first two or three meetings," thought one Scott director, "it was just spectacular. The people he let go were the people he should have gotten rid of. The people he kept were those he should have kept. Then, Al became Al. He repeated himself a lot. He became more overbearing and his ego was much more obvious. At that stage, he began to roll over the board. Al became insufferable. All he wanted to do was brag about what he had done."

Dunlap had, of course, reason to brag. He had become a legitimate hero to Wall Street and Scott's investors. He had done many of the things Lippincott had been trying to do for years, but had simply failed to get done. When Kimberly-Clark agreed to buy Scott Paper for $9.4 billion, Scott shareholders saw their investment in the company rise by 225 percent. Under Dunlap's leadership, the company's market capitalization went up by an extraordinary $6.3 billion. "The Scott story," he boasted, "will go down in the annals of American business history as one of the most successful, quickest turnarounds ever. It makes other turnarounds pale by comparison."

Shockingly, few Wall Street analysts and reporters closely examined his record at Scott Paper, even after Kimberly-Clark immediately stumbled badly after acquiring Dunlap's company. In the first combined quarter, Kimberly's performance was held down by excess inventory of Scott paper and tissue products, the result of Dunlap's efforts in pushing for unsustainable sales and earnings growth. The company's chief financial officer publicly laid the blame for the earnings surprise on Dunlap's notoriously aggressive inventory stuffing.

Kimberly's red-faced CEO, Wayne R. Sanders, who once proclaimed that Dunlap was "a wake-up call to a lot of CEOs" and was "good for American business," was in a difficult position. Already under pressure from shareholders who saw their stock in the company sharply trail the market and rival Procter & Gamble, Sanders would not admit that he had paid too much for the acquisition. "Al didn't stick us with anything," he later said. "We got exactly what we paid for."

Going into the merger, however, Scott's budget projected income of $100 million in the fourth quarter of 1995. Instead, Kimberly-Clark lost $60 million on Scott's business, according to company insiders, a profit swing of $160 million that did not include a massive $1.4 billion restructuring charge the company declared to cover its "integration plan for Scott." Among the acquisition's hidden costs was a hit of $30 million on the promotion credits for the discounted sales Scott gave retailers to build inventory. In the first three months after the takeover, Kimberly spent nearly $30 million more on plant and equipment maintenance that had been postponed under Dunlap. "We had to get the condition of our equipment back to where it should have been," explained Ballas, who spent fifteen months with Kimberly-Clark to assist with the transition.

Among other things, Ballas found himself undoing "80 percent of what we did the year before" under Dunlap. On one of the company's most important products, Scott Towels, Dunlap had reshuffled the product line so the standard paper towels could be sold in rolls of 60, 120, and 180 sheets each, rather than the 80 and 120-sheet rolls that previously existed. The change, Dunlap believed, would allow the company to make $80 million more if it could merely sell the same volume. The alternation, designed to delude consumers into paying more for less product, miserably backfired. The result: Scott lost 30 percent of its volume in Scott Towels in 1996. Kimberly reversed the strategic blunder eight months after taking over, but more than two years after the merger it still could not recover its lost market share. Kimberly was forced to take a second restructuring charge of $810 million in early 1998 to close plants and slash 5,000 workers, bringing total job cuts since the Scott merger to 11,000.

ONCE OUT OF SCOTT, Dunlap found it none too easy to find another job. Of course, he didn't need one. He had made his first millions at Lily-Tulip, where he took away some $8 million in gains. With Sir James, he had collected far more loot, bringing in $25 million in one of the three years he worked for Goldsmith. Dunlap had left Kerry Packer in Australia nearly $40 million richer. His brief stint at Scott brought him $100 million.

Yet Dunlap loved the limelight and yearned to move into it once again. He openly spoke about wanting to lead General Motors or Westinghouse or Eastman Kodak, all troubled American institutions that Dunlap believed he could turn around. But no one called. "Al has an ego about the size of the United States," said Gary Roubos, the Scott director who was instrumental in bringing him to the company. "He began to think so much of himself that he thought he could turn around GM. He sat around for nearly a year waiting for somebody to come to him, and nobody did."

Instead Dunlap, eager to find work again, began calling his contacts, trying to nudge them into putting his name into play for whatever jobs he could get. Thomas Neff, the silver-haired chairman of headhunters SpencerStuart, who helped bring him to Scott in the first place, took his telephone calls regularly. Every time a newspaper or magazine article would note that Neff's firm was searching for a chief executive, Dunlap called to ask that his name be put into the hopper.

"He kept bugging me," remembered Neff. "He'd say, 'Why aren't you considering me for this or that? Why aren't you getting me a job?'"

Neff, who had been quietly distancing himself because of Dunlap's often outrageous comments in the media, basically told him to forget it. "In light of all the publicity, your best opportunity would be running a company controlled by an investor who didn't care about the PR," he told him. "Or maybe running a major company in Europe where people may be less aware of what happened here."

With investment fund managers Michael Price and Michael Steinhardt the two largest Sunbeam shareholders, the appliance company appeared to be a perfect fit: an impatient chieftain for restless investors in an impatient world. It was on an airplane, some 36,000 feet into a soaring sky, that Steinhardt's representative on the board of directors first realized that Albert J. Dunlap just might be the ideal candidate. There, Shimon Topor, fifty-two, an Israeli lawyer, banker, and Steinhardt partner, discovered Dunlap in a magazine article. It was one of those "puff jobs," as Dunlap himself would call them, that extolled the virtues of his tough leadership style at Scott, without closely examining the facts behind the numbers. "I didn't know anything about him, other than what was in the magazine," recalled Topor. "But the article raised my curiosity so I came back and said 'I think this is the guy we need.'"

Topor, who speaks with a thick Israeli accent, first contacted Price's lieutenant on the Sunbeam board, Peter Langerman, and then headhunter Jim Boone of Korn/Ferry's Atlanta office. Dunlap was what Roger Schipke wasn't: bold, decisive, outspoken, powerful, loud, and arrogant. His ruthless cost-cutting ways appealed to Topor, who, at Sunbeam board meetings, seemed only interested in costs. In late May Topor flew down to Dunlap's home in Boca Raton, spent four hours with him, and left convinced that he was the man for the job. "He was full of confidence, and we needed someone who knew what could be done and how to do it," said Topor. "He had a proven track record of success. He did it. He wasn't just reflecting confidence, he did it. He seemed to be a person who would devote 150 percent of his time to it."

Topor's session led to another, in early June, with Langerman and Ray Garea, another key analyst for Price who kept a watchful eye on Mutual's investments in financial services and health care. Price's men met Dunlap in New York for lunch and were equally impressed with him. They too were certain that he could assume strong control and that his track record would virtually guarantee a recovery in Sunbeam's slumping stock.

But it was Price, Dunlap later acknowledged, who persuaded him to join the company. The investor had briefly met Dunlap only a few months earlier for an informal breakfast in New York. It was nothing more than a get-acquainted session. But Price left the meeting impressed with Dunlap's tough, no-nonsense style. The investor especially liked the fact that he had worked for demanding people in the past: Sir James Goldsmith, Lord Jacob Rothschild, and Australian media magnate Kerry Packer. In Price's mind, that was an important endorsement. "I know Packer," said Price. "I had met Goldsmith. So I knew he had worked for very tough people, and I believed his track record was good."

Truth is, if Michael Price were Dr. Frankenstein, he could not have fashioned another creature more like-minded. Dunlap knew how to satisfy someone like Price, who incessantly demanded quick turnarounds on his investments.

For as Price himself admitted, one of Schipke's failings was that he lacked what the investor obliquely termed "urgency." Someone more blunt, perhaps more honest, would have plainly said that he was in it for whatever short-term gain he could extract. But Price was not that someone. "As managers of a fund," Price opined, "we have an urgency. We are not short-term traders, but the urgency is still there. We have this burning in our stomach every day. It doesn't mean you buy and sell businesses every day. But you constantly evaluate your investment, and the urgency is always there to hold management accountable for performance." Dunlap shared that burning sensation with him.

Like Schipke before him, though, Dunlap had some reservations. He wanted to ensure that he would have no meddling from Price or Steinhardt. "He wanted control of every facet of the business," recalled Price. "He wanted to put a guy or two on the board. He didn't want to be interfered with."

Getting Dunlap wasn't going to be an inexpensive proposition. But Langerman and Topor would have to take care of the finer details. It was less of a negotiation than it was Dunlap naming his price. "He more or less laid out the terms he wanted," recalled Topor, who met again with Dunlap to hammer out the details of the contract. "There wasn't much of a negotiation. He made it clear that this was his final position."

The deal Price eventually signed guaranteed Dunlap a $1 million annual salary, $2.5 million in stock options, and 1 million shares of restricted stock worth $12.25 million alone. Price also agreed to allow Dunlap to buy $3 million worth of stock from Sunbeam's own treasury at $12.25 per share, the closing price on July 17, the day before Dunlap's appointment was announced. That allowed him to benefit from any rise in the stock due to his appointment. Indeed, his entire stock package was pegged to this lower price, effectively permitting him to benefit from the inside knowledge that he would become CEO within twenty-four hours.

He demanded six weeks of paid vacation annually and compensation at year's end for any unused vacation days. He got Sunbeam to buy the Mercedes he already owned, even though he alone would use the car afterward, and he required the company to buy him a new car every two years. He wanted to retain the chauffeur and bodyguard he had hired at Scott, so he asked that the company also pay for his full-time driver "for security and safety reasons."

Sunbeam gave him a virtually unlimited expense account, allowing for first-class travel and lodging for both Dunlap and his wife as well as all initiation fees and monthly dues for his country club membership. It agreed to pay the legal, accounting and tax advisers who helped negotiate and prepare his contract and to reimburse him annually for financial-consulting advice. And the company agreed to pay his additional income taxes on the perks.

On July 18, as some contract minutiae were still being negotiated, the Sunbeam board met in New York at the law offices of Skadden Arps. Sunbeam's executives found it an odd meeting because they quickly realized they did not have the full attention of the board's key directors. When chief financial officer Paul O'Hara breezed through his review of the latest financial results, there were few questions. He thought it odd because the numbers were not good.

Then Langerman was called out of the room for a telephone call. Topor and Charles Thayer, a director who was serving as interim CEO of Sunbeam, stepped out as well. Richard Ravitch, a new director who ran a New York real estate firm, remained. Weary and tired, he had been up all night long, worried that his son might be aboard the TWA flight to Paris that crashed the day before after taking off from Kennedy Airport.

For at least an hour, maybe longer, Sunbeam's executives waited for Langerman and the other directors to return. They did not know that Langerman was verifying the contents of the deal that would bring Dunlap to the company. Once that was done, he walked into the conference room with a mischievous smile on his face.

"The meeting is over," announced Langerman in a melodramatic tone. "We've just hired Al Dunlap."

"Oh shit!" said Richard Boynton, Sunbeam's household products chief.

"There's no sense in finishing up the presentations," Langerman added. "Take your plans to Fort Lauderdale on Monday and present them to Al."

Within days, the executives would gather around the boardroom table in Fort Lauderdale and meet the man who had completely won over Michael Price and the board of directors.

4
PIRATES AND TRIBES

THE SUNBEAM CORP. that Al Dunlap joined was an American icon. When America gathered around the radio to listen to *The Shadow* and later watched *Ozzie and Harriet* on a flickering black-and-white tube, Sunbeam was the brand that occupied a favored place in the home. For more than half a century, the company supplied the gleaming appliances that allowed a flourishing middle class to toast its bread, blend its drinks, and press the wrinkles out of its shirts.

Sunbeam was the company that grew up with modern America. Its ingenious inventors devised the first automatic coffeemaker, the first pop-up electric toaster, and the first mixmaster, a convenience that made it easier for housewives to bake cakes, scramble eggs, and beat mashed potatoes so they were lump-free.

Like the country itself, the company was in constant metamorphosis. Founded in 1897 as the Chicago Flexible Shaft Co. by two illustrious entrepreneurs, John Stewart and Thomas Clark, the company developed early products that suited the times. It churned out agricultural tools, sheep-shearing machines, and the flexible shafts employed to balance or propel them. Stewart and Clark began using the Sunbeam name in the early 1900s, when they moved into the production of electrical appliances. Their toasters, irons, and mixers became so successful that by 1946, just as America's veterans were settling back to start new lives, the company officially changed its name to Sunbeam Corp.

By 1960, after prospering on the growing affluence of postwar society, Sunbeam gobbled up rival Oster Co., famous for its blenders, barber clippers, and electric blankets. The newly combined companies boasted sales of well over $1 billion and a reputation for having the finest brands in small appliances after General Electric Co.

But in the 1980s' tidal wave of hostile takeovers and mergers, Sunbeam found itself swamped by the forces of the markets. It fended off an unwanted takeover from IC Industries in 1981, only to fall into the "friendly" arms of an ambitious conglomerateur by the name of Robert J. Buckley. The Sunbeam acquisition completed Buckley's transformation of Allegheny International Inc. from a specialty-steel maker to a sprawling consumer products conglomerate. It also was the event that divided Sunbeam's history into a before and an after.

UNDER THE PORTLY BUCKLEY, the appliance company with some of America's beloved brand names became a victim of neglect and abuse. Sunbeam was compelled to return nearly all its profits to Allegheny's corporate center in Pittsburgh, and was starved of capital to update its factories and refresh its product line. The returns from Sunbeam and all the other divisions in the Allegheny empire helped to fund the indulgences of a businessman who savored a regal lifestyle.

As chief executive for over a decade from 1975 to 1986, Buckley knew nearly every extravagance. The "Allegheny Air Force," a fleet of five luxurious jets, flew him and his colleagues all over the globe, even ferrying guests to the wedding of one of Buckley's children. He entertained his executives at posh gatherings in the Bahamas and in Boca Raton, where $10,000 ice carvings graced the tables. With company money, he purchased apartments in New York, a resort condominium beside an exclusive golf course on the Rolling Rock estate in Pennsylvania, and a majestic Tudor home in Pittsburgh to entertain himself and clients. (These properties remained company assets and were subsequently sold by Sunbeam.) An elegant wine cellar, stocked with more than $100,000 worth of vintage bottles from a wine collection that once belonged to J. P. Morgan, was installed in his home by an Allegheny subsidiary. His lavish salary and bonus, over $1 million in 1984, was supplemented by company-subsidized loans of more than a million at an interest rate of only 2 percent.

Buckley's free-spending ways and his forays into more risky and speculative ventures, from real estate to oil and gas deals, led to a corporate meltdown. Profits fell steadily through the early 1980s until Allegheny began racking up sizable losses in 1985. The stock plummeted to new lows. Buckley lost his job in 1986, and new management began downsizing the company, ditching a third of its workforce, freezing managers' salaries, and selling off some two dozen businesses. But the company's freefall continued. Four months after the stock market collapse on October 19, 1987, it filed for bankruptcy, overwhelmed by loads of debt and a balance sheet that made bankers cringe.

It took nearly two years for investment fund managers Michael F. Price and Michael H. Steinhardt to capture control of Allegheny in what became the first hostile takeover of a company in bankruptcy. Through a pair of former Goldman Sachs & Co. investment bankers, Paul B. Kazarian and Michael Lederman, the rechristened Sunbeam-Oster Co. was adroitly restructured and made highly profitable again. An intense workaholic, Kazarian engineered a turnaround that allowed the investors to bring Sunbeam public and that brought the company from a loss to $120 million in profits by 1992. He was, however, as penurious and eccentric as Buckley was wasteful and flamboyant. Little more than two years into his stint as CEO, Kazarian's eccentricities led to a management coup that won quick support from the two Michaels. In a legal dispute that was ultimately settled, Kazarian claimed they wanted him ousted so they could cut him out of the money he deserved and could more easily control their investment in Sunbeam.

After the Kazarian battle, the investors hired Roger Schipke, a veteran of the General Electric Co. Compared to the frenetic and volatile Kazarian, the company's new chief was like a dose of Valium. Paradoxically, Schipke's most appealing attributes at the time, his reassuring and calming personality, led to his own failure. His inability to assert strong leadership over a company racked by political infighting caused Sunbeam's earnings to fall like a rock. Schipke quit in May 1996 after a little more than two and one-half years as CEO, before Price and Steinhardt could fire him. Only two months later, Albert Dunlap was brought in to halt the company's decline.

For all of Dunlap's bluster, many of Sunbeam's survivors initially discovered something refreshing about their new boss. Finally, something was going to happen. All the delays, the inaction and indecisiveness of the Schipke era had come to an end. Dunlap was the man who was getting things done, revitalizing the company, pumping new life into the enterprise. The executive offices that once had the feel of a funeral parlor now buzzed with the frenetic commotion of a Grand Central Station rush hour.

Executives huddled in offices to discuss sales of assets, plant closings, layoffs, and the elimination of unprofitable products. Consultants roamed the halls, interviewing staffers in every department of the company. A seemingly endless parade of analysts and reporters made their way into Dunlap's office. And nearly every day, people were being discarded or hired for what Dunlap called his "Dream Team for Sunbeam."

All of a sudden, there was an electricity about the place. It was filled with energy—and tension. "We went from a guy who had trouble making decisions to a guy who couldn't wait to make a decision," said James Wilson, the vice president of human resources. Though many of Sunbeam's managers feared the loss of their jobs, many more believed they at least were going to have an impact on what had been a lifeless and lethargic organization.

"For a lot of people, it was a very exciting time," recalls Rich Goudis, the boyish-looking director of corporate planning. Earlier in the year, he had become so frustrated with things that he seriously considered leaving. "We were looking for strong leadership, and we hadn't had it for a while. With Al, I thought now we're going to get down to business here. There was so much low-hanging fruit to harvest. I was having a blast. We were knocking down all the walls. We were creating a new corporation."

Dunlap's most immediate impact was on people: not only deciding whom to discard and whom to keep, but also whom to hire from outside the company. From his first day at work, he had begun to summon the keepers to his office during short breaks from his antics in the boardroom. Wilson was brought in after lunch at 1 P.M.

"What do you think of the people in that room?" asked Dunlap.

Wilson gave his honest assessment of each man, one by one.

"You know the board did say you had a tendency for candor," said Dunlap. "Do you want to be part of the team?"

"Well, if you're asking me whether I would like to stay around and try to fix some of the things that I helped to screw up, the answer is yes."

It was the right answer. By day's end, Dunlap would tell Wilson that every senior executive was in jeopardy, except general counsel Fannin and him.

IN EVERY NEW SITUATION, Dunlap took on the persona of a pirate captain. He dangled munificent riches before business mercenaries who understood that the work would be tough and dirty, but that it also would be short-term. It was pirates' wages for pirates' work. Instead of gold coin and a secret journey at sea, Dunlap's men gained lucrative stock options and a rather wild business jaunt. Laying off thousands of people was not pretty work. Picking up the pieces of an organization you had just thrown into utter chaos was not easy work. Everyone toiled at a horrendous pace. Ronald L. Newcomb, recruited from Black & Decker as Sunbeam's manufacturing chief on Dunlap's seventeenth day, likened it to war. Newcomb, whose skin began to peel off his palms because of the stress, called the conference room off his office "the war room." He told his wife, "It's just like the people who went off to war in World War II. You know it's going to be over someday and then you're going to cash in."

Dunlap reminded recruits that sixty-two of his executives and managers at Scott Paper became millionaires when they cashed in their stock options after Kimberly-Clark purchased the company. That "turnaround" and sale took all of twenty months. Sunbeam, he predicted to his closest associates, would take no more than six months to a year. If all worked well, the key people would walk away with enough loot so that they might never have to work again.

The most important qualifications for a Dunlap-led business journey, however, were trust and loyalty. Whether hiring people for the company's key jobs or recruiting directors to fill board seats, Dunlap first sought friends, acquaintances, and former business associates. From Dunlap's perspective, they were far less likely to resist his often outrageous demands. They already knew what it would take to survive him and the job.

No one was more trustworthy or loyal than his very first hire at Sunbeam: Russell Kersh. Dunlap had discovered him at Lily-Tulip in 1983 when Kersh was a novice financial analyst. After a swift promotion to corporate treasurer, Kersh soon became Dunlap's most trusted aide and confidant. The two worked side by side for six years during

Dunlap's stint with Sir James, then had a falling out when Kersh declined an offer to follow Dunlap to Australia. Instead Kersh went off to work for Adidas America. At Scott Paper, he rejoined Dunlap as his right-hand man and constant crony.

With a Chaplinesque mustache and a bad haircut, Kersh was a competent and creative accountant, though it was his unwavering loyalty to Dunlap that was the foundation of their longtime association. It was, said some, a father-son relationship, without the teenage rebellion years. Dunlap called Kersh his "alter ego," but he was hardly Dunlap's second self. Kersh was so openly a sycophant that some outsiders felt pity for him. One Sunbeam consultant, meeting Dunlap and Kersh for the first time, considered Kersh "a trained puppy because he was totally subservient to Al."

Dunlap made him a multimillionaire and often reminded him of that fact. "Russ is the smartest guy I ever made," Dunlap frequently boasted. "Russ is worth $20 million and I made him." At Scott alone, Kersh took away $16.4 million, money to indulge his passions in NASCAR racing and monster trucks. If not for Dunlap, some wags joked, Kersh would be playing the electronic keyboards at a Holiday Inn in Columbus, Ohio. "He's like a greaser who got lucky in life," laughed one analyst.

Though Kersh would never defy Dunlap, he knew how to communicate with him. He would typically listen in silence to the long-winded rants and raves, always seeming to agree with Dunlap, and then throw out a suggestion or consideration that gently showed he really didn't agree. "Russ understood Al, and he could take whatever Al dished out," said a Sunbeam director. Yet Kersh clearly knew the limits of their friendship. He once confided to a colleague that he doubted Dunlap knew the names of his children. At Sunbeam, however, Kersh became the gateway to Dunlap. He counseled others on how to communicate and deal with the man. "The rule with Al," he said, "was you take the punch, you go down, and you stay down."

IT WAS CERTAINLY the allure of fast money that brought Dunlap's next major hire out of retirement. Newt White was a Scott Paper Co. veteran, a sales-and-marketing guy who had tallied up twenty-eight years at the company before Al Dunlap arrived there. White was a handsome executive, six-foot-four, with a strong, chiseled face, piercing eyes, and a full head of dark hair with just a touch of gray. His good looks earned him the nickname "pretty boy" from Dunlap. White headed up the worldwide away-from-home business, selling paper products to restaurants and hotels. It was a highly lucrative part of the Scott business, largely because of White's dedication and perseverance.

When Dunlap was firing people right and left at Scott, White asked him why he too shouldn't leave. "Because I'm going to make you a rich man," Dunlap responded. White stayed, and Dunlap kept his promise. He left Scott with more than $25 million, including a cash payment of $4.5 million in a noncompete agreement.

Most of White's colleagues considered him a better Al Dunlap than Al himself. He was both smart and decisive, could think strategically as well as tactically, and knew how to get the most out of people. Like Dunlap, he was a no-nonsense executive who could fly into a rage at a moment's notice. But his rage was usually directed toward some sensible business purpose. At Scott, he had been the only internal candidate to succeed CEO Phil Lippincott.

When Dunlap called him at his dream house in New Mexico, White had doubts. Frankly, he did not like or respect Dunlap. He had butted heads with him many times at Scott. Early on, when White was touring Scott's European facilities with Dunlap, he fell victim to one of Dunlap's most irrational tirades. For an entire flight from London's Gatwick Airport to Manchester, Dunlap berated him for not firing Scott CEO Phil Lippincott. It was bizarre criticism: Since Lippincott was White's boss, he could hardly have fired him. Yet Dunlap insisted that any executive worth his salt knows how to get rid of someone who won't change.

White's initial hesitancy about joining the new Sunbeam team, however, was quelled by the giant stock option package that Dunlap threw at him as well as Dunlap's anticipation of a quick exit. "Al and Russ were confident that we could bring this to an endgame within six months to a year," he said. "That was an okay idea because there was a lot of confidence that we could bring the stock to $30, which would have made me $10 million. Why did I go? In one word: money."

That was a hardship White could accept: $10 million in potential stock option gains for no more than a year's work. His new title, executive vice president of Sunbeam's consumer products, didn't fully reflect the scope of his job. White really would function as the chief operating officer of the company, reporting directly to Dunlap.

White quickly recruited dozens of key executives, many of them trusted colleagues from Scott Paper who had also survived Dunlap. He brought in Lee Griffith, former head of Scott Canada, to become vice president of sales; Dixon Thayer, a key executive in Scott's away-from-home business, to become Sunbeam's international chief; William J. Kirkpatrick, another Scottie, to run the company's barber's clipper business and drum up more appliance sales from hotels and restaurants.

Soon enough, three tribes of talent were emerging at the company. First, there were those who had worked with Dunlap before: Kersh; logistics chief Jack Dailey, who hailed from Lily-Tulip and Scott; and White and his band of Scotties. Then there were the Sunbeam survivors like general counsel Fannin, human resources chief Wilson, corporate planner Goudis, controller Bob Gluck, investor relations head John DeSimone, and new product leader Paula Etchison. Finally there was the tribe composed of newly recruited professionals, like marketing chief Donald R. Uzzi, manufacturing head Newcomb, and marketer Kevin McBride, who like Uzzi had also worked at Pepsi, P&G, and Quaker Oats.

ONLY SIX DAYS after his arrival at Sunbeam, Dunlap was sitting in his Fort Lauderdale office with all the members of his self-styled "dream team" operating committee. Russ Kersh was there, along with Newt White and David Fannin. It was Monday, July 29, the day that Dunlap ordered all the file cabinets in his office thrown away because "there was nothing in them."

Leaning back in the green leather chair behind his desk, Dunlap began to discuss the nitty-gritty of what he did no matter where he went, the restructuring and downsizing of the company. He talked about the sales of assets, plant closings, layoffs, and the elimination of low-margin products. Already Don Burnett's Coopers & Lybrand consultants were swarming over the company to come up with the restructuring plan that was his hallmark.

During the conversation with his key executives, he tossed off a startling question to everyone in the room.

"How many plants will we get down to?" he asked.

The inquiry hung in the air like something stale. To simply hazard a guess required great hubris and impudence. It also required knowledge.

Kersh, White, and Fannin had no idea at all. Why should they? None of them was capable of making that determination. Not yet, anyway. Kersh and White had never entered a Sunbeam plant. Like Dunlap, Kersh had been on the job for only six days; White for even fewer. Fannin was the only executive in the room who had ever walked into a Sunbeam factory. But the lawyer knew next to nothing about manufacturing or production, and he could hardly assess the viability of a factory. Sunbeam, moreover, had twenty-six plants and sixty-one warehouses scattered around the world, including its state-of-the-art complex in Hattiesburg, Mississippi.

"Christ," Fannin ventured, "I don't have a damn clue. I know we have plants running well below full capacity, and we still have to consolidate some of the factories into Hattiesburg."

Dunlap, of course, already had a number in mind. Although new to the company and the industry, and completely unfamiliar with the strengths and weaknesses of each of Sunbeam's twenty-six factories, he confidently predicted Sunbeam would have no more than four or five plants by the time the restructuring was complete.

The guesswork appalled Fannin and White, but they soon realized that Dunlap was keen on making a statement at Sunbeam. Layoffs and plant closings would be made not only because they were necessary, but also for effect. It made Fannin, at least, queasy that someone could so carelessly and with total indifference talk of causing so many people and communities pain.

"I have a reputation to maintain," Dunlap insisted. "I don't want people to think I've lost my touch. I want big numbers."

Dunlap was deadly serious. Though he claimed to despise his most popular alias, Chainsaw Al, Dunlap cheerfully volunteered its origins to anyone willing to listen. It was the nickname given to him by the famous British naturalist John Aspinall, who, Dunlap said, told him he was like a chainsaw that cuts away the fat and leaves a great sculpture. Dunlap joked that the epithet made him sound like a serial killer. He much preferred the designation given to him by his mentor Sir James Goldsmith, who dubbed his American friend "Rambo in Pinstripes." "You're like Rambo," Sir James once told him. "You go into chaotic situations and clean up in business what he does in war."

Dunlap regarded the Rambo appellation as a great compliment, and he was determined to live up to it and his own reputation for savagely attacking costs and people. On downsizing, Dunlap's underlying belief was profoundly simple: like a street fighter with a sharp blade, he always cut big, deep, and a little wild. "My philosophy is to err on the side of too much," Dunlap wrote. In his own mind, he wanted to take people out all at once and never have to do it again. Dunlap always justified the cutbacks as a way to provide a more secure future for the survivors. It did not always turn out that way.

Still, there were few executives anywhere in the world who had so clearly and fully built their success on laying people off. He was the fiercest advocate, perhaps the only willing public advocate, in favor of downsizing. At Lily-Tulip, he cut headquarters staff by 50 percent and one of every five salaried employees. At Crown-Zellerbach, he axed 22 percent of the workers and reduced the conglomerate's distribution centers to four from twenty-two. At Consolidated Press Holdings, Dunlap sold off 300 of 413 companies. At Scott, he laid off 11,200 workers, some 35 percent of the payroll, within months of his arrival. And now at Sunbeam only six days, it was becoming clear that Dunlap was seized with the idea that this should be the biggest downsizing of them all.

FOR SOMEONE WHO had made a career out of downsizing, Dunlap did not seem to be overly anxious to fire many people himself. More often than not, he would instruct others to deliver the news, then wait anxiously in his office to hear how the executed took it. When Dunlap ordered someone fired at headquarters, he would often give specific instructions on what time the person should be told so that he would not even be inside the building. "He would say do it at 11:45 A.M. and he would be in that damn car of his by 11:30 A.M.," recalled Wilson, who carried out several of his termination orders as head of human resources. Indeed, at Sunbeam, where Dunlap would announce the layoffs of 11,100 people in all, the only employee he would personally fire was Clegg.

No one in the company was more disturbed by Clegg's firing than his good friend Richard Boynton. Though they had vastly different personalities, they had worked closely together ever since Clegg hired Boynton as a national sales manager five years earlier from Polaroid, where he had worked in sales for thirteen years. By his own reckoning, Boynton could be unusually volatile and brutal. He spoke with a strong Bostonian accent, was highly opinionated, and had a fiery temper. Though he was in his early forties, he still maintained a muscular body by lifting weights and working out. As a student at Nichol College in Massachusetts, he boxed in the Silver Mittens and Golden Gloves to raise money for the school. He was also a rugged defensive end on an impressive college football team that won the New England Conference Championship four years in a row.

Like Clegg, he was a superb salesman, someone who could sell air conditioners to Eskimos, as one admirer put it. He had expanded Sunbeam's business with retailer Walgreen's from $1.5 million to $13 million. With every promotion that Clegg won, Boynton followed him upward. So Dunlap's shabby treatment of his buddy both angered and sickened Boynton. "I was in shock for a few weeks after that," says Boynton. "You've got to understand: He killed himself for the company. Jim Clegg was Sunbeam-Oster. In the customers' eyes and in the employees' eyes, he was the company. Al Dunlap was an impostor. Schipke was sitting on Clegg's throne. Everyone in the company thought Clegg would get the job."

Though Dunlap initially deemed Boynton a keeper, Boynton believed his days were surely numbered. He had been too closely aligned with Clegg for things to be otherwise. Infuriated over Dunlap's treatment of his friend, he was determined to do everything he could to make life difficult for Dunlap and his new team. He often refused to take phone calls from either Kersh or White. When he did take them, he often refused to do what they asked him. During one heated telephone conversation with White, Boynton slammed the phone down after yelling into the receiver: "I don't know who you think you're talking to but don't ever threaten me." Most of the arguments focused on Dunlap's plans to close the company's Schaumberg, Illinois, sales and marketing offices, where Boynton was based.

"Pittsburgh? Providence? Fort Lauderdale? What's next?" wrote Boynton, making a pitch in a memo for Dunlap to move the headquarters to Chicago.

Informed that Dunlap had decided to consolidate the sales and marketing offices in Florida, Boynton told White, "Boy, that's a bright decision. What are you going to do? Move it to Boca Raton? Do you guys know we don't have any customers in Florida except Eckerd Drugs? Do you understand why we're here? It's because we're a stone's throw from Sears, Walgreen's, Costco, Montgomery Ward. That's why it's here. To save money. We're a one-hour flight to Minneapolis to visit Target. We're a thirty-five-minute flight to Detroit to see Kmart. We're a one-hour flight to Memphis, where Service Merchandise is. We're a one-and-one-half hour flight to Wal-Mart."

At one point, Boynton circled all the locations of Sunbeam's customers on a map of the United States and then circled Florida with the words "Please explain!" and faxed it to Dunlap. From his friends in Fort Lauderdale, Boynton heard that Dunlap was enraged by the games he was playing. Word got back that Dunlap said he was going to get a two-by-four, come out to Schaumberg, and hit Boynton with it. Boynton's response to White: "Why don't you come out and try it. I'll shove it up your ass."

By early August, Dunlap had had enough. He ordered White and Wilson to fly to Chicago and fire Boynton as well as Michael Beauregard, vice president of strategic planning. Wilson telephoned the pair and told them to be at the Hancock Tower in downtown Chicago, the location of Sunbeam's international business at 10 A.M. on August 7.

Boynton immediately knew their mission was to terminate him. "I was being very belligerent," he admits. "I was being disrespectful and insubordinate." Three days before their visit, Boynton and Beauregard were e-mailed the separation agreements by a headquarters' friend who wanted them to be prepared so they could negotiate better deals for themselves.

On August 7, before departing for what would become their execution, Boynton had gathered together all the employees of his household products group to bid them farewell. As many as 100 staffers crammed into a conference room. They lined the walls and the outside hallways. Many of the managers were openly crying, knowing that Boynton was about to be fired.

In an angry and impassioned speech, a visibly upset Boynton told them he was proud of the team he had created and what it had accomplished. Each of them, Boynton warned, would now go through a challenging and disturbing period, but he would no longer be there to lead them.

"No one was going to tell me how to do things," he said. "No one is going to tell me how to live my life, except my dad. Take care of yourselves. Don't worry about me. I will rise like a phoenix out of the ashes."

The assembled employees were just as shocked as the executive team in Fort Lauderdale had been only a few weeks earlier. "Everyone wondered what the hell is going on," remembered one manager. "It was bedlam. Most of the people there were visibly sad. Some were crying. People also were upset not only because Rich was going to lose his job. They also were worried that they would be next. We were already trading lists of recruiters, and everyone had their résumés up on their computer screens."

When Boynton finished his speech, the crowd burst into applause. Boynton and Beauregard were escorted by colleagues out of the building and into a waiting limo for the trip to downtown Chicago. Once there, Boynton was invited into Spencer Volk's office first by White, who quickly told him he was being terminated. Known for his volatile personality and hot temper, Boynton exploded.

"Can you tell me why I'm being fired?" he shouted.

But Boynton wouldn't allow White to give him an answer.

"Newt," he said, "don't even waste my time. You couldn't even carry my jock. For you to even evaluate my performance is such a fucking joke. Don't bother. I wouldn't work for you and that scumbag boss of yours on a bet. You can shove all your paperwork straight up your ass. My customers won't be happy with this, Newt."

"They are our customers," White replied, "and if you were a professional, you wouldn't contact them."

"Go fuck yourself," yelled Boynton, as he walked toward the door and stormed out of the office. "This is my company," shouted Boynton. "This is not your company. This company belongs to me because of my relationships."

Wilson then met with Boynton to hand him his separation agreement.

"This ain't enough," Boynton said. "I've talked to one of the best labor lawyers in the United States and he said it ought to be double what you're offering."

"Well, Rich, I don't know who your labor lawyer is but let me give you a piece of advice. I've only worked for Dunlap for seventeen days, but you can litigate this until you're seventy-five years old, and you'll never get another nickel. Go home, sign it, and send it back to me and be happy you're getting what you're getting."

"We'll see," Boynton shot back.

White had already fired Beauregard, who took his papers from Wilson and left the office.

Within fifteen seconds the phone rang. It was Dunlap.

"How did it go?" he asked Wilson. "What happened?"

"Beauregard is fine, but Boynton was a problem."

Wilson told Dunlap exactly what Boynton had said and Dunlap went ballistic. "He was screaming and yelling into the receiver," remembered Wilson.

"That dirty son of a bitch," Dunlap shouted. "If he's going to fuck with me, I'll show him who's boss. Goddamn it, Wilson. You go back and you tell him . . . "

"He's gone, Al."

"Well, what did you tell him?"

Wilson's reply satisfied Dunlap, who then ordered Fannin to keep on top of Boynton.

"You follow up on this thing and if that son of a bitch doesn't sign that severance agreement in the allotted time, pull the offer from him."

ROB JOHNSON, then forty-five, had worked at Sunbeam longer than any of the other apprehensive executives gathered in the boardroom on Dunlap's first day. In fact, he had never worked anywhere else in his life. His twenty-six years with the company began in the late 1960s, when he was nineteen years old. During the day he had attended classes at Jones County Junior College in Ellisville, Mississippi, some forty-five miles away from his home in Waynesboro. At night he had cut vast rolls of fabric for electric blankets at the same plant that had employed his mother for well over a decade. For years the mammoth 887,200-square-foot plant was the company's largest, a place all the locals simply called "the blanket factory."

For Johnson, Sunbeam became the ticket to a lifestyle that his father, an auto body repairman, could only dream about. In early 1970 he transferred out of the factory and into the office as a full-time clerk. A few years later Johnson helped to relocate the Hanson Scale Co., a new acquisition in Northbrook, Illinois, to Neosho, Missouri, where the company produced outdoor grills. By the time Kazarian had taken control of Sunbeam in 1990, Johnson was vice president of marketing. Rob Johnson was a good-looking man, with wavy blond hair and warm blue eyes, handsome enough to have starred in one of the company's "Buy American" television commercials only a couple of years earlier. With his easygoing manner and his soft and casual Mississippi drawl, Johnson claimed that cheaper, imported furniture would quickly rust, while Sunbeam's aluminum products would not.

To the delight of Kazarian, the commercial coaxed major retailers to remain loyal customers and to curtail their orders of imports. Johnson, handsomely rewarded with lucrative stock options by Kazarian, won another step on the ladder upward: to senior vice president of sales and marketing. When Schipke ousted his boss, Richard D. Davidson, in late 1995, Johnson became the acting president of Sunbeam's outdoor grill and furniture businesses.

It was a big job, making him one of the top four operating executives at Sunbeam, along with Clegg, Boynton, and Volk. His division accounted for almost 40 percent of Sunbeam's $1.2 billion in sales. But he left Fort Lauderdale wary and uneasy about the future. Dunlap, Johnson believed, hardly instilled confidence. "My impression was that he was going to apply a cookie-cutter approach to the company," says Johnson. "No one cared to know anything about the business. It was: 'This is what we've done before, and this is what we're going to do now. If it doesn't work, it's your fault.' That was his attitude."

Still, he had more immediate worries. Johnson had only two weeks to prepare for one of the most crucial rituals on the business calendar, the immense National Hardware Show in Chicago's McCormack Place. Every year as many as 100,000 customers would converge on the convention center to look over the new products of nearly 8,000 suppliers. This year Johnson's division was unveiling more new products in outdoor furniture and barbecue grills for the following season than at any time in its history. Sunbeam would send twenty-five employees to the event, where it leased one of the largest areas of any company at the show.

Dunlap's arrival, however, gave many customers the jitters. "I have no choice but to treat Sunbeam very judiciously," said George Schwartz, a vice president of Pergament Home Centers, which depended on Sunbeam for 80 percent of its outdoor business. "I may look to give them 50 to 60 percent and fill in with other vendors. Right now, nobody at Sunbeam can give me a comfort zone because they don't know what's going to happen. If Sunbeam gets sold and they divest the outdoor furniture division, where does that leave me?"

Johnson sought to answer such questions continuously during the four-day show that began on August 14. In fact, nearly all his time was consumed by questions about future supply. Will Dunlap cut products from the line that they wanted in stock? Will the company be able to fulfill its orders? To quell their doubts, Johnson tried to assure them that furniture and grills were core products at Sunbeam, and he promised he would honor all his sales commitments to them. Still, several retailers began to reduce their orders and arrange for new suppliers.

Even Johnson had doubts. Furniture was a low-margin business, and it had veered back and forth between profit and loss for several years. Dunlap had dispatched his newest hire to the show, P. Newton White, a Scott Paper alumnus who was now Sunbeam's executive vice president of consumer products worldwide. While strolling the convention floor with Johnson to survey the competition, White asked: "Why are we in this business?"

It was not an idle question. After the show closed on Wednesday, August 17, White told Johnson that Dunlap planned to sell the outdoor furniture division, getting rid of nearly 3,000 employees and eight plants, shutter the division's Nashville offices where twenty were employed, and close one of the two outdoor grill factories. The news was upsetting, especially because only a day earlier Johnson had made promises to customers he had known for years. "I found out I had been lying to them," he later said. "I had worked hard to build good relationships with the retailers. I had a reputation for honesty and for trust."

He flew back to Nashville on Thursday, only to receive word that same night that now White wanted him in Fort Lauderdale first thing on Friday morning. "By that time, I had known there were things that were going to happen that I would not agree with and would not take part in," he recalls. It wasn't that Johnson was opposed to any retrenchment. He had spent a good part of the past year working on and getting approval for a downsizing plan that would close four plants and lay off 800 to 1,000 employees. Every rank-and-file employee, under that plan, would have been given one to three months of severance pay, and as many as 300 to 500 of them would have been offered the chance to relocate to other factories.

He was already closing down one of the ten plants and consolidating its operations into another. Dunlap would later take credit for that closure, even though it was completed by the time he announced his own restructuring plan. But what Dunlap was now proposing was not only too draconian, in Johnson's view, it was also inhumane to the people who would lose their jobs, for in an offhand remark, White had told Johnson, "We don't typically pay severance."

On Thursday evening Johnson ruminated over what exactly they wanted. Did White want him in Fort Lauderdale so he could fire him in person? Or did he want him to work on plans to cut back even more? "If it was to fire me, I was going to save them the trouble," Johnson says. "And if it were the plans, I didn't want any part of it."

The next morning, instead of boarding a plane to Florida, he called Jim Wilson and Fannin and told them he wasn't going to Fort Lauderdale.

"If you want to talk about the business, we can do that by phone," he recalls telling Wilson. "If it's about something else, I'm not coming down. It's a beautiful day in Nashville. I think I'll play golf."

"Fine," replied Wilson. "If you're resigning please leave the office. We'll have your things packed up and delivered to you."

"That's great," said Johnson, who quickly left for the nearest golf course, where he shot eighteen holes.

To the boy who had become a man at Sunbeam, a resignation seemed more honorable than a firing. "I walked away from a year to eighteen months' severance pay and some stock options that I wasn't fully vested in," says Johnson. "At the risk of sounding self-righteous, it was worth it to me."

In little more than a month on the job, Dunlap had lost or fired three of the top four operating executives responsible for 90 percent of Sunbeam's revenues. He had lost or tossed away their forty years of company experience. Only Volk, president of international, remained. His critics inside the company had dubbed him the "armadillo" because, said one, "he had a knack for bullshitting and surviving, no matter what." During his two years at Sunbeam, the company's international business fell into the red, losing $17.6 million in 1996, after earning $10.1 million in 1994, a profit swing of nearly $28 million. By November, however, even the smooth-talking Volk was gone.

5

ANOTHER DOWNSIZING

THE TRUE ARCHITECT of the downsizing was C. Donald Burnett, a senior partner at Coopers & Lybrand, a consultant Dunlap had relied on for advice and counsel through much of his career. Burnett lacked the spit and polish of a McKinsey & Co. man. He looked a little like the corner druggist in an old-fashioned pharmacy in Iowa. Completely bald with huge ears, the bespectacled Burnett wore wide suspenders under often rumpled suits. He was amiable and helpful, if not a deep or introspective thinker. When Dunlap bought his time, he gained a loyal mercenary. Burnett, it was said, was one of the few people who could stand toe to toe with Dunlap. Yet he was always eager to oblige Dunlap's appetite for dramatic and wrenching change, especially for the ruthless cutbacks that earned Dunlap his reputation as Chainsaw Al and Rambo in Pinstripes.

Burnett began working for Dunlap when he was at American Can in 1977, and he had worked for him everywhere since. He helped chop heads at Lily-Tulip, Crown-Zellerbach, and Scott Paper. He helped plot strategy and reorganize operations. He analyzed potential acquisition targets, from BAT Industries to Pan Am Airlines, when Dunlap worked for Sir James. He screened candidates who hoped to work with Dunlap and then counseled them on how to deal with the man once hired. He advised outside contractors who were ready to throw their hands up in disgust.

Few people understood Dunlap better than Burnett. Fewer still thought of Burnett as a good friend. Though Dunlap and Burnett often engaged in volcanic arguments in which the CEO often threatened to fire him, Burnett considered Dunlap a close pal. The consultant told associates that Dunlap would "always be my friend," no matter what. They played tennis together several times a year, and the Burnetts often socialized with the Dunlaps, even throwing an occasional dinner party for them in New York. When Coopers sponsored a junket to the Ryder Cup, flying guests over to England where they boarded the QE2 for a cruise to Spain's Mediterranean coast and the world-famous golfing event in late September, Dunlap went along for the ride.

As a senior partner at Coopers, Burnett often handled the bigger and tougher clients. He found that no one was more demanding than Dunlap. During the peak of a consulting job for Dunlap, Burnett typically spent two or three days a week on the premises, becoming an integral part of Dunlap's management team. Through two decades of work, Burnett absorbed remarkable abuse from him. "He expects you on call twenty-four hours a day," Burnett told others. "Nobody pushes like he does. He can be a bastard, but a fair bastard. He's very loyal and demands the same. If you're not, you're dead meat."

Burnett knew the rules, and he adhered to them. In exchange, his relationship with Dunlap was highly profitable for him and his firm. Though Dunlap often beat him down on price, Burnett's own review of his long association with Dunlap found that nearly $30 million of Coopers & Lybrand consulting work could be directly or indirectly traced to him. So Burnett was one of the first people Dunlap called when he landed the Sunbeam job.

By the Friday of his first week, Burnett's troops had already begun crawling all over the company. Eventually, a dozen consultants worked at company headquarters. They set up a command post of sorts in a conference room and fanned out in teams by each function of the company, from finance to human resources. Another dozen worked in the field, visiting Sunbeam's factories, warehouses, and sales offices; interviewing managers; compiling facts. Always, they were rushed to conclusion: Dunlap would never wait for the final result of the study. Instead Kersh met with Burnett and some of his charges every few days for the up-to-the-minute reports that Dunlap demanded several times a week. At one point, when the Coopers team came back with some initial estimates of the layoffs that didn't quite meet Dunlap's expectations, Dunlap quipped that Burnett was "getting weak-kneed in his old age." So the pressure was on to come back with a bigger number.

While Burnett's people hastily studied Sunbeam and put together the restructuring plan, Newt White assembled sixteen profit-improvement teams to examine every aspect of Sunbeam's business. The goal of each team was to determine how a specific business or function, like household products or new business development, should be overhauled and repositioned. Virtually all the direct management of the company were team members, along with many of Burnett's consultants. Rich Goudis, an insider who intimately knew Sunbeam's problems, was named White's top aide, with the title of vice president of planning and strategy.

The goal for all of them was to create the master plan that would allow Dunlap to turn the company around, just as he had done at Scott Paper. But he was not only restructuring Sunbeam to put more air in its stock. He also was reorganizing the company's all-important board of directors to gain greater control over a group of men that had long been dominated by Price and Steinhardt.

FROM THE EARLIEST point in the negotiations, Dunlap insisted not only on money but also on control, and Price so badly wanted him that he and Steinhardt acceded to every demand Dunlap made. "We put the kitchen sink in that contract and they accepted everything," confided a Dunlap associate. "Al got exactly what he wanted." While the monetary inducements attracted most of the attention, other details were truly unusual. Dunlap's employment contract allowed him to personally select at least three new board members—a right that gave the CEO effective control of the board and would eventually permit him to replace every director other than Price's hand-picked representative, Peter Langerman. The contract also gave him "without limitation the power of supervision and control" over the company, a peculiar clause Dunlap inserted into the contract to ensure that he would be free of any meddling by Price and Steinhardt.

Considering how much control Price had exercised over Sunbeam in the past, these were extraordinary concessions. But Price went further than the contract required. He asked a new board member, whom he had personally recruited only weeks earlier, to resign his seat.

Sometime in June, Price and Peter Langerman had visited with Raymond Troubh at his offices in New York to invite him to join the Sunbeam board. A former Lazard Freres investment banker, the seventy-year-old Troubh was a lawyer and a professional director. When he was named a director on July 2—two weeks before Dunlap was named CEO—Sunbeam became his seventeenth board.

From the start, Dunlap didn't want him. He disliked the notion of professional directors, had driven them off the board at Scott and immediately sought Troubh's resignation as well. So within two weeks of Dunlap's arrival, the director received a telephone call from Price and Langerman.

"You did us a favor by joining the board," Price told him. "But Dunlap doesn't want any professional directors. He doesn't like them."

"Well," said Troubh, "I don't want to hang around with a fellow who from the beginning doesn't like the definition of my being."

Troubh graciously resigned after being on the board for exactly one month and never attending a meeting. He would not be the last to lose his board seat, however.

Intent on shaping the board, Dunlap soon went after another director, Richard Ravitch, who had been recently invited onto the board by Michael Steinhardt. Formerly chairman of New York's Bowery Savings Bank, Ravitch was head of his own real estate management firm in New York. His first board meeting as a Sunbeam director was the one at which Dunlap was named chief executive. After he attended a couple of sessions with Dunlap, it was clear to Ravitch that the CEO wanted him off the board. Dunlap told others that he was kicking him off because Ravitch fell asleep in the boardroom, a contention that Ravitch later called "utter nonsense." "It was very clear that Al was not looking for advice or independent judgment," thought Ravitch.

He called his friend Troubh and asked his opinion.

"Am I correct in thinking that the last thing this man wants are independent directors?" Ravitch asked Troubh.

Troubh, never having met Dunlap, didn't know what to think.

"Well," said Ravitch, "the investors want him. It's their business. It's their money. It's their capital."

Ravitch wrote Dunlap a polite letter, claiming that personal commitments made his time unavailable. Suddenly the board's two newest members—installed by Price and Steinhardt to replace the two directors who had resigned over the investors' undue influence over the company—were gone. After Steinhardt closed his investment fund and distributed Sunbeam's shares to partners and investors, his representative, Shimon Topor, departed the board as well.

Finally, in early April 1997, Dunlap sent general counsel David Fannin to see Charles Thayer with the message that Dunlap did not want Thayer to stand for reelection to the board. Other than Langerman, he was the longest serving Sunbeam director and probably the most knowledgeable as well. An ex-banker, Thayer had been on the board since the company was taken out of bankruptcy. He had served as acting chief executive on two occasions when the investors tossed out Kazarian and then Schipke. He also had recruited Fannin to the company. "As questions would come up, it was not uncommon for new directors to ask me what I thought about what Al was proposing," Thayer said. "I didn't disagree with any of the decisions, but I don't think that Al liked it." Thayer agreed to resign as well.

Dunlap, meantime, had begun to stack the board with longtime friends and allies. Besides Kersh, he invited his personal attorney, Howard G. Kristol, to join the board. A small, hunched-over man who wore owl-like spectacles, Kristol was a partner in the New York law firm of Reboul, MacMurray, Hewitt, Maynard & Kristol. For nearly two decades, the Harvard-educated attorney had looked after Dunlap's personal affairs, negotiating his employment contracts from his days at Lily-Tulip to the present and setting up trust funds for him and Kersh. When Dunlap brought public one of Kerry Packer's U.S. companies, Valassis Communications Inc., Dunlap put Kristol on the board to serve as his "eyes and ears" while he remained in Australia.

After Kristol helped Dunlap get his extraordinary compensation deal at Scott, Dunlap put the lawyer on the Scott Paper board. Other board members expected a complete sycophant, but they were pleasantly surprised when the lawyer asked challenging questions in the boardroom. After he assisted Dunlap to gain his new employment contract at Sunbeam, Kristol was brought onto that company's board—it was the third Dunlap company at which the lawyer served as a director.

To replace Ravitch, Dunlap enlisted Faith Whittlesey, a passionate and outspoken Republican conservative, whom he had met through Sir James Goldsmith. A widow for over two decades, Whittlesey looked like a grammar school principal. She wore glasses, dressed modestly, and displayed a good deal of nervous energy. She was a lawyer and policy wonk who had raised three children and devoted herself to conservative and Christian causes that aligned her with the Reagan White House. Under Reagan, she served as ambassador to Switzerland from 1981 to 1983 and again from 1985 to 1988. Between those tours, Whittlesey served as a member of the senior White House staff, heading up the office of public liaison. It was at the Reagan White House that she struck up a friendship with Sir James, a frequent visitor, and then Dunlap.

She shared Dunlap's conservative views, attempted to more deeply involve him in Republican politics, and greatly admired the man's tenacity and grit. Indeed, Whittlesey considered him a "real American hero," a self-made man and an exemplar of the American dream. Like Kristol, she had served as a board member at Valassis Communications, and when Dunlap was being pilloried in Philadelphia for his massive layoffs at Scott, she had written an op-ed piece for the *Philadelphia Enquirer* in defense of downsizings. Whittlesey served as chairman of the New York–based nonprofit American Swiss Foundation, a group devoted to promoting better understanding between the United States and Switzerland.

In Thayer's place, Dunlap named a local banker, William Rutter. Rutter had been among a team of colleagues who had won Scott's commercial banking business for First Union Bank. A personable man who ran First Union's private banking department, he helped to manage the money of some of the wealthiest of Boca Raton's residents. Rutter may have lacked the credentials to be on the board of a New York Stock Exchange company, but he knew everyone worth knowing in Boca Raton. His bank had some of Sunbeam's commercial banking business, and as Rutter became better acquainted with Dunlap, First Union gained the opportunity to help arrange the transition of new Sunbeam executives to Florida. Rutter thought the CEO a "dynamic leader" and an "extremely charming" golf partner.

Of all Sunbeam's new directors, however, none had come to so openly admire and praise Dunlap as a Harvard-educated attorney and Stetson University law school professor by the name of Charles M. Elson. An earnest and diminutive man, who at age thirty-six still retained his boyish looks, Elson had met the CEO by accident. In

August 1994 Elson received a somewhat mysterious telephone call from Peter Judice, Dunlap's personal public relations adviser. Dunlap had read an essay Elson had written for the *Wall Street Journal* eleven months earlier, in which Elson had argued that all directors of public corporations should receive their board fees in the form of company stock. He reasoned that stock ownership would strongly motivate directors to be more independent of management and more closely aligned with the interests of shareholders.

Elson studied the issue and found that board members with insignificant equity holdings were far more likely to overpay their chief executives than directors who owned $100,000 or more of stock.

During the phone call, Judice, an unassuming PR veteran with the Burson-Marsteller agency in New York, told Elson he represented the chairman of a company who had read his opinion piece and who wanted to eliminate all cash and perks to his directors in favor of outright grants of stock.

"What do you think?" Judice asked.

"I think it's fabulous," said Elson, surprised and delighted that his essay might have an impact on the real world. At the time, only one other major American corporation, financial services giant Travelers Inc., paid its directors solely in stock.

Judice, ever the clever pitchman, wanted to direct reporters to Elson so that Dunlap's action would gain support and credibility, reaffirmed by an academic who had studied the issue.

"Well," said Elson, "whoever it is, tell them the market is going to be very receptive to this idea. I bet your stock will bump up a full point or more."

Judice was doubtful, but he thanked the professor and said he would be in touch. The following day, on August 30, he faxed Elson a draft press release announcing Dunlap's pay plan for Scott Paper directors. The news added $2.125 to Scott's stock, pushing it up to a record $65.875.

Delighted by the market's reaction, Dunlap invited Elson to Philadelphia headquarters for lunch. Inside of a week, the young professor found himself munching sandwiches with the chairman of Scott Paper. Elson remembers that listening to Dunlap, whose hearing was impaired because of artillery fire at West Point, was "like listening to a radio turned all the way up."

Over lunch, on an eerily quiet and vast floor of empty executive offices, they agreed to work together to promote the idea of stock ownership among directors. The meeting sparked a professional friendship that helped make both men fixtures on the corporate governance scene. Five months later, in February 1995, Dunlap delivered a speech at Stetson on stock ownership, and later in the year Dunlap and Elson began serving on a blue-ribbon panel of the National Association of Corporate Directors in Washington, D.C. The committee was studying the issue of directors' compensation, and the duo were intent on pressing their point of view.

When panel member William Adams, the CEO of Armstrong Industries, spoke in favor of recommending increased cash pay to directors, Dunlap perked up. "You know," he said, "it's interesting that you would say that. I would expect nothing less from you, given the incredibly pathetic and mediocre performance that you've delivered at your company." Adams looked mortified and did not try to respond to the attack, which hushed the room, until someone shifted the discussion elsewhere. From that moment on, however, the anti-stock side collapsed, and the committee drifted toward Dunlap's position. Still, few agreed that directors should be paid solely in stock because that policy might be an imposition for some who might need the cash, particularly academics and executives from nonprofits. A draft of the group's report urged companies to pay directors "with equity representing the majority of pay from 50% to 100%."

After panel member Barbara Franklin took issue with the language, it was softened so that the report eventually endorsed the view that equity represent "a substantial portion of the total, up to 100%." It was a minor compromise, one that allowed some measure of interpretation, but it enraged Dunlap. At a June 1996 press conference, called to announce the committee's findings, he did not hold back from insulting her.

"What do you have against professional directors?" asked Franklin, a former government official who serves on numerous boards and is considered a professional director.

"I think, Barbara, that professional directors have a lot in common with the world's oldest profession," Dunlap responded. "They do it for the money, and they are not selective about their clientele." Appalled, Franklin walked away in disgust.

Though embarrassed himself, Elson nevertheless admired the CEO's impudence. With the professor's help and connections in the burgeoning governance movement, moreover, Dunlap began to cultivate an image as an advocate for shareholder rights. The issue nicely dovetailed with Dunlap's long-stated belief that companies should be run only for the benefit of owners—not employees, communities, or any other constituency.

When Dunlap left Scott Paper and first contemplated writing a book, he asked the professor if he would be interested in ghosting it. Though Elson declined, he agreed to help Dunlap find a writer and to edit the final manuscript. So when Dunlap began to reconstitute Sunbeam's board, he telephoned Elson.

"I'm thinking of putting a shareholder advocate on the board," Dunlap told him.

"Who are you thinking of?" asked Elson, thinking it might be Nell Minow, a prominent shareholder activist.

"How about you? Would you be interested? I don't know if I can do it yet. I have to talk to my board. But would you do it?"

"Yeah, I think I would," Elson said.

A week later, Dunlap called Elson again and said he would name the professor to the board but he would have to hold 5,000 shares of Sunbeam stock. Elson had already purchased 2,000 shares and told Dunlap so.

"I want you to have 5,000," Dunlap said.

"That's $100,000, Al. That's a helluva lot of money for an academic."

"I know, but I want you to sweat. Some academic once wrote that unless you had $100,000 in company stock you shouldn't be a director," joked Dunlap, referring to Elson's own writings.

Elson, thinking this was his chance to become a guinea pig for his academic theory, agreed to take the money from his savings and put it into Sunbeam stock. Like everything else, Dunlap hoped to get some complimentary media coverage for being one of the first chief executives to ever name a shareholder activist to his board.

But the plan backfired. On September 26, Elson's phone rang at 7:30 A.M. On the line was Judice in New York.

"Have you seen it?" Judice asked nervously.

"What?"

"The story," he answered. "Al's very upset. I've never had anyone scream at me like he did. He wants to talk to you. I've got to warn you. It's coming."

"Well, let me go and get it."

Elson hung up, dashed out, and drove straight to the nearest newsstand, at Walgreen's Pharmacy a few blocks away. He picked up a copy of the day's *Wall Street Journal* and hurriedly opened it to page B9. Under the headline "Sunbeam's Chief Picks Holder Activist and Close Friend as Outside Director," the story said that Dunlap's close relationship with Elson raised questions as to whether he could act independently of Sunbeam's strong-willed chairman and CEO.

A quotation from Sarah Teslik, who headed up a trade group of more than 100 of the largest pension funds, made Elson nearly gasp for breath. "From my viewpoint," she said, "Mr. Dunlap is closer to Elson than he is to his wife." The academic, Teslik added, "is not just a yes man. He's a yes lap-dog." The story was written by management writer Joann S. Lublin, whom Elson had invited to moderate at Dunlap's Stetson University appearance.

Back home, he tossed the paper over to his wife, Aimee. "I want you to read this and tell me what you think."

"Lap dog?" she said. "How could she say that about you? That's awful!"

Within minutes, the phone rang again. It was Dunlap. He was, as Judice warned, livid. But to Elson's astonishment, Dunlap was not only angry, but he blamed Elson for the story's disapproving spin.

"It's your fault," he shouted. "You're the one who introduced me to that reporter in the first place."

"Al, come on."

"I'll never give her a story again!" he vowed.

"What's done is done," said Elson. "People who know me know it's not true."

What Elson did not yet know, or could ever imagine, was that he would someday be placed in a position where he would have to prove his independence.

ON WALL STREET, where companies that were laying off people, restructuring operations, and doing mergers and acquisitions were routinely rewarded, the expectations of a monumental downsizing at

Sunbeam were high. "The stock has gone up in anticipation of this announcement, and he's going to have to satisfy everyone's expectations," said Susan Q. Gallagher, an analyst who covered Sunbeam with Nick Heymann at NatWest Securities Corp. "But he's done it before."

The consensus on the Street was that Dunlap would eliminate 30 percent of Sunbeam's workforce through layoffs and sales of operations. No one thought he could hit the 35 percent number he had achieved at Scott Paper. After all, this was a company that only a few years earlier had gone through massive layoffs and restructuring during the Allegheny bankruptcy and the leadership of Paul Kazarian.

On November 12, less than two months after Elson joined the board, Al Dunlap stood before his board of directors in New York and outlined the restructuring plan cobbled together by his consultants. By now the board included Dunlap, Kersh, Langerman, Thayer, Kristol, Ravitch, and Elson. Whittlesey and Rutter had yet to join, while Topor had already resigned because Steinhardt Partners were now out of the stock. The seven board members met in a conference room at the Rockefeller Center law firm of Dunlap's personal attorney, Kristol.

The cutbacks Dunlap proposed were so draconian that they would invite criticism from Wall Street, the U.S. Secretary of Labor, and a host of management gurus and experts. Dunlap said he would eliminate half of Sunbeam's 12,000 employees, scrap 87 percent of its existing products, and sell or consolidate thirty-nine of its fifty-three facilities, including eighteen of its twenty-six factories and thirty-seven of its sixty-one warehouses. He also would divest several lines of business, including Sunbeam's outdoor furniture operations, clocks, scales, and decorative bedding. He would close six regional offices as well as the company's Fort Lauderdale headquarters and move to a single office building in Delray Beach, Florida. The downsizing, he said, would save the company $225 million a year and would result in a one-time pretax charge of $300 million.

"We planned this like the invasion of Normandy," Dunlap told the board. "We attacked every aspect of the business."

The downsizing king, however, also presented an aggressive growth plan. Dunlap promised to introduce at least thirty new products a year in the United States, expand sales abroad, and double the company's revenue to more than $2 billion by 1999. Some $600 million of the sales gain would come from new products, while another $600 million would come from joint ventures and licensing agreements overseas. Dunlap said Sunbeam would spend $12 million on a new advertising and marketing program under the slogan "There's a New Sunbeam Shining."

Hearing all these details for the first time in a three-hour board meeting, the directors sat stunned at the aggressiveness of the plan. None of them had received any written materials on the massive upheaval in advance of the board meeting. Dunlap said he was making final changes up to the last minutes. Of them all, Langerman posed the most questions, poking into the plan's details, especially Dunlap's assumptions on future revenue growth. With each query, however, Dunlap came back firmly and convincingly.

Some board members thought it odd that Dunlap presented the cutbacks so dramatically and with so much hyperbole. Though he played up the 50 percent reduction of the workforce, a full 6,000 jobs, only 2,800 people would actually get laid off. The remaining 3,200 employees worked in businesses that Dunlap planned to sell. Other chief executives, eager to downplay the social costs of a massive restructuring, would have emphasized the smaller figure. "It was accurate, but it was vintage Dunlap in its hyperbole," said a director.

What truly caught their attention, however, was Dunlap's ambitious growth plan. Langerman and Thayer had been on Sunbeam's board since the company was purchased out of bankruptcy. They saw first-hand how difficult it was to get growth out of a mature yet highly competitive industry that was being squeezed by foreign competition and the mass merchants who sold Sunbeam products. "I was a little concerned with the sales side of the plan," said Thayer. "I didn't think it could be done domestically, but I agreed that the company never took advantage of its international opportunities. I had no clue whether he could hit that sales growth number."

The board not only unanimously approved the plan, but directors quickly went public in supporting the drastic nature of it. "It wasn't a question of whether we cut too many or too few," director Kristol told the *Wall Street Journal*. "It's a comprehensive plan designed to match what the company wants to accomplish." Charles M. Elson also was impressed. "It's very Dunlapesque in many respects," he said. "It's very coordinated and focused. He capitalizes on the company's strengths and positions it for what I think will be a substantial future."

Whether exaggerated or not, the size and scope of the plan was so great that even Wall Street, which almost always rewards cutbacks with rising stock prices, was taken aback. Sunbeam's stock lost 50 cents to close at $25.375 on the day Dunlap announced the restructuring. "I can't believe this guy would come out with something so aggressive just to set himself up to fail," said PaineWebber's Andrew Shore. "If he pulls it off, this is a $30 stock."

In percentage terms, it was one of the largest single cutbacks ever announced by a corporation, anywhere in the world. AT&T Corp. had recently shocked its employees with an announcement that it would eliminate 40,000 jobs, but that reduction amounted to only 13 percent of its total workforce. Some management experts warned that Dunlap's plan was so severe that it could cause utter chaos within the company, ravaging employee morale, efficiency, and productivity. "There is no excuse for treating employees as if they are disposable pieces of equipment," remarked Labor Secretary Robert Reich upon hearing the news.

WITHIN DAYS of the announcement of the cutback plan, human resources chief Wilson was summoned to Dunlap's office. Dunlap began asking him lots of questions about Don Uzzi, the Quaker Oats executive who had been hired as marketing chief.

"Al, why am I answering these questions?" Wilson asked.

"Newt's sick," Dunlap told him. "When the pressure gets on, it's hard on Newt. It happened at Scott. He doesn't need the money anymore, and he doesn't want to put his health at risk."

Contrary to what Dunlap told his associates, however, White quit on November 16 not because he was ill but because he knew Sunbeam was no quick turnaround. A full month earlier, White had confided to some colleagues that he was going to leave as soon as the board approved the restructuring plan. White's friends said he had forgotten how much he despised Dunlap. Only after going to work for the man again had he realized that it was a mistake. At times he would emerge from heated meetings with Dunlap, his face beet-red.

White could have tolerated the abuse and the pace, but he had concluded that there was no way Dunlap or anyone else was going to make a quick exit from Sunbeam. This was not a six-month assignment. It could not be done in a year or two either, White thought.

"The stock was talked up quickly to the point that I could see there wasn't going to be a viable merger candidate short-term," said White. "I also could see that it was a two- to three-year fix-up, and I had no intention of staying there that long. It would have taken an enormous amount of change to turn the company around. We had to develop an entire cadre of managers and get them smart in the business: That was two to three years of grinding work."

White harbored significant doubts about the Coopers plan as well. "It wasn't realistic," he said. "It was Al's Achilles' heel. He was trying to put ten pounds in a five-pound bag. That was one of the main reasons I couldn't stay. There was no way I could do what Al wanted in the time frame we talked about. You can't turn around a billion-dollar company in six months."

No one fully realized it, not anyone inside or outside the company, but White's departure was to become an abrupt turning point. Months and years later, many Sunbeam executives marked his resignation as the beginning of the end. "The day he went back to Santa Fe," thought Wilson, "was the day Sunbeam started going into the tank. I didn't know it at the time, but Dunlap has to have a terrific operating executive with him, and Newt was that person."

6
COPING WITH THE AL DUNLAPS

MICHAEL PRICE was not aware of the importance of Newt White to Sunbeam. All he knew in the aftermath of Dunlap's restructuring announcement was that someone was finally taking aggressive action to move the company forward. The stock price certainly reflected the optimism about Dunlap's likely success. Price's investment alone had risen by more than $230 million since the executive joined the company.

No one, not even the gung-ho analysts on Wall Street, was as generous in his praise or as quick to defend Dunlap as Michael Price. "One of the main things that society has to do is learn to cope with the effects of the Al Dunlaps," Price declared. The star investor argued that it was the Al Dunlaps of business who were making society more productive by laying people off and closing plants. "Those jobs were gone anyway," Price said, without a trace of sympathy. "It's part of our economy. Look at France. They protect jobs there, and the whole economy suffers."

By aligning himself with the poster boy of downsizing, Price had done what his humble mentor Max Heine would never do: He became an outspoken proponent for a new kind of capitalism. Indeed, his emergence as a public figure reflected the death of the sleepy and quiet world of mutual fund investing and the birth of a small but noisy group of new activists. Price remained true to his roots as a value investor, searching the market for underperforming and distressed securities that he thought could be rehabilitated. But as it became more difficult to buy the truly beaten-down stocks that once had formed the core of Mutual's portfolio, Price increasingly assumed the role of a bully with money. He was no longer content to sit on the sidelines as a passive investor. Instead he became a vocal and impatient one. He bought shares in lagging companies and then began to prod management to take actions that would raise the price of the stock and his own investment.

In the 1990s, when greater power in America shifted to the generally faceless managers of the big mutual and pension funds, Price found himself at the center of this new capitalism. Armed with record sums of investment capital, Price and other money managers were no longer relegated to the sidelines. They were using their stock ownership and newfound aggressiveness to make themselves into the new power brokers in Corporate America.

The pressure that institutional shareholders placed on corporate managements led to a sea change in the way the public corporation was governed. Where it had once been fashionable to manage a corporation for all its stakeholders—employees, communities, suppliers, customers, and shareholders—it was now recognized that investors stood first in line. Price, among others, was not shy in reminding executives of their new priorities.

Only a year before hiring Dunlap, he had prodded Chase Manhattan Bank, a key investment, into a merger with rival Chemical Bank, a deal that led to the layoffs of 12,000 employees. Price showed up at Chase's annual shareholders' meeting in 1995 to denounce its CEO in public. "Dramatic change is required," demanded Price. "Unlock the value, or let someone else do it for you." He lobbied other large shareholders of the bank to enlist them in his bullying tactics. The eventual Chase merger with Chemical gave Price's fund a windfall of more than $500 million on his investment.

Forcing the two financial goliaths to the table was something Heine never would have done. Humble and gentle, he might have considered all the bullying somewhat unseemly. "We were just asserting our rights," Price insisted. "It's about getting respected. It's about being right. We feel as if we own these companies. I know I do. When you're an owner, you really feel that the board and management reports to you. And they should report good things. If they don't, they should have good reasons for their failures. And if they don't, then something needs to change."

The transfer of power to investors from management struck the corporate landscape like a devastating earthquake. It altered the tectonic plates of what was right and wrong. Soon the corporate elite began to talk about "maximizing shareholder value" and aligning their objectives with their shareholders. The change led to massive downsizing and restructuring, with hundreds of thousands of white- and blue-collar employees losing their jobs in the service of greater profits and higher stock prices. In the background, Michael Price and others like him kept the pressure on for change.

AL DUNLAP'S most important benefactor at Sunbeam probably would have preferred to play football than to become one of Wall Street's smartest investors. Though he was so fascinated by the stock market that classmates noted in his senior yearbook that he would someday become a tycoon, his hero was neither J. P. Morgan nor John D. Rockefeller.

Instead Price worshiped Ray Nitschke, the indestructible middle linebacker for the Green Bay Packers. What most appealed to Price was not his sheer athleticism, but his toughness. On the field, Nitschke's rage and intensity terrified rivals. "He wasn't the flashiest," said Price, "but he was tough. He was in your face." Several decades later, when Price discovered that his caddie at the exclusive Balustrade Golf Club had once carried the clubs of his idol, he peppered the young man with questions. It had to be the ultimate accolade years later when Price made the cover of *Fortune* magazine under the headline "The Scariest S.O.B. on Wall Street."

In high school Price excelled in athletics rather than academics. He made the freshman baseball team, played football all four years, and dabbled in lacrosse, water polo and skiing. His love of football—and what he concedes were his "lousy grades"—led him to attend the University of Oklahoma. It seems a peculiar choice for a Jew from Long Island until one understands that his options were limited. Price's father had done better, going to the University of Pennsylvania's Wharton School for Business until inability to afford the tuition led him to drop out.

Price's father, who had become a co-owner and chief buyer for a West Coast chain of women's apparel stores, landed Price a summer job working for his stockbroker, Max L. Heine, who also lived in Rosyln, Long Island. A gentle and humble man, with a shock of wavy white hair, Max Heine distinguished himself as an astute investor in an unconventional area: bankruptcy investing. From such legendary bankruptcies as the Penn Central, Boston & Maine, and Reading railroads, he ran up monumental returns on behalf of fellow refugees, family and friends. He quickly learned that there was great, untapped value to be found in bankrupt companies whose bonds could be bought for as little as 8 to 10 cents on the dollar. And for thirteen years, from 1975 until his death in 1988, Heine taught Michael Price how to be a phenomenal stock picker.

To Heine, Price became the son he never had. Soon after Price joined Heine's company in 1975, they began a close and nurturing relationship. "Max used to tell people that he'd be thinking of something and I'd say it, or I'd be thinking of something and he'd say it," recalled Price. "It was kind of this invisible brain wave or vibe, a way that we both communicated with each other." Under the tutelage of this grandfatherly teacher, Price became a master of value investing. Like Heine, he had an unerring instinct for buying the beaten-down stocks of lagging and distressed companies and squeezing profit out of them.

"Max taught me that if you really wanted to find value," said Price, "you had to do original work, digging through stuff no one else wanted to look at." By the early 1980s he had become the dominant presence at Heine Securities, and his mentor worked out a deal under which Heine remained the principal owner of the firm but the profits were split equally between the two men. By 1986, when Heine was seventy-five and ready to retire, he worked out another deal so that Price would eventually become the sole owner of the firm. Heine died two years later, and Price purchased the company for little more than $4 million, perhaps the single greatest investment Price ever made. He would sell his four mutual funds to Franklin Resources Inc. in 1996 for more than $800 million.

Through the years, Price became expert in the financial esoterica of the bankruptcy world. His success enticed millions of dollars from eager investors wanting to take a ride on his instincts and calculated gambles. His funds' returns, among the highest on Wall Street, attracted a powerful array of investing clients, including some of New York's most cynical and insightful financial journalists. Always they could depend on Price for ideas that were bold and different. Few of them were as daring and unusual as the way he became involved in Sunbeam Corp.

THE OPPORTUNITY to make great sums of money off the debt-ridden and bankrupt Allegheny International Corp. was not initially seen by Price. Instead the mess caught the eye of Charles Davidson, then a general partner at Steinhardt Partners, the $1.5 billion hedge fund run by Michael Steinhardt. Much of the wild dealmaking of the 1980s, the leveraged buyouts done by overzealous gamblers backed by junk bonds, was beginning to unravel. One highly leveraged company after another was looking for saviors or declaring bankruptcy. Davidson, eager to play the bankruptcy game, was shopping for the best buys. Allegheny seemed a natural—a company with misguided management, a bloated cost structure, and underperforming assets. "Buckley ran this place as his own fiefdom," says Davidson. "It was a horribly abused company with some great consumer brand names that were so strong you couldn't destroy them."

After a superficial analysis, Davidson became sufficiently intrigued to move the company to the top of Steinhardt's list of prospective investment candidates. He retained Japonica Partners to take a closer look on his behalf in the spring of 1989. The partnership was headed by a former Goldman Sachs & Co. investment banker, Paul B. Kazarian, thirty-three, and included ex-Goldman colleague Michael G. Lederman, thirty-six. "What I needed from them was a thorough research job of what the business was really worth," says Davidson. "If I know the company's worth, I can play the hand. If it's value is $100 million and I can buy it for $50 million, that's good. If I can only buy it for $150 million, that's bad."

The math wasn't nearly that simple. But with a weekly retainer of $25,000 plus expenses, the wiry and intense dealmakers began to untangle the company's assets and liabilities and soon became convinced that Allegheny was a prize worth capturing. Kazarian found that the current management, hoping to buy the company on the cheap, had undervalued foreign subsidiaries, understated the true profitability of several divisions, and overstated the company's exposure to risk. Allegheny's executives, for example, forecasted that they would have $100 million in cash after their reorganization plan lifted the company out of bankruptcy. Kazarian claimed the number was closer to $300 million, all of which could be used to help finance the acquisition.

Davidson, who had met Kazarian while running the bond trading desk at Goldman, agreed to pony up $60 million in cash for what would become the first hostile takeover of a company in bankruptcy. But Kazarian and Lederman needed at least twice as much to mount a successful attempt to win the company. That's when they decided to visit Michael Price, the powerful mutual fund maven, the man with the money.

In October 1987 Price was already one of Wall Street's most successful investors, managing hundreds of millions of dollars in his highly popular Mutual Series funds. Yet he was not much older than the dealmakers who came to see him. At the age of thirty-eight he was pear-shaped plump, with a long oval face, a high forehead, and a double chin. Even though his suits were custom-made, sewn with a label that read "Made Expressly for Michael F. Price," he almost always looked rumpled and disheveled. Price spoke as if he was always in a hurry, with clipped questions and answers, and phrases that showed he was well-versed in the lingo of Wall Street and high finance. He spoke about converts and basis points, cash flows and subordinated debt, liabilities and liquidity. Price was a phenomenal stock picker and a clever risk taker, ingenious at finding and then pouncing on hidden opportunities.

Kazarian, whom Price had initially met at Goldman Sachs, had brought him one of those opportunities only recently. Price kicked in $5 million to help Kazarian finance a proposed leveraged buyout bid for Chicago Northwestern Corp., owner of the Chicago and Northwestern Railroad. Though the bid failed, Price, Steinhardt, and a few other investors doubled their money in a year's time.

For Price a $60 million investment to purchase Allegheny was a huge deal, one of the largest his funds had ever made in a single company. More importantly, though, this deal differed greatly from what Max Heine had taught him. His old, humble mentor preferred to play a passive role in his investments, cleverly and quietly buying bankruptcy bonds for cents on the dollar. He never courted the spot-light and never wanted to assume the role of a raider or takeover artist. Price's differing philosophy, he explained, had to do with different times. "It's not as easy to get a clean dollar's worth of value for fifty cents as it was in 1975," he said. "But I think Max would understand and bless most of the things we do."

The Sunbeam deal also differed because of its size. "It was a big commitment," recalled Price. "It was more of selling me on the size of it and going for control. When we did large bankruptcies in the past, we always stopped short of control. We always needed liquidity, and we didn't have the management to put into a company."

The investor had closely watched Allegheny, in part because Price's Mutual Series fund had owned stock in several companies it had acquired, including Sunbeam. Buckley's acquisition spree was usually done in cash-and-stock deals, and Price had always unloaded the Allegheny stock from his fund. "We never really liked Buckley," he says, "and we never really liked Allegheny . . . So we got out of them." After Allegheny filed for bankruptcy protection, Price closely followed the company's troubles in the newspapers. "It was kind of a back-burner item that we were watching," Price said, "like every night at 11 o'clock you sit down to watch the next episode of *Cheers*."

Impressed by Kazarian's analysis, however, Price seemed favorably disposed toward putting up the money for the deal. But he wanted one last crack at grilling the young deal makers before agreeing to commit an initial $30 million of his funds' money. Price invited them out to his offices in Short Hills, New Jersey, a sprawling block of brick and glass populated with stockbrokers and insurance salesmen, across the street from an upscale shopping mall. He had only recently moved the firm there from its cramped, catacomblike offices on Broad Street in Manhattan.

On the second floor, behind a pair of glass doors that opened onto a small marbled reception foyer, was Price's world. The formal entrance to Mutual Series was flanked by solid white pillars that led to a large securities trading room transported from Wall Street. Inside, the eyes of a dozen or so analysts and acolytes were riveted on a bank of computers. In his shirtsleeves, Price sat like a monarch at the head of a T-shaped trading desk under humming fluorescent lights and a set of screens blinking constantly with information. The offices were relatively spare, with the exception of Price's faux-Venetian boardroom with its deep red walls and crystal chandeliers.

After Kazarian and Lederman spent most of the day being interrogated by Price and one of his top lieutenants, Peter Langerman, a lanky bankruptcy lawyer, they went to dinner at Price's home. The duo followed Price's car through the rolling countryside of New Jersey's Somerset Hills, a secluded region of farms and estates about fifty miles west of New York City, where country club Republicans live in grand houses set on vast well-tended fields. Price's neighbors in Far Hills included the late magazine publisher Malcolm Forbes and King Hassan II of Morocco, whose 456-acre estate spilled over two towns.

It was, perhaps, an odd place for a Long Island–bred Jew, a less-than-motivated student who grew up knowing neither privilege nor wealth, to settle. Yet one of Price's greatest passions was an anglophile diversion—polo. He played the sport frequently, and he played it vigorously. He said it was one of the few team sports that an out-of-shape man could enjoy. And Price was never really in shape since his days at Roslyn High School out on Long Island, New York, where, in the late 1960s, he blew out a knee playing middle linebacker for the Roslyn Bulldogs.

Price's relationship with his wife, Bunny, was deteriorating. In a few years they would agree to a divorce that would cost him $50 million of his net worth. That evening she refused to greet his guests, preferring instead to remain in the upstairs quarters while uniformed servants fed the trio in the mansion's dining room. "It was at one of these tables that sit eighteen people," recalled a wide-eyed Lederman.

After dinner Price walked them through his stables, introducing them to several of his revered ponies. He was, they thought, clearly showing off his wealth and his success. Price's stables alone were more immense than any home Lederman had ever been inside—and probably more imposing than any house either ever expected to call his own.

He was, believed Lederman, showing them what one day could be their own if they worked like animals for him.

In contrast to the earlier interrogation, Price now seemed genuinely friendly. His guided tour revealed a personal side that the investor often kept hidden. He spoke of his love of polo and of the muscular, athletic horses in his barn. And as they sat together on the wooden benches that lined the walls of the stables, Price picked up a riding crop and began using it as an animal trainer in a circus might use a whip.

He walked over to a wooden horse, draped with his dark brown leather saddle, and suddenly began to strike the frame as hard as he could.

"You guys are my slaves and you're going to work like hell for me," he declared, smacking his whip on its side. The shrill sound echoed through the cavernous stables, startling the handsome ponies and the two young men.

"You guys are going to make me millions," he proclaimed, unleashing his riding crop again. The slap of the leather against the wood traveled through the stables as Kazarian and Lederman looked on in silent astonishment.

"You're going to make millions," Price bellowed.

"It was not threatening," recalls Lederman. "It was not mean-spirited. It was Price doing an imitation of an Oklahoma football pep rally. But he wouldn't be doing it if there wasn't a huge level of seriousness to it."

Their day ended at 10:30 P.M., soon after Price's impromptu pep talk. They stepped outside in the cool autumn evening and walked across the grounds to the driveway at the side of Price's mansion. Confident that they had finally won over Price, they comfortably settled into the backseat of a waiting limo for the hour-and-a-half journey to New York City, a little closer to the biggest and most important deal in their lives.

FOR THE NEXT few months they were the visible deal makers, running interference, blocking and tackling, investing their own sweat equity so that the two Michaels could remain largely in the background. Largely with Price's money now behind it, Japonica launched a formal offer for the company in late November 1989. Allegheny's board scoffed at the bid, however, repeatedly refusing to meet with Kazarian and Lederman. The board's ice-cold reaction became a precursor to a more insidious strategy to gain control of Allegheny. If the company would not seriously entertain an outright bid, why not begin to buy Allegheny's debt from banks and insurance companies?

In a bankruptcy, the debt of a company effectively becomes its equity because creditors stand first in line to get paid off. Stockholders are often wiped out. When they are not, they usually receive mere token consideration for their losses. The purchase of debt also offered another advantage to a would-be raider: Investors who acquire debt escape regulatory scrutiny. In contrast, when someone buys more than 5 percent of a public company's stock, he must file with the government a statement of his holdings and his intentions. It was easier, cheaper, and far more surreptitious to buy debt that could later be converted into the equity of a newly reorganized company. "I don't think anyone ever conceived of doing it in such a predatory way as we were considering," said Davidson.

They didn't have to convince Price. "Buying the bank debt of Sunbeam was exactly what Max would do," said Price, who had been purchasing bankruptcy debt since 1979. Only three years earlier he had pulled off an extraordinary coup, gobbling up 35 percent of the total debt of bankrupt Storage Technology Corp. for little more than 47 cents on every dollar. His annual returns on that prescient investment approached 40 percent for years. "In a bankruptcy, the only way to be certain of having some profit is to buy out banks or the public bonds. If you just make a bid for the company and you lose . . . you don't make any money after all this work."

With the men concealing the identity of Price as a key investor, moreover, they were more likely to snap up the debt at bargain rates from jittery bankers desperate for cash. As Price put it: "Once we show up as a buyer of bank loans, the word goes around that Mutual's buying . . . They know we're big . . . they know we have a good track record in the stuff, and they're less likely to sell at good prices. Some guy named Michael Lederman, soliciting a bank, they don't know who he is."

It was a role they fully embraced, eager to take the steps that would allow them to win the company. "All of this, from the very beginning, was Michael Price," says Lederman. "He was pulling the strings. We were all puppets in one way or another. Some of us were puppets with brains. Others were puppets with money or strategic sense. But behind nearly every major decision from the earliest days was Michael Price."

By early September 1990 Japonica had outwitted the management team hoping to buy Allegheny and could finally claim victory. Price and Steinhardt wound up paying about $210 million for the prize, the amount used to bankroll the purchase of the company's debt. The partnership borrowed only $125 million from banks because they were able to use some $325 million in cash from the company itself. Their own costs, largely fees for lawyers and consultants, amounted to less than $15 million. Before the deal formally closed on September 28, Kazarian and Lederman went to see Price again in Short Hills to go over its final details and savor their victory. "This was a raise-your-glass, have-a-cigar meeting," recalls Lederman. Just the three of them gathered in Price's private office, a modest space overlooking the John F. Kennedy Parkway and the Short Hills shopping mall. It was an unpretentious room for someone who had become a Wall Street tycoon, an office so uncluttered that, as one observer noted, it was "as if the last person in it was the interior decorator." The only indulgence was a near life-sized portrait by Lionel Edwards of a master of the fox hunt seated stiffly on his tall horse.

It was an upbeat meeting, filled with backslapping and congratulations until Lederman made a rather innocent and perhaps naive observation. "This gives us the opportunity," he said, "to take an American icon and turn it into a great company. We can really build value over the long term."

At first Price and Kazarian seemed bemused by his comment, but then they began to openly snicker. "They laughed me out of the office," remembered a bewildered Lederman, though Price does not recall the conversation. "They ran me out. They just thought that was the stupidest thing they ever heard. I was totally serious, and they were appalled. I thought one of the reasons we got this billion-dollar entity was to build value from it. That wasn't going to be the case."

THE PRIZE they captured was hardly a prize. It didn't include the thriving Sunbeam of the postwar era. Instead it was a decayed and neglected enterprise that sorely needed rejuvenation. Some of the factories were of World War II vintage, filled with machinery produced by companies long out of business. Sunbeam's product line was as old and tired as its plants. Most of the company's blenders, irons, and can openers had been designed over a decade ago. More visible and innovative rivals, from Black & Decker to Braun and Cuisinart, were gaining shelf space and prestige. Warranty costs on many of Sunbeam's products were at recklessly high levels because only scant attention was given to quality. Sunbeam and Oster logos had no standardization, with as many as thirty different versions of the Sunbeam name on packaging. As one insider put it, "almost everything we touched was rotted away."

Yet among the rot was enormous opportunity. So badly was the company neglected that it was possible to move money-losing operations into the black quickly. With the help of the company's managers, Kazarian set ninety-day objectives and then knocked them off one by one. He consolidated eleven divisions into four, organizing teams to pitch the company's entire business line to major retailers. He brought together the purchasing operations of each of those units in order to better leverage the company's buying power. His partner, Lederman, was like a hound dog in pursuing every claim and asset on the company's books, even flying to Buckley's home in Florida in hopes of collecting on the seven-figure loan the former CEO still owed the company. Buckley wasn't home, but Lederman left his business card with a note that read: "When are you going to pay?"

"There was money lying everywhere," recalled Clegg, who emerged under Kazarian as a key Sunbeam executive. "You could pick it up with a snow shovel. If you walked through this company with your eyes open, you could tell there was a lot of money to be made here. What they bought the company for was the great train robbery." The deal makers uncovered nearly three-quarters of a million dollars in bank accounts not accounted for on its books. They found other cash in escrow accounts and property worth many millions more.

The first year was a whirlwind. The raiders had taken over the company, renamed it Sunbeam-Oster, consolidated divisions and closed facilities, sold off unwanted assets, moved headquarters to the Citizens Plaza building in downtown Providence, restaffed corporate headquarters, and begun preparations for taking the company public. Stripped down to its essential businesses in consumer products—appliances, hair clippers, electric blankets, outdoor grills, and furniture— the company was swiftly restored to profitability. Operating earnings hit $96 million in 1991, a dramatic reversal from the company's $95.3 million loss in the previous year.

By August 1992 Kazarian successfully took the company public. Sunbeam raised $250 million, selling 23.8 percent of its common shares. Price and Steinhardt were elated. They had essentially acquired Allegheny for $1.50 per share. The company went public at $12.50 a share, bringing their total investment of some $130 million to a value of

$1.1 billion. It was a spectacular success for a once-bankrupt company that had only one full year of audited financial statements under its belt.

In Kazarian, Sunbeam's investors could not have asked for a more dedicated and focused chief executive. As CEO, Kazarian routinely put in seven days a week, demanding perfection from everyone and micromanaging every aspect of the company's affairs. He created training programs for Sunbeam's managers. He issued a set of management principles ("Wear out the soles of your shoes before the seat of your pants" and "There are not mature markets, only mature managers who need to be rejuvenated or replaced.") His relentless focus helped to significantly increase Sunbeam's market share to number one or number two in virtually every category in which the company competed. A Harvard Business School case study celebrated Kazarian's success and won him invitations to lecture Harvard's MBAs.

Kazarian, however, was a tough taskmaster to tolerate. Managers and employees viewed him as a peculiar and eccentric boss. He insisted that his executives double up in budget motel rooms on business trips. He demanded that executives rent compact cars and book only discounted airline coach seats, even if it meant staying over on a Friday or Saturday night away from their families. He refused to order such basic office supplies as paper clips and pens, requiring managers to save clips that came in the mail or use pens from suppliers and customers.

When Kazarian held an off-site meeting at a hotel, he would invariably refuse to have lunch or dinner catered by the establishment. To save a few bucks, he would simply give a lieutenant $20 and send him to a nearby McDonald's to fetch what he could. The person would return and toss the contents of a McDonald's bag on a conference room table, leaving managers to scramble for food.

It was not uncommon for executives to receive phone calls from Kazarian at all hours of the day and night. One time he led a team of managers through a Tupperware plant in Tennessee at 3 A.M. to inspect the facilities for a possible acquisition. Management meetings with him often began as early as 6 A.M. and continued into the wee hours of the night. Frequently they were held on Saturdays. He required executives to sometimes work the third shift at factories and then attend 8 A.M. meetings. During new-product review pow-wows, he handed out rubber pig noses and cow bells to every participant.

Kazarian demanded that if the managers thought little of a new product idea, they should put on their pig noses and shout oink, oink. If, on the other hand, they saw great potential in a new product, they should loudly ring their cow bells, signifying their belief that the idea could be a cash cow for the company.

Kazarian's behavior, said several senior executives, went beyond mere eccentricity. One time, he threw a pint of orange juice at the company's controller. Later, in explaining the incident to a reporter, Kazarian maintained he wasn't trying to hit the executive. "I threw it at the wall behind his head," he said. On another occasion, according to one associate, he began firing a BB gun at vacant chairs of executives. Kazarian later conceded that he shot the gun in the company's offices, though he could not recall where he aimed the weapon. He charged that he was the victim of a smear campaign.

Kazarian's conduct rankled some of Sunbeam's executives and they soon began to plot a revolt that would lead to his dismissal. The coup was orchestrated by none other than Lederman, Kazarian's partner and friend who had been feuding with him for months over their partnership agreement. Eventually, however, some two dozen of the company's top managers, many of them millionaires thanks to the stock options Kazarian handed out, promised to quit if the board failed to fire the CEO. It was Lederman who brought the news to director Peter Langerman, Price's right-hand man.

Circumspect, Langerman was a lawyer's lawyer. He was pencil-thin, with nerdlike spectacles and thinning hair. One figured him to be clumsy on a basketball court, but adept in a classroom. Earlier in life, when he was majoring in Russian studies at Yale University, he had toyed with the notion of becoming a spy. Instead he became a Stanford University–educated bankruptcy lawyer whom Price hired from the New York law firm Weil, Gotshal & Manges in 1984.

Though he had studied with the famed value investor for over a decade, Langerman was not known for sniffing out a great investment or digging through esoteric financial documents to sense a lucrative deal. Nor did he know very much about management or operations. "Peter," explained one former Sunbeam director, "was a decent guy, but his total focus was the stock price." Langerman was the man who, as another colleague put it, "crossed the t's and dotted the i's" for Price and made sure all the legalities were taken care of. When asked his opinion on Sunbeam matters, he often would defer to an absent Price with the words, "I'll have to talk to Michael about that."

Still, his link to Price made him the most important director on Sunbeam's cozy six-person board. Langerman and Davidson were the designees of Price and Steinhardt, respectively. Kazarian and Lederman were the board's two insiders. The remaining two directors were supposedly complete outsiders: Charles J. Thayer, the retired banker who joined the board at Kazarian's invitation, and Roderick M. Hills, a Washington, D.C., lawyer who was named a director by the bankruptcy court judge to look after the interests of Allegheny's creditors.

Thayer was not a disinterested party. He had met Kazarian in the mid-1980s when Kazarian was at Goldman and Thayer was chief financial officer of Citizens Fidelity Corp. in Louisville, Kentucky. During the Allegheny bankruptcy battle, Kazarian enlisted Thayer as a paid adviser to help negotiate a settlement with some of the banks. Once the deal makers won the company, Kazarian invited him on the board. That made Hill, who was not known as a particularly involved or vocal director, the only independent outsider among the six board members. A year after Kazarian was dismissed, two Columbia University professors named the Sunbeam board one of the worst in America due to its "paucity of independent directors."

Alarmed by the scale of the revolt, Langerman and his fellow directors fired Kazarian on January 9, 1993, after he delivered nine consecutive quarters of profit during his tenure. If Price was disappointed in Kazarian's removal, he did not show it. "He was fine for the first six months or year, then he wanted to stay," the money manager said later. "It went well, and he just burned his bridges with his management group. They didn't respect him. He was incredibly intense, and intensity in business is an attribute. But if it gets carried too far, people can't stand working with you. He carried it too far. The guys said, 'We can't take it.'"

Kazarian, however, may simply have handed Price and Steinhardt a convenient reason to ditch him. His partnership agreement with them gave Kazarian the power to veto any stock distribution for five years. By the end of 1992, each investor's Sunbeam stake was worth $500 million, yet they could not unlock the gains without his approval. As the company's stock rose further, the value of Kazarian's interest soared as well, to more than $200 million. Kazarian claimed that his investors' representatives on the board became both furious and jealous when they saw his net worth balloon well beyond theirs. Langerman and Davidson denied Kazarian's charge was true.

Nevertheless, it was Price and Steinhardt who allowed an investment banker with little experience in managing people or operations to become chief executive of a sprawling company with some 10,000 employees. "Paul was brilliant in leading an unfriendly takeover of the company, but that did not make him competent to run Sunbeam," director Hills said years later. "It was incredible to think that anyone with his background in investment banking could run a marketing company of Sunbeam's size."

WITHIN DAYS of his ouster, many of the accusations against Kazarian leaked into the media. Largely quoting anonymous sources, the *Wall Street Journal* ran a shockingly detailed story of Kazarian's eccentricities under the headline: "Out of Control: Fired Sunbeam Chief Harangued and Hazed Employees." *Business Week* weighed in with a similar treatment under the title "How to Lose Friends and Influence No One." Even the supermarket tabloid the *National Enquirer* took a shot, calling Kazarian "The Worst Boss in America." After the initial press flurry, *The American Lawyer* ran a lengthy piece that took Kazarian's side, entitled "Framed?"

The coverage helped fuel a legal fracas that engulfed the company. Price and Steinhardt sued Kazarian to remove him from the board and dissolve their partnership with Japonica. Kazarian's partner Lederman and key associate Robert Setrakian filed a lawsuit against him. Kazarian, in turn, accused all of them of a conspiracy to ruin his reputation and bilk him out of his partnership money. With every filing and motion, with every new affidavit and counterclaim, they savaged each other in the courts and the papers.

What emerged from the court documents was an unflattering portrait of a heavy-handed Price, who, Kazarian alleged, often sought favorable treatment as an investor in Sunbeam. From the very beginning, he charged, Price and Davidson constantly angled for control and advantage. After Sunbeam's first-quarter earnings were released in 1991, they wanted to flip the company to get out their money. They quickly sought the initial public offering and wanted the proceeds to go to them instead of back to the company.

In the course of these various proceedings, Kazarian charged, Price pressured him to extend as much as $10 million in credit to a near-bankrupt R. H. Macy & Co. in late 1991 when the investor also had a significant investment stake in the retailer and was a director on its board. Kazarian said Price told him to "open the floodgates" to Macy in early November 1991, just before the all-important Christmas season. Worried that Macy's might slip into bankruptcy, Kazarian was forcing the retailer to pay for goods it had already received before more would be shipped. According to Kazarian, Price responded: "You may lose a million, but I'll lose a lot more." Price denied he ever made the statement, but conceded that he had called Kazarian on behalf of Macy's.

On another occasion, charged Sunbeam general counsel Lederman, Price called and pressured him repeatedly for confidential information on Carter Hawley Hale Stores Inc., a bankrupt department store chain in which Price had acquired millions of dollars in distressed bonds. Because Sunbeam was a major creditor of the chain, Lederman was on Carter Hawley's creditors' committee and privy to non-public information. According to a Lederman memo dated September 25, 1991, Price wanted to know on that day if an offer to take over the company would succeed. "I know you can talk because Paul's at a lunch I set up for him, so tell me the real scoop and I'll tell you what to do so we can get this done," Price said, according to the memo. Earlier, Lederman charged, Price called to remind that he was "paying his salary" at Sunbeam. Price denied the charges.

Still, in mid–1993, only months after Kazarian was fired, Price and his firm were being investigated by the Securities & Exchange Commission for the third time in his career. In 1988, the money manager and his mentor Heine agreed, without admitting liability, to be censured by the SEC for not disclosing that they received some $2.4 million in brokerage commissions from a brokerage firm affiliated with their mutual fund company. Only a year earlier, the agency began an inquiry into whether Price traded Macy's securities with inside information. The probe was dropped, without any charges being filed against Price.

This time, the agency looked into whether the brokerage firm, once partly owned by Heine, benefited from insider information available to Price. The brokerage house heavily traded Sunbeam-Oster warrants in June 1991 when Price and only a few others were in a position to know that Sunbeam would likely go public. That information was crucial to outside investors because they were betting that they could someday exchange the warrants for more valuable stock. Price denied doing anything wrong. "You know," he said at the time, "you don't have to cheat. Ivan Boesky didn't have to cheat. He could have made money just carefully following the rules." The SEC later dropped the investigation. But along with Kazarian's allegations, the publicity did little to enhance Price's image.

The bizarre battle between Kazarian and his investors and partners made it nearly impossible to attract credible CEO candidates, until director Thayer stumbled onto Roger W. Schipke. His résumé frankly looked too good for Sunbeam. Unlike Kazarian, he had racked up years of operating experience. From 1981 to 1989 Schipke had run General Electric's mammoth $5 billion appliance business in Louisville, Kentucky. While there, Schipke had served on the board of directors of Thayer's bank and had become acquainted with him.

Reached at Ryland Group, the Maryland-based home builder where he was CEO, Schipke hardly seemed interested in Sunbeam. The last thing he wanted was to lead a company with two dominant and meddlesome shareholders wanting nothing but to make a fast buck. Ultimately it was a dinner meeting with Michael Price at the Washington, D.C., home of director Rod Hills that helped make up his mind. During cocktails in Hills's drawing room, Schipke told Price that if he was searching for someone to build the company over the long haul, he had his man. If not, Schipke said, he was the wrong choice for the job.

Desperate to find a trustworthy CEO who could allay Wall Street's fears, Price told Schipke he was interested in nothing but the long-term health of the company. On that answer, a $1 million base salary and a handsome pile of stock options, the former GE executive quit his job at Ryland and joined Sunbeam as CEO not much more than a week after Price settled Kazarian's $3.2 billion lawsuit for a reported $160 million. Before year end, Schipke moved the company out of Providence and down to new quarters in Fort Lauderdale, only a five-minute drive down the road from where his friend Thayer lived.

AFTER KAZARIAN, SCHIPKE BROUGHT calm to the company. Though he was an accomplished executive, he was as bland as a low-salt, no-fat diet. The former U.S. naval officer viewed Sunbeam as his final step toward retirement after having spent twenty-nine years at GE and three years at Ryland. He was only fifty-six years old, but his interests were elsewhere and his final years at General Electric had taken their toll. It was under his watch as head of GE's appliance division that GE took a $300 million after-tax write-off in 1988 to replace faulty rotary compressors in GE refrigerators. The screw-up cut his division's profits to $61 million in 1988, down from $490 million. Schipke fixed the problem, but he left GE two years later emotionally and physically spent. Still, during his eight years as group executive, GE's major appliance sales grew to $5.6 billion from $2.5 billion. Those earlier years were among his best. He enjoyed growing a business and looked forward to doing that at Sunbeam through acquisitions and new product development.

To his dismay, Schipke soon found that Sunbeam was nothing like the operations he had managed at General Electric. What he inherited was a company run, as he put it, as if it were a leveraged buyout. Everything was done on the cheap. It was a company, concluded Schipke, with second-rate manufacturing, unsophisticated financial procedures, and virtually no marketing. The computer systems linking the company's operations were nonexistent. Many product lines had been starved for investment. The company's senior management team had to be totally recast, believed Schipke.

Though he gained approval for a new $80 million production facility, Schipke also formed the view that the company's backers were none too eager to invest in the future. Within months of Schipke's arrival, Price and Steinhardt wanted to sell down their significant Sunbeam holdings. With things still going well, the investors wanted to capture more of their gains. To do so Schipke hired investment banker Merrill Lynch & Co. and reluctantly went on the road in both the spring and the fall of 1994 to sell potential investors on the stock. This helped Price and Steinhardt make two secondary offerings that reduced their Sunbeam stakes to 57 percent from 70 percent.

But the road shows were time-consuming ordeals that required three weeks of preparation. Schipke had to put together slides and scripts, and to rehearse presentations internally and with the investment bankers before going out for two weeks at a time. "He wasn't a kid anymore and Merrill Lynch would have him making presentations in Milwaukee in the morning, New York in the afternoon, and Atlanta at night," said James Wilson, vice president of human resources. "That was not an easy thing to do for a guy close to sixty." Price, who agreed that it was a huge management distraction, was not sympathetic. "Who else is going to tell the story if you want to see stock?" he asked. "It's too bad. It was something he had to do. I felt sorry for him." Price added sarcastically: "I think he chartered a private plane to do it."

By early 1995 performance began to slip. Conflicts between corporate headquarters and the field began to erupt as Schipke was perceived to be indecisive and ineffective. The huge investments the CEO was making in the company's infrastructure had yet to pay off. Material costs were rising, and Sunbeam was unable to pass the higher costs on to retailers like Wal-Mart and Kmart, who were increasing their market power and leverage over suppliers. Warranty costs on a poorly made breadmaker produced by a Chinese supplier climbed into the millions.

Then, in mid-1995, not much more than a year after Price assured Schipke he was in for the long term, the two Michaels decided to sell out completely. In the past both Price and Steinhardt would periodically bring up the possibility of flipping the company. It was the easiest way for them to collect a big check and walk away from their investment. But Davidson, Steinhardt's partner, always counseled against it. He didn't believe that Sunbeam had a logical buyer. To run an auction, Davidson thought, you'd better have several potential buyers in mind or you'll likely risk an aborted sell-off. "It's better not to run an auction than to do one and get nowhere," said Davidson, who left the board when he began his own investment company. "Because whenever you run an auction, management starts to think about selling and not running the business. It becomes another excuse for not dealing with your problems."

Davidson was replaced by Shimon Topor, an impatient Steinhardt partner who wanted nothing other than to unload the stock. Sunbeam executives and some of his fellow directors concluded that Topor had no interest in and no knowledge of the company's business. He failed to show up for some board meetings, and when he did appear, he would ask a battery of questions only about costs, nothing more. They hired investment banker Merrill Lynch & Co. in October to shop the company. That process, and the "due diligence" it would require, burned up months of work and brought the internal workings of the company to a virtual halt—just when Sunbeam could least afford it.

As the company's problems worsened, its chief operating officer James Clegg complained to directors about Schipke's lack of leadership. He secretly met with directors Thayer and Paul Van Orden, a newly recruited board member who had at one time been Schipke's boss at GE. Schipke discovered that Clegg was undermining him, and he also blamed him as COO for many of the company's problems. Schipke made the journey to Price's Short Hills, New Jersey, office and asked for the investor's blessing in getting rid of Clegg. Price granted his approval, but soon changed his mind after speaking with Langerman, who believed that ousting Clegg would harm Merrill Lynch's search for a buyer. Rather than disrupt the process and hurt their chances of cashing out, they refused to allow Schipke to fire his chief operating officer.

Costs, largely associated with a new underused plant in Hattiesburg, Mississippi, and escalating warranty costs on the defective breadmakers, were running out of control. Thayer estimated that the company had added $150 million in extra costs in the last eighteen months alone. Sunbeam would have to double sales to show any increase in earnings at all. In the fourth quarter of 1995 the board began to actively consider whether Schipke should go.

Of them all, Langerman was most reluctant. He didn't want any headlines that would hurt Merrill's chances of selling the company. Thayer proposed getting rid of Clegg. He believed the board should hire a headhunter to officially conduct a search for a chief operating officer but really aim for a CEO to take over from Schipke. Once they had the candidate in house, they could allow Schipke to stay on for another six months to ensure a smooth and quiet transition. But the plan went nowhere because Langerman and Topor were still hoping that Merrill would find a buyer.

A customer proved elusive, and the auction was proving little more than a costly diversion. Merrill, which initially thought it could get two or possibly three bidders for Sunbeam, could only interest SEB, a French consumer products company. It spent weeks visiting the company's facilities and meeting with its executives, but ultimately decided against an offer. The distraction posed by the auction only prolonged the downturn and the crisis. In early April 1996, with the sale a dismal failure, three of the company's five directors believed it was time to move Schipke out. The company's decline was all too obvious and painful. It had now missed five straight quarters of earnings forecasts, dating back to the first quarter of 1995. And it was on its way toward missing a sixth.

These were not near-misses by any stretch. In the first quarter of 1995 the company fell short of its internal sales target by $26 million. In the next quarter it missed the goal by $86 million, nearly a fourth of the $389.1 million in revenues it expected. After Sunbeam issued a downward revision on the third quarter Langerman remarked to chief financial officer Paul O'Hara: "If you don't make that number, not only do you have to worry about your job, but I've got to worry about mine."

But Sunbeam failed to make even its revision, and for the year 1995, revenues were $208 million under plan. The profit picture at Sunbeam was turning so bad that Schipke began a series of quarterly pilgrimages to Price's Short Hills offices, where he would go over the increasingly bad news with Price and Langerman just before announcing the numbers. Price was always disappointed but always polite, asking a few questions here and there, eager to know what was happening before any other normal investor did.

He, Langerman, and Topor, however, did not fully understand the extent of the deterioration. The company's own internal market share numbers in key categories were falling fast. In blenders it fell to 37.9 percent in 1995 from 41.3 percent in 1993. In food mixers Sunbeam's share dropped to 18.7 percent from 24.9 percent two years earlier. In toasters it declined to 2.7 percent from 4.1 percent. In gas grills market share dropped to 44.2 percent from 48.8 percent in 1993. In folding outdoor furniture it plummeted to 43.6 percent from 57.6 percent.

Van Orden, Hills, and Thayer proposed firing the indecisive leader. They believed Schipke had the brains to do the job, but lacked the energy and the confidence. Langerman and Topor opposed the move. They didn't want to risk another major disruption, and they didn't realize how badly the company was troubled.

"No, no," said Langerman. "We can do this quietly."

When it was pointed out that they had the votes to can Schipke, Langerman became insistent.

"Look, you guys," he said. "It's not going to work that way. It's not going to go the way of a vote. We control the company. We'll just have a meeting of the shareholders and dissolve the board."

"Well, then, I'm out of here," said a disgusted Van Orden.

"So am I," added Hills, to Van Orden's surprise.

They abruptly got up and left the boardroom, unable to participate in the farce they believed the board had become under Price and Steinhardt. To stay, they believed, would have been immoral and unethical. "This company can do a whole lot better in the future than in the past, but it requires a first-class management team with vision and tolerance for the details of the business," Hills said.

Though overruled by the investors, Thayer remained on the board. On April 1 he was elected vice chairman, and the board quietly sought a successor to Schipke. Within days Thayer moved into Fort Lauderdale headquarters and the top executives began reporting to him. Though no public disclosure of the change was made, Schipke no longer had a real job at Sunbeam. He stopped coming to work, finally resigning in May just after first quarter profits fell by 42 percent.

Sunbeam badly needed strong leadership, not an interim chief like Thayer, not a careful lawyer like Langerman. The company needed a new, permanent boss, and the deeper its problems became, the more likely Sunbeam required someone who was an expert at turnarounds. With costs out of control, market shares declining, an enormous expansion of plant capacity, and a company rife with political conflict, Sunbeam needed a powerful and forceful leader.

That was when Al Dunlap was named Sunbeam's corporate savior.

7 RAMBO

ON A BRIGHT, temperate day in the early fall of 1996, David Fannin was at his desk, tending to the mountain of paperwork that every corporate counsel confronts on an almost daily basis. Suddenly he was abruptly disturbed when Dunlap's bodyguard rushed into his office with an urgent plea.

"Quick!" he shouted. "You've got to come to Al's office. Something is wrong."

Thinking the worst, Fannin jumped from his desk and hurried down the hall toward Dunlap's executive suite. All sorts of horrific possibilities ran through his head. Perhaps, he thought, his boss was suffering a heart attack. But when he entered Dunlap's domain, Fannin nearly had a heart attack himself.

Standing on a desk like a military statue in a New England town square was Dunlap. He was toting a pair of automatic weapons with bandoleers of ammunition crisscrossing his chest. Under his eyes, he wore large black stripes of war paint, and a black band was tied tightly around his head.

Dunlap broke into hearty laughter as Fannin's face displayed nothing but shock. The executive was all decked out as a business version of Rambo so a photographer could shoot a promotional picture for his book. The only prop he declined to wear was a bulked-up rubberized chest the photographer picked up at a costume shop.

Dunlap later regretted the masquerade but joked "at least I didn't pose in a wedding dress like Dennis Rodman."

With Dunlap, executives learned, you could often expect the unexpected. For all his egotistical rants, he could sometimes be refreshingly straightforward and playful. He was not above pulling a witty prank or engaging in a bit of mischief. Yet there was something menacing about the man, and his murderous pose atop a desk betrayed a hint of the danger that always seemed to lurk around him. For while he could pull a prank, he could just as unexplainably pull a tantrum.

Early one Monday morning, not much more than a month into Dunlap's reign as CEO at Sunbeam, Russell Kersh walked into James Wilson's office at 8:30 A.M. with a rather frightening admonition.

"Al wants to see you," he said tersely. "I hope you have a thick skin today."

"What does that mean?" Wilson asked.

"You're going to get beat up, real bad."

Thinking that Kersh must be joking, Wilson got up and went straight to see the boss. He did not shy from confrontation. As a navigator, Wilson had flown thirty-five missions over Vietnam, from cargo planes to B-52 bombers. He had beaten back cancer at least twice in his life. Wilson had been working overtime to help recruit new talent and plan for the eventual downsizing. For the previous week Wilson had been trying to lure to the company Don Uzzi, the former beverage division president of Quaker Oats who was responsible for Gatorade's phenomenal success. He had left his job after the company's debacle with Snapple, a failure he had foreseen but was unable to prevent. The talks were not going well. Uzzi was holding out for more money and a bigger stock option package.

Without a word Dunlap closed his office door and fired a chair across the room at the perplexed executive.

"You son of a bitch!" he screamed. "Don't you know who you work for?"

"Yes, I do," said Wilson.

"I didn't ask you to talk. Shut your mouth!"

Dunlap then went into an extended tirade, suggesting that Wilson hadn't kept Kersh fully informed of his negotiations with Uzzi. Dunlap, believed Wilson, was under the mistaken impression that he had made an offer to Uzzi that exceeded the approved parameters Dunlap had set. In fact Wilson hadn't made an offer at all because he knew it wasn't going to be enough to lure the executive to Sunbeam.

Dunlap's fusillade of rage silenced him until Dunlap began knocking his fist on an imaginary door.

"Well, hello," he said mockingly. "Is there anybody there?"

"Yeah," Wilson replied, "I didn't think you wanted me to—"

"Who asked you to talk? Shut up. You don't deserve to speak."

Fortunately for Wilson, Dunlap's secretary interrupted the beating to let Dunlap know that his next appointment had arrived.

"Get out of here!" Dunlap yelled at Wilson.

The battered executive skulked out and turned down the hall, only to realize that dozens of people in his own department were standing in the corridor in total shock. They had heard every word of Dunlap's diatribe, making the words sting yet again. Wilson, thinking of nothing but quitting, rushed back to the safety of his office.

The next day Newt White stopped by.

"Welcome to the team," he said with a smile. "I understand you have been baptized."

"If that's what it is, I guess I was."

"You know, once Al gets started, all you can do is let him go," White advised. "It's like a force of nature, like a hurricane. There's no way you can stop it. All you've got to do is let it blow itself out."

No one at any Dunlap-run company was immune from the gale winds he could unleash at a moment's notice. Wilson could understand why Dunlap felt he needed the unusual item he charged to the company on his first expense report: Dunlap made his own employees hate him. As head of human resources, Wilson had to sign off on the CEO's expenses and his eyes widened when he spotted an item that Dunlap's predecessor never would have purchased: a bulletproof vest. "I knew it was a different world," he said. Later Wilson would approve Dunlap's purchase of a handgun for himself.

As he and the other executives soon learned, Dunlap's concern for personal security was not trifling, nor did it represent mere paranoia. The massive publicity he attracted for his layoffs and outspoken views brought bundles of hate mail to Fort Lauderdale headquarters. Knowing of his fondness for his German shepherds, someone anonymously sent him a photograph of a couple of dead dogs on a road. One person even erected an Internet site using the Sunbeam logo to spell out "Sunbeast." The site urged people to boycott Sunbeam and Oster products because of Dunlap. Even some Sunbeam shareholders, who had plenty of reason to cheer Dunlap at this point, sent him dreadful letters.

"Hi Scum Bag," began one letter dated August 11, 1996, from a woman who described herself as a disgusted stockholder.

"If there's justice in this world, the thousands of people you have ruined for a bloody buck should be able to dissect you piece by piece.

"You think you are worth the millions you have accrued by climbing over dead bodies is justified . . . just think of some people who have amassed fortunes without a brain in their head . . . Mike Tyson, to name one.

"I hope you never draw a happy breath for the rest of your miserable life."

The writer, Virginia Egan Dale, was a personal friend to people at Scott and Sunbeam who had been fired by Dunlap. Her husband, in fact, had once supervised a young Jim Clegg at Bristol-Myers before he had joined Polaroid and Sunbeam.

Since Dunlap joined Sunbeam, someone had smashed the sunroof of his 1995 S500 Mercedes while it was parked in his driveway. A year earlier, a fountain centerpiece had been stolen from his lawn along with a concrete pineapple from atop a garden wall. Dunlap was unsuccessfully trying to get his neighbors at the Boca Raton Resort and Club to foot the annual bill for as much as $270,000 of armed security service.

Dunlap had learned to live with the threats and incidents from his days in Wisconsin over two decades earlier, when he received calls and letters from people who said they were going to blow up his car or shoot him in the company parking lot. It was why Dunlap insisted that the company pay for a personal security guard to accompany him no matter where he went. Sean Thornton, his bodyguard, was six-foot-two and built like granite. A former Wackenhut guard, he had once chased drug smugglers for the U.S. Coast Guard and watched over figure skater Katarina Witt. "If I was going to be in a foxhole, I'd like him to be at my side," said one Sunbeam executive.

THE PERSONAL SIDE of Al Dunlap was mostly protected by himself. His carefully crafted image belied a dark and troubling side. Not only did he have a controlling personality and a constant need to be at the center of attention, he had a tremendous temper and an enormous ego. And for reasons that few understood, he often felt the need to either exaggerate the experiences of his life or simply reinvent them.

He painted an Horatio Alger portrait of himself, as a boy who grew up poor in the slums of Hoboken, New Jersey, the deprived son of a Woolworth's store clerk and a dock worker who frequently was laid off from his job in the shipyards that sat in the shadow of New York City. He told associates a childhood story that had driven him throughout his life. The incident had happened when, Dunlap said, his family was crowded into a basement apartment under a beauty parlor in Hoboken. "He was playing with a friend whose mother came along and said, 'Johnny, you can't play with Al because he lives in the tenements,'" recalled a Dunlap colleague. "It was a defining moment in his life. That incident burned into his brain. He said, 'I'm going to show those folks that I'm better than them.' It was his Rosebud."

But Dunlap was no Citizen Kane. His childhood was hardly lost, and his parents were never impoverished. By his sister's account, he was a pampered boy raised in the comfort of generous and loving parents and grandparents from the day of his birth on July 26, 1937. As a baby he lay under blankets adorned with his initials. As a youngster he donned the finest clothes, whether it was a leather bomber jacket or a well-pressed suit. "Al was the shining light of everyone's existence," said Denise Dunlap, his only sibling. "He was not only loved, he was adored, almost to the point of obsession. It was a very comfortable childhood."

His mother, Mildred, was short and heavy-set, opinionated and introverted. A woman of German and Irish descent, she doted on his every need. After high school dates, Dunlap would come home to sit at the foot of her bed and speak expansively about his day and his life. His Anglo-Irish father, Albert, whose handsome looks and demonstrative personality made him a ladies' man, often seemed to vie with the son for his wife's attention. After the younger Dunlap graduated from West Point, his grandfather created something of a shrine to him in a corner of their Hoboken home. He proudly placed Dunlap's cadet hat under a glass dome and hung an array of pictures of the good-looking cadet on the walls of his living room.

Until Dunlap turned eleven, he spent the better part of his life in a three-story, red-brick row house on Garden Street in Hoboken, not far from where Frank Sinatra was raised. Then, in 1948, his family moved to Hasbrouck Heights, New Jersey, a middle-class community of peaceful, tree-lined streets and modest homes largely populated by first- and second-generation German and Italian immigrants.

Though something of a loner, Dunlap excelled at Hasbrouck Heights High School. His report cards were filled with A's, and he earned letters in football as well as track and field. He exuded confidence, if not cockiness, often drawing stars on his school papers. He lifted weights as often as three times a day and didn't hesitate to show off his well-developed muscles to some classmates. The solidly built, blond adolescent cut a dashing figure, towering over his shorter parents in the family album pictures.

Even as a youth, though, Dunlap was short-tempered and obstinate. His younger sister remembers that things often flew through the air when her brother was angry. "He would just spin on you in a second," she said. During one rage, she says, he even threw darts at her dolls. "Things had to go right, or his face got red," said Andrew Kmetz, his high school football coach. "He sure did have a temper, an aggressive one. If someone knocked him on his butt in a game, he was going to knock the guy back twice."

After he graduated in 1956, Dunlap's good grades and good looks got him into West Point. He was the first resident of his town to ever win an appointment to the military academy. Of the more than 1,000 incoming cadets who reported to West Point that July, Dunlap was among the 608 who survived "beast barracks," the first eight weeks of verbal hazing in plebe year. "I didn't like it," said Dunlap. "You had to be a total masochist to like it, but I knew I had to survive it."

He was always the underdog, the fighter who had to succeed. In those early days the harassment seemed relentless. Upper-class cadets terrorized and violently abused the raw recruits, forced them to run a gauntlet of senior cadets, all for the purpose of putting "iron in their souls." Dunlap endured the cruel treatment, with the support of his parents and sister, who frequently drove up from New Jersey on the weekends. "Al was not happy and was always ready to jump out of there," remembered Denise Dunlap. "My parents would go up and give him the old pep talk. They were faithful to him. They were very proud of him."

Up against stiffer academic competition, Dunlap hung on thanks to friends who helped tutor him through the difficult material. He often studied late into the evening, putting blankets over the windows of his room so the upperclassmen wouldn't know he was up after the 10 P.M. lights out. "He had a hotshot attitude, but he kept us laughing a lot," recalled Ken Sindora, who was assigned to company G2 with Dunlap. "He didn't let the stuff get him down." Once, in the electricity lab, he and Dunlap had to hook up generators with long cables in a class assignment. Suddenly there was a loud bang and smoke poured from their experiment. "We damn near blew up the lab," added Sindora. "We ended up making it through that course and the academy, but I look back on that and wonder how we ever got through it."

Above all, Dunlap survived by reminding himself he was the underdog and he had to stay up longer, work harder, do whatever it took to make it through. In the boxing ring at West Point, his coach scored fighting cadets on how much leather they could throw and how much blood they lost. Dunlap had a wicked left jab, punched up a storm, and rarely bled. "He was aggressive and tough to hit," said Philip A. Tripician, Dunlap's roommate for six months. "He didn't show you much. He fought out of a crouch, and all you would see was his head. And when he hit you, he stung you."

Soon after graduating in 1960, 537th out of his cadet class of 550, Dunlap was to begin a mandatory three-year military stint at a nuclear missile base in Maryland. Before reporting to duty as a first lieutenant, he met a striking redhead at a dance club in West Orange, New Jersey. Gwyn R. Donnelly was a young, impressionable eighteen-year-old woman with the looks of a *Vogue* model. Slender and tall, with high, sculpted cheekbones and blue-green eyes, she had just graduated from high school and was at the club with a fake ID and a girlfriend. Dunlap strolled over to their table to ask her for a dance. "We danced the rest of the evening," she remembered, "and at the end of the night he asked for my number."

In Dunlap she saw a man with dreams and the ambition to fulfill them. "He knew he wanted to be successful, going all the way up the ranks in the military or in business," she said. "He always wanted money and power." Donnelly, the daughter of a plumber, shared his desire to make a better life for herself. "We thought the same about a lot of things. I was taken by him. He was caring and attentive. We just clicked."

When Dunlap reported to duty after training at Fort Benning, they maintained their relationship long distance. She sent him home-baked cookies in the mail. He sent daily love letters in return, telephoning relentlessly to check on her. On September 10, 1961, less than a year after they had first danced together, they married in a military cere-mony at Holy Trinity Church in her hometown of Westfield, New Jersey. He was twenty-four. She was all of nineteen now, a showroom model for a New York maker of cocktail dresses and evening wear.

It did not take long for her to discover that the handsome cadet she had married was an angry and at times tortured individual. Returning from their Bermuda honeymoon, Dunlap took her along on a curious expedition at the request of his mother. Emotionally distraught over her husband's infidelity, Mildred Dunlap asked her son to drive to a stranger's home and confront the woman she suspected was her hus-band's lover. Soon, Donnelly found, Dunlap's mother was consumed by the idea of her husband's infidelity. She had been calling that home for days, trying to break up an affair that apparently did not exist. "His mother was all upset," she says. "Al was trying to help." They drove to the home, knocked on the door, visited briefly with the woman, her husband, and three children, and left. The only time Donnelly would see her husband cry was in a car, driving home. The tears ran down a son's face, angry at his father for terribly hurting his mother. It was not the first time his mother had called attention to his dad's wanderings. Some thirteen years earlier, when Dunlap was eleven years old and his sister was just five, Mrs. Dunlap put both her children in a car to chase down her husband, who she believed was cheating on her in a hotel in Philadelphia. "My mother took us there because she had heard that my father was in the hotel with someone else," recalled Denise Dunlap. "My father's wandering started when we were children, but he wasn't so much a philanderer as he was seeking some sort of connection. My mother was cold in some ways, and Al and my dad were always in com-petition."

The rivalry surely ended with Dunlap's marriage in 1961.

That year Dunlap left New Jersey, his parents, and his sister, more or less for good. He and his bride moved into a modest ranch house on the military base on the eastern shore of Maryland. Almost from the start, according to the divorce complaint she would later file, their marriage was full of "wretchedness and misery." Her husband, she said, demanded that she dye her hair blond even after the dye caused a rash and blisters on her scalp. He told her he liked the way it looked on a former girlfriend, the same woman for whom he had bought the engagement ring he later gave Donnelly. Coming home from work, he would conduct military-like inspections of the house, ducking his head under the mattress of the bed and moving chairs away from the walls to see if he could find even a trace of dust. If he did, Dunlap went ballistic.

When she told him she was pregnant in May 1962, according to the complaint, Dunlap became violent. He told her he would divorce her and move to Europe so he "would not have to support you and your brat," the complaint alleged. Four months later he ordered her out of the house, forcing her to get a job because she was "bringing in another mouth to feed." During the Cuban Missile Crisis in October, when Dunlap was confined to the base, she was left in their military home with no food or money. Dunlap had even taken their savings book so she could not draw funds from the account. Desperate, she telephoned her mother and sister for help. Two weeks before her due date, Gwyn Dunlap became ill enough to be rushed to the base hospital, where Dunlap asked the doctors to induce her labor to avoid an additional $25 admission fee.

The abuse, she claimed, was both physical and emotional. Dunlap would allow her $15 a week for all the family food and would check the supermarket register tapes to see if she had spent all the money. On several occasions, she claimed, he became violent over the small amount of groceries she got for his money, pushing her up against the refrigerator or stove. He would look into her pocketbook for hidden money, and even go through her closet for clothes he disliked. He took them to a nearby thrift shop and sold them.

He talked about how rich he would be from the insurance if she were dead and threatened her with weapons. According to the complaint, he once pointed a bowie knife at her and remarked: "I often wondered what human flesh tasted like." At other times, when he sat at home cleaning what was described as a "small arsenal" of guns, Dunlap allegedly told her: "You better watch out and toe the line."

Still, she stayed with him and by him. Divorce, she thought, was an admission of failure. She was a Catholic, reared to believe that you live with the vows you make in a church. No one in her family had ever been divorced. For the sake of their child, Troy, and her own religious convictions, she was determined not to be the first. Even the thought of divorce scared her. She wondered if she could get a job again, if she would be able to support her child. With Dunlap's three years of active duty coming to an end, they would have another change in their lives, a change that might be good for all of them.

In 1963 the military offered no war that would allow Dunlap to scramble up the ladder of the military echelon. And it became increasingly clear to him that although he could accumulate power in the army, it was unlikely he could accumulate much wealth. He had paid back his debt to West Point with three years of service. Now it was time to move on. After months of searching for a job from his in-laws' home in Westfield, Dunlap landed with Kimberly-Clark Corp.

The Dunlap family moved into a two-bedroom garden apartment in New Milford, Connecticut, not much more than a brisk walk from the non-union paper mill where Dunlap began on the plant floor. He threw himself into the job, coming home exhausted every evening. But the change of venue did not alter his behavior toward his wife or his son. Every day he drove his canary-yellow Thunderbird to work, stranding them at the red-brick complex, because he refused to allow her to use the car. If he saw his son's fingerprints on the living room cocktail table, he would command his wife to immediately clean them off the veneer. Nearly every day he barked orders and expectations, and criticized her housework, her friends, and her appearance.

It was during the Christmas holidays of 1963, while at her parents' home in New Jersey, that Dunlap shoved his wife so hard that she fell over a coffee table and onto the living room floor. "You son of a bitch," he screamed, "I will kill you and step all over you and take that baby," he shouted. Just then, the telephone rang and Dunlap yelled at her to give him the phone or he would bash her over the head with it.

By early November 1964, with their only child, Troy, only months shy of his second birthday, she had enough. She had quietly contemplated waiting until her boy turned five. But she began to ask herself a simple and telling question: "If I were a child, would I want Al as my father?" Her answer was always a resounding no. Dunlap had carefully mapped out Troy's entire future. He would get nothing but A's at school. He would be successful in life. She wondered what fate would befall her son if he didn't share her husband's vision of the future. Ultimately she came to the conclusion that she had to leave for Troy's sake as well as her own.

When Dunlap returned from work on the evening of November 2, he insisted on conducting another inspection of their home. He had warned her to keep their child locked in his room to prevent the baby from messing up the apartment. So when Dunlap discovered his son's fingerprints on the living room coffee table, he flew into a terrible rage, screaming and cursing at her and insisting at 11 P.M. that she polish the furniture spotless.

Before he left for work the next morning, according to the complaint, Dunlap grabbed a knife off the kitchen table, pointed it at her, and told her she better have the house clean and the ironing done by the time he returned. The same morning, her parents were driving north from their Westfield home to visit her and Troy. When they arrived, she took her mother aside and asked if she could return home. She had kept Dunlap's mistreatment of her a secret, but it was a burden she now had to unload. Her father did not have to hear too many of the details.

"Okay, let's go," he said.

And they began to hurriedly gather her belongings and cram them in her father's Chevy Impala until there was barely room for the four of them. She piled in most of her own clothes, the boy's outfits, a portable television set, a small broiler, and her son's toys. "I remember when my dad was loading up the car with Troy's toys, my father was putting them in one side of the car and Troy was pulling them out of the other," she now laughs.

For months Dunlap tried to win her back. He called her aunts to make his plea. He blamed her mother for the decision to leave. At one point Dunlap spotted her pushing Troy in a stroller down the main shopping district in Westfield. He pulled over his Thunderbird and began pulling her into the car. Another motorist, thinking she was being abducted, stopped her car and began beeping the horn hoping to attract the attention of the police. Dunlap's wife broke free from her husband and rushed over to the stranger, who drove her and Troy directly to the police station. Finally Dunlap even enlisted her father in efforts to save his marriage. After listening to the young man, her father thought she should give it one more try. Dunlap came to her parents' home and sat, with her father, in the living room, waiting for an opportunity to make his case. She refused to come out of her bedroom. "Finally my mom put an end to it," she says. "I was too young to realize that when somebody is calling you up to find out what you are doing every second of the day, that is about control, not love."

All in all, her divorce complaint is a remarkable document filled with shockingly vivid allegations of cruel and abusive behavior. Dunlap dismisses the charges as "ridiculous" and vigorously denies them. "Anyone taking the time to look at the grounds for divorce before no-fault divorce laws were passed in the 1970s knows that lawyers had to be very creative in establishing grounds for divorce," Dunlap maintained in a written statement.

The judge, however, found Dunlap guilty of "extreme cruelty," and granted her divorce in November 1966, giving her sole custody of Troy. Dunlap's ex-wife, now remarried and living in the northwest, stands by the allegations she made more than three decades ago. "I didn't make up one thing," she insisted. "The attorney didn't stretch one thing." At the time she was so afraid of Dunlap and anxious to break all ties to the man that she didn't request alimony and accepted, without question, the $15 a week in child support Dunlap offered. At the divorce proceeding, she recalled, the judge leaned over the bench and jokingly asked her class rank in high school, wondering why she would possibly settle for so little for her child and nothing for herself. "Are you sure you want this, now?" he asked. "I so desperately wanted a divorce," she says, "I didn't ask for anything."

WHEN HE WAS served with the divorce papers on October 13, 1965, Dunlap had already placed a couple of thousand miles between himself and his family. He had moved to Wisconsin for Kimberly-Clark, setting himself up in a small apartment on 334 Naymut Street in Menasha. He eventually met his next wife on a blind date arranged by his new boss, Ely Meyer of Sterling Pulp & Paper. Meyer not only wanted to be Dunlap's employer, he wanted to be his matchmaker as well. Every year Meyer threw himself a birthday bash at the local country club, inviting as many as 200 people at a time. Dunlap sat next to the boss at the first party and soon found himself the recipient of a lecture for coming without a date. That evening Meyer promised to find him a "nice girl" and arranged a blind date the very next night at his home over dinner.

The woman who showed up, Judy Stringer, was a teller at a drive-in window for the local bank. Dunlap, who had made work his entire life since Gwyn had walked out on him, found her beautiful and intelligent. She thought him brash and aggressive. Even so, they continued to date and within six months were engaged. Dunlap hoped to marry her before the end of the year for tax purposes. He figured the $600 he would save from the tax reduction would be enough to pay for the wedding. Stringer resisted on the grounds that it was terribly unromantic, and they married on March 30, 1968, some sixteen months after his divorce was finalized. Dunlap's sister came out for the wedding, but his parents were not invited. The new Mrs. Dunlap seemed far more tolerant of her husband's temper and far more understanding of her place in his world. "There are three things that are important in Al's life: his business, his dogs, and his wife, in that order," she said. "Being third isn't all that bad."

She also understood from the beginning what Dunlap was all about. "People were saying things to my parents about 'How can Judy marry this terrible person? He's firing people, and he's cold and cruel' and all the words that I heard, and I sat down one night and started crying. And Al said, 'Sit down. We're gonna have a talk. And we're going to have this talk once, and if you can't live with what I'm going to tell you, then maybe we're not meant to be.' He said, 'I came here not to win a popularity contest. I came here to save a company. And, if I have to get rid of 30 percent of the people so that 70 percent of the people have job security, that's what I'm going to do.'"

IF HIS NEW WIFE was alarmed by the talk of her husband around town, she might also have wondered why Dunlap had virtually no contact with his only son. Indeed, he apparently treated the boy as if he had been just another faceless employee terminated in a Chainsaw downsizing. After marrying for the second time, Dunlap did nothing to contact Troy Dunlap. He didn't acknowledge his birthdays or graduations. There were no telephone calls, letters, cards, or gifts. The child support checks, of $15 a week and later $150 a month when Troy turned twelve, were sent from the home of Dunlap's in-laws in Wisconsin. Mrs. Donnelly, meantime, never discussed Troy's father with him until he was in the second grade and came home one day to tell his mother that his classmates asked why his last name was different than his mother's. He told the other children that his father had died in the Vietnam War a hero.

"That is when I felt I wasn't doing my son a favor," Donnelly says. "I told him he came from good stock. 'Honey,' I said, 'you don't have to make up a story. You can be proud of your dad.'"

It was not until 1985, when Troy was twenty-one years old, that he saw his father for the first time since he was two years old. He had read a magazine story about Dunlap's success as chief executive of paper cup maker Lily Tulip Co. and decided to seek him out. At his own expense, Troy briefly visited with his father at Hilton Head, North Carolina, where Dunlap had taken up residence. It was, by Troy's account, an unemotional reunion.

At one point, his father arranged to get him a job in a paper mill plant in Portland, Oregon, that was part of Sir James Goldsmith's empire. But the son quit within a year when his supervisors, realizing he was Dunlap's son, put him to work in a storage room. Troy would only see his father a couple more times during his life. In 1995, when Dunlap toured one of Scott Paper's facilities in Everett, Washington, less than a half-hour's drive from Troy's home in Seattle, his son only found out about the visit by reading the local newspapers. "It was pretty pathetic to hear that he was there," says Troy, who had last seen his father in 1988. "He didn't even bother to call." Still, the son later managed to create some semblance of a relationship with his father by telephone until Dunlap discovered that Troy had spoken to a reporter in 1997. "You may get your five minutes of fame," warned Dunlap, "but I guarantee you and your mother a lifetime of aggravation."

By the late 1980s and early 1990s, as Dunlap spent more time in England and Australia, he had severed almost all contact with his family back in New Jersey. In 1989, while he was working as an aide-de-camp to Sir James Goldsmith, his sister called him with a plea for help. "My mother had stopped walking," she said. "My father and I asked if he could pay for a housekeeper to take care of her. His reply was that 'a nursing home would be good for her. She'll learn to sing songs.' I went ballistic. 'Someday you'll sing songs, Al.'"

Eventually her father had to sell the family home and move into a small apartment to pay for his wife's two-year stay in a Cape May, New Jersey, nursing home. "Al never visited her," she said. "The first thing she would always say when I saw her was, "Have you heard from Albie?' I would say he's really busy but you know he loves you." His only contact with his mother was a card that came through the mail on her birthday.

Her father, she said, was tortured by the way his son had turned his back on the family. "I don't understand your brother and why he is so selfish," he told her. When Dunlap sent newspaper clippings on his exploits in Australia, she shared them with her father, who cried at what he read. Albert Dunlap, Sr., could not believe that his son said he grew up dirt-poor, or that his father worked as a dock worker or that his mother worked in a five-and-dime store. "My father wasn't a dock worker," Denise said. "He was a boilermaker for United Engineers, which built power plants, and my mother never worked a day in her married life. My father asked: 'Why does he have to tell these stories?' He was crushed. He couldn't understand it."

When their mother died in December 1992, Dunlap, who was then working for Kerry Packer in Australia, failed to attend her funeral. He said he was too busy to make the trip. Six months later his father was rushed to a hospital in Camden, New Jersey, after being hit by a pickup truck. He hung on for three days, during which time Denise Dunlap tried to get her brother to come home for a final visit with their dying father. "He didn't have much of a reaction," she said.

Their father's funeral drew only seven mourners: Denise Dunlap, her two daughters, his lady friend, her son and wife, and a neighbor. Dunlap refused to attend that funeral as well. Again, he said, he was too busy to make it. The son apparently had written off the father he had lost respect for so many years ago.

Back in their father's apartment to sort through the family's belongings, Denise Dunlap called her brother to ask if he wanted her to look for anything in particular.

"I don't want anything," he told her. "Just send me whatever pictures of me you can find."

She made up an album of photographs from the better days and put it in the mail. Although their father left a $5,000 life insurance policy in his daughter's name, she says Dunlap received the check and kept the money because, as he explained to her, he had paid for their father's funeral.

HIS ONLY FAMILY seemed to be himself; his wife, Judy; and their dogs. Judy would occasionally bring the dogs to Sunbeam headquarters, especially on a late Friday afternoon when the dogs were sometimes set free in Dunlap's office. Judy, said friends, was a perfect soul mate for Dunlap. An excellent athlete and a twelve-handicap golfer, she displayed the outward strength and the expansive personality of an actress. She was made of sterner stuff that made her resilient and independent. Certainly, she could more easily tolerate and forgive his temper tantrums. Once, during a business trip to Chicago for Sunbeam, Dunlap began to publicly berate her in a hotel lobby for leaving $500 in cash on her bureau. His criticism was so unrelenting that his business associates assumed that Judy had left the money in their hotel room. Instead, it was on her bureau in Florida, in a home protected by a sophisticated alarm system, two dogs, and numerous electronic gates. Judy Dunlap, however, took his harangue with great poise, never showing any of their guests even the slightest sign of upset.

Dunlap often compared her to Nancy Reagan because she would defend him as vigorously as Nancy had the President. She wouldn't hesitate to lecture her husband's executive minions, often in the exact language he himself would use. If things turned sour, she would remind them that "Al is out there killing himself. What are you guys doing?"

She took a keen interest in his business, often calling up the company to ask about the price of the stock or to be patched into a conference call to hear her husband answer questions from Wall Street analysts. But she was hardly a calming influence on the man. Coopers' Don Burnett once told associates that "Judy absolutely encourages him and fires him up" when he's angry and upset.

Friends found her good company. She was unassuming, affable, and gregarious. Yet, like her husband, she was capable of getting right to the point. At one social gathering, when some of Dunlap's colleagues advised him to take it easy or he would end up with heart trouble, Judy snapped to the amazement of their guests: "Al doesn't get heart attacks. He gives them."

Indeed. In early November, a week before Dunlap was to present his restructuring plan to Sunbeam's board of directors in New York, David Fannin was eating a turkey sandwich in the small downstairs café at Fort Lauderdale headquarters when he began to experience chest pains. Fannin returned to his office and collapsed. An ambulance was called and he was carried out on a stretcher to a local hospital. Technically, Fannin had not suffered a heart attack, but he certainly was ill with heart trouble. Several of his arteries were clogged, and his doctors ordered an angioplasty to clean them out.

Like everyone at Sunbeam, he had been working overtime, keeping up a wild pace. He had never had heart problems before. His wife, Lucille, had unplugged the telephone to allow him some rest at the hospital. At one point, Fannin was sleeping while his wife kept a vigil. Suddenly, Fannin jolted awake.

"Al's here," he said.

"What?" his wife asked.

"Al's here!"

"You're having nightmares," she told him. "Just calm down, David, and get some more rest."

Within seconds, however, they both clearly heard the booming voice coming closer and closer until Dunlap strolled into the hospital room carrying a large basket of fruit.

"This same thing happened to me at Scott Paper," Dunlap said.

"You had a heart attack?" asked Fannin's wife.

"No, not me." Dunlap laughed. "My corporate counsel at Scott had a heart attack. David, if you wanted some time off, why didn't you just ask for it? You didn't have to do this in order to get out of the office."

8
THE BLANKET WITH A BRAIN

THE COOPERS & LYBRAND restructuring had turned Sunbeam upside down, inside out. Managers and employees were being fired every day. Departments and functions lacked the people to get a normal day's work done. Plants needed to produce goods for retailers were being shut down. Computers no longer worked. Some of the surviving factories lacked the parts' inventory to make their products.

Coopers' Don Burnett, Dunlap's pal, had left the company an utter mess, or as a top executive indelicately put it: "It was as if Coopers took a shit on our desks and left us with knives and forks. That's exactly what they did. We couldn't get all this stuff to work. We couldn't run our financial systems. We couldn't invoice our customers. We couldn't process our returns. It was total bedlam."

Wal-Mart, the company's largest single customer, threatened to drop the appliance maker as a vendor after losing $9 million in sales on 300,000 irons that Sunbeam failed to deliver. The retailer's buyers groused about bar-coding problems with three major shipments. Sears, Roebuck complained of having to deal with three different sales reps from Sunbeam in six months. Other retailers claimed they received shipments past the cancellation dates on their contracts.

Much of the turmoil was attributed to Burnett's work. Sunbeam executives said Coopers took a highly numerical rather than studied approach to a business. "They come as accountants even though they think they are consultants," said Dixon Thayer, vice president for Sunbeam's international business. "They come at it with the numbers. Al basically told them, 'I want 50 percent of the workforce out,' so they knew the answers before they got there."

Many of the executives interviewed by his staff found the Coopers visits "perfunctory and political," designed merely to validate answers that Dunlap wanted to hear. In almost every case, they cut not merely fat, but pure muscle, right down into the bone of the organization. In human resources, for example, the Coopers plan decimated a staff of seventy-five employees, leaving only seventeen. The dramatic reduction was proposed after Jack Bonini, one of the lead consultants under Burnett, assured the vice president of human resources that the cutback would be twenty-eight or thirty employees. The first time Coopers informed him of the more severe number was during its presentation to Dunlap when Wilson and anyone else was less likely to complain.

After the meeting, HR chief James Wilson sought out Bonini to protest the cutback of people who also would suffer the indignity of having to fire nearly 3,000 others before getting the chainsaw themselves.

"This makes no sense," Wilson complained. "I can't manage a function that goes from seventy-five to seventeen. You can't do that."

"Jim," Bonini replied calmly, "it's all ratio. Most people have maybe one [HR manager] per hundred employees. We're going to give you one for every 300. That's the way the ratio works."

He made no apologies for sandbagging Wilson into believing that he would cut his staff to twenty-eight or thirty and then surprising him in front of his boss. Stunned, Wilson realized that Bonini and Burnett were simply playing to Dunlap's demands, cutting people on the most arbitrary basis possible, with no regard to the level of work they had to do. "From an operational viewpoint, the Coopers work was superficial," said Wilson. "It was from 50,000 feet and don't ask me to go to 49,000 because the closer I get the more I can't answer any of your questions."

Even worse, the cutbacks failed to account for any natural attrition or the chance that talented survivors would quit in outrage over the poor treatment accorded their friends. In one case after another, executives and managers who failed to get the ax soon resigned for other jobs, leaving shortages of skilled and experienced talent throughout the corporation. The vast changes led to humiliating mishaps. When a new marketing executive booked a get-acquainted session with Wal-Mart, he mistakenly took a flight to Fayetteville, North Carolina, instead of Fayetteville, Arkansas, where the retailer is headquartered. The executive reportedly failed to realize his error until he attempted to take a taxi to Wal-Mart and the driver responded with "Which one?"

Burnett's sheaf of recommendations, made hastily with little input from the company's management, was filled with strategic blunders. The consultants assumed that Sunbeam could have a completely flexible workforce that would allow it to significantly cut production of seasonal products such as electric blankets and grills during the off-season and ramp up production when the products were needed. But Coopers failed to account for the fact that employees needed year-round jobs and if you laid them off, you probably wouldn't be able to hire them back when you started up production again. Nor did the consultants consider how much inventory needed to be built before the products' season rolled around. "We had a helluva time keeping workers and hiring workers," explained an executive. "There was very little recognition that Sunbeam manufacturing was not very good. The engineering designs were not kept up to date, the specs weren't right, the planning for production was not good, the inventory to parts wasn't right. So we had all these fundamental problems, and then Coopers started moving stuff and it was an absolute disaster."

Among other things, Coopers urged that Sunbeam fire its computer staff and outsource the entire information processing function. Dunlap fired technicians making $35,000 a year who quickly discovered they were worth $125,000 a year elsewhere. To replace them, Dunlap had to hire far more expensive help, including some of the people just fired at consulting rates three or more times what they had once been paid. In the midst of all this, the company attempted to upgrade its computer systems, with no backup system in place in case something went wrong. The result: the computers were down for months. Sunbeam began to manually invoice customers such as Wal-Mart and Sears, Roebuck.

Managing the mess fell largely to Donald Uzzi, the marketer who had effectively become chief operating officer when Newt White abruptly quit in mid-November. Of all of Dunlap's early recruits, few brought more credibility to the management team than the short, high-strung executive whose résumé overflowed with credentials gained at American's best marketing companies: Procter & Gamble, PepsiCo, and Quaker Oats. Crowned "marketer of the year" by *Advertising Age* in 1995, he was well known to Wall Street analysts as a savvy brand-builder.

Uzzi looked a little like a model on the pages of *GQ*. He was a handsome man, in his mid-forties, with dark slicked-back hair that curled up over the back of his shirt collar. He wore the casual look of a wealthy man who vacationed on Nantucket, Massachusetts. He favored Polo shirts, pleated trousers, and Gucci loafers without socks, and he drove a red Porsche that seemed to compliment his supersmooth professionalism. Though his marketing presentations were as polished as a Broadway production, he was an Irish-Italian street fighter from a Bronx blue-collar family.

From his very first meeting with Dunlap, he sensed trouble. During the job interview, Uzzi was asked just one critical question: "Can you do this job?" Then Dunlap spent the next hour, recalled Uzzi, talking about himself. He left, thinking that Dunlap had turned Scott Paper quickly and made fortunes for many of its executives. "At the outside, I thought Sunbeam would take a year," he said. "My dad used to say you can shovel shit against the tide for a year. I figured I would make a lot of money."

Now, mired in the turmoil created by Dunlap and Coopers, turning Sunbeam around didn't seem all that easy. "We couldn't bill our customers," he said. "We couldn't keep track of our shipments. We didn't know what we were shipping. We had customers calling day and night, asking where their orders were. Some had three orders instead of one. Others had the wrong order. Our customers were irate. Manufacturing was in shambles. We couldn't plan future materials requests to make goods or to schedule production. We fell into a black hole."

Having worked for exacting bosses before in fiercely competitive environments, Uzzi was no stranger to high pressure or great adversity. But he believed the cutbacks were so severe and so wrenching that they made normal operations impossible, never mind the exceptional work Dunlap demanded. Yet when Uzzi or any other executive came to Dunlap to point out the difficulties, Dunlap would inevitably refer to the Coopers study again and again in bullying them to hit the sales and profit targets, no matter what.

"Coopers said it can be done!" Dunlap yelled. "Go do it! Just fuckin' do it!"

Uzzi now understood why Newt White had told him shortly after being hired that he should be grateful that he would not have to report directly to Dunlap. "Don," White advised, "you want to be as far away from this guy as possible. If I could figure out how not to report to him, I would do it."

Since gaining White's job, Uzzi saw firsthand how difficult it was to work with and for Dunlap. He quickly came to the conclusion that it was virtually impossible "to have intelligent, strategic, in-depth business conversations" with his new boss. When Uzzi recommended that Sunbeam's strategy be more focused on North, Central and South America, for example, Dunlap's response was that the idea was "bullshit."

"You don't know what you're talking about," Dunlap told him. "That won't sell on Wall Street."

And when Dunlap began to belittle manufacturing chief Ronald Newcomb for failing to hit Coopers's savings projections, Uzzi saw Dunlap lapse into bizarre, unrelated anecdotes about his past experiences.

"Do you remember when we started up that plant at Lily?" he asked Kersh. "We did that in weeks." Kersh nodded in agreement, and Dunlap continued his tongue-lashing.

"We make tinker toys," he shouted. "Anybody can do this!"

The remark infuriated Uzzi and others because it denigrated their efforts to hold the company together and move it forward. "It was like your dumb uncle escaped from the basement," said Uzzi. "He would go into these examples for twenty or thirty minutes and just berate you, bringing up examples that had nothing to do with our situation at Sunbeam."

When the chaos inside threatened the company's grill business with Wal-Mart, Uzzi and Dunlap took a chartered jet to the retailer's headquarters in Arkansas. While Uzzi tried to brief his boss for the meeting, Dunlap kept watching a movie video on the jet, headphones covering his ears. At the time, in early 1997, Sunbeam had nearly 90 percent of Wal-Mart's outdoor grill business, a stake worth some $175 million in

Sunbeam annual sales. Yet, disenchanted with Sunbeam's ability to deliver quality product on time, Wal-Mart was seriously considering dropping the company as a supplier.

Dunlap did little to help Sunbeam's cause. Meeting with several key executives and buyers, he seemed more intent on handing out autographed copies of his book. He arrogantly boasted about his past exploits, giving short shrift to Wal-Mart's worries over Sunbeam's supply problems. On the trip back home, Dunlap openly wondered how anyone could possibly live in Arkansas and then watched another video. Shortly after their return, Uzzi got a call from one of the Wal-Mart executives, who warned him never to bring Dunlap back again.

Whenever Uzzi felt he was finally getting things under control, Dunlap almost always intervened with some new idea or project that often would wreak only more havoc on the company.

Just as the company was embarking on its massive restructuring, Dunlap insisted that the corporate headquarters be moved north to Delray Beach, not far from his home in Boca Raton. It was the worst possible time to relocate. His management team had flung itself into the dauntingly tough tasks he assigned and could scarcely deal with the disruption over the Christmas and New Year holidays. But he had picked out a location just off Route 95 in a low-slung, two-story building that faced six lanes of concrete at 1615 South Congress Avenue. Across the street was an apartment complex where guests were forbidden to own pickup trucks or motorcycles. In the back of the building was a set of railroad tracks and Route 95. Whenever a train came by, the building would creak and shake.

Dunlap's office, at one end of a U-shaped second floor, was three times the size of the one he left in Fort Lauderdale. It was a dimly lit getaway, with smoky blue carpeting and a blue leather couch and chairs. Its decorations evoked Dunlap's take-no-prisoners style: On the table behind his desk, a small statue of a paratrooper served as a reminder of his military days. Next to it were two small flags. One was Old Glory, the other, a miniature reproduction of an American Revolution flag with a coiled snake above the phrase "Don't Tread on Me."

The building's dominant theme was predatory. The company's modest lobby contained gaudy portraits of feline predators similar to the two large oil paintings behind Dunlap's bleached-wood desk. An iron desk lamp of a prowling lion and a trio of brass sharks placed in circle formation on a nearby coffee table reproduced the theme in his office. Other executives on the floor felt obliged to hang wildlife paintings on their walls or place predator sculptures on their desks. Flowers were judged a bit unmanly. "I just love predators," Dunlap told everyone who entered his office. "They can't just call up room service when they get hungry. They must go out and hunt and kill to survive."

Displaying his own appetite for blood, Dunlap began to insist that the company undergo yet another downsizing "refinement" soon after getting settled in its new quarters. The Coopers plan would take the headquarters staff down to 124 from the 308 employed at all of Sunbeam's main offices. To the bewilderment of Sunbeam's key executives, Dunlap wanted another reduction, even before the Coopers downsizing had been completed.

"I only want 100 people in the headquarters," he told Kersh and Uzzi. "Fire everybody else."

"Al," asked Uzzi, "how did you come to this conclusion?"

"Look," he said, "we could do this the hard way or the easy way. We are going to have only 100 people."

Uzzi tried to reason with Dunlap in the hopes of getting him to reconsider his decision. "I had the shit kicked out of me for it," said Uzzi. "I figured that either we did it or I would have to resign. So we ended up firing people who were trying to get things done."

Coopers was called back, and more people were given the boot. Yet over 70 percent of the company's cost structure was in materials, not people. Of course, Dunlap's reputation was based on chainsawing people out of organizations. His early notices at Sunbeam had struck fear and apprehension in the mayors and governors of every city and state in which the company had a plant. The governor of Mississippi telephoned Dunlap in his first week on the job to inform him that he wanted Sunbeam to stay in his state. A third of Sunbeam's total workforce and one-third of its sales were generated from products made in Sunbeam's six Mississippi factories. The state had provided some $120 million in financial incentives and tax credits to lure Sunbeam's new Hattiesburg complex. The governor's telephone call didn't make much of a difference. When Dunlap announced the largest revamping in the company's history on November 12, he said he would sell or consolidate eighteen of Sunbeam's twenty-six factories, including four of the six in Mississippi and two small plants in the modest rural town of Bay Springs, Mississippi.

Compared to all the facilities Dunlap had shuttered and all the people he had laid off, the pair of factories in Bay Springs was certainly small potatoes. The cinder-block plant in the downtown district employed only around 125 people. The other facility in Bay Springs's industrial area to the north of the town employed another 150. Though the loss of those jobs would be devastating for such a small community, there were plenty of other Sunbeam closures that would have far greater impact. In Shubata, Mississippi, the factory that made Sunbeam scales employed 350 people in a town of 577 residents. In Coushatta, Louisiana, where the company made irons and toasters, Sunbeam's $10 million annual payroll supported nearly 500 workers in a town with a population of 2,300.

Yet what made the closure of Sunbeam's south plant in Bay Springs stand out above the rest was that it was an economically foolhardly decision, a decision made to maintain Dunlap's image as a self-styled apostle of cost cutting, a decision partly made out of little more than personal vindictiveness.

BAY SPRINGS is about 130 miles north of New Orleans. It is situated in the east central part of the country's poorest state, where the blacktops of a pair of state highways, 15 and 18, intersect. Where those once dusty roads of the Deep South crisscross is where the bay trees grew tall and strong on the clear waters of a free-flowing spring. A handsome white gazebo now marks the spot of the artesian well that gave the town its name.

In an era of Wal-Marts and Gaps, of massive shopping malls that have gutted downtown districts all across the United States, Bay Springs is an anachronistic town within an anachronistic state. "Folks say that Mississippi is twenty-five years behind everybody else," quips John Few, editor of the *Jasper County News*, a weekly that has kept tabs on crime, poverty, and progress in Bay Springs since 1890. "A lot of these smaller towns are twenty-five years behind Mississippi. Bay Springs is like that. It's like stepping back in time."

It is a cozy rural place, with a population of only 2,200 people and no strangers on the sidewalks. The telephone company remains locally owned by the Fails family, who started it some seventy-five years ago with a single switchboard in Mrs. Fails's bedroom. The homemade pies at Bayless Restaurant continue to draw patrons from dozens of miles away. The storefronts along Third Street and Highway 528 are well-maintained and crammed with shoppers on an ordinary Saturday.

Dominated by teetotaling Baptists, whose churches outnumber those of any other religious denomination in town, Bay Springs was completely alcohol-free until recent years. It was even illegal to drink a beer in your own home. Unaware of the ban on alcohol, a newly transferred plant manager for the Sunbeam factory was arrested by the police for sipping a beer while mowing his lawn in the early 1980s.

On the fringe of the city's limits, outside its compact five square miles, most people make a living by raising chickens, hogs, cows, and steers. For high school students the local 4-H and Future Farmers of America livestock competitions remain a serious matter. A Georgia Pacific Corp. mill tears into 130 trailer loads of pine trees a day, spewing out two-by-fours and other lumber. The goat shipping and receiving station on Highway 15 holds a monthly auction where a well-bred goat can fetch tens of thousands of dollars.

The very first factory to ever locate in Bay Springs was the Sunbeam plant on the south side of Highway 528. Originally built in the early 1950s as a clothing factory, it was taken over in 1955 by the inventor of the electric blanket, Pop Russell, and his Chicago-based, family-owned and -run Northern Electric Co. A quaint engineer with a passion for ideas, Pop had a vision in the early 1900s to make electric heating pads that would replace the hot water bottle. After a number of failures, he managed to hit on a successful version and began selling them through drugstores in the early 1920s. The entrepreneur's most innovative product came by accident. The proprietor of a tuberculosis sanitarium in Saranac Lake, New York, called to ask if Pop could make heating pads as large as blankets to cover the patients who slept outside in the cold on the institution's immense wraparound porch. Pop obliged, creating in the 1930s the forerunner to the electric blanket by using stiff, asbestos-coated heated wire. During World War II, his two sons, Sam and Ed, began working with air force engineers to create heated flexible wire to sew inside the flying suits of pilots to keep them warm at high altitudes.

Through the years, the Russell family frequently traveled through Bay Springs on their way to the Gulf Coast where they spent holidays.

Tiring of Chicago, Pop Russell moved the company's operations into Mississippi, opening his first factory in the state in tiny Bay Springs. Soon, however, the business became something of an orphan passed from one pair of hands to the next. Oster Co. bought out Pop Russell's Northern Electric Co. in the late 1950s, Sunbeam Corp. acquired Oster in 1980, and Allegheny International gobbled up all of them a year later. Through all the ownership changes and financial machinations, the Bay Springs plant continued to churn out the thermostats and wires that went into its electric blankets.

But it was not until the mid-1980s that the factory played a crucial role in helping Sunbeam completely dominate the business. Working with a Scottish wire maker, Sunbeam engineers contrived a flexible heated wire that did away with the lumpy thermostats that lined the fabric of most electric blankets. It took nearly a decade of development work to produce the high-tech wire that adjusted heat levels by sensing the body's temperature. Sunbeam began to sell the new blankets in the mid-1980s, quickly devastating the competition with the innovation and capturing nearly 100 percent of the market for electric blankets—more than a decade before Dunlap renamed the product "The Blanket with a Brain" and falsely touted it as one of his "new product" introductions.

If Sunbeam made anything that was technologically superior and proprietary, it was the PTC (positive temperature coefficient) wire made in the clean and orderly Bay Springs plant. To give the wire its self-limiting characteristics, it was bombarded with a stream of electrons in the radiation vaults with concrete walls that were four feet thick. "For years we teased each other that if you went into the vaults long enough, you'd glow in the dark," laughed Earle Maxwell, a twenty-four-year Sunbeam veteran who once ran the plant.

History, of course, doesn't mean much to someone like Al Dunlap. Corporate traditions and customs are as quickly discarded as people in the companies that Dunlap has run. For the most part, that is not an indictment against him or modern management. It is the way it is, a circumstance of a vastly altered economic world where competition is unforgiving and knows no boundaries. It is what has made downsizing and layoffs part of the price of becoming competitive, and it is, frankly, what has helped to make the American economy the envy of the world again. But laying people off is, sadly, what Dunlap did time and time again to build his career and his notoriety. Bay Springs wasn't going to be an exception.

THE MAYOR of Bay Springs is a tall, lanky, bearded Mississippi-born man who first moved to the town in 1962 when he was eighteen years old. Mayor Jerry Evon Smith, whom the locals call J.E., owns a real estate firm, a used car lot, and a convenience store in town. He also is widely credited with rejuvenating the downtown district. Soon after Dunlap became chief executive of Sunbeam, Smith began hearing rumblings of closures and layoffs from employees at the two Bay Springs plants.

He was not surprised that Dunlap would close the north facility. Through the years, its employment ebbed and flowed with the unstable production of too many low-margin products, from fans to comforters. But when Smith heard that Dunlap planned to shut down Sunbeam's south plant, he was outraged. He knew it was one of the company's better factories, with skilled employees producing a critical product. For the more than thirty years of the county-owned plant's operation, the company never paid a cent of taxes or rent on the property. So anxious was the industry-starved county for business in the 1950s that it turned over the plant for free so long as its owners produced a payroll of $300,000 a year.

"They didn't pay anything," sniped Smith. "No school taxes, nothing. Until the day they moved out, they never paid a dime in taxes or on the lease of the building."

Dunlap was not only closing a 59,000-square-foot plant that Sunbeam occupied for free, Sunbeam also would have to shell out between $8 million to $10 million to relocate the plant forty miles to Waynesboro, Mississippi, where the company assembled its electric blankets. Sunbeam then would have to spend millions more to hire and train a new workforce to assume the jobs of those Dunlap was firing in Bay Springs. The move would save the company less than $200,000 a year in transportation costs. To close the plant that employed skilled laborers in Sunbeam's only sophisticated manufacturing process was economic madness.

Smith believed his town should be accorded the same dignity and respect any major employer would expect from the community in a time of trouble. Other companies had left Bay Springs in the past, but they had departed honorably. When a local sewing plant shut down, the officials came to see the mayor, explained their situation, gave generous severance pay to the employees, and helped them gain jobs elsewhere. "Mr. Dunlap operated totally in a different manner," said Smith. Based on reports from employees, the mayor believed Dunlap had no intention of paying severance to the laid-off workers, and, to his mind, even tried to cheat them out of collecting unemployment benefits. The company offered employees jobs in Hattiesburg, about sixty-five miles south of Bay Springs. "They couldn't drive 200 miles a day for $6 or $8 an hour and he knew it," said Smith. "He was offering them jobs so he wouldn't have to pay them unemployment."

A feisty and obstinate man himself, the Bay Springs mayor was hardly mute about what he considered an injustice and a reckless business decision. He "raised hell" on local television and in interviews with the *Jasper County News*, the *Mississippi Clarion-Ledger*, the *Wall Street Journal*, and *Newsweek* magazine. He called Dunlap on the telephone twice and wrote him an angry letter as well. He complained that Chainsaw Al was treating Sunbeam's workers "like a depreciating piece of equipment." "He used them up and threw them out on the street," Smith said bitterly. He questioned Dunlap's financial acumen. "It doesn't take a genius to figure out it would take thirty to thirty-five years to get the payback to save $200,000 a year," he scoffed. "If you can't profit in a free building with no taxes, how are you going to make a profit in an $8 million building in Waynesboro?"

Dunlap was enraged by the mayor's verbal assault. Several executives urged him to reconsider the decision on economic grounds, but Dunlap would hear none of it. "That plant was closed because the mayor of Bay Springs created a big deal in the newspapers," said a Sunbeam executive. "Al said, 'Fuck 'em! We're closing the plant.' He made us move that plant because the mayor in that little town created a stir. My daughter will not live long enough for that investment to pay out."

When Don Uzzi heard of the decision, he immediately went to Kersh to raise his objections.

"Russ, it makes no financial sense to close that plant," Uzzi told him. "It will cost us money to close the plant. Plus we'll have to hire and train new employees and take the risk of starting up another facility. You've got to bring it up to Al."

"Forget it," replied Kersh. "I've already talked to him about it. His mind is made up."

"Well, you have to promise me you'll talk to him again."

"Al doesn't want to hear about it," said Kersh.

Later on, when Uzzi found himself next to Dunlap on an airplane, he tried to bring up the subject and Dunlap cut him off in mid-sentence.

"It's done!" he said brusquely. "It's closing!"

It was, thought general counsel David Fannin, one of the worst calls he had seen Dunlap make. "It was the dumbest decision on the face of the earth," recalled Fannin. "The plant was running well for decades. What it basically did was give Al another plant to close. When I heard this, I began to really question it. It didn't make any sense. I understood this guy's reputation was built on cost cutting, but it ought to have been for some rational end or logic. None of this ever made the slightest bit of sense. Yet if anybody dared question or challenge the great man, he was to be crushed. Even a little mayor in a small town."

Fannin went to see Ron Newcomb, the gung-ho head of manufacturing, who helped to implement the closures. But Newcomb was then a Dunlap believer, fixated on the challenge of moving the sophisticated machinery in the plant and not willing to push back on the decisions made by Dunlap and Burnett's swarm of consultants. He made some excuses that the plant lacked the capacity to produce enough wire to supply electric blankets overseas. But there was no reason that the Bay Springs plant could not produce more wire with little if any additional capital expense. Later Newcomb would admit that it made no economic sense to close the plant. For now, however, the decision was made. It was recommended by Burnett and made by Dunlap, who refused to reconsider it in light of Mayor Smith's public protests.

THE NEWS that Dunlap was closing the plant struck Cherrie Mae Gammage like a hard slap in the face. She had first walked through the steel doors of the factory on September 23, 1966, happy to gain employment for the minimum wage. For the next thirty-one years, she toiled away in the plant, just a couple of blocks away from her home, working up to a wage rate of $10.89 an hour. Over those years she had worked in most of the factory's departments, manning the twister machines that coiled the blanket wire and the machinery that once fashioned thermostats for the electric blankets. She had been there when the plant made electric toothbrushes and hair dryers as well. She had worked each of the three shifts at the plant, starting at 7 A.M., 3 P.M., and midnight. And she had worked there at the factory's peak, when 700 employees toiled behind its concrete walls.

On the money she made in the plant, Gammage bought a modest home and raised and nurtured five children through high school and college. The concrete factory was more than a place of work. It was as familiar as her home, and it was filled with people she considered family. Like most of her coworkers, she cried when a Sunbeam manager gave the bad news to assembled employees in the plant. "It was a wonderful place to work," she said. "I had good supervisors and good coworkers. To me, that plant was like one big family. I guess I spent more time there than at home. The plant had been good to me."

Gammage, then sixty-three, was nearing retirement. She was less concerned about herself and far more worried about the younger people in the plant who would be losing their jobs and their livelihoods. "It was sad," she said. "We cried. It affected a lot of people, especially younger people who had just bought homes and cars and were trying to send their children to school. The Lord was good to me. I stayed there long enough. But I was very sad for the people who needed those jobs."

It took Sunbeam more than a year to close and move the plant to Waynesboro. At one point, the new employees who would operate the same equipment in Waynesboro moved to Bay Springs for nearly three months of training. Some workers refused to teach them how to run the machinery. "A lot of people were real harsh about it," recalls Gammage. "It was sad to me that a lot of people didn't want to help them learn their jobs."

Some saw it as an inexcusable affront, a final humiliation. "It just wasn't right, I figure," said Jack Montgomery, who had spent thirty-eight and one-half years working in the factory. Montgomery was a small man, only five-foot-five, but the seventy-year-old laborer was known as one of the hardest working employees at the place. His friends said he could outwork any three people. In exchange for his severance pay, Montgomery and three or four other employees were asked to travel to Waynesboro back and forth every day for three months to install some 140 machines from the plant. "There wasn't anything you could do about it. If Al hadn't come along, I figure the plant would still be in Bay Springs. All he done was cut jobs and move plants and done this and that. That's the only way he could show anything on the books."

Many of the plant's employees were, in Gammage's way of looking at things, "harsh" toward Dunlap. They cursed and despised him. They dreaded his power and their powerlessness to do something about it. Yet Cherrie Mae did not share their hatred or their dislike for the man none of them had ever met. She prayed for him as well as for her friends at the Bethlehem United Methodist Church. "You have to know the reason he closed the plant before you can judge him," she says plainly. "That's my opinion of things. I wondered if he did it out of greed or not caring about people's welfare. I was thankful for one thing. With his wealth and his power, he could have done whatever he wanted to do. He could have took all them plants out of Mississippi. I did understand why they called him Chainsaw. He cut back so much stuff."

Like Gammage, Paul Strickland bore no ill will toward Dunlap either. He had begun working in the plant at the age of eighteen, just three months after getting married. He had been there, working the machines and doing maintenance, for twenty-six and one-half years of his forty-four years. "I just have to pray for the man because he hurt a lot of people," said Strickland. "I ain't going to talk bad about the man. I hope he is satisfied with what he done because he sure messed up a lot of people. I hope he is right with the Lord because I think he's done some wrong stuff."

Gammage left the factory for the last time on December 12, 1997, just two weeks before Christmas and almost thirteen months to the day after the closure announcement was made. "I felt something you can hardly describe," she said. "You think about this place, where you have spent your whole lifetime. I knew I would never see a lot of the people I worked with all those years. Everyone tried to stay cheerful, but it was rough for some people. A lot of them couldn't hardly find a job. It really hit hard for people with small children. That was a sad Christmas for everybody." There was no company Christmas party that year. Still, Gammage had crafted ornaments for the artificial tree in the plant's sterile lobby. She had written the names of the remaining employees on decorative balls so that each of them could take one home as a memento of their days in the plant.

About the same time that the last few workers were filing out of the plant in Mississippi, Albert Dunlap was cutting into a steak in a restaurant in Florida, in the thick of negotiating a new contract with Michael Price. The contract would later be conservatively valued at $46.5 million. It was enough money to employ 620 workers for three years at an average salary of $25,000 per year, a sum more than most of the employees made at the Bay Springs plant.

Although Dunlap did not want to pay severance to the town's employees, Mayor Smith's pressure tactics gained the workers up to six weeks' pay and six months of medical benefits. The local banks extended the car and home loans to Sunbeam's laid-off employees until they got back on their feet. After her thirty-one years at the company, Gammage was handed a check for $2,614 before taxes, her six weeks of pay. She collected unemployment checks for six months until signing up for Social Security. "It's a lot different than my pay," she says, "but we're making it."

On a dull and lazy Mississippi day in March, it fell to Montgomery and Strickland to finally close down the place they too called home. By then all the machinery was up and running in Waynesboro, and many of the employees had been drawing unemployment benefits for three months. The two men walked the dusty floors of the dark and lifeless plant, making sure all the power was off and all the windows and doors were locked tight. Strickland then carried the keys over to Jasper County attorney William R. Ruffin and dropped off a meaningful part of his life.

"We were hurt and aggravated," said Strickland. "I considered the people in that plant some of the finest I ever worked with. We knew each other. We knew each other's families. If you got sick, everyone in the plant knew and within a day or two, you probably got several calls from some of them wanting to check on you. I loved those folks like they were part of my family. It was pretty tough."

Mayor Smith, meantime, worked hard to find a new tenant for the abandoned building and succeeded in landing a business that reworks automobile starters and generators. The place employs fewer than twenty-five people, but it does pay $25,000 a year in rent to the county. He's not apologetic about the ruckus he raised over Dunlap. "This guy," said Smith, "doesn't know what it is not to have the money to pay your rent. He's a nut if he thinks the mayor of the town wouldn't raise hell over the closing of a plant. We've survived two World Wars, floods and hurricanes. We will survive Chainsaw Al."

9

A QUIET REBELLION

WORD OF AL DUNLAP'S latest downsizing spread like an epidemic through the company's far-flung network of factories and plants. Over the first week of the announcement, Sunbeam executives were dispatched to the hinterlands to small towns in Mississippi, Tennessee, Louisiana, and Texas to deliver the bad news in person.

One place they didn't visit during that mid-November was the rural town of McMinnville, Tennessee, where some 700 employees worked in a brick-faced factory making Oster shearers and hair clippers. Located on the highland rim of the Cumberland Mountains, midway between Nashville and Chattanooga, McMinnville has a population of not many more than 11,000 people. The Oster plant had been an integral part of the community for nearly four decades, at its peak providing enough work to employ one of every ten persons in town. After the Bridgestone radial tire factory and the Carrier air conditioner plant, Sunbeam's Oster facility was the area's third largest employer.

Once the New Year began, most of the factory's employees believed they had been spared. But during the third week of January, two unexpected visitors came to town from headquarters. Human resources chief James Wilson and manufacturing head Ronald Newcomb flew to Nashville, rented a car, and drove the seventy-five miles southeast through the fertile farmlands of eastern Tennessee to McMinnville.

Accompanied by two armed security guards, sent to the plant by Dunlap's own bodyguard, Wilson and Newcomb strolled into the factory during the first shift. The noisy machines were shut down. The production lines were quiet. A few hundred employees on the first shift were herded into an area of the plant in front of a makeshift platform designed for the event.

Newcomb, a short, well-built man with a mustache, climbed atop the platform and positioned himself behind a podium. Reading from a prepared statement, he tensely spoke into a small microphone.

"The world is changing," he said. "The market is no longer domestic. We must compete in the world market."

Newcomb claimed Oster had lost market share in the past year. He said rivals were sourcing cheaper products from China and elsewhere. As a result, some 550 employees would soon lose their jobs to Mexico. First Sunbeam would move out production of the least expensive products, the hair clippers and trimmers sold at retail. Then it would move the higher-margin products sold to professional hairstylists and animal groomers. Some 150 jobs would remain, only for those who made the professional carbon steel blades.

What Wilson and Newcomb saw that day would haunt them years later. As they scanned the sea of nervous faces, they saw hope disappear from the young people who had recently joined the company. They saw shock grip the more weathered faces of older employees who had worked in the plant for decades. Many of the faces were contorted with confusion and pain, either spilling tears or holding them back. "It was bad, really bad," recalled Wilson.

One of the tearful faces belonged to Charlotte Redmon, a tireless assembly worker who had put thirty-two years of her life into the plant. Less than a year earlier, Redmon had buried her husband of twenty-seven years. Now, at age fifty-three, she was losing the job that provided her sole source of income and medical benefits. "I was devastated," she said. "It was as close to death as anybody can come. I knew we had plenty of orders and a good business. There was no reason to close the plant, except greed. They thought nothing of the people there."

Marsha Dunlap, no relation to Al Dunlap, stared at the executives in disbelief. She earned $9.30 an hour after working in the factory for nearly thirty-four years. The job provided her family's only pension and health insurance coverage. "They always said we had done good," said Dunlap, who began work on a production line after graduating from McMinnville High School in 1964. "We had been a moneymaking plant. If we lost money, I could understand it. A lot of people dedicated their lives to that plant. These were hardworking people who were losing their jobs. They were good workers. Like me, factory work is all they have ever known."

From Dunlap's start, many of the employees at the McMinnville plant discounted the rumors that he would close the plant. After all, the factory was running seven days a week, three shifts a day, cranking out highly profitable products. Every day the plant produced 15,000 hair clippers and trimmers, a record 3.3 million units in 1996 sold in Wal-Mart, Kmart, Target, and other major retailers. It also churned out more than 375,000 professional models, used by beauticians and animal groomers, and 1.2 million sets of replacement blades.

It was a classic niche business, all self-contained in McMinnville, throwing off net profits of more than $40 million a year on sales that approached $110 million. No other business at Sunbeam boasted higher profit margins. It was the proverbial "cash cow," the term strategists commonly used to describe a business that could be milked and milked for profits with little investment. The clipper operation consistently turned in net margins of 38 percent, four times the profitability of Sunbeam blenders, more than double the profits of the company's electric blankets. The margins on the professional models topped 50 percent, while those on the carbon steel replacement blades made in McMinnville exceeded 65 percent.

Without knowing the numbers, the constant shipments from the plant were enough to assure the employees that they were part of a wildly successful venture. But the production line employees were not privy to the fierce fight being waged by the plant's managers to keep Dunlap's chainsaw at bay.

WHEN THE Coopers & Lybrand consultants descended on the factory shortly after Dunlap took control, it was as if the decision to move it to Mexico had been predetermined. Mexican workers made $1 an hour in wages and benefits, less than one-tenth of what Marsha Dunlap and Charlotte Redmon brought home. Sunbeam already had three underused Mexican plants. To the cost cutters, it seemed a no-brainer to close down McMinnville and consolidate its operations south of the border.

Don Burnett's freshly minted MBAs marched through the plant, making its managers feel as if they had just been captured in a war. "All of us were considered the enemy until proven otherwise," said Mark A. Bohling, the factory's head of manufacturing. Bohling had joined Sunbeam in the spring of 1994 after spending thirteen years with General Electric Co. He was all of thirty-six years old then, a bright and ambitious Stanford University graduate with a degree in industrial engineering. Five-foot-ten with blue eyes and a full head of brown hair, he was an engaging manager with strong people skills. One of the reasons Bohling was chosen for the job was to improve relations between management and the employees who only narrowly turned down a union vote the year before he arrived. The attitude of the consultants troubled him. "They didn't solicit opinions on anything. No one was brought in for any kind of strategic or business discussion. They only wanted our data on costs and production. They obviously didn't respect what we had to say."

Yet, after the visits, Bohling and the plant's general manager, John Davenport, had been led to believe by Newcomb and Newt White that the plant would survive. They would have to run an already efficient plant more efficiently, but the initial assessment seemed positive. It wasn't until one day late in September 1996 that Bohling received a telephone call he said he would never forget.

"Look, Mark, there has been a little change in direction regarding McMinnville," said Newcomb ominously. "Dunlap has decided to shut it down."

In the maddening moment in which he heard those words, Bohling was shocked into silence.

"I'm sending a couple of people down tonight," Newcomb continued, "and they'll be there in the morning. I want you to spend tomorrow working with them on a detailed plan to shut it down by the end of December."

"You've got to be fucking crazy," Bohling finally blurted. "It can't be done."

To move the factory that quickly, Bohling knew, would cost the company millions of dollars in lost sales. The plant was so efficient, able to turn out products to order, that it built no inventory and ran around the clock. Closing down within two months would severely damage Sunbeam's relationship with its customers.

"No, no, that's what Al wants done," insisted his boss. "You need a detailed strategy on how McMinnville can be shut down in two months."

Bohling hung up, determined to stop it. He later discovered that earlier the same day, during the morning hours, the Coopers consultants were in Dunlap's office providing an update on their downsizing plan. Dunlap, unhappy with the estimate of the cost savings, wanted at least $20 to $30 million more in annual savings. The consultants obliged, telling Dunlap that the only way to cut that much more out of the business was to shut down McMinnville and transfer it to Mexico. Dunlap said simply: do it.

At 7 A.M. the next morning, Bohling met the Mexico City plant manager and Robert Terhune, a project manager on Newcomb's manufacturing staff, at the plant. He brought them through the factory that day, spending most of his time attempting to convince them that closing the plant made no sense from either a financial or a technological point of view.

Demand for the plant's products was so high that it would be virtually impossible to stockpile inventory, increasing the likelihood of a costly disruption of supply to customers. Making clippers, argued Davenport and Bohling, required skilled labor able to run expensive and sophisticated milling, grinding, and stamping equipment. The cost to move the factory would reach $14.4 million. Shipping goods from Mexico would increase transportation costs. The quality and work ethic of the labor force in Mexico, moreover, paled in comparison to the McMinnville employees, many of whom had spent the better part of their lives in the plant. The plant's non-union workers boasted a twenty-four-hour turnaround on orders that eliminated the need for inventory and warehouses. They boasted a warranty level on professional clippers that was minuscule. Besides, in McMinnville, Sunbeam had a sweetheart lease on the 169,400-square-foot plant, paying only pennies per foot in rent, some $29,000 a year.

Anxious to fulfill Dunlap's demands to get $225 million in annual costs out of the business, Burnett's team tossed in the McMinnville plant, believing that its closure would save the company roughly $28 million a year. "It was a good business," conceded Burnett. "It ran by itself. It was doing well from that point of view. You could leave it alone, and it would be perfect. But you could get much more money out of it by moving . . . much more income for Sunbeam if you moved the easy part down to Mexico."

The day after Dunlap announced his restructuring plan on November 12, Bohling was given a script to read to the plant's employees. The message to them was work hard, do better, and you'll probably survive under Al Dunlap. The truth, however, was that Bohling was secretly working on the plan with Terhune to shutter the plant by Christmas time. "The whole experience sickened me," he said. "After that, I made up my mind that I was not going to become part of the Dunlap program."

Bohling, growing ever more antagonistic, continued to press his reasons for leaving McMinnville alone. At times, the arguments with his boss grew ugly and heated. Whenever he attempted to explain why it made no sense to close the plant, Newcomb retorted that he had successfully moved several product lines at Black & Decker into Mexico and South America.

"You don't know what you're talking about," maintained Newcomb.

"I've done this stuff before, and I've done this very successfully. This thing can be pulled off, and pulled off very fast."

Bohling's continued resistance was beginning to place him in jeopardy. At one point, he received a phone call from James Gitney, another manager on Newcomb's staff who had known Gitney at General Electric Co. Now Gitney was calling Bohling to warn him to put an end to his rebellion.

"Look," Gitney told him, "let me give you some personal advice. You are getting a reputation for being a very negative, non–team player. I suggest that if you want to keep your job, you better start nodding your head in a different direction."

Bohling had no intention of doing so. He believed the McMinnville decision was not only ethically wrong, but uninformed and foolish. "Newcomb didn't have the balls to tell Al Dunlap anything he didn't want to hear," Bohling thought. Newcomb, who had been savagely attacked by Dunlap in front of his peers, was, like many, terrified by Dunlap.

If he was going to be successful at stopping the move, Bohling concluded he probably wouldn't get much help from Newcomb. After getting a look at the assumptions Coopers plugged into its economic model to justify the plant's closure, the young manager was shocked by the shoddiness of the work. The consultants vastly overstated the expected savings by double-counting cost reductions and underestimating the amount of excess scrap and rework that would likely be necessary in a Mexican plant.

Among other things, Coopers also assumed that the factory in Mexico would be just as productive as McMinnville after a twelve-month transition period. That might have been possible if Sunbeam were moving an inefficient Rust Belt plant with bitter, unionized employees. That was not McMinnville. It also was simply not possible to make that assumption in a region of Mexico where the employee turnover averaged 10 percent a month, 120 percent a year, compared to virtually no turnover at all in McMinnville. "The numbers were so overstated that I had no confidence in them," said Davenport, the plant's general manager. "It was all wishful thinking. The learning curve to take production into a new facility with brand-new staff was longer than they anticipated. When we started going through their evaluation, the cost savings started shrinking immediately."

As Davenport and Bohling rebutted many of the Coopers arguments, the consultants were forced to cut their cost savings estimate in half, two separate times. The initial $28 million number fell to $14 million, and finally $7 million, a figure, it turned out, that would be overly optimistic as well.

By tearing apart the Coopers assumptions, the pair convinced headquarters at least to reconsider the decision to close the plant by year end. But on December 19, the Friday before the Christmas holiday, Newcomb called Bohling again. This time he told him that Dunlap agreed to keep 150 employees in McMinnville to manufacture the carbon steel blades for its professional clippers and trimmers. The balance of the jobs would be transferred to Mexico by the following December.

Over the Christmas holidays, Bohling decided he had reached the breaking point. "There was absolutely no logical or rational reason to move the business," he said. "I worked as hard as I could to bring some sense to the process, and I wasn't going to be part of something that was wrong. It was morally wrong, and it was wrong from a business perspective." He had been offered a job as vice president of operations for MagneTek, the maker of electric motors, and had decided to take it. Newcomb asked him to stay for three weeks, until the decision was announced to McMinnville's employees.

In January, before the announcement of the McMinnville shutdown, Uzzi was on a Northwest Airlines flight to Detroit with Dunlap. They were on their way to visit Kmart. Determined to make an issue of it with the CEO, Uzzi wanted to prove to his boss that closing both McMinnville and Bay Springs made no financial sense. They were bad business decisions. The company wouldn't see a payback on them for years, if ever.

But Dunlap cut him off as soon as Uzzi began to speak about the closures.

"Forget it," he told him.

Uzzi tried to bring up the subject several times during the flight, but it was futile. Dunlap had made his decision, and he was obviously sticking with it, whether it made sense or not. Uzzi grabbed the documents and shoved them back into his briefcase.

BOHLING NEVER would have guessed it, but his campaign to keep the plant open had won a new and important ally at corporate headquarters in William "Kirk" Kirkpatrick, a former Scott Paper executive. Bohling had mistakenly dismissed him as just another greedy, self-important pirate who signed on with Dunlap to make some fast money at the expense of the company and its employees. He was partly right. Kirkpatrick was there for the money, but he came to share Bohling's belief that the closure of the plant would be a complete disaster.

A trim and athletically built man, Kirkpatrick is six feet tall, 165 pounds, with graying brown hair and a sizable nose that he attributes to his Rumanian immigrant mother. He is also a Vietnam War veteran. As a lieutenant in the U.S. Marines, he led an infantry platoon of nearly fifty men in combat. One day, while peering above a foxhole, he took a round through his face, a hit that cost him one of his eyes and the use of an arm. When he returned to the States, he taught math at Chester High School, just outside Philadelphia, while attending graduate school at night at Widner University for a business degree.

When he felt little aptitude for teaching, Kirkpatrick began working at Scott Paper Co.'s plant in Chester as an engineer. His father was an electrical engineer, and he had earned an engineering degree at the University of Pennsylvania on an ROTC scholarship before joining the Marines in 1967. Kirkpatrick loved the work and moved up through the years, from one plant to another, until gaining a job at Scott headquarters in research and development in the early 1980s. When Dunlap took control of Scott, he was working in Japan for Newt White, attempting to develop a commercial business in the country. Kirkpatrick left the company after it was acquired by Kimberly-Clark, ending a twenty-six-year career with the paper concern.

At the age of fifty-one, he was taking graduate courses in education, thinking that he might want to teach high school again, when he received a telephone call from White in October 1996. Enticed by an option grant on 50,000 shares, he took the job to develop a commercial business for Sunbeam and to manage its professional clipper business. Dunlap had made him a millionaire at Scott, one of sixty-two who cashed in on the stock options that Dunlap made extremely valuable. Sunbeam was his chance for more. "The Scott guys who went in had seen this act before," he acknowledged. "We knew we would be driven unmercifully. We knew what the game was, and we all signed up and said fine. Our expectation was a twelve-to-eighteen-month threshold."

When Kirkpatrick first visited the McMinnville plant in early November 1996, he was unaware of the fight Bohling and Davenport were waging. Indeed, he did not know that Dunlap planned to close the facility. Walking the factory floors, Kirkpatrick was immediately impressed with the plant and its diligent employees. "The McMinnville facility was just a jewel," he thought. "Many of the people in the assembly area had been doing their work for twenty-five or more years. They could do their jobs with their eyes closed. This was a small family where people had worked side by side for years. They had a wonderfully committed workforce. The employees had tremendous values. Certain areas of the plant were working overtime for a couple of years. They had flexible production. If there was a surge in demand, they knew how to deliver. "

The tour of the plant was an uplifting experience for him, until he met with Terhune, the engineering manager who would be responsible for moving the plant to Mexico. "When he started showing me what he planned, I nearly went into shock," said Kirkpatrick. He was stunned because the same Coopers plan that would essentially eliminate the plant also called for him to increase sales by 30 percent in the same year. He could not believe that anyone could expect a huge increase in volume in the same year in which a plant would be shuttered and its operations moved. "The Coopers plan allowed virtually no learning curve," he said. "According to the plan, there would be no disruption in supply. I had done a lot of plant work, and I knew what it takes to move a well-operating factory. That is one of the reasons I was scared to death of shutting down McMinnville."

Kirkpatrick, fearful he would have no product to sell if McMinnville was closed, began his own efforts to save the place. He wrote a white paper on the risk of moving the plant, arguing that he could make more money driving the revenue side than the company could save in costs by a move. But like Davenport and Bohling, he faced a Newcomb who was hell-bent on getting the consultants' plan implemented. His ten-minute meeting with the manufacturing chief went nowhere. Newcomb was so distracted that he began reading other materials on his desk when Kirkpatrick attempted to make the argument in favor of the plant. His attitude, Kirkpatrick said, was that "Coopers made the decision. Al signed off on it. Now it was, get it done. No one was going to go to Al and try to talk him out of it."

Undaunted, he went to Uzzi, unaware of the executive's futile attempt to bring up the subject with Dunlap in January.

"Don't get involved in this," Uzzi warned him. "You're not responsible for this."

"I have to get this stuff on the street," Kirkpatrick argued.

"Don't worry about it," Uzzi replied. "We'll stockpile it, and we'll have it."

Uzzi already knew it wasn't possible to get Dunlap to change his mind. Whenever he tried to do that, Dunlap would inevitably tell him he didn't want to hear it. Instead, Dunlap viewed every legitimate discussion on a business issue as an excuse to explain nonperformance or justification for altering a decision he had made.

IN McMINNVILLE, meantime, Redmon and her colleagues began to train the Mexican employees who would take over their jobs. The workers, who could not speak English, arrived in town in batches until some 100 of them were taught how to use the machines that had long been the source of money, dignity, and purpose for many of the town's citizens. The McMinnville employees greatly resented the company's orders to train their replacements, especially when many of the Mexican students showed little interest in learning the jobs. Yet they did what was expected of them. "It was hard," said Redmon, "but I knew it wasn't their fault. It wasn't them to blame. They were difficult to train. They didn't care all that much about the work. They were late coming back from breaks."

Terhune, nonetheless, followed Newcomb's orders to unbolt the machines, put them on a caravan of flat-bed trailers, and move them south. Redmon lost her job in the first wave of terminations in the spring and remained unemployed for the following year. By March the equipment to build the retail clippers had been moved to the company's plant in Mexico City. Of Sunbeam's three Mexican plants, however, the Mexico City operation was the weakest. It was a dirty, unproductive plant, poorly managed and filled with meagerly paid, unmotivated employees. In an industrial section of the city, the factory made blenders and waffle irons. Bohling had toured the cramped and cluttered place in October and immediately concluded that the plant would be incapable of precision machining or fabrication work.

"There was trash all over the place," said a young marketer at Florida headquarters who was enlisted to help get production out of the plant. "Few of the workers could speak English. There was no communication. It was just chaos. It was absolutely crazy. It was brutal. You had no planners, no systems. They couldn't get trucks in because there wasn't a traffic department to control it. There was no pride among the employees. When you have people making $5 a week, they don't care."

At times the production lines turned out versions of products that were unneeded. At other times assembly lines were shut down for days because the plant lacked needed components, from parts as basic as plastic casings to motors. At least one time the lines were stopped for three days because the plant ran out of screws. Quality problems became rampant. When the factory attempted to make blades they quickly rusted, forcing the factory to depend on McMinnville for its supply. On another occasion the employees put the products in the wrong packaging.

In the first month of operation, in April, the plant turned out 80,000 units—less than one-fourth its expected output. The following month it managed to get out 100,000 clippers. In June the factory turned out 200,000. Bedeviled by the shortages, Sunbeam's sales staff broke promises to angry retailers who failed to get their orders. "There was hate mail between sales and marketing, and then sales and operations," explained one marketing manager. "Each department blamed the other for the screw-up." The lost production destroyed profits, wrecked market share, alienated customers, and consumed great amounts of organizational energy.

So shorthanded was the company that the young marketer, hired only months earlier out of college, was compelled to go down to Mexico on a weekly basis to schedule production runs and try to ensure the plant had ample supplies of components to make the clippers. "I should have been coming out with new products and marketing campaigns to drive the business," he conceded. "Instead I was flying down to Mexico to get products out of the plant. I was afraid to start projects because I thought they would get fucked up because there was no process in place. A few product extensions would have put the company far ahead of the competitors, but they had to be put on hold indefinitely."

Only a small portion of Kirkpatrick's product line was affected by the move. His division lost virtually its entire customer base on a line of cheaper motorized clippers, having to short major customers because he lacked supply. However, Kirkpatrick used the massive problems in Mexico to forestall the plans to move production of his line of professional clippers. He sat in meetings and moved, as he put it, "from my quiet phase to being an asshole." "I knew if we moved to Mexico, I would have a complete disaster on our hands," he believed. "Under no circumstances did I want that plant to close. I was selfish."

Kirkpatrick appealed to the frantic desire to make his numbers.

"We've got to stop this because you're not going to have any product to sell," Kirkpatrick told Uzzi, his boss. "If you want to continue to throw money away, that's fine. Fire me now, because if you move it and I don't have anything to sell, you'll have to fire me later."

He won support from an exasperated Luis Silberwasser, who was in charge of selling the retail hair clippers. "You guys have been unable to meet the numbers you promised," Silberwasser complained. "You're now going to take another piece of the business and throw it away?"

Troubled by the move's impact on sales, Uzzi flew to Mexico City for three days to investigate the problems. What he saw confirmed Kirkpatrick's worries and stunned him. The plant was not large enough to house both raw materials and work-in-progress. "No one did a footprint of the plant to make sure we had enough space," said Uzzi. So Sunbeam had to lease at least three warehouses to store the raw materials it needed for the assembly lines. The limited bathroom facilities were inadequate for the number of new employees. "People were waiting in line to go to the bathroom," said Uzzi. "It was like halftime at Giants' Stadium."

Uzzi concluded that Sunbeam should close the plant and sell the property. When he returned to headquarters, he tried again to convince Dunlap to reconsider his decision to shutter the McMinnville factory.

Unsuccessful, Uzzi resorted to what so many Sunbeam executives and managers were doing: for the good of the company, they were conspiring behind Dunlap's back, engaging in guerrilla warfare, to prevent patently bad business decisions from being carried out. Without Dunlap's knowledge, Uzzi put the rest of the McMinnville move on hold and arranged to ship some machinery back to Tennessee. Kirkpatrick's appeals had paid off.

Marsha Dunlap, who had received a termination letter that assigned July 4, 1997, as her last day of work, and a few hundred other employees won a reprieve—at least until the company could straighten out its manufacturing problems. Meantime, though, Kirkpatrick quietly refused to build inventory. "I told my guys to drive the living crap out of the market," he said. "I didn't want to close this plant. If growing my business prevented them from building inventory and moving the plant, then that was it. I wasn't going to increase the inventory to let them close it down."

By slashing prices on key products, Kirkpatrick met his goal of increasing revenues by 30 percent to $60 million and prevented the plant's near total shutdown. But the Mexico City foul-ups cost his colleague, Silberwasser, as much as $17 million in lost revenue and nearly $6 million in lost profit in 1998. More than a year into the transition, the Mexico City plant still was unable to equal the quantity or quality of product once made in McMinnville. Yet it was not atypical of the widespread chaos inside the company. Nearly everything and everyone at Sunbeam was caught up in a messy jumble caused by the man at the top.

10 THE SECRET ROOM

WHEN ANALYST Andrew Shore made his second visit to Sunbeam headquarters on June 30, 1997, he was greeted with much more enthusiasm by Al Dunlap. Though the PaineWebber analyst hadn't lost his skepticism, his reports on the company became both brighter and more favorable as the stock climbed ever higher.

Dunlap beat Shore's first-quarter profit estimate by three pennies a share, prompting Shore to concede that "Dunlap might pull it off." "Without a doubt," Shore told investors, "Sunbeam has made enormous progress, faster and greater than originally thought. Sales in the quarter were three percentage points higher than our estimate, the highest level achieved without acquisitions since it went public."

This time, meeting in Delray Beach, Shore did not incur any ugly glares or awkward silences from Dunlap. Minutes after arriving at the company's headquarters, Dunlap personally greeted him. After a briefing by investor chief Rich Goudis, Shore was brought into the boardroom for a private lunch with the CEO. "I almost felt like a relative coming over for Thanksgiving dinner," recalled Shore.

Dunlap was anxious to convince the analyst that he was not merely a slash-and-burn executive but was capable of growing a company. Indeed, Dunlap had become extremely touchy about criticism that he could not build a company through product innovation and savvy marketing. At Scott Paper, he had claimed to introduce 107 new products, but nearly half of them were nothing more than changes in packaging for a single product and the upgrading of another. Dunlap, for example, counted twenty-two "new products" by wrapping Scott Clean paper towels in a new package in twenty-two countries and another twenty-two by making its basic Baby Fresh wet wipes slightly thicker in those same countries.

Virtually all the real new products at Scott were hatched before Dunlap's arrival, though he took full credit for them. The same routine was occurring at Sunbeam. When Richard Boynton, former household products president, told a reporter for the *Wall Street Journal* that many of the new products launched by Dunlap were developed before he arrived, Boynton was sued by Sunbeam because his comments violated the muzzle clause in his severance pact. Though Boynton was right, he sent a letter of retraction to the *Wall Street Journal* to end the litigation.

To counter the image, Dunlap created what his public relations' handlers dubbed "the secret room." The six-by-six foot space at headquarters was little more than a bland storage room filled with a dozen or so makeshift contraptions. Before Shore and his associate analyst, R. T. Quinn, were allowed to enter the room, they had to sign confidentiality agreements. Many of the plastic and Styrofoam mockups elicited quiet laughter from Shore. There was an electric fan with blades covered in toilet paper that was supposed to be the first completely safe fan, a crock pot with a self-stirring handle, and prototypes for two new products that Dunlap believed would be blockbuster hits.

The two mockups would bring Sunbeam into new product categories, the air and water purification markets. Its water product, a pitcher that filtered water, was called Freshsource. Its air product, which eliminated invisible particles from the air, was dubbed Allergysmart. The company was entering these markets after competitors had invested millions in building well-known brand names and gaining significant shelf space in retail stores. But Dunlap saw them as crucial to the company's success and his own image.

On the return flight to New York, Andrew Shore slipped a yellow legal pad out of his briefcase and laid it on top of his fold-down tray. He and R. T. snickered about the secret room, joking that it looked like a large broom closet. "This was part of Al's PR machine," thought Shore. "Create the allure. Seduce us. Bring us in. Get the world to believe they really have some kind of big secret going on."

So on the airplane going back north, Shore wanted to assess what he considered the true potential of some of the products likely to come out of the secret room.

"Okay," Shore said, "let's make a grid on this stuff. What do you think they can do in sales?"

Water? They forecast $50 million. "How about $15 million?" said Shore. "Nah, never. Maybe $10?" The numbers kept going further and further down.

Even so, when Shore returned to New York and wrote up his visit to Sunbeam headquarters, he seemed as seduced as anyone by what he saw in the refashioned broom closet. "In anticipation of strong consumer acceptance of some of these 'secret room' products as well as the company's 1998 grill line-up, we have raised our sales growth expectations for 1998 from 15–16 percent to 20 percent," wrote Shore. "The new Sunbeam is not a commodity appliance company . . . Our meeting re-confirms our belief that Dunlap is not a CEO you want to bet against."

THE NEW AIR AND WATER products so critical to Dunlap's growth campaign were the brainchild of Paula Etchison, a Sunbeam veteran who had survived through the Kazarian, Schipke, and now Dunlap eras. She had joined the company in 1992, the same year she and her husband divorced, and flung herself into her work as a product manager in the appliance group. Her colleagues described her as a diligent thirty-something trooper who knew how to get things done on a shoestring. Over the years Etchison had brought along a number of new products, from breadmakers to a refreshed line of irons. When Dunlap arrived, she was invited to move from the Schaumberg office to Florida, lured with options on 50,000 shares and a promotion to head up new business development. "I was a greedy son of a bitch along with everyone else," she concedes. "I said, 'I have a chance to make a lot of money,' and I thought there would be a good education here, one way or another."

She bought a townhouse in Boca Raton, just ten minutes from Delray headquarters, and made Dunlap's domain her life. All the products introduced under the CEO in the early months had been in development when he came aboard, and Etchison had her hand in most of them: a rotisserie, a redesign of the blenders, and the toast logic toaster, an innovative product with a computer chip that Sunbeam claimed turned out perfect toast every time. What earned her the key promotion was the idea to investigate the air and water filtration markets. She was given a team of two other marketers: Susan Robertson, who closely worked on the development of the water filter product, and Rich Seligson, whose time was devoted to the air filter. Robertson, an intense workaholic, had racked up marketing expertise at Quaker Oats, SmithKline Beecham, and Fruit of the Loom before joining Sunbeam in January 1997. Seligson, recruited from Alberto-Culver a year before Dunlap joined the company, was assigned to the team in March 1997. For Seligson, who tended to look a bit unkempt because of the white wrinkled shirts and baggy pants he often wore, the job was a demotion. He had spent the previous four months trying to come up with a new "safe" hair dryer that would never damage hair. After a Taiwanese vendor failed to perfect the heating element in the dryer, the project was dropped and about $1 million was lost.

Etchison's projects, however, seemed far more promising and ambitious. Through a couple of contacts, she was able to bring new technology and breakthrough positioning to markets Sunbeam had never penetrated. One outside inventor, for example, created a laser-activated allergen detector for air cleaners and air monitors that would automatically turn on or off based on the level of airborne pollutants in a room's air. Another innovation was a water purification pitcher with faster and more effective filtering than the best-selling models by rival Brita.

Etchison, Robertson, and Seligson worked frantically to harvest the ideas into saleable merchandise. They labored under insufferable conditions, a mere trio striving to invent new products that were supposed to generate $100 million of sales in a single year—half the time truly required. The team had no administrative support, no marketing or financial analyst dedicated to the project. Managers with six-figure salaries and hefty stock option grants of 50,000 and up were answering their own phones, making their own flight arrangements, booking hotels, filling the paper trays at the copying machines, and sending out faxes and packages. Some even bought their own office supplies because it was too time-consuming and difficult to get them from the company. "There weren't enough people to execute stuff," said

Etchison. "The budgets kept getting reduced. Everything was starved of resources. It was a disaster."

Lacking help from purchasing, Etchison's team had to negotiate terms and costs with outside vendors. She had to put together the pro formas of financial projections because no one from finance was available. She even had to scramble for engineers to design and tool the new products. "There weren't enough tool engineers or process-development people to make sure the manufacturing lines were well-organized and well-designed," she said. "You were constantly fighting for resources, yet Al had made this a top priority."

The team gained little support from the company's other departments. Because of the Coopers cutbacks, they were already working overtime to move product out the door. "I came from companies similar in size that had in-house market research and logistics and production planning support," said Robertson. "In our case, Paula and I really had to do all that stuff on our own." Predictably, arbitrarily set deadlines were missed, and Dunlap grew angry. "Al would scream at Uzzi, and Don would come back and scream at everyone else," recalled Etchison. It did not help the cause when Seligson was fired in August by Kevin McBride, Uzzi's hand-picked marketing chief whose "people skills" were not top of the line.

Etchison, of course, was not the only person shorthanded. Virtually every department, every function, every remaining plant was hungry for more people. The new product team in the company's lucrative hair clipper business was shrunk to one person from six. The results: new product development came to a halt. To aggressively develop sales to the lodging and restaurant industries, a heavily recruited executive was supposed to have a team of five people. Instead he initially got only one young person, who had no background in sales, to build what was a $1.5 million business into one with $25 million in revenues. He fell short of the budget goal by $17 million, only to earn Dunlap's caustic wrath in front of his peers.

Yet whenever anyone dared to ask for additional resources, he or she was routinely given short shrift. When the complaints reached Dunlap, he would command his secretary to summon Coopers' Don Burnett on the telephone. "His intention was to chew out Burnett," recalled general counsel David Fannin. "But when Don insisted the number was correct, Al would turn to whoever was complaining and say, 'It's the right number. Don says it's the right number!'" The Coopers study, however inadequate, became gospel, its goals and objectives enforced by a hostile Dunlap. Soon Uzzi and the other executives didn't bother to complain because they knew it was pointless. Dunlap would only scream at them for asking for desperately needed resources.

Outside vendors were contracted to develop the prototypes for Etchison's new products. A San Francisco industrial design firm put together the water filter by June. Minutes after opening the Federal Express pouch that contained the first sample, Robertson first showed it to her boss, Etchison. She poured colored water into the pitcher, and the unit turned the liquid crystal clear. Uzzi soon saw the demonstration and was so thrilled with the results that he sought out Dunlap. Two hours after receiving the prototype, Robertson found herself doing a demo for Dunlap himself.

Again it worked like a charm, and Dunlap was delighted.

"Great work! Great work!" he enthused. "Let's go tell the world about it!"

All they had was a sample, kluged from a white coffee maker. Yet within a few weeks Sunbeam began showing the product in its "secret room" to Wall Street analysts and newspaper reporters. Soon after that it began taking orders for shipment from retail buyers—even though some of the demos were embarrassing failures. On at least one occasion, for example, Etchison showed the product to a buyer from Costco. During the demonstration water spilled from the unit, creating a small pool of liquid on the table, and then began spitting a stream of water directly in the face of the bemused buyer.

Undaunted, Uzzi and McBride began to insist that Etchison's team get the new products out by the fourth quarter of 1997, a deadline originally agreed to by Etchison but wrecked by the paucity of resources. "We did everything too soon," says Robertson. "We didn't know if the product would be reliable. We didn't have safety testing on it. We would say, 'It's too soon, it's too soon. The product isn't reliable. We have a lot of debugs that have to happen.' I'm constantly fighting to say the product doesn't work. Commit some resources to fix it. There was a general denial of the realities of the business. There was no commitment, no resources, to finish anything right."

Meantime, as the team struggled to produce Sunbeam's most

important new products in years, Dunlap was telling the outside world that he had successfully shrunk the time it took to create products to only a quarter of what it used to be. "We have changed our product development cycle," boasted Dunlap at NatWest Securities' Best Ideas Conference in Montana in April of 1997. "It was over two years, which was ridiculous. Who knows what will happen over two years in the future? Now it's six months. How did we do it? Again, it was very simple. We have R&D reporting to marketing, not to the chairman. We focus only on the best prospects and throw everything else out. We do the consumer research upfront, and we partner with technology companies that can accelerate developments so that we can come out with a substantial amount of new product." At Sunbeam, however, there was no R&D department and there hadn't been one in years. Etchison's products, moreover, were still far from ready, even though she had already been working on them for a full six months.

AT SUNBEAM the cruelest demands often came from woefully naive expectations made by Dunlap and Kersh for the purpose of boosting Sunbeam's stock price. Some time during the oppressive Florida summer, Kersh would make one of the more magnificently wrong forecasts the company would ever trumpet. Etchison and Robertson were out of the office when yet another Wall Street analyst arrived for the usual "secret room" tour. Curious about the sales prospects for the air and water projects, the analyst asked Kersh for a rough estimate of Sunbeam's projections. Uncertain, Kersh asked a finance staffer who had only assisted the new product team to come up with one on the spot. "They dug back through our files and found this old piece of paper with some numbers on it," recalls Robertson. "They handed it to Russ Kersh and he massaged it and came up with projected sales of $100 million in the first year. When we came back to the office that suddenly was our number: $50 million on air and $50 million on water. That was so far away from anything that had to do with reality."

The team believed they could rack up $20 million in revenue on water filters in the first year, but only if Sunbeam spent $8 to $10 million in advertising to support the product's introduction. Even the $20 million estimate may have been optimistic because the Sunbeam products would have to go up against some tough, established rivals. In the water filtration category alone, at least ten major competitors had a head start on Sunbeam. Many of them, from Clorox's Brita to Teledyne's Water Pik, boasted greater resources, had invested more advertising money than Sunbeam spent over its entire line of appliances, and dominated retail shelf space. Clorox, for example, was spending $25 million to $30 million annually in advertising for its market-leading Brita line. Besides, the entire market was worth only $160 million. How could Sunbeam, coming into the category years late, seize a third of the market share with minimal advertising support?

Robertson, concerned about the unrealistic sales goal, initially persuaded McBride that the $50 million figure could only be reached if they were in full production for the entire year and selling both domestically and internationally. "But as time went on and things changed, it ended up becoming my domestic number for 1998," says Robertson. "I would tell them we weren't going to make it, and they would say, 'Yes, you are.'" Under the Dunlap-imposed mandate to reduce all costs, including advertising, Uzzin limited the ad budget for the water product to just $3 million for the first year.

Even the pricing of the water filter became an issue. The team believed that the product should sell at retail for $60 a unit. The water filter business was similar to the razor and blade business. The idea was to gain market share by selling the base product at a low-margin profit so you could later sell consumers the high-margin replacement filters. Uzzi and McBride, however, insisted that the product should sell for $84 a unit, despite consumer testing that demonstrated it was too high a price. "Don wouldn't let us change the price on the base unit because if we did we wouldn't meet corporate margin hurdles in the first year," said Robertson. "It looked pretty on paper but it was not reality because it was impossible to get the volume we needed to make a profit at that price."

The air cleaner also would go out at a hefty premium to rival products. The company planned to sell the units in two sizes, a 200-cubic-feet-per-minute model that would retail at $219, and a 125-CFM model that would retail at $179. The team's repeated warnings about the pricing fell on deaf ears. "I give you credit for persistence," said Uzzi. "I have heard you. I don't want to hear it again." Uzzi believed that the products should command higher prices because the company's proprietary technology made them superior. Besides, he said,

Etchison was over budget, so if the products couldn't fetch a premium, they wouldn't be worth producing.

McBride, initially their immediate boss, was more to the point. "Look, none of us are going to be around to manage this," he told them. "It's all about making it look good to sell the company."

Forced into a crash-and-burn timetable, Etchison tried to rush the products into production at Sunbeam's huge, modern plant in Hattiesburg, Mississippi. But the paucity of resources continued to conspire to prevent a trouble-free launch. With no materials experts on staff, Sunbeam went to vendors for the least expensive parts to assemble the water product. Sometimes the wrong materials were shipped and used because initially no one at the plant checked to ensure that the parts ordered were those that had arrived. The water seal didn't fit properly, and the product continued to leak. Eventually the company hired a consulting firm to help debug the product.

That was a feat in itself, however, because Sunbeam had become so cost-conscious that it required vice presidents to sign off on Federal Express packages. As it became even more difficult to make the numbers later in 1997, it only got worse. Kersh insisted that Uzzi, the top operating executive at Sunbeam, had to give his approval for a Fed Ex mailing. To make the numbers, Sunbeam even began to refuse to pay its bills. One headhunter enlisted a member of the board of directors to get paid. Another recruitment firm walked away from Sunbeam's business when the company refused to pay the full invoice. A small supplier of marketing and packaging materials who had a five-year relationship with Sunbeam had to regularly beg for payment. "The vendor was calling me every other day asking to get their bills paid," said Etchison. "Uzzi didn't want to sign off on the invoices." Uzzi later maintained he refused to approve them because Etchison was way beyond budget, and he wanted to see the full documentation for the work.

Ultimately Sunbeam agreed to pay the supplier six months late, but only after insisting that the invoice be reduced by as much as 25 percent. "They approved the budgets and then whacked the vendor on $50,000 on an order of a couple hundred thousand," recalled Etchison. "They told him, 'You can give us a $50,000 break or not work for us in the future.' When it got to that point, I said, 'Now you are messing with my personal integrity.'"

Robertson was just as frustrated. "It was personally humiliating," she said. "I couldn't tell for sure if they were simply pinching pennies or [it was] because we were short on cash. Later on it became apparent it was the latter."

The stress and pressure hit uncommonly high levels. Like most staffers, Etchison worked twelve to fourteen hours a day, six to seven days a week. Marc Haberman, a category leader in appliances, insisted that his employees turn in weekend schedules so he could reach them on Saturdays and Sundays. Ailments of one kind or another were not uncommon. One human resources staffer at headquarters suffered a heart attack over the summer. The engineer partly assigned to Etchison's team, Don Kaminski, died of a heart attack during the project. "He was a great guy who jumped through hoops to get anything done," said Etchison. "He was a heavy man, but the stress and strain of the project certainly was a contributor."

ON OCTOBER 8 an ebullient Dunlap stood before nearly 100 Wall Street analysts and reporters to proudly unveil the new inventions at the opulent Plaza Hotel in New York. Under the crystal chandeliers in the hotel's Rose Room, Sunbeam's entourage built a large display of the new products. Dunlap was at his charismatic best. He shook hands with technicians setting up the presentation. "Al Dunlap, howya doin'?" he said, beaming. He cracked jokes with Etchison and Robertson, who helped to prep him for questions on the new products, especially when he struggled to pronounce the word "cryptosporidium," a microorganism that Freshsource's filter could trap.

At one point Dunlap asked general counsel David Fannin how much he could say about the shortcomings of competing products. "I'll stop you when you've said too much," quipped Fannin.

"Great, I'll be a deaf-mute up there," Dunlap said.

On stage Dunlap was hardly that. "These two products represent the very best of the new Sunbeam," he crowed. "We were able to bring these products to market in eight months, from idea to production, and they both solve the most significant consumer complaints associated with current products in the marketplace."

Etchison demonstrated the air filter, bringing up an analyst to dribble some dust in front of the unit. Robertson did a demo of the water filter, inviting analyst Andrew Shore to pour green-colored water into the pitcher and turn it on—just as she had done for Dunlap only four months earlier. Shore ambled on stage, feeling that he was being used by Dunlap. "I kept thinking this is just okay," he said later. "I couldn't believe I was doing it."

Once again the water poured out as clear as if it had just flowed from a fresh spring. The audience applauded. Wall Street was dazzled. Dunlap was so pleased with the presentation's success that once the room cleared, he kissed both Etchison and Robertson on their cheeks. "Great job," he told them.

The products, however, were not ready to launch. It would take many more months to get the bugs out of them. Yet Dunlap told the analysts the products would come out in limited distribution for the 1997 holiday season, with full availability in January 1998. "We were telling them something we didn't think would be true," said Robertson. Of course it didn't make much difference if Dunlap could sell Sunbeam, a goal he still intended to accomplish.

Returning from the triumphant launch in New York, though, Robertson and other executives began to doubt Dunlap's ability to pull it off. At Scott rumors of a buyout by Kimberly-Clark had begun to surface publicly within eleven months of his tenure there as chief executive. Within fourteen months, reports had emerged of negotiations between Scott and Kimberly. A month later, or fifteen months into his reign as Sunbeam CEO, the acquisition of Scott was finally announced. Yet there was no sign of a buyer for Sunbeam. "We better sell this pig soon or it's going to come crashing down," thought Robertson. "We had done a lot to make the 1997 returns look good, and we knew that the first quarter of 1998 would be bad. I finally figured out around October that nobody was going to buy this pig. If anyone did the 'due diligence,' they would realize it was a farce. They did this on every project. It was all fantasy."

Given the constraints, the lack of advertising support, the high pricing, the poor quality of the product, there was no way that Dunlap could get what he promised Wall Street: $100 million in new revenue from two products that still had bugs in them. At the Hattiesburg plant, they could not stop the water filter from leaking in several places. There were small leaks from the pitcher, but there was a catastrophic leak from the seal between the pitcher and the base units that held a motor and the filter. "It was the kind of debug we knew we had to do but we never had the time or resources to do it properly," said Robertson. Even as the engineers in the plant continued to test the product, the company began to ship its first units to customers in late December 1997. They would be promptly recalled when it was determined that the leaks still were not fixed.

Yet in the immediate aftermath of the launch in early October, even perpetually skeptical Andrew Shore seemed to be losing some of his doubts. "Sunbeam enters 1998 with a potent combination: two exciting and innovative new products, Freshsource and Allergysmart, which, even if they are not absolute home runs, should provide completely incremental sales at better than corporate average operating margins, and an enhanced grill line-up against a weak grill showing in the first half of 1997," wrote Shore to his clients, unaware of all the problems associated with those products. "Unless Sunbeam has Thomas Edison stashed away in the 'secret room,' momentum should slow for Sunbeam in the second half of 1998."

Shore, noting with caution a large jump in inventories and receivables on Sunbeam's balance sheet, was positive enough to upgrade the stock for the second time. He put out a buy on October 28 from his earlier attractive upgrade, as the stock dipped temporarily into the high $30s. He no longer believed Dunlap could sell the company, however. "We agree that Sunbeam may be too rich to be taken over, but we do not believe that this means Sunbeam is overvalued," wrote Shore. "Sunbeam possesses an intangible asset, the Dunlap factor, that none of its potential targets possesses . . . yet. The real potential for another round of meteoric stock price appreciation comes if Sunbeam can make a strategic acquisition, using Sunbeam stock as the currency, at a modest premium that doesn't already factor in all of the cost-cutting potential. If Sunbeam can pull this off, shareholders may be getting two Dunlap turnarounds for the price of one. Now that's a bright idea."

11
THE DITTY BAG

WORKING ON THE front lines of a company run by Albert Dunlap was like being at war. The pressure was brutal, the hours exhausting, and the casualties high. Dunlap and his consultants had imposed such unrealistic goals on the company that virtually everyone understood he was engaged in a short-term exercise to pretty up the business for a quick sale. That had to be the goal because there was no way to sustain the performance Dunlap demanded.

To double total revenues to $2 billion by 1999, Sunbeam had to perform five times better than any of its rivals in the industry. To boost operating margins to 20 percent in little more than a year, Sunbeam had to improve its profitability more than twelve-fold from the measly 2.5 percent margins it had. To generate $600 million in sales through new products by 1999, the company had to virtually smash home runs with every at-bat.

The expectations were impractical. Dunlap, however, refused to acknowledge either the difficulty or the impossibility of meeting the goals. By sheer brutality, he began putting excruciating pressure on those who reported to him, who in turn passed that intimidation down the line. It went beyond the ordinary pressure to do well in a corporation. People were told, explicitly and implicitly, that either they hit the number or another person would be found to do it for them. Their livelihood hung on making numbers that were not makeable.

At Sunbeam Dunlap created a culture of misery, an environment of moral ambiguity, indifferent to everything except the stock price. He

153

did not lead by intellect or by vision, but by fear and intimidation. In that way he was not unlike the most infamous corporate leaders who used fear as a weapon, people like ITT's Harold Geneen or Oxidental Petroleum's Armand Hammer. Unlike them, however, Dunlap imposed expectations that were more often than not irrational and unrealistic. "No matter what happened, Al was driving for more and more," said manufacturing chief Newcomb.

In Dunlap's presence, knees trembled and stomachs churned. Underlings feared the torrential harangue that Dunlap could unleash at any moment. The pressure was beyond tough. It was barbarous. "There are tough people and then there are mean people," explained a Sunbeam executive. "Tough people keep you up at night, worried about getting things done. Mean people make you piss in your pants. They scare the absolute shit out of you. They are violent. They beat on you. Al is a mean man."

At his worst, when his sound and fury were at full bore, Dunlap became viciously profane, even violent. He would throw papers or furniture, bang his hands on his desk, knock glasses of water off a table, and shout so ferociously that a manager's hair could lift from his head by the stream of air that rushed from Dunlap's screaming mouth. He made himself all the more threatening because he often carried a handgun, wore a bulletproof vest, and had a bodyguard nearby. One Sunbeam executive found a gun under a sofa cushion in Dunlap's home. If that were not enough, many were terrified because they witnessed the unusual, if not vindictive, behavior by Dunlap toward members of his own family. Shortly after an argument with his son, Dunlap summoned a lawyer to his office to write him out of his will. Dunlap so openly disliked his sister, Denise, that he insisted that his secretary, Denise Valek, be addressed only by the letter "D," essentially forbidding anyone from using her real name.

Dunlap's executives believed that he didn't care about the details of the business, and oftentimes he would tell them that directly when they tried to explain a business situation to him. The upshot: It was virtually impossible for executives to tell him the truth.

Everyone's performance was compared unfavorably to the work of others at companies he previously ran under Sir James Goldsmith or some other executive.

"In a meeting with Al, you are not there to tell him anything," said

Bill Kirkpatrick, who worked with him at both Scott and Sunbeam. "You are there to listen. If you didn't hit your numbers, he would tear all over you. The lines would be pat."

Dunlap's face would turn florid red, and then the words would shoot out of his mouth like bullets.

"I have thousands of résumés from people who would work here for free," Dunlap screamed, inches from his victim.

"You are being paid to work here, and you can become rich because I've given you all these options. And you're letting me down. I'm working hard for you on the street, and you're letting me down."

In the field, Sunbeam's sales force felt the same pressure. "It was like your job or your life," explained a top salesman. "But it was a combination of the carrot and the stick. You were constantly reminded of the huge financial payoff if it worked out."

The payoff would come in stock-option gains that would become available if the company was sold. Stock options were huge and plentiful. Soon after arriving at Sunbeam, Dunlap won approval to hand out options and restricted stock on as many as 16.5 million shares. He could give as many as 250,000 options to a single executive in one year. The top 250 to 300 executives and managers at Sunbeam all received option grants, typically twice the size of what they might get at other companies. General managers were given grants on 50,000 to 75,000 shares, and additional awards were routinely doled out when someone received a promotion or performed exceptionally good work. Later on Dunlap gave minimum grants of 100 stock options to every employee who had a year's service under his or her belt.

But in some cases Dunlap's generosity had a perverse impact. The outsize rewards made it easier for employees to do things they might otherwise refuse to do. Some of the company's executives were sitting on millions of dollars of option gains that may have served to undermine their integrity. Option grants vested over a three-year period. So if an executive was dismissed, he or she would lose all the options not yet vested. In many cases that could mean the loss of more than a million dollars in option gains. Dunlap had managed to transform a carrot into a stick.

Some referred to their paper gains as "dream money" and occasionally huddled behind closed doors to imagine themselves cruising the highways in a new Porsche or Ferrari or piloting a new boat on the

Intercoastal. In Dunlap's option-laced culture, long-lasting improvements in operations were often traded for stock market thrills that fueled those fantasies.

Every option granted by Dunlap, moreover, had an unusual feature: a muzzle clause. Managers with options could not speak to analysts or reporters. If they left the company, that prohibition remained in force for two full years after their departure. If anyone talked, Dunlap could cancel all their options, even forcing the return of stock or cash on grants that already were exercised.

After ordering his staff to meet unrealistic sales goals, Dunlap left it to Uzzi to prod managers to reach the targets. Uzzi often reminded them of their stock option gains. It was, he thought, the only way to motivate the troops. The hours were bad. The morale was dreadful. The CEO made impossible demands. Uzzi figured the hell was tolerable only because of the money. He would dangle the value of a salesman's stock options over his head, insisting that he go out and "get the job done."

Amazingly, for the most part, they did. In the first quarter of 1997, the cost savings in manufacturing projected by the Coopers consultants failed to materialize. Production chief Newcomb simply could not get the numbers to work. It was taking much longer than anticipated to close plants and consolidate production. The marketing and sales staff was pressured to protect the margins. To make the quarterly numbers required a fierce dash to every quarterly finish line. Yet they did it, surprising Wall Street and bringing more cheers and ovations for Dunlap. The company outdid the Street's projections for the first quarter of 1997, earning 24 cents per share, 2 cents better than expected. Its second quarter earnings of 30 cents per share were right on the Street's estimates. Sunbeam turned in a blowout third quarter, with earnings of 34 cents a share, beating the analysts' consensus by a penny.

Inside Sunbeam, however, there was little enthusiasm. The survival tactics of kissing up and kicking down sowed widespread bitterness and frustration. Many of Uzzi's people began to deeply resent him, and some of them, in turn, were resented by their own subordinates. After all, Uzzi had what they called "fuck you" money. A wise and frugal investor, he had accumulated a good deal of wealth for himself during his years at P&G, Pepsi, and Quaker Oats. But Uzzi, thought some, failed to use his savings to effectively stand up to Dunlap. "Don had 'fuck you' money so he could walk into Al's office and tell him regardless of what you think, this is what is happening in the business," said one executive. "He had the money to stand up to Al, and he didn't do it because he wanted more. Newt used his 'fuck you' money, and Don didn't."

Uzzi saw it differently. Though he worked his people exceptionally hard, he also believed he was one of the few holding the place together. He wasn't going to walk out precipitously. Like Newt White before him, Uzzi also saw himself as something of a barrier between Dunlap and the people beneath him doing the work of the company. He sometimes struggled against Dunlap and Kersh to reduce their outrageous expectations, but was invariably overruled time and time again, until it reached the point where he no longer wasted his breath or else quietly subverted their will. "It was like banging into an electrical fence," said Uzzi. "Once you hit into it the first and second time, it hurt so bad you decide you don't want to hit into it again. So you avoid it."

Though many of his subordinates did not see it, Uzzi increasingly evaded the highly charged fence and began to view his boss with near total contempt. He marked his own time at Sunbeam in the same way that a combat solider in Vietnam might, taking out a calendar to cross off every new day of a year-long sentence. Just as he had opposed Dunlap in holding off the complete move of the clipper business to Mexico, he also quietly began to defy Dunlap in other ways. When the CEO demanded that Uzzi fire manufacturing chief Newcomb, for example, he delayed the firing for four months so that at least some of the executive's stock options would vest. He would do the same for McBride before firing him by the end of 1997 at Dunlap's insistence.

By the fourth quarter of 1997, as it became more difficult to meet the numbers, a new and rather menacing management technique was invented. Kersh called it "tasking." The idea was to gather the company's top executives in the Delray Beach boardroom and then ask each to run through the numbers for their businesses. If one area was running behind, someone in the room would be asked to make up the difference so Dunlap's forecasts to Wall Street could be met. "They would say, 'I don't care what your plan was. I don't care what you delivered last month,' recalls Dixon Thayer, head of international sales. "'We are going to task you to this number.' Russ and Don would give you a revenue and profit number and say, 'We don't want any bullshit!

Your life depends on hitting that number!' These numbers got to be so outrageous they were ridiculous."

Yet, under fierce strain, many of the executives caved in to the pressure, agreeing to meet irrational objectives. Cynthia Vahlkamp, who ran the outdoor cooking business, signed up for 35 percent margins on Sunbeam's grills, a pledge that could only be fulfilled by nearly doubling the product's sales. She never hit 20 percent.

Thayer was appalled by the willingness of some managers to agree to such fatuous targets. "When you were in these reviews, Al would march around the table menacingly and people would say, 'Yes, sir, I will do it.' They came in wanting to be loved by Al, so if he said 'You need to double your profits for the month, the answer was 'Yes sir,' as opposed to 'There ain't no way in hell.' It was like trying to be loved by a shark," thought Thayer. "When its brain says it is hungry, it's going to eat. Its brain says it is tired, it's going to sleep. That's Al Dunlap. He's not thinking about the long-term success of the company or the elegance of a strategy. It's what do I have to say on Wall Street this week to make it happen."

In an effort to meet their tasked numbers and hang on to their jobs, Sunbeam's managers began all sorts of game playing. Bills routinely went unpaid. Some vendors were forced to accept partial payment on their invoices. More work was shuffled to outside suppliers. Product was heavily discounted to get retailers to buy more than needed. Credit terms were extended for the same purpose. Commissions were withheld from the company's independent sales reps. In brief, every shortcut was taken, every trick was employed to make a number, even if it would threaten the business in the future. What difference did it make? Many of the executives hoped that the day of reckoning would be put off by a sale of Sunbeam or an acquisition that could be used to camouflage the downturn that would surely come because of their short-term schemes.

"We gave customers extra dating or discounts if they brought it in early," said a top salesman. "We were jamming inventory at people like you couldn't believe. Most of the stuff I had done before for solid companies. We just took it to another level. We did it every quarter, with every customer, on every product. We pushed the envelope like we never did before. We used to think we were cowboys at the old Sunbeam. Compared to these guys under Al, we were Jesuits."

THE GAMES did not go completely unnoticed, even on Wall Street. There are two kinds of analysts on the Street. Story analysts pay scant or no attention to the fundamentals of a stock. Instead they buy into the story spun by the company and the market. Few executives could rival Dunlap as a master storyteller. The company's ever-rising stock price was a tribute to his success at persuading Wall Street that Sunbeam was a story worth buying.

Technical analysts adopt the opposite tack. With a spreadsheet, a calculator, and some healthy skepticism, they pore over the financials like forensic detectives. They search for clues that tip off any number of common games that might inflate earnings but are a harbinger of bad news in the future. Of all the analysts who followed Sunbeam, William H. Steele of Buckingham Research Group in San Francisco was perhaps the most technically driven.

Steele was born and raised in San Francisco, and educated at Berkeley in conservation and resource studies, and then made a detour into business by getting his MBA from the University of Boulder. The thirty-something analyst had been watching and rating companies since 1988, specializing in the consumer product industry. Unlike Shore, who also was considered a technical analyst, Steele won Dunlap's immediate favor because he put out a buy on Sunbeam stock the day the company announced it had hired Chainsaw. Dunlap later surprised the analyst, coming to visit him shortly afterward with television cameras in tow. Steele, then with Dean Witter, said the right things on camera and Dunlap was grateful. When the analyst moved to Buckingham, Steele got a personal recommendation from the CEO of Sunbeam.

What he saw in the company's numbers for the first six months of 1997, however, greatly troubled him. Inventory in the second quarter hit $208 million, up $60 million from first quarter levels. "That told me that orders were not as strong as the company indicated or that its gross margin performance was artificially inflated because the plants were running faster than the orders received," Steele said. He also noticed that changes in cash from working capital were a negative $36 million. A year earlier, it was a positive $1 million. "When your working capital is going negative, you are not efficiently selling your goods," said Steele.

The analyst believed the deterioration in those numbers was enough of a warning sign to become cautious. Steele understood that a weakening in the balance sheet is often a precursor to lower-than-expected earnings so he downgraded the stock to neutral in July while most analysts were still in the midst of an extended honeymoon with Dunlap. His downgrade did little to dampen the enthusiasm of investors or other analysts who either still believed in Dunlap or thought the market would not react to changes in a company's balance sheet it probably wouldn't fully understand. Shore, for example, noted the same changes but chose to hold off on a downgrade because he believed the stock would continue to rise.

NO ONE, not Steele or Shore or any other outsider, could fully appreciate the extent of the turmoil inside Sunbeam and what the company was doing to make its overall profit and sales numbers. Of all the ploys, few were as controversial and daring as the "bill-and-hold" sales the company began making in early November. Anxious to extend the selling season for its gas grills and boost sales in Dunlap's "turnaround year," the company hoped to convince retailers to buy grills nearly six months before they were needed. In exchange for major discounts, retailers agreed to purchase merchandise they would not physically receive until months later and would not pay for until six months after billing. In the meantime, the goods would be shipped out of the grill factory in Neosho, Missouri, to third-party warehouses leased by Sunbeam where they would be held until wanted by the customers.

The program had at least some legitimate basis. In the previous year, Sunbeam's supply of grills fell short and it failed to meet retail demand. By building inventory earlier and then shifting it onto the retailer, Uzzi believed the company could better balance supply and demand and increase market share. If Wal-Mart and Costco bought Sunbeam grills, whether delivered or not, they would not be purchasing competitors' product. But there was also an instantaneous benefit to the company's numbers. Even though customers failed to accept the goods in their stores and warehouses, Sunbeam was able to immediately book the sales and profits as if they had. The downside was just as evident: Sunbeam was clearly booking what would have been future sales in the present. It was likely that these early sales would diminish future revenues.

The concept of doing bill-and-hold sales came out of a brainstorming meeting earlier in the year at which sales staff and managers were tossing around ways to increase sales. Griffith apparently had done similar transactions at Scott Paper and suggested the idea to goose the sales of electric blankets during the second quarter of 1997, when few retailers would be interested in buying a product that only sold during the winter months.

From the beginning, it was a controversial move. Bill-and-hold sales are not standard practice, as Dunlap and Kersh would later insist. The Securities & Exchange Commission has explicitly called such transactions "a departure from the general rule of revenue recognition." The regulatory agency first issued guidelines on such sales in 1981, to Mattel Inc., the toy maker with a highly seasonal business. The SEC then made clear that the practice was not acceptable if a customer—not a supplier—failed to have "a compelling business purpose" for it. Even then the agency demanded that a supplier had to meet a set of seven stringent "conditions" and consider six additional "factors" before it could book a bill-and-hold sale.

Among other things, buyers, not sellers, had to request that the transaction be on a bill-and-hold basis, and customers had to make fixed commitments to purchase the goods, preferably in writing. The rules also obligated the seller to provide a fixed delivery schedule, and buyers had to assume the full risks of ownership. Even if a company met all seven conditions, however, the SEC maintained that the sales could still fail to meet the requirements for revenue recognition. That was because the agency required accountants and auditors to consider a series of other issues. Before approving a bill-and-hold transaction, for example, they had to consider whether normal billing and credit terms were modified, whether the buyer assumed the risk of losses if the goods declined in value, and the seller's past experiences with such sales.

The accounting treatment of these sales, as well as every other decision dealing with accounting, had to go through controller Robert Gluck, who reported directly to Kersh. A tall, thin, and angular man with a receding hairline, Gluck was a master accountant who put in ungodly hours of work. His subordinates judged him a humorless introvert, weak on people skills. Gluck brought a rare intensity to his job, and he was particularly adroit in the intricacies of the SEC's reporting rules. "If you had a question about revenue recognition or the proper way to account for something, you would always go to Bob," said a colleague. It was the kind of knowledge that could be employed to keep a company on the straight and narrow or used to skirt along the very edge of propriety.

Unlike so many of the fresh faces around Sunbeam, Gluck was a true survivor. He was one of the few high-level executives who still remained from the Kazarian era. He had been hired from the accounting firm of Ernst & Young by former general counsel Lederman, who regarded him as "professionally competent." Initially Gluck was somewhat reticent about the bill-and-hold transactions. Unlike Mattel, which faced a Christmas season lasting little more than a single month, Sunbeam's selling season for electric blankets or outdoor grills typically was four to five times as long. So it might have been a stretch to contend that Sunbeam had a "compelling business purpose" to turn toward bill-and-hold sales. Besides, it was Dunlap's managers who were aggressively advocating the transactions rather than the customers, as required by the SEC. Sunbeam, moreover, extended credit terms far beyond what might be considered "normal." Customers were given a full six months, instead of the more typical thirty days, in which to pay their bills. Some were told that the sales were essentially guaranteed so that the goods could be returned if they were not sold at retail, another clear violation of the SEC's rules.

Though Dunlap and Kersh would later publicly maintain that the sales were made to balance production with sales, Sunbeam had never resorted to bill-and-hold transactions in the past.

So beginning in November, Sunbeam's sales staff rushed around the country to shove discounted grills onto retailers in a bid to satisfy Dunlap's impossible goals. Unable to get enough revenue in the United States, Uzzi asked international sales chief Thayer to advance sales outside the country. Thayer wanted no part of it. He had been meeting his goals for international sales and felt no reason to move what would be future sales into the present.

"I'm not going to do it," said Thayer. "I'm so far ahead of plan there is no reason to do it. If I put my first quarter into the fourth quarter, I'll get fired for not having a first quarter." Other than a bill-and-hold sale in Mexico in 1997's fourth quarter, the practice was not moved overseas.

"More and more, it became impossible to make the kinds of numbers that Al thought should be made," conceded a top executive. "It was the only way we could get even remotely close to the numbers Al wanted. He thought the numbers should be made because he willed them. In a reasonable environment with good management we knew what the right things to do were. But Al was so concerned about revenue that we sacrificed margin. He was aware of the grill sales, and they were reviewed with him."

It wasn't until three months later when the board of directors first learned that Kersh and Gluck had been booking the unusual grill sales. On January 26 the board's audit committee met to hear the results of the previous year's audit by Arthur Andersen. William Rutter, the director who chaired the audit committee, was at Sunbeam's Delray Beach headquarters, while directors Howard Kristol and Charles Elson were patched in by telephone for the three-hour meeting that began at 10 A.M.

Shortly into the discussion the bill-and-hold sales were brought up, but not by Kersh, Gluck, or Sunbeam's director of internal audit Thomas Hartshorne. Instead Philip Harlow, the Arthur Andersen partner in charge of the company's audit, said the directors needed to be aware of a few issues. At the top of his list were the controversial bill-and-hold transactions.

Harlow said the transactions were part of the company's "go to market" strategy to coax retailers to commit early to purchases by offering favorable pricing and terms. Because the retailers lacked warehouse space during the Christmas season, Harlow said the inventory had been stored at third-party warehouses leased by Sunbeam. The auditor, according to minutes of the meeting, said he "saw no particular issue with this procedure in light of the explanation of the company's marketing strategy for 1998."

Director Kristol was not so sure. Years earlier he had been involved in a case as a lawyer in which a furniture maker booked bill-and-hold sales to Sears, Roebuck & Co. The sales later turned out to be completely bogus. So a somewhat skeptical Kristol began posing questions about the Sunbeam transactions.

"Is this conservative under GAAP?" asked Kristol.

Gluck attempted to reassure him that the sales were legitimate and met the SEC rules. Kersh immediately jumped in to support Gluck. Kersh, according to the board minutes, added "that these kinds of 'go to market' programs are precisely the sorts of things the company should be doing in order to be responsive to the requirements of selling seasonal products." Kersh and Gluck, however, did not tell directors that Sunbeam had first begun bill-and-hold sales on electric blankets in the second quarter of 1997. During a portion of the meeting closed to them, the board members asked internal auditor Hartshorne to work closely with Arthur Anderson to ensure that the transactions were done as conservatively as possible under accounting rules. Hartshorne, whom Kersh had hired at Scott Paper, was recruited to Sunbeam by Kersh again to establish an internal audit department. Until then, Sunbeam farmed this work out to the accounting firm of Ernst & Young.

Six-foot-two with white hair and a weathered face, Hartshorne had worked as an auditor at W.R. Grace & Co. before meeting Kersh.

At the audit committee meeting, directors recalled, he expressed no reservations about the unusual sales nor did he tell the board members about the considerable worries of the only other member of the internal audit department. Unbeknownst to the board, Deidra DenDanto had been challenging a number of practices at the company, including the bill-and-hold sales, ever since Hartshorne hired the young accountant in late 1996. Her skepticism, DenDanto later came to believe, was not what anyone at the company would have expected. "I think I was hired because I was young, and they thought I was controllable," she said later. If so, Hartshorne might well have hired DenDanto on little more than first impressions. Gregarious and cute, she appeared much younger than her twenty-five years. She had only two years of auditing experience at Arthur Andersen's West Palm Beach, Florida, office. It was her first job after graduating with a degree in accounting from Florida State University in 1994. She hadn't yet sat for the CPA exam. Yet, with Hartshorne, she was part of a two-person internal audit group for a billion-dollar New York Stock Exchange company.

What she lacked in experience, DenDanto more than offset in diligence and smarts. She commonly worked 65-to-70 hour weeks, arriving at 7 A.M. and leaving at 8 P.M., often skipping lunch. During her nineteen-month stay at Sunbeam, she did more than a dozen audits and worked on a host of high-priority projects, from Dunlap's sale of the company's Biddesford, Maine, blanket plant to Sunbeam employees to assisting with the implementation of a new corporate-wide computer system.

Almost immediately, she passionately struggled to bring management attention to deficiencies that caught her eye. DenDanto's audit report in 1997 on Sunbeam's high rates of product returns from customers urged the company to impose greater accountability on managers for returns. It was a material issue because Sunbeam technically had a no-return policy that allowed the company to set aside small reserves for what should only have been minor, unanticipated returns. Yet customers were sending back millions of dollars in product every month.

When Hartshorne and she composed a written no-return policy and urged its adoption, the plan was opposed by a senior finance official because, he said, it would constrain Sunbeam's ability to make its quarterly numbers. "How do I sell it, if I can't take it back later?" asked Al Lefevre, who approved many of the sales transactions at corporate headquarters. When DenDanto and her boss brought the issue to Kersh, he seemed all ears, telling them both he wanted internal audit to be "the storm troopers of the company."

But then little follow-up would occur. "Nothing would happen," she said later.

The returns still flowed into the company, to the point where Sunbeam began to hold "truckload" sales in late 1997 to unload the returned goods. The sales were often run off the back of trucks in tents erected in parking lots or in abandoned storefronts that would be taken over temporarily by Sunbeam. After studying these all-cash deals, DenDanto found there were inadequate controls over the cash receipts, the cash deposit process, and the inventory. Yet, she said, her concerns about them were met with a comment from Kersh that the company planned to have only a couple more before the end of the year.

In another report, DenDanto urged the company to upgrade what she discovered were incomplete and less-than-accurate records of the fixed assets on its books. "But no one was ever made responsible to change things that needed to be changed," she recalled. "The priority was always on making revenue."

To DenDanto's chagrin, management's exaltation of the short-term came up time and time again. During a discussion of the company's preparedness for Y2K, the millennium computer bug, she heard Kersh say, "What do I care? Do you think I'm going to be around then?"

It was Sunbeam's bill-and-hold transactions, however, that most disturbed her. DenDanto had become a fearless and persistent critic of the sales, challenging the practice from the very first mention of it in early 1997. Asked by a top Sunbeam salesman if she considered the accounting treatment of such a sale legitimate, she flatly replied no. Her opinion was based not on the SEC guidelines but on standard accounting principles that made it clear that revenue could not be "recognized" until a sale was complete or substantially complete. Reporting revenue six months before goods would be delivered seemed to her a violation of those accounting rules. She also was suspicious that in some cases Sunbeam was booking sales on grills it did not yet have in inventory.

Over the course of several months, DenDanto made her doubts and displeasure known to Hartshorne, LeFevre, Gluck, and Kersh. She alerted a visiting Arthur Andersen staff auditor to look into the issue, instructing him "to get your hands around this." Yet, to her increasing disillusionment, little changed. They would usually listen to her concerns, attempt to discount them, and then redirect her efforts elsewhere. "Whenever I got upset and frustrated," DenDanto said, "they would change my focus. When I became interested in bill-and-hold or sales processes, they put me on systems implementation." Powerless to make a difference, she felt herself a lone conscientious voice in an organization consumed with boosting revenue and its stock price. "My work at Sunbeam," DenDanto later recalled, "had become constant frustration, constant aggravation, and constant stonewalling by others."

IN THE FOURTH QUARTER, however, no amount of game playing, no manner of beating up people, could produce the numbers Dunlap willed onto the organization. So the celebrity CEO turned to the kitchen and his long-time ally and chief financial officer Russell Kersh. While he may have obeyed the very letter of accepted accounting practices, much of his bookkeeping was later challenged.

Accounting is hardly an exact science. It's far more like an art, open to broad degrees of practice and interpretation. Generally accepted accounting principles, the so-called GAAP, leave wide areas of discretion for financial managers. That flexibility sometimes makes it difficult to know when a company has crossed the line from aggressive earnings management to outright fraud. Generally, though, the line is crossed when a company's financial statements obscure the reality of its actual condition.

In the often esoteric interpretations that are made in accounting, Kersh was rarely conservative or bashful about his creative competence. In a self-congratulatory tone, he would point to his chest to remind fellow executives that he was "the biggest profit center" the company had. Dunlap knew it as well. At meetings, Dunlap would say, "If it weren't for Russ and the accounting team, we'd be nowhere." "Make the goddamn number," Dunlap shouted again and again. "And Russ, you cover it with your ditty bag."

The phrase itself was a military term. A ditty bag was used by sailors to hold small articles of gear. At Sunbeam it was the collection of accounting techniques that Kersh could employ to pad the company's net income and sales.

Throughout the 1997 year Kersh had been regularly dipping into the bag to help create a "turnaround" for his boss. One common recipe was simply to reverse the excess funds that had been placed in reserves when Dunlap took his big restructuring charge. Like many chief financial officers, Kersh took a bigger write-off than he would ever need so he could later bleed the excess into income. Until the fourth quarter, however, his reversals were fairly minimal. He took into income only $500,000 in the first quarter, $4.5 million in the second, and $1.5 million in the third. With the year's final quarter a hopeless mess, Kersh fully opened up the tap and poured $21.5 million from reserves into income.

Besides reserving far more money than needed, Kersh made a number of changes that artificially boosted earnings. In the second quarter, for example, Kersh began capitalizing the inventory of manufacturing supplies. Previously these inventories were charged to operations when purchased. The change increased Sunbeam's operating earnings by $2.8 million in 1997.

The accountings also took full advantage of the sales practices Lee Griffith was employing to pump up the numbers. Besides offering retailers massive discounts, Griffith's sales force was making sizable guaranteed and consignment sales. Under the former, a customer is given the guaranteed right of return at full cost. Under the latter, a customer accepts the product but Sunbeam retains title to the goods. The company could only recognize the revenue and profit from consignment sales when the goods were actually purchased by consumers. Historically, Sunbeam often guaranteed the sales of electric blankets.

Under Dunlap's management, these sales and consignment deals not only mushroomed, but many of them failed to pass muster when reviewed a year later. Some consignment sales, for example, were immediately recognized as revenue before customers bought the goods. In effect, some merchandise on retail shelves actually belonged to Sunbeam. To goose sales and profit, Kersh and controller Gluck approved $36 million in guaranteed and consignment sales and $17 million in pretax profits for 1997. Pushing so much product out to retailers, of course, meant that more merchandise would likely be returned from them. By failing to account in a reserve for those returns, Kersh and Gluck were able to hold off the potential deduction of those sales from 1997 revenue and profit. This move alone allowed Sunbeam to book $16 million more in sales and $6 million in pretax profits than the company actually had.

Kersh and Gluck also brightened the financial picture by the way they accounted for Sunbeam's bill-and-hold revenues. Only days before the close of Sunbeam's fourth quarter, Gluck went into a panic when Griffith and his finance officer, Al Lefevre, failed to have all the documents necessary to cover the quarter's bill-and-hold sales. From the start the financial controller had been chary about such sales. He had handed out copies of all the rules that needed to be followed. He even called another accounting firm, Ernst & Young, to check on the procedures for bill-and-hold. His worries now seemed prescient. Griffith and LeFeure could produce letters for only a small portion of the $35 million in bill-and-hold sales. Some managers said that only $3 million of the $35 million sales were covered a mere three days before the quarter's close.

Instead of individual customers composing such letters to cover the transactions, as is often customary, Sunbeam itself drafted form letters and scrambled over a few days to get them signed. Some customers refused. Many others failed to return the documents in time for Sunbeam to recognize the deals as sales under accounting rules. One customer returned the document, but only after typing in the words: "As per our discussion, we have the right to return this within six months." Nonetheless Kersh and Gluck booked the sales and profit from all of the $35 million in bill-and-hold transactions. When outside auditors later reviewed the documents, they reversed a staggering $29 million of the $35 million and shifted the sales to future quarters.

In doing the audit Harlow and Larry Bornstein, his Arthur Andersen colleague, questioned the accounting treatment of some transactions. But in almost every case Gluck defended them on the basis that they were "immaterial" to the overall audit. In one instance, for example, Sunbeam made some consignment sales on a more than $5 million order from a distributor. Harlow believed the sales shouldn't be recorded. Gluck disagreed. The revenue went on the books because Gluck convinced Harlow it was not material to the audit. In another example Sunbeam entered into an agreement to sell its replacement parts inventories to a company and booked an additional $11 million of sales in the fourth quarter even though Sunbeam hadn't yet completely valued the inventory it moved over. Harlow later felt obliged to bring this issue up before the audit committee of the board. Yet the auditor passed on the transaction, he said, because he did not see any "material issue" with the contract.

After a while, of course, immaterial issues pile up and become quite material. In those cases, a controller or chief financial officer might concede a few transactions to get the auditor to sign off on the financial statements. In Sunbeam's case Gluck did not have to disallow any substantive accounting transactions. Harlow and Bornstein largely agreed with Gluck that the questioned transactions were immaterial. Arthur Andersen gave its approving imprimatur to the company's financial documents, and the 10K, the annual report filed with the SEC, was signed by Dunlap, Kersh, and Gluck, who assumed management responsibility for the numbers.

Yet Sunbeam's fourth-quarter financials still disappointed Wall Street. When Dunlap finally reported the numbers on January 28 he turned in earnings of 47 cents per share, a cent short of analysts' expectations. The shortfall caused Sunbeam stock to fall nearly 10 percent, to $37.625. Dunlap publicly attributed the stumble to sales of electric blankets, which were $15 million less than expected. He blamed warm weather in the northeast as well as a shortage of king- and queen-sized blankets to meet customer demand—a consequence of his and Burnett's hasty cutbacks and poor planning.

What investors didn't know would have caused Sunbeam stock to suffer a total collapse and might have caused Dunlap's immediate firing. Shifting the $21.5 million from reserves into income enabled Kersh to disguise the company's calamitous erosion in profit margins. It helped to cover up the deep discounts given to customers by Sunbeam to stuff and load the retail channels. If not for the reserve, the company's pretax margins would have collapsed in the quarter, falling to only 12.1 percent versus the 18.5 percent Kersh reported. Grill sales made under massive discounts, extended credit terms, and "bill-and-hold" transactions artificially inflated the company's fourth quarter sales by $50 million. Without them the quarter's profits would have been reduced by more than $5 million more. Instead of reporting sales that were up 26 percent to $338.1 million, Sunbeam sales would have increased by only 7 percent.

Kersh was right. He was, sadly, the company's biggest profit center.

12

"DON'T YOU THINK I'M A BARGAIN?"

ALL THE UNSEEN TURMOIL and chaos within Sunbeam did little to daunt the enthusiasm of investors. Sunbeam managers and executives struggled mightily to keep up the facade of what the outside world believed was a sleek and fast, hyper-performing company, an enterprise that had been adeptly turned around by a celebrated and charismatic leader. Many of the company's insiders privately joked about the gullibility of Wall Street, and they wondered when and if the whole thing would finally topple like the house of cards it had become.

But the investment community had its hero and savior, and he was Al Dunlap. No one sung his praises more consistently and with greater fervor than Michael Price, the powerful investor, who kept a photo of Dunlap near the computer on his trading desk in Short Hills, New Jersey. The rumpled mutual fund maven even began to use some of Dunlap's pet phrases. "I want the management of a company that we have stock in to have fire in their belly," he said, an expression that often spilled out of Dunlap's own mouth. "That sometimes gets criticized," Price added, "but what does it do at the end of the day? It rewards shareholders."

When reporters asked him how he felt about the people Dunlap threw out of work, Price quickly rose to the defense of the man who

171

had become his favorite chief executive. "Those jobs were gone anyway," he argued, just as Dunlap would. "It's part of our economy. Look at France. They protect jobs there, and the whole economy suffers."

Whenever Sunbeam stock hit a momentary plateau, Price seemed ready to blow still more air into the bubble. "You gotta love Sunbeam," Price boasted to a reporter in the fall of 1997. "It's like owning a football team with Johnny Unitas as quarterback. Wall Street says it's overpriced, and they've been wrong, wrong, wrong. Al is going to do something very smart, you watch."

Sunbeam was no longer a classic value stock, but Price couldn't bring himself to sell down Mutual Shares' 21 percent stake because he thought there was still more upside to be gained. It was as if Price, gripped like so many other investors in the enthusiasm of greed, had forgotten what his old mentor Max Heine had taught him about the true value of a company. Heine, like legendary investor Benjamin Graham, believed that a stock price must always reflect a company's fundamentals, the numbers on its balance sheet and income statement. Analyst William Steele had based his downgrade on those fundamentals. Andrew Shore, reading the numbers and investors' view of them, determined that shareholders hadn't yet caught up to those basics.

Price knew better than anyone that investors often ignored these basics when blinded by exuberance or fear. If Price failed to notice what two Wall Street analysts plainly saw, it was because he was charmed by Dunlap and what he had done to Sunbeam's stock. Every extra dollar of value Dunlap added to Sunbeam enriched Price's funds by more than $17.5 million. By the fall of 1997, with the stock reaching into the low $50s, Price's windfall alone exceeded $650 million on a relatively small company in a mature, low-margin industry under attack by cheap imports.

Greed was good, after all. Price's public admiration of Dunlap was shared by every investor who bet on the celebrity CEO. Dunlap could not walk down a New York City street or thorough an airport without turning heads. For any player of the market, for any person who worshipped greed, Dunlap had become an icon of the decade of Wall Street. He not only talked the nineties game of creating "shareholder value," he walked the fast-money walk. Shareholders at Sunbeam were faring even better than those delirious investors at Scott Paper Co.

who gleefully applauded Dunlap's ability to increase the value of the paper maker by $6.3 billion.

Dunlap breached the common divide between Wall Street and management. His tactics and methods, all calculated to generate fast money, broke the natural antipathy that has long existed between the managers of companies and the investors who plop down their dollars on them as if betting on horses at a racetrack. The money drawn to a Dunlap company was blind to the pain of employee layoffs, the need for long-term investment, and the social responsibilities of a public corporation. This kind of impatient money chased immediate gratification, which is exactly what Dunlap was known to deliver.

As he delivered those unrealistic returns at Sunbeam, other active investors dreamed of getting him into poorly performing companies that they were trying to squeeze for swift profit. One of them was a little-known lieutenant to Hungarian-born financier George Soros named Robert Jermain. Shortly after joining Soros Fund Management as a managing director, Jermain placed a sizable bet on Dunlap at Scott Paper that promptly established him as a man with the golden touch. Jermain's investment on behalf of Soros was no small bet. Over more than a dozen meetings with Dunlap, during which the two formed what Dunlap called a "tight, friendly relationship," he amassed more than 5 million Scott shares, becoming one of the company's largest investors.

Jermain, however, also steered Soros into another company that didn't do nearly as well: Waste Management Inc., a trash hauler based outside Chicago, whose earnings and stock were severely depressed. Without a Dunlap at the helm, Jermain's $1 billion bet in Waste Management with Soros's money was going nowhere. He was not alone. Lens Fund, an activist investment firm that also profited from Dunlap at Scott, invested $20 million in Waste Management.

There were links between the two money managers. Soros was the largest single investor in the Lens Fund, having handed over $50 million to Lens founder Robert A. G. Monks to invest on its behalf. A Harvard-educated lawyer and intellectual, Monks was among the first activists to invest in a handful of laggard companies and then pester them relentlessly into radical changes that would cause their stocks to rise. Directly or more subtly, Monks would exert pressure, hectoring the CEO and his board with letters, meetings, media campaigns, proxy battles, even lawsuits. He was a rebel, a revolutionary capitalist, who believed the way to improve the efficiency of public corporations was to make them more responsive to their shareholders.

For Monks and his Lens colleagues, activism was simply an investment strategy, not unlike Price's value investing or Steinhardt's hedge investing. They considered lobbying a chief executive or board of directors a skill, every bit as vital to maximizing their returns as another investor might consider balance sheet analysis. "Boards of directors are like subatomic particles," said Nell Minow, one of Monks's partners and a prominent and passionate advocate of shareholder rights. "They react different when observed. We observe them very hard."

Monks and Minow were masters at using the media to pressure poorly performing management into action. In his first campaign at mass retailer Sears, Roebuck in 1991, Monks paid for full-page newspaper advertisements that pictured Sears' board of directors under the headline "Non-performing Assets." His steady badgering at American Express, Eastman Kodak, and Westinghouse helped to fuel the dissent that led to the firing of the CEOs at all those corporations.

Ironically, Scott Paper was one of the few companies in which Monks invested that he did not campaign for the ouster of the chief executive. He had met with Scott CEO Philip Lippincott in September 1993 and left confident that Lippincott had a good plan to restore the paper company. Seven months later Lippincott was gone and Dunlap was in the job, much to Monks's surprise and later delight. Monks admired Dunlap, considered him a "godsend," and saw Lens's initial $2 million investment in Scott Paper grow by more than 225 percent thanks to the man. "We made more money in Scott than anything else and had nothing to do with it," Monks said.

From the start of Soros's investment in Lens, there were disagreements within Monks's partnership over how the money should be used. Usually Monks and his partners would decide which companies to target based on screens of total shareholder return. Those results are then compared against industry peer groups. If a corporation miserably trails its competitors, as Scott Paper and Waste Management did, it becomes a potential target for Lens, Inc.

Soros, bringing more cash to the militant money manager than Monks had ever seen, had another idea. Soros's lieutenants initially wanted Lens to stalk the managements of companies it would identify.

Minow, a Chicago-trained lawyer and daughter of former Federal Communications Commission Chairman Newton Minow, objected. She did not want Lens to function as a hired "have-gun-will-travel" for Soros or any other investor. It was a strategy fraught with potential for conflict, and it also reduced their role to one of essentially public relations and lobbying. Monks viewed Minow as "the canary in the coal mine," the moral compass of the organization. She was sensitive to conflicts of interest and insisted on a wide margin of safety. Minow won the argument, though Lens's relationship with the Soros Fund would soon spark another disagreement between her and Monks.

With his investment in Waste Management looking more and more like a massive blunder, Jermain was hoping to enlist Lens's support to make something happen at that company. Waste had just lost a newly recruited chief executive as well as its chief financial officer on October 29. The board had hastily appointed one of its directors, Robert S. "Steve" Miller, as acting chairman and CEO.

In a meeting with Minow, Jermain wanted to get her actively involved in moving Dunlap to rescue his disaster of an investment. He knew that she and Dunlap were somewhat close, having forged a friendship through their governance activities. She had served on the same commission on director pay with him. Indeed, when Dunlap left Scott, he asked her advice on which companies he should examine as a potential employer. Minow sent Dunlap a letter listing a wide range of possibilities: AT&T, Aetna, Digital Equipment, Hart-Marx, Kmart, RJR-Nabisco, Tenneco, Toys "R" Us, Time-Warner, Westinghouse, Woolworth, and even Waste Management. Jermain now hoped that she might use her influence and friendship with Dunlap to move him to his troubled investment.

"It's time to get Al out of Sunbeam and into Waste Management," Jermain told her.

"What do you mean?" asked Minow. "He's got a job he isn't likely to leave."

"We're going to take care of that," Jermain replied. "We're working on something."

Exactly what, he didn't say. But one of Jermain's associates, Brian Corvese, was "working full-time taking care of that problem."

In any case, Waste's previous management had scheduled meetings with its major shareholders in New York. Those sessions were initially prompted by Minow to prod the company into more fundamental changes to fix its inefficient operations. Now that Miller was the new acting CEO, there was a strong possibility that those sessions—a perfect opportunity to promote the idea of drafting Dunlap into Waste—would be canceled. Minow insisted that Miller show up. Otherwise, she menacingly warned, Lens would give his company virtually the same treatment it gave Sears, Roebuck years earlier. Minow told Miller she had reserved space in an upcoming issue of the *Wall Street Journal* to run an ad referring to Waste Management's directors as "long-term liabilities." He agreed to come, the ad space was canceled, and a new and bizarre Dunlap episode would soon unfold.

AS TURNAROUND SPECIALISTS GO, Miller was no slouch. As chief financial officer of Chrysler Corp. in the early 1980s, Miller helped to craft the innovative financial restructuring with the federal government that rescued the auto company from bankruptcy. He was an accomplished and erudite executive who in recent years found himself drafted into unusual service. Before the board of Waste Management named him acting chairman and CEO, he had fulfilled the same role at auto supplier Federal Mogul Corp. Before that, he had been pressed into service as chairman of Morrison Knudsen Corp. when that company went through a tortuous restructuring.

Miller knew Dunlap only by reputation. His estimation of Dunlap's abilities was not favorable. When Miller became acting CEO, he assured the company's 58,000 employees that he was loath to bring in a leader like Dunlap. "I would not support a Chainsaw Al," he said. "This is a great asset. We're not going to rip the place apart and destroy things."

Yet, on November 18, as Miller sat across from some twenty shareholders in two meetings at the New York offices of Kekst & Co., a financial public relations firm, he heard several investors urge him to hire Chainsaw Al. His reaction was immediately negative. Miller considered Dunlap little more than a slash-and-burn opportunist, not a true leader or a builder of businesses. He rejected the idea as soon as it was suggested.

"Look, I know what you're thinking," said Minow at the afternoon meeting. "Your personal style is completely different. But your heart is actually similar. At least you should meet with him."

THOUGH AL DUNLAP *said he grew up poor in Hoboken, he graduated from this very typical suburban high school in Hasbrouck Heights, New Jersey.*

IN HIS *high school yearbook, a clean-cut Dunlap was described as a "grid star, rugged, studious."*

AL DUNLAP *with his mother, Mildred, at West Point Military Academy after graduating in 1960 near the bottom of his class.*

DUNLAP WITH *his most important mentor, Sir James Goldsmith.*

RUSSELL KERSH *was "discovered" by Dunlap at Lily Tulip and became Dunlap's most loyal business confidant at Scott Paper and Sunbeam.*

C. DONALD BURNETT, *a longtime Coopers & Lybrand partner, functioned as Dunlap's personal consultant for downsizing and restructuring for over a decade.*

AL DUNLAP *recapped his life, career, and business philosophies in a 1996 book entitled* Mean Business.

AL DUNLAP *during the Scott Paper era.*
*(Photo by Ed Hille/*Philadelphia Inquirer.*)*

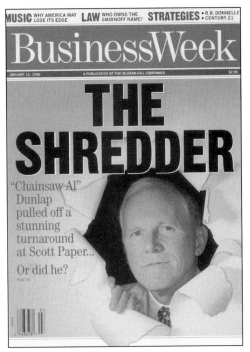

THE AUTHOR'S *first major story on*
Dunlap challenged his assertion that he had
turned around Scott Paper Co. (Courtesy of
Business Week *magazine)*

NEWT WHITE, *a Scott Paper veteran, was*
among Dunlap's first recruits to Sunbeam
and the first key executive to become
disillusioned.(Photo by Jerome Lukowicz)

AL DUNLAP *in a reflective mood.*
(Associated Press photo by Adam Nadel)

MUTUAL FUND MAVEN *Michael Price, dubbed by* Fortune *"the scariest SOB on Wall Street," helped to recruit Dunlap to Sunbeam and became his most vocal champion. (Photo courtesy of Mutual Shares)*

MICHAEL STEINHARDT, *a superstar hedge-fund manager, put up the original money with Michael Price to gain control of Sunbeam in 1990. His personal representative on the Sunbeam board was instrumental in bringing Dunlap to the company. (Photo by John Abbott)*

AL DUNLAP, *in his trademark dark eyeglasses, speaking at Sunbeam's annual shareholders' meeting in 1997. (Associated Press photo by Hans Deryk)*

THE ONLY PROP *Al Dunlap, who enjoyed the nickname "Rambo in Pinstripes," refused to put on during this photo shoot in Sunbeam's boardroom was a bulked-up, rubberized chest. (Photo by Andrew Itkoff)*

PETER LANGERMAN *was Michael Price's top lieutenant and personal representative on the Sunbeam board. (Courtesy of Mutual Shares)*

DUNLAP'S *personal attorney, Howard Kristol, was among his first appointees as a director on the boards of Scott Paper and Sunbeam. (Photo by Douglas Levere)*

THOUGH NOT *a board member, Michael Price (here with Al) helped negotiate Dunlap's employment contract and his purchase of Coleman Co.*

DUNLAP PUT *Faith Whittlesey, former U.S. ambassador to Switzerland, on the Sunbeam board after knowing her for years through Sir James Goldsmith. (Courtesy of American-Swiss Foundation)*

WITHIN TWO MONTHS *of joining Sunbeam, Dunlap invited friend and law professor Charles Elson onto the board. Elson would later make the boardroom motion to fire Dunlap. (Courtesy of Stetson University)*

DUNLAP *and his wife, Judy, walking their beloved German Shepherds. (Photo by Liu Xin)*

DUNLAP *in Sunbeam's product showroom at corporate headquarters in Delray Beach, Florida. (Photo by Liu Xin)*

DUNLAP *hoped to get big growth out of a new air cleaner and a water filter, but both products became huge failures. (Courtesy of Sunbeam Corp.)*

N THEIR *Boca Raton, Florida, home, ...eneath a grand portrait, the Dunlaps share ... kiss. (Photo by Liu Xin)*

DAVID FANNIN, *Sunbeam's general counsel, told the board of directors that the company's sales were far worse than Dunlap and Kersh admitted. (Courtesy of Sunbeam Corp.)*

ANDREW SHORE, *a PaineWebber analyst who followed Sunbeam, was the first on Wall Street to sound the alarm that something was badly amiss. (Photo by Douglas Levere)*

BILLIONAIRE *financier Ronald Perelman, a shrewd dealmaker and investor, engineered a deal that made him Sunbeam's largest single shareholder. (Associated Press photo)*

JERRY LEVIN, *a Perelman loyalist, stepped in as chief executive after the board fired Dunlap. (Courtesy of MacAndrews & Forbes)*

Before the day was over, Minow called Dunlap to let him know that he would soon be getting a call about Waste Management. Miller had already called Dunlap and left a message. That same day Dunlap agreed to meet with Miller at his home five days later on Sunday.

Minow considered her job done. "I got Steve to call Al, and Al to talk to Steve," she said. "I thought okay, I did my job."

But her investment colleague Robert Monks wanted her to fly down to Florida for the meeting between the two executives to help prod the process along.

"You can do it," Monks told her. "You've got a good relationship with both Al and Steve. The Soros people will love us forever. "

"Bob," she said, "I've got them to talk to each other and now I'm out of the business of being a matchmaker."

"You have to do it," pleaded Monks. "You're the only one who could do it, and it would make our number one client happy."

Minow, however, wouldn't budge. "I'm not going to do it," she insisted.

When Monks asked why, Minow expressed her doubts over Dunlap's ability to get the job done. He was generating huge amounts of publicity for himself and making too many egotistical comments that made her question whether he could do with Waste Management what he had done at Scott. Just as she had won the earlier disagreement with Monks, Minow won this one as well.

Miller, meantime, began to prepare for his own private meeting with Dunlap. He bought a copy of Dunlap's book. He read a few more newspaper clippings about the man. And he had a telephone conversation with a member of Kimberly-Clark's board of directors. The board member had a rather unkind view of Dunlap's management style. He told Miller that to inflate Scott Paper's profits, Dunlap had stripped operating management to the bare bones and eliminated all scheduled maintenance on the costly machinery in the paper company's plants.

Nonetheless, to keep his investors happy, Miller was on an airplane on November 23, reading through Dunlap's book while flying from his home in Oregon to Fort Lauderdale. A driver and car met him at the airport on a sunny Sunday and quickly drove him to the Boca Raton Resort & Club, a vast complex of Mediterranean-styled homes with barrel-tile roofs, immaculate golf courses, and clay tennis courts.

Miller was surprised by the extraordinary security precautions he had to go through to reach Dunlap's home at 422 Addison Park Lane. First his driver had to pass through a security gate at the perimeter of the resort. Then he had to drive through an electronically controlled gate to get to the exclusive fifteen-home compound of Addison Estates and Dunlap's street. Finally he had to go through yet another security gate to gain access to Dunlap's driveway.

The moment Miller stepped from the car, all he could hear were dogs viciously barking as if they were preparing for an enemy assault. When Miller reached the Moorish-style house, Dunlap and his wife were at the door holding back Brit and Cadet, their barking German shepherds, on taut leashes. Once the dogs were told that Miller was "okay," they became docile, were taken off their leashes and allowed to roam the vast 6,500-square-foot house on their own.

Dunlap gripped Miller's hand tightly, and the Waste Management director let Dunlap know that they shared an unusual connection. Miller was on the board of Pope and Talbot, a company that now owned the paper mill in Eau Claire, Wisconsin, where Dunlap had worked three decades earlier for Ely Meyer's Sterling Pulp & Paper. The two men settled into an upstairs sitting area around a coffee table where Miller heard Dunlap retell, in a voice several decibels above normal, many of the stories he had just read himself on the flight.

When it came to the Waste Management job, Dunlap left no uncertainty about his interest. Dunlap said he was trying to sell Sunbeam and might pull off a sale in the near future. If so, that would free him for something else. "He said he thought this was an opportunity that would be very suited for his talents, and he would be very interested in it," recalls Miller.

It was a friendly visit. Dunlap gave Miller a detailed tour of his home, guiding him through all the rooms, past the pool with its lions sculpted from stone standing guard. He proudly showed him the crest of a lion's head painted on the wall over the entrance to his home office, the place he called the "lion's den." Wherever Dunlap brought him, Miller noticed that there hung at least one picture or painting of the man and his dogs, a testament to his ego and his love for the dogs. Yet Dunlap was a gracious and engaging host, and Judy Dunlap served them an agreeable, if no-frills, lunch of sandwiches and potato chips. They ate the food around the glass-topped table in the kitchen.

However, nothing he heard during his near three-hour visit with Dunlap changed his mind about the man. Miller left the house after telling Dunlap he certainly was a candidate for the Waste Management job, but he did not offer him the job and had little intention of doing so. Dunlap was not pleased. He expected to be wooed and flattered by Miller, not merely visited, and he soon called Soros's people in New York to complain about Miller's look-him-over visit.

On his flight back to Oregon, Miller mulled over his doubts. "Is he a one-trick pony?" he asked himself. Miller certainly thought so because Dunlap never built any company he had ever worked for. "With the warning I got from Kimberly-Clark, I wondered if he had a sustainable business model," he says. "I was afraid these fund managers simply wanted to see the stock pop before the chickens came out to roost." Miller decided to check out other candidates who, as he put it, "build organizations rather than destroy them."

Two weeks after the trip, Miller was at a dinner for shareholders in Boston organized by Michael E. Hoffman, an analyst with Credit Suisse First Boston Corp. Asked by shareholders about Dunlap again, Miller said, "I'm not sure if he's the right person for the job, but he is campaigning for it."

Hoffman gave Miller's comment wide circulation when he issued a report on Waste Management. Suddenly Sunbeam stock began tumbling on fears that Dunlap was about to jump ship. The remark angered Dunlap, who on December 19 issued a statement of his own in which he denied campaigning for the Waste Management job, even though he had spoken directly with Soros's lieutenants about the position. "That statement is completely untrue and a total fabrication and Mr. Miller knows it," Dunlap said. "I can only conclude that he and others are attempting to trade on my name in order to prop up their sagging stock . . . I clearly am the CEO that [Waste Management] needs; however, with their current board culture and the attitude of Mr. Miller and others like him, I would not consider heading that company." Fannin had to convince Dunlap not to include in the press release still further attacks on Miller, including one in which he laughingly called him a "Dunlap wannabe."

Stunned by the statement and the publicity it generated, including a lengthy front-page story in the *Wall Street Journal*, Miller called Dunlap's office to apologize.

"I'm sorry," said Denise Valek, Dunlap's secretary, "he won't take your call."

UNBEKNOWNST TO MILLER, however, he had handed Dunlap a valuable card to play in a game with Michael Price, for there was no way that the investor was going to lose his corporate version of Johnny Unitas. Only a month earlier, in October, Dunlap had informed Langerman that he wanted a new compensation deal, even though he was only fifteen months into his three-year employment contract. Dunlap's first package, largely negotiated by Langerman, was not only extremely rich, helping to set the stage for an even bigger contract now, it was also severely flawed because all of Dunlap's 2.5 million stock options vested in the first two years. That meant that Dunlap essentially would work the third year of his contract for only his $1 million-a-year salary.

To Dunlap, little in life was more important than money. As he told associates, "I never made a dollar that I didn't love like a brother." He meant it. Yet he did not live an exceptionally extravagant life. He did not fill his home with pricey antiques or fine art. He did not gamble his money on risky ventures or investments. Other than a few million invested in Sunbeam stock, he put virtually all his money into risk-free Treasury bonds during the biggest bull market in the history of the stock exchange. He told one Sunbeam colleague that stock was a "fool's game."

Indeed, Dunlap would strangely husband his dollars. His friends thought him a cheap and stingy man, one who would venture to the main building of the Boca Raton Resort and Club to read the newspapers and magazines because they were free there. His colleagues and acquaintances said he would fight you for a nickel on the table. When his only son, Troy, reached the age of eighteen, he sent his final child support payment to his first wife with the word "maturation" scribbled on the check. All told, Dunlap paid less than $20,000 of child support for a son he had left at the age of two. When Troy later wanted to see his father as a teenager, the boy and his mother had to pay the airfare for the trip. Dunlap didn't even cough up a penny of the boy's college tuition. In 1997 he donated his artificial Christmas tree to the company so that he could buy a new one for his own home and put it on his corporate expense account. He displayed such unusual frugality because money was important to him only if it could be piled high and counted.

"How do you know when you're rich?" he asked colleagues and associates. "It's when you can't spend the interest on the interest on the interest. Russ," he said, turning to Kersh, "tell them. I can't spend the interest on the interest on the interest."

Money was the very index of his success. He measured his self-worth by it. He measured the distance he had traveled by it, "from Hoboken to Palm Beach," he proudly told friends. Never mind that he lived in Boca Raton. "Would I love to be a billionaire?" he asked. "Yeah, because it would say I achieved [something] that everybody said was beyond somebody like me." Friends said Dunlap was angry at *Forbes* magazine because it failed to include him on its annual listing of the richest people in the United States. While most dreaded the publicity, Dunlap craved it. He told colleagues *Forbes* failed to properly calculate his net worth, which he claimed to be as high as $600 million. Now he wanted more.

As his hopes for the company's sale began to fade, Dunlap realized that a quick exit from Sunbeam wasn't likely. If he had to pursue a strategy of acquisitions, Dunlap wanted new deals for himself, Kersh, and Fannin. For running a relatively inconsequential company with little more than $1 billion in sales, Dunlap was insisting on a contract that would pay him more than the chief executives got at General Electric, General Motors, Microsoft, or Intel. But his most outrageous demand was for another mammoth grant of free stock, with no restrictions attached, currency that virtually no chief executive ever receives. In Dunlap's first contract, he got 1 million free shares. This time he wanted even more, and he wanted a sure thing.

His initial demands were so staggering that Michael Price decided to negotiate the contract with Dunlap himself during Price's weekend trips to his Palm Beach, Florida, home in the winter months. The renowned investor had become so sensitive about losing his favorite CEO to Soros that he even began to publicly belittle Soros's investment in Waste Management as a sorry attempt to replicate his own investment strategy. "That guy buys a huge stake, forces them to do a buyback, a management change. They do it, and the stock is nearly ten bucks below where he bought because the asset values aren't there," Price told a journalist. "A lot of people make mistakes and think they can push companies around, but they haven't bought the stock cheaply enough."

Desperate to keep Dunlap in the job, the value investor was not able to come up with a value contract for Dunlap. Price was able to shift more of the free stock that Dunlap wanted into stock options. In any case the final outlines of the deal were dizzying: Price agreed to double Dunlap's base salary to $2 million a year. He handed him 300,000 free shares, worth more than $11 million, as well as options to buy 3.75 million shares, one of the most lucrative option grants ever awarded. Under the deal, Kersh's annual salary would more than double, to $875,000 from $425,000. He would get 150,000 shares of restricted stock, worth over $5.5 million, and 1.125 million stock options. Fannin's annual pay would rise to $595,000 from $313,233. He would get 30,000 shares of restricted stock, worth $1.1 million, and 750,000 stock options.

Everyone on the board, with the exception of Dunlap and Kersh, thought the contract's numbers were obnoxiously high. Though he and the other directors were elated with the company's performance, director Charles Elson believed Dunlap's first contract had rewarded him amply. At a January 20 dinner with Dunlap and his wife at New York's Four Seasons restaurant, Elson told the CEO he was concerned with the "optics" of the deal and openly wondered if it was truly necessary.

Dunlap blew up. "If I don't get the contract," he said, "I'm going to walk. I'm serious. There's a world of opportunity out there. People are interested in me. Either get this done or I'll go. I want that contract."

Dunlap, however, had no desire to leave South Florida or the lifestyle he enjoyed there to take on a new challenge. Indeed, he seldom traveled to Sunbeam's plants or its customers, or anywhere else for that matter, other than to New York to go on television or meet with Wall Street analysts or reporters. He had no real offers from anyone, including Waste Management, because Miller was determined not to hire a man for whom he had little respect.

Over the weeks since the contract first came up in October, Dunlap had made similar threats to Langerman as Dunlap and Price discussed the shape of the package. Yet if Dunlap and Kersh walked, Price feared, Sunbeam stock would lose its rather sizable Dunlap premium. At a minimum that was worth $1 billion and possibly $2 billion in market value. The damage to the company's stock, he believed, would be far more substantial than the cost of the contract.

Still, the directors on the board's compensation committee—Langerman, Elson, and Faith Whittlesey—had serious reservations. At a telephonic committee meeting on January 26, Kersh gave them further pause when he explained that the contracts would result in a $31 million charge to Sunbeam's earnings in the first quarter. It was an extraordinary write-off, one of the largest ever for executive compensation. Though accounting rules allow companies to hand out stock options to executives as if they are free, with no impact on the income statement, cash or outright grants of stock must immediately be charged to earnings. Since the package would award Dunlap 300,000 free shares of stock, Kersh 150,000 shares, and Fannin 30,000 shares, the contracts would have an immediate impact on Sunbeam's bottom line. The cost of those shares would have to be deducted from Sunbeam's earnings, along with the company's agreement to pay Dunlap's income taxes on his perks and earlier restricted stock grants. Dunlap told Langerman that the reimbursement on taxes was non-negotiable.

When the three directors agreed to delay a vote on the matter, Kersh threw a wicked tantrum.

"Goddamn it," he said, "we've worked really hard. Don't screw with us, or we'll leave."

He stormed out of the meeting, leaving Fannin on the telephone with the three dazed directors. All of them wanted more time to think about the deal and its consequences, though they clearly acknowledged that Dunlap had the upper hand. He was in demand, as the dance with Waste Management had proven. They believed there was no one else in the organization who could succeed him because Dunlap had rarely paid any attention to management development. Unaware of the accounting games and chaos within the company, they believed he had turned in a spectacular performance. Still, they refused to immediately vote on the package.

Though accustomed to Dunlap's volatile personality, they had never seen Kersh lose it. Elson soon called Kersh up to find out why he had overreacted.

"What's going on?" Elson asked.

"There's a lot going on here," Kersh said. "We're working very hard. There's a lot of pressure."

Elson explained that as a lawyer he just needed to stew on it. The delay had nothing to do with a lack of confidence in him or Dunlap. It was a big package with a major impact on earnings. He said their decision wouldn't prevent them from voting on it the following week when the full board planned to meet at Sunbeam headquarters in Florida.

The evening before the February 3 board session, the directors converged with Dunlap and his wife for dinner at a Chinese restaurant in the Boca Raton Marriott complex. After the meal Langerman, Elson, and Whittlesey remained to discuss the deal yet again for about an hour.

Though all three were uneasy about the contract's size, they took the threats of both Dunlap and Kersh seriously.

"It's stiff," said Elson. "It's really high."

"Yeah, but you should have seen where it started," replied Langerman. "Michael thinks this is as low as we'll get him.

"I know these are big numbers, very big numbers," he added. "But what is the alternative? Let's assume Al picks up his chips and walks and his senior management team does the same. Where are we and what are our alternatives and options for the company?"

They agreed. They believed he had them over the proverbial barrel. The board had far more leverage than it imagined. If Dunlap resigned before July 18, 1998, he would have forfeited the still unvested portion of his original stock options and his restricted stock grant, a full third of the total equity package. It was highly unlikely that Dunlap would walk away from what was then worth $35.7 million to him. It was just as unlikely that Dunlap would allow himself to lose tens of millions more if Sunbeam stock lost its "Dunlap premium." Because of restrictions on the sale of stock by insiders, Dunlap would have had no choice except to sell his Sunbeam shares after quitting his job—after the shares would presumably tumble because of his departure.

Taking his threat seriously, however, the directors badly misjudged their own negotiating position. Besides, both Elson and Whittlesey took some comfort in knowing that at least Price, the company's largest single shareholder, had negotiated the contract with Dunlap. If the owner of more than 17 percent of the company agrees that Dunlap is worth the money, they reasoned, who are we to say no?

Before the vote the next day in the second-floor boardroom at Delray Beach headquarters, Dunlap was at his very best. He spoke convincingly of building Sunbeam into a larger and more powerful consumer-goods company. He spoke movingly about himself and his career.

"This is my swan song," he told the directors. "This is my last big deal. By approving the contracts, you'll be sending a signal to the market. You'll assure the marketplace we'll be around to build this company into a powerhouse of brands."

After the speech, Dunlap and Kersh left the boardroom. Whatever concerns were raised by the directors were swept aside because they unanimously voted in favor of the contracts. Dunlap, whose actual net worth probably exceeded $200 million, had gained the biggest of a long string of oversize compensation packages he had ever received.

Elson's early concerns about the "optics" of the package proved right. The deal was roundly criticized once it became known. "Dunlap is no Rambo in Pinstripes," said Graef "Bud" Crystal, a well-known critic of excessive pay. "He is, rather, Wally Peepers wearing an ill-fitting Rambo costume." The new contract, negotiated by value investor Price, would award Dunlap $46.5 million if Sunbeam's stock rose only 5.5 percent a year, the same level of return investors could make on a risk-free Treasury bond, estimated Crystal.

In a conference call with Wall Street analysts on March 2, when Dunlap's new contract was announced, the pay package quickly came up. Bear, Stearns's Constance M. Maneaty, who waited longer than any other influential analyst to upgrade the stock after Dunlap's arrival, awkwardly addressed it.

"Can you talk a little bit about your employment agreement?" she asked. "What the terms of it are, and if there is anything in there in terms of options that might have an impact on earnings?"

"You know, firstly, as I say in my book, you can't overpay a great executive," Dunlap answered. "And being the biggest bargain in corporate America . . . essentially my contract is very, very heavily oriented toward stock options and stock, as are all of my contracts. I still don't get an annual incentive or a long-term incentive, but a very heavy stock position. This will be filed by the end of the week, with the 10K [the annual statement every public company must file on its business operations]."

"Hmmmm," said Maneaty, clearly frustrated by Dunlap's response. Neither he nor Kersh would disclose what they and the board already knew: that the contracts would result in a material charge to the company's earnings in the first quarter, a write-off equal to nearly a third of Sunbeam's entire net income the previous year. After an awkward pause, Maneaty simply gave up, deciding it was worthless to pursue the issue.

"Okay," she said with resignation.

"Don't you think I'm a bargain, Connie?" Dunlap asked.

"Well," she responded, "you're one of a kind."

"That's a fact," Dunlap agreed.

13

"A TRIPLE!"

IN THE FACE OF improbable odds, Al Dunlap still clung to the dream that he could sell Sunbeam and make a wealthy and triumphant exit from the appliance company. That was always Dunlap's intent, the way he meant to unlock his own millions of dollars of profit so he could march off to his next challenge.

All of Dunlap's hopes to pull this off rested with William H. Strong, the unflappable Morgan Stanley investment banker, whose job was mission impossible. Dunlap had been so skillful in touting the company's "turnaround" and Kersh had been so adept in presenting the financial results that Sunbeam stock traded at too high a premium to interest anyone in buying the company.

A handsome man with salt-and-pepper hair, Strong was never a Master of the Universe star during all the Wall Street deal making of the 1980s. He just didn't fit the picture. Strong lacked the Ivy League pedigree that Dunlap so often poked fun at. He had earned his accounting degree at Purdue University, before picking up a master's in management at Northwestern—not Harvard or Wharton. He prided himself on honesty and integrity, always putting his clients' interests ahead of his own. After being described as "chubby" in *Barbarians at the Gate*, an ego-bruised Strong took up running and lifting weights to shed a good number of pounds.

Still, he had been at the center of some monster deals, helping to engineer the $6 billion sale of Fort Howard paper to James River and serving as the lead honcho for Sears, Roebuck in its $20 billion spin-off of insurance subsidiary Allstate in 1995. The affable Indiana-born banker and former accountant was even a bit player in the largest takeover in Wall Street history, the dramatic battle for RJR-Nabisco in 1988. He tried to put together a joint $3 billion bid for Nabisco between Solomon Brothers and Hanson Trust, the British conglomerate, to counter the attempt by the cookie company's management to buy out Nabisco. It was gutsy, but too late. The day he was going to quietly begin buying a position in Nabisco was the same day that financier Henry Kravis made his takeover bid public. It was less than a year later that Strong hooked up with Dunlap and Sir James Goldsmith, who was winding down his holdings.

Most of the Goldsmith work was done not by Strong, who then headed up Solomon's fledging mergers and acquisitions group, but by a highly ambitious and more junior member of the Solomon team, Mark C. Davis. A bright dealmaker educated at Dartmouth College, Davis eventually helped to orchestrate what many considered a deal made in heaven. Goldsmith would trade his Crown-Zellerbach timberlands for Hanson's 49 percent stake in Newmont Mining, a gold company. The $1.3 billion transaction, which included the purchase of a Goldsmith company in the Cayman Islands, saved Sir James some $300 million in taxes. The "trees-for-gold swap" was not only a brilliant deal, but, more importantly, it made Dunlap something of a hero in Goldsmith's eyes because he got much of the credit for it.

The transaction cemented what would become a lucrative and highly beneficial relationship between Dunlap and Davis. When Strong quit Solomon for Morgan Stanley, it was Davis who led Sir James's next big move, the sale of half his stake in Newmont for $600 million, even though other Wall Street bankers had more expertise in selling equity. When Dunlap moved to Australia to work for Kerry Packer, he turned to Davis again for the spin-off of his U.S. interests under Valassis Communications Inc. The initial public offering of Valassis raised $1 billion for Packer.

Davis not only assumed the role of Dunlap's banker, he became a loyal friend, talking up Dunlap with headhunters and boardroom directors to help his client win his next job at Scott Paper. Davis even prepped his client for his meeting with Gary Roubous, the Scott director who headed the board's search committee. Once at Scott, Dunlap turned to Davis again to sell the company's publishing papermaker,

S. D. Warren Co. Scott had already hired Goldman Sachs & Co., but Dunlap tore in half his copy of the firm's exclusive contract so Davis could get in on the action. Davis responded with a $1.6 billion deal that Dunlap later called "the linchpin of my strategy" because it allowed him to clean most of the debt off Scott's balance sheet.

Davis then pulled off the transaction that made Dunlap a true Wall Street celebrity: he convinced Kimberly-Clark to buy Scott, a deal that garnered one of the largest investment banking fees Solomon ever collected, $28 million. Davis even had a hand in working out the juicy details of the severance and noncompete pacts for Dunlap, Kersh, and four other top members of his team.

When the opportunity to join Sunbeam came up, Davis intervened again, calling both Peter Langerman and Michael Steinhardt to recommend Dunlap for the job and helping his client cut the first rich compensation contract with Sunbeam's big investors. It was no surprise, then, that Dunlap would bring Sunbeam's investment banking business to Davis, who had now left Solomon and moved to Chase Securities to build a mergers and acquisitions business from scratch.

His first Sunbeam deal, however, turned out to be his last. He sold the company's outdoor furniture business to U.S. Industries Inc., but was able to get only half to a third of what Dunlap wanted. After taking a write-off of $39.1 million on a business that had only $227.5 million in sales, Sunbeam had to book another write-down of $22.5 million after ditching the furniture unit because Davis could get only $60 million in cash for it. Dunlap somehow believed Davis didn't work hard enough on the sale and had taken him for granted, and was determined to teach the banker a lesson.

A month after Sunbeam took the second write-down on the furniture business, Bill Strong got an unexpected phone call in his office on the thirty-seventh floor of a nondescript skyscraper on South Lasalle Street in Chicago. It was Kersh, who wanted to know if Strong was interested in bidding for the opportunity to get Sunbeam's investment banking business. Strong jumped at the chance. He had assumed his old colleague Davis had Dunlap's business locked up. So did Davis.

Strong marshaled the firepower of what he thought was an unbeatable team, including partners James Stynes and Robert Kitz in Morgan's New York offices. They flew down to Sunbeam's Delray Beach headquarters on April 22 and put on a polished show for the business. By then Sunbeam stock was trading as high as $38 a share. It had tripled in value since Dunlap joined, while the shares of the Standard & Poor's 500 had risen by not much more than 20 percent.

With Sunbeam stock trading that high, the team concluded a sale of the company wasn't going to be in the cards. Instead of trying to persuade Dunlap they could flip Sunbeam for a quick profit, they argued in favor of an acquisition. They ran through a list of eighteen potential targets, reviewing the strategic and financial "fit" each one had with Sunbeam. They told Dunlap that three of the eighteen companies had the "highest availability." One of the three was Coleman Co., the camping equipment maker.

Dunlap encouraged the team to talk to possible acquirers, but Strong told him the likelihood of a Sunbeam sale was very small. The investment banker agreed to pursue the possibility for Dunlap, but he urged him to focus on acquisitions. "The right thing to do for the shareholders," said Strong, "is to make an acquisition if you can do to it what you've done to Sunbeam."

Everyone was impressed. In typical Dunlap fashion, however, the Sunbeam chairman squeezed every page of work product out of the team for months on end without a fee, dangling in front of them the prospect of getting all of his business. Though it would take Sunbeam until October to formally announce Morgan Stanley's hiring "to explore strategic options," Strong, Stynes, and Kitz had already logged hundreds of hours on Dunlap's behalf over nearly six months.

The group worked overtime to come up with a buyer, calling on a network of contacts around the world at Gillette, Black & Decker, Brunswick, Rubbermaid, Maytag, Whirlpool, the Dutch electronics giant Philips, Electrolux AB of Stockholm, and Matsushita of Japan. The Morgan team even tried to renew the interest that the France-based SEB group expressed years earlier when Merrill Lynch shopped the company under Schipke. No deal. Even though Dunlap would later mislead a journalist into reporting that Philips was keen on buying Sunbeam for more than $50 a share, no one was the least bit interested.

What Davis had told Dunlap and Kersh early on was true. Sunbeam could not be sold at a price north of $30. Anxious for a quick exit, Kersh had long ago become exasperated by Dunlap's constant trumpeting of the stock. All his pronouncements and chest thumping had pushed the value of the company to unrealistically high levels, from $1 billion to more than $4.1 billion. "Goddamn it," Kersh told some of his colleagues, "if I could just get Al to shut up. If this thing was where it ought to be in the high $20s, we could get this thing sold." Regardless of Wall Street's lovefest with Dunlap, Sunbeam simply wasn't worth the lofty $45 price it commanded by the fall of 1997 in an irrational market.

Within the industry, moreover, rumors circulated that Dunlap's self-styled turnaround was all smoke and mirrors. Many potential buyers were justifiably skeptical of Dunlap and his reputation. They had watched Kimberly-Clark become mired in trouble since it acquired Scott Paper and wanted no part of a company run by a slash-and-burn manager. No one—not a single potential suitor—bothered to look through the more than dozen boxes of Sunbeam documents the company had shipped to Skadden Arps in New York for a "due diligence" review.

Strong's failure to produce even a modicum of interest enraged Dunlap. In numerous meetings, on the phone and in person, Dunlap would upbraid and beseech him to find a buyer for the company.

"Raise your game," he intoned. "Strong, goddamn it, raise your game. Don't be a white-shoe banker. Goddamn it, look what you've got here. You've got a turned-around company. You've got a perfect company. Anybody could sell this."

Often he would tell Strong that he had fought to hire Morgan Stanley, which was not true. He told Strong that they could have just as easily hired Goldman Sachs, which also was not true, because that investment banking firm had declined an invitation to compete for the business due to a conflict with another client in the same industry.

"Bill, we go back a long way," Dunlap told him. "Don't let me down! Goddamn it, get the job done."

Strong, as Midwestern calm and reassuring as Dunlap was Hoboken volatile and unsettling, had had all kinds of people yell and scream at him over the years. He had arrived home to all types of irate telephone calls from clients. It was part of his job, he thought, not to get rattled. So he calmly absorbed the blows, just like everyone else who learned to withstand a Dunlap assault. The survivors understood that you took the punch, kept your hands down, and never fought back.

Even though Strong had told Dunlap from the start that chances of a Sunbeam sale were slim, the investment banker assured Dunlap that he and his partners were making every effort to find a buyer. Often Strong would tell Dunlap that he knew this or that person and could make the contact that might result in a sale. He told Dunlap that John J. McDonough, the chairman of Newell Co., a consumer products company that Dunlap viewed as a potential acquirer of Sunbeam, was a neighbor of his in Lake Forest, Illinois. Amused by all the names dropped by Strong, Dunlap quipped that he wondered "how many houses away from Bill do you have to be to get counted as one of his neighbors."

"You and your white-shoe buddies are supposedly the best in the business," Dunlap told him. "The board wanted to hire somebody else, but I went to bat for you. I got you this assignment, and now you're letting me down."

"Al," Strong mildly replied, "we're putting a lot of resources into this. It's difficult for a lot of reasons."

"You guys are supposed to be so great," Dunlap screeched at him during one telephone conversation. "Are you telling me that in this entire universe you can't find a single buyer interested in this company? You're incompetent. I'm going to give you guys a black eye on Wall Street. It's all your fault. This is a great company for somebody to buy, and it's your job to find them. Goddamn it, do it!"

Strong explained that some companies, particularly Gillette, wanted to see a longer period of sustained growth in profits and sales before they would even think about a deal. The investment banker clearly touched a raw nerve with his explanation. He learned, rather quickly, that it did not take much to set Dunlap off. For he interpreted Strong's reply as a challenge to him and to what he had convinced himself was a Sunbeam turnaround. How dare they think that Sunbeam wasn't completely revived, Dunlap said.

"I'm not the person to run the status quo," he said. "I make an obscene amount of money for what I do, and then I move on and do it again."

WITHOUT A BUYER Dunlap wasn't going to move anywhere. He was stuck. Though Dunlap still held out hope of a sale, Strong increasingly attempted to steer him in the direction he always believed was the only option: Sunbeam, Strong explained, could use its high-priced stock as currency to acquire other consumer product companies and play the role of a consolidator in a highly fragmented industry. Sunbeam could cobble together a stable of valuable brand names, use its distribution network to expand sales and strengthen its relationships with the massive retailers like Wal-Mart and Kmart. It made great strategic sense, even though it failed to satisfy Dunlap's desire for a quick exit. So the Morgan team went to work compiling an even broader matrix of potential takeover candidates.

They mulled over tiny franchises, like First Alert smoke alarms and Signature Brands' Mr. Coffee, as well as larger and less likely targets such as Whirlpool Corp. and Maytag Corp. Yet, with Dunlap in the picture, even an acquisition strategy wasn't all that easy to execute. "As the bankers approached different companies, many of them told us to go pound sand," said one associate involved in the effort. "They would rather sell to the devil than to Al Dunlap. Because after you sell, you have to listen to Dunlap tell the world what a lousy manager you were. None of the companies that would create real value would talk to us."

At one point Dunlap even contemplated a hostile takeover of Black & Decker, whose management had no interest in being acquired by Chainsaw. The Morgan team, however, thought it would be like trying to take over the Alamo. The appliance maker was incorporated in Maryland, where state law made hostile buyouts a difficult and costly proposition. It just didn't seem worth the money and trouble, so they passed on that idea as well.

One day Dunlap's secretary raced through the halls, frantically looking for him. On the phone was David Whitwam, the chairman and chief executive of Whirlpool, the Michigan-based producer of large appliances. He was responding to a letter drafted by Morgan Stanley for Dunlap to explore whether the company was interested in negotiating some kind of combination.

When Whitwam came on the line, Dunlap put him on the speaker phone so Kersh and Fannin could hear the conversation. A wicked grin broke out on Dunlap's face as they heard Whitwam stiffly read a dull legal statement that had clearly been drafted by Whirlpool's lawyers. "We have received your expression of inquiry in our company," said Whitwam nervously. "We have no interest in it."

When he hung up, Dunlap chuckled indulgently, pleased in the knowledge that he had at least spooked a rival, however improbable it was that much smaller Sunbeam could ever attempt a takeover of a company that was four to five times its size. Yet Whitwam's obvious jitters again showed just how big and powerful a figure Dunlap had become in the world of business. He was feared not only by the people who worked for him but by those who thought there was even a slim chance that Dunlap could become part of their business life.

Ironically, the first serious possibility emerged not because of Strong and his Morgan team but because of Mark Davis, the investment banker Dunlap dumped in favor of Strong. During the summer of 1997 Davis had first raised the possibility of Sunbeam acquiring Coleman, the camping-gear maker controlled by billionaire financier Ronald Perelman. Initially the idea was dismissed out of hand by Dunlap, who so badly wanted to sell rather than buy. That's why Strong didn't initially pursue it, even though Coleman was on his original list of eighteen possible acquisitions back on April 22. Besides, Perelman's in-house investment banker, the chain-smoking Jim Maher, formerly of First Boston, suggested to Davis that it would take a large premium to get Coleman. Maher suggested he had an offer for Coleman of $28 a share from Brunswick Corp. When asked, a director of Brunswick said the company had no interest in Coleman, whose shares were then trading in the low teens.

Over the intervening months, however, Davis kept contacting Dunlap and Kersh, trying to play matchmaker between the two oversized egos. Davis's motives were simple. Davis hoped to capture Dunlap's business, even though Strong and his team had been working for months. He knew Perelman wanted out of Coleman, and he believed it could make a good fit with Sunbeam. So Davis kept plugging away, trying to get a deal off the ground from the sidelines, even though he was retained by neither Sunbeam nor Coleman.

Perelman, who had once considered hiring Dunlap to run one of his companies, viewed him as a tough guy who knew how to make money. When Dunlap was scouting around for quote blurbs to put on the jacket of his book, Perelman obliged with a laudatory comment. "Lively, funny and provocative," he wrote. "No one feels neutral about Al Dunlap—you either love his ideas about running a business or hate them."

Perelman, of course, could have just as easily made the same statement about himself. The brusque and balding fifty-five-year-old tycoon was a feared corporate terrorist and raider who amassed one of the world's largest fortunes through ruthless dealmaking. His business conquests amounted to a vast hodgepodge of companies, from Marvel Entertainment Group to Revlon Inc. An enormous cigar seemed perpetually implanted in his mouth, and a seemingly computer-generated young model always seemed to be on the arm of the thrice-married financier.

Of all the companies in his MacAndrews & Forbes empire, run out of a townhouse on New York's Upper East Side, Coleman was hardly a gem. Perelman had picked up the Kansas-based company in 1989, when its management was attempting to take it private through a leveraged buyout. Perelman jumped in with a $545 million all-cash offer and won control. Then, in 1992, he sold a small portion of the company to the public, at just under $13 a share. Five years later the badly stumbling company was still trading in the teens, roiled with financial troubles. Perelman owned 82 percent of Coleman, with the rest of the stock held by only 700 or so shareholders.

Coleman's camping products competed at the low end of the scale, not unlike Sunbeam's small appliances, where the margins are razor-thin and larger retailers pressed hard for every extra penny of profit. Earlier in the year, news reports surfaced that the camping equipment company was near bankruptcy. It had lost $41.9 million in 1996 and was well on its way to a $2.5 million loss in 1997. Coleman, which made write-offs and restructuring charges a common occurrence, hadn't reported a profit since 1995. The company had had to amend its credit agreements at least twice in the past year and one-half. Perelman's stake was pledged to the banks in exchange for debt, and the $350 million in goodwill on Coleman's books completely wiped out its $290 million in shareholder equity. Though there was talk on Wall Street of a turnaround by Jerry W. Levin, the former Revlon chairman whom Perelman installed as Coleman's CEO in February, it had yet to materialize. Indeed, Perelman had chided Levin over the results, asking him why he couldn't work the same kind of turnaround magic for which Dunlap had become famous.

All of investment banker Davis's behind-the-scenes nudging came to nothing until early one Saturday evening in late November when Perelman's consignore, Howard Gittis, received an unexpected telephone call from Michael Price at his winter home in Palm Beach, Florida. A short and stocky lawyer from Philadelphia, Gittis had long been Perelman's most trusted confidant and partner. He had known Price for years, even having represented the investor's mentor, Max Heine. And Price went way back with Perelman, having known his father, Ray, and having invested from time to time in Perelman-controlled companies. Gittis's Palm Beach residence, a handsome historical home, was only a couple of blocks away from Price's retreat.

"What are you doing?" asked Price.

"I'm about to go out to dinner," replied Gittis.

"Well, why don't you stop by for a drink?"

It was not unusual for the two men to socialize every now and then. So Gittis, along with a lady friend, got into his car and drove over to Price's house. Walking up to the door, Gittis was surprised to hear loud voices flow out of an open window. He wasn't expecting to meet anyone other than Price. Instead, he found Price quickly introducing Al Dunlap, Russ Kersh, and a woman who was Price's cousin.

Gittis had met Dunlap before, through Mark Davis. But he had never met Kersh. "It seemed really strange," thought Gittis. "What the hell am I doing here having a social drink with Dunlap? We made a lot of chit-chat and then we broke up and went to dinner."

The next week, Price called Gittis again, and it became clear to him why the mutual fund maven wanted him to meet Dunlap.

"Al," Price said, "would really like to buy Coleman."

"Mike, you know, it's really early," said Gittis. "The turnaround has just started, and the stock market isn't reflecting the true value of what Jerry [Levin] has done there."

"Al is really interested," Price said. "Real interested."

"It's too early to talk about it because we're going to look at what its value is eighteen months from now, and you're going to look at what it traded at yesterday," said Gittis. "It's going to be hard to do a deal."

"Well, Al wants to try," said Price. "Can you get us some information?"

The telephone conversation led to a New York meeting in early December between Kersh, Fannin, and Price's right-hand man and Sunbeam director Peter Langerman with Coleman CEO Levin, general counsel Paul E. Shapiro, and chief financial officer Steven F.

Kaplan. The session went extraordinarily well. The Sunbeam team left the pow-wow with the clear impression that Perelman wanted to sell Coleman. The Perelman crowd believed that Dunlap could possibly be a buyer willing to pay a premium price for the troubled company.

Soon after the meeting, Price telephoned Gittis yet again.

"Al is more interested than ever," he told him. "We'd really like to get together."

"Look, Mike, I've talked to Ronald, and he's not going to be interested in selling this based on what the market price is. Ronald knows what Jerry is doing there. It's just not timely right now."

"Well, Al really wants to meet with you guys," continued Price. "We have to do it."

"With the holidays coming up, it's going to be hard to meet," Gittis replied. "I'm going away. Ronald is going away. I'm sure you're not going to be around, either. But let me talk to Ronald."

Gittis and Perelman arranged to fly down to Palm Beach from New York so that a meeting could be held between them and Price and Dunlap at 5 P.M. on Thursday, December 18. The following day, Gittis would fly off to spend the holidays with his children and grandchildren, while Perelman planned to go to St. Bart's.

For the big rendezvous, Dunlap, Kersh, and Fannin were to first meet Price at his Palm Beach home to plot strategy. Then Dunlap and Price were to go on to see Perelman. Soon after the Sunbeam group arrived at Price's place around 4 P.M., the powerful money manager poured orange juice for all of them and then leafed through the documents prepared by Morgan Stanley. Strong's team had put together a book filled with extensive charts and an elaborate matrix that displayed different potential cash-and-stock offers.

Strong had concluded that Sunbeam should pay no more than $24 a share for Coleman. Even that seemed generous because Coleman's stock hadn't traded at that level for nearly two years. During a raging bull market, Coleman stock had been going nowhere, collapsing to a low of $12.38 only recently. Morgan Stanley advised Dunlap to begin negotiations at a price of between $18 to $20 a share. Price's own analysis concurred with that assessment. The $24 upper limit assumed that Dunlap could squeeze huge costs out of Coleman, just as he had done at Sunbeam and Scott.

"I think that's about right," agreed Price, who then asked about the "due diligence" they had done on Coleman. His primary concern was environmental. Organic chemicals from Coleman factories had contaminated groundwater and soil at sites in Kansas and South Carolina. Coleman was claiming that the future costs to deal with these issues wouldn't be substantial. Price wasn't so sure. In any case, no one in the room had an answer to satisfy Price.

Fannin conceded they hadn't done any real "due diligence" on Coleman at all. It was still too early to look that deeply at the company. Yet so certain was Dunlap that a deal would get done quickly that every member of his board of directors had already been advised to keep their calendars clear before the end of the year so a special meeting could be called to approve the acquisition.

The strategy session over, Dunlap and his driver followed Price in his car to Perelman's house, while Kersh and Fannin drove back to Boca Raton and Fort Lauderdale.

The negotiators pulled to a stop in front of the gate of a large, handsome home, Casa Apava, the $16 million mansion of the part-time Palm Beach resident. Thornton, Dunlap's bodyguard, followed Price through the gate and up the driveway to the house, where Perelman and Gittis came out to greet their guests. It was not long after they shook hands and walked through the front door and into the library and den that Perelman and Dunlap began negotiating.

"Ron," opened Dunlap, "I'd really like to acquire Coleman."

"Al, I'm not in a rush to sell it," replied Perelman, a cigar in one hand and a Diet Coke in another. "Jerry's back in there and in six months to a year, the stock market will reflect it. So why would I want to sell it now?"

"No, no," interrupted Dunlap. "Now's the right time to sell. We're a good fit."

Perelman, playing the shrewd dealmaker that he is, seemed indifferent to a quick deal, a prospect that appeared to agitate Dunlap, whose ruddy face began turning red, a stark contrast to the white turtleneck he wore.

"Look, Al," said Perelman, "if you really want to do this, I'm not going to sell this for under thirty bucks a share."

"Well," replied Dunlap, "we could do a share-for-share exchange. One Sunbeam share for one Coleman."

Perelman had no interest in merely exchanging stock, a deal that would have been worth far less than the $30 a share he wanted.

"Al, I've had First Boston calculate it out and if the numbers are right, the transaction is accretive [with an immediate payback] to you at $30 a share. Why would I sell you something that good for less money?"

Dunlap, already in a sour mood due to a bout with the flu, appeared to grow only more perturbed. After all, Coleman stock had closed on the market that day at only $16.44. Perelman was demanding a premium of nearly double the stock's current price. Dunlap, his face becoming redder still, finally lost it.

"Ron," he snarled, "you're a pig. You know your company is a piece of shit. You'll never see it worth thirty dollars a share in your lifetime. It's only worth twenty bucks and that is an early Christmas present."

"It's Hanukkah," retorted Perelman, a devout Jew.

"Both rolled into one!" yelled Dunlap with contempt.

Perelman and Gittis began laughing as Dunlap became more agitated.

"Well, fuck you," Dunlap finally roared. "Screw you. You guys don't know what you're talking about."

"Fuck you!" retorted Perelman.

"I'm going to save this company for you," Dunlap shouted. "I'm going to do what I did at Scott and Sunbeam. I'm going to cut all the costs out."

"Look, Al," said Gittis, "don't get yourself so excited. You're going to have a heart attack here."

"I don't get heart attacks," insisted Dunlap. "I give heart attacks, and I'm going to give you a heart attack!"

As the argument grew louder, Perelman's security guards peeked through the windows of the house to see what was going on.

"Calm down," replied Gittis. "This is only business. Whether we make this deal or not, Ron is not going to be any more or less rich, and I'm not going to be more or less rich. It's not going to change any of our lives. I don't think it's going to change yours. I know it's not going to change Mike's."

"Fuck you guys," screamed Dunlap again. "You'll never make a deal. I told you, Perelman, you should never listen to lawyers."

Dunlap then stormed out of the house, shouting, "Fuck you and fuck your company."

Price sat and watched in stunned silence, like a child witnessing a fireworks display for the first time.

As the door slammed little more than ten minutes into the meeting, Price was left in Perelman's library staring at Perelman and Gittis. "We all kind of sat there speechless," recalled Price. "I didn't know he was that volatile. I knew Al was a vociferous type, but he did get a little more vociferous than I thought he would."

"Mike," asked Gittis, "what the hell is the matter with this guy? This is a business transaction. There's no sense in getting that upset about it. If we do a deal, fine. If not, it's not the first deal we couldn't get done, and it's not the first deal you couldn't get done. What the hell is wrong with him?"

"Gee, I'm sorry all this happened," ventured Price, trying to calm things down. "Guys, maybe there is some sense in trying to do something here. Maybe we can patch something together. If you guys can be more reasonable, maybe he would be more reasonable."

Perelman and his men just thought Dunlap was cracked. "We thought the guy was crazy," Gittis told friends. "We were just trying to do a deal. He went off like a wild man. We didn't know what to think. We were mystified."

There would be no more discussions that day. Still, Price claims he didn't view Dunlap's violent eruption as a red flag. Price had pulled some wacky stunts in his day to get deals done, including the time he cracked his riding crop to extol Kazarian and Lederman to work like slaves on his behalf. To him, deal making was a little like dating. You never knew, he said, when you're going to hit it off. "It was unusual but some people negotiate in unusual ways and it can be very effective," he says. "I give plenty of room for personal style. He could have been setting the stage to come back the next week."

Price, moreover, shared Dunlap's conviction that $30 was far too pricey a sum to pay for Coleman. "We really cared at nineteen or twenty bucks," he said, "and a dollar or two long-term doesn't matter. Ten bucks does."

IN THE BACK LEATHER SEAT of the company's Mercedes, Dunlap immediately got on his cell phone, dialed Kersh's home phone number, and told him what happened.

"I put Perelman in his place," Dunlap crowed.

Kersh listened to the news with a sense of uneasiness. He knew there was little chance that Strong could find a buyer for Sunbeam, and he desperately wanted out. He concluded that Dunlap had blown an important opportunity simply because he could not control his temper.

If Dunlap had met Kimberly-Clark CEO Wayne Sanders before Sanders bought Scott Paper, the same thing probably would have occurred. The biggest deal of Dunlap's life, the deal that had made millions for Kersh, would have blown up just as this one had. That was a reason why Dunlap had never met Sanders until the signing ceremony, at which only Dunlap's signature was required. At that point, as one associate put it, "he couldn't fuck up the deal" that married Scott Paper with Kimberly-Clark.

"It's over," Kersh told Fannin on the telephone. "It's dead."

"What are you talking about?" asked Fannin.

"Al just called me from his car and it's over. He blew up at Perelman and stormed out. It's over."

NOT EXACTLY. Within days of the dustup at Perelman's home, Price reached Gittis again. He immediately apologized for Dunlap's behavior and tried to see if a deal was still possible.

"Would Ron do a deal at twenty-five dollars?" asked Price.

"Ronald is a very simple guy," replied Gittis. "If he tells you he'll do a deal at thirty dollars, then he'll do a deal at thirty dollars. Calm down. Just wait. We're not selling to anybody else. If we don't do a deal now, maybe we'll do one six months to a year from now. There's no rush."

Within a month, word got back through William Reed, a Morgan Stanley analyst who followed Perelman's company, that a deal for Coleman was still possible. Business is business, he was told. The blowup in Palm Beach was history. Perelman still wanted to sell Coleman, but he was firm on the price. Davis, just as disgusted as Kersh with the outcome of the earlier meeting, was now out of the picture.

By then, yet another last-ditch hope to sell Sunbeam had evaporated. Strong was trying to arrange a meeting with Philips at the Chicago hardwares show in mid-January. Kersh and Fannin flew out in hopes that the session would come off. It didn't. So a week or so later, when Morgan Stanley brought back the news that Perelman was still interested in a deal, Kersh urged them to quietly begin negotiations.

"If this is ever going to happen, we have to keep Al out of it," said Kersh. "And the other side should keep Ron out of it."

Strong agreed. His team took control of the negotiations, keeping Dunlap at a distance to ensure he wouldn't blow up the deal. "We are not going to get these two guys in a room together ever again," is the way one of the dealmakers put it.

Dunlap, of course, was not merely a buyer now. He was what every seller so badly wants: a desperate buyer. The financial alchemy Kersh worked in the quest to sell Sunbeam would soon be laid bare unless they could hurriedly complete a major deal to camouflage Sunbeam's troubled condition. Sales were falling. The retailers were loaded to the gills with product. By making a significant acquisition, Kersh could obscure Sunbeam's own deteriorating results by taking more write-offs and restructuring charges on the newly acquired company. More than Dunlap or anyone else at Sunbeam, Kersh relentlessly drove the Morgan team to complete the deal as quickly as possible. So did Perelman's team when they realized that Dunlap was coming around to the $30 a share their boss first demanded. Their due diligence was cursory at best. No one came to review the roomful of Sunbeam documents at Skadden Arps, and no one bothered to interview Don Uzzi, who was running the company's day-to-day operations. "It was a good deal for us," explained Jerry Levin. "It was a very good price for the business, and there seemed to be some element of desperation there [to get the acquisition done quickly]."

Price could not have been more elated by the prospect of a deal. In an interview with *Barron's* in early February, he telegraphed the acquisition and predicted that it would have a positive impact on Sunbeam's stock price and earnings. "Our favorite company, even though the management is a little bashful, is Sunbeam," quipped Price. "Now that they are running their business better, what Sunbeam's management needs to do is take their skills at turning things around and apply them to businesses that haven't turned around. Looking forward, earnings will be terrific this year. Then, when it buys another company, dropping that company's turnaround and its earnings into Sunbeam's share base, it'll be really terrific."

By February 19, Strong's Morgan team completely revived the deal. Initially Perelman's inner circle wanted the entire offer for Coleman in cash, something that would defeat the purpose of using Sunbeam's premium-priced stock. Strong tried to focus their attention on the combined synergies of the two companies and was able to convince them to take a mixture of cash and Sunbeam stock. Although his lieutenants pressed him to push for as much cash as possible, Perelman grew more enthusiastic about taking a sizable chunk of Sunbeam stock. Though Perelman "didn't trust Al farther than he could throw him," explains one associate, he believed "the story would have positive momentum. Ronald was a believer, Ronald more than the rest." Yet he also wanted an escape clause. So the deal was structured so that Perelman could sell some Sunbeam stock after holding on for only three months. He could completely liquidate his position within nine months.

Morgan, proceeding at breakneck speed to get an agreement, ran various scenarios of stock-and-cash offers. To help rush the deal through, the team decided to keep the stock portion below the 20 percent level that would trigger a shareholder vote under New York Stock Exchange rules. They eventually settled on a 14 percent stake in Sunbeam. As the negotiations moved forward, Dunlap met Perelman at a social gathering in Florida. It was by mere chance that they bumped into each other. Dunlap had planned to attend a benefit dinner for the Stevens Institute of Technology at the posh Everglades Club in Palm Beach. The Dunlaps, however, were turned away from the door because Judy was wearing a pantsuit instead of a dress. Offended, Dunlap stormed away and toward a nearby cocktail party attended by Perelman. The financier came up behind Dunlap, put his arm on his shoulder, and told him, "It's great to see you again." The two struck up a pleasant, if brief, conversation, the first since their "fuck you" meeting in December, and Dunlap left the party interpreting Perelman's approach as a new overture to do business again.

"See," he told associates back at the office, "we put him in his place, and now they're coming back."

When the talks entered their final stage in late February, Kersh and Goudis met directly with Coleman CEO Levin and his associates at Morgan Stanley's New York offices. The Sunbeam executives laid out their strategy for the combined companies and astonished Levin by focusing on little more than drastic cost-cutting. "During the presentation, they never mentioned people or teamwork," said Levin. "Yet, my experience taught me that the success of every organization is based on people. It's getting people motivated to do the right things."

No less surprising to Levin was Kersh's plan to centralize all the company's vast and diverse operations, from headquarters to the sales teams that Dunlap believed could call upon retailers to sell the entire array of Sunbeam and Coleman products. "It would be like running General Motors with one division," believed Levin. "Coleman alone sold to thirty different buyers at Wal-Mart. If we had one or three people calling on Wal-Mart as a team, we'd have ten minutes to talk about grills, while our competitors had two hours. It could not work." Levin's observations were cast aside, and he determined to sell his Coleman stock the moment the deal went through.

Morgan, meantime, had also brought to Dunlap two other smaller companies controlled by Boston financier Thomas H. Lee. Both of them, First Alert smoke alarms and Signature Brands' Mr. Coffee, were simple product extensions for Sunbeam. Dunlap believed he could strip out the entire cost structure for the companies, keeping only the brand names. The products could then be made in Sunbeam factories or simply outsourced to low-cost producers in Asia at enormous savings. But like Coleman, they were not strong and healthy companies. First Alert hadn't earned a profit since 1995. It lost $15.7 million in 1996 and $6.1 million in 1997. Though the maker of Mr. Coffee was profitable, its growth had completely stalled due to greater competition and a dearth of new successful products.

Strong's team commenced intense negotiations on all fronts, with a goal of pulling off all three acquisitions. Sunbeam agreed to pay about $1.6 billion for Coleman in stock and cash and to assume $440 million in Perelman debt. For a badly troubled company, it was a rich price to pay—roughly $30 a share for a stock that had traded for $14 only a month earlier. It was the same price, in fact, that sparked the clash between Dunlap and Perelman only three months ago. Sunbeam grossly overpaid for not only Coleman but the Lee companies as well. In total, Dunlap paid more than twenty-two times the earnings generated by the three companies. In the same month Borden Inc. bought Corning Inc.'s consumer housewares business with such brands as Pyrex, Corning Ware, and Revere, for only 6.7 times earnings. Three months later, in June, Windmere-Durable Holdings Inc. would acquire Black &

Decker's household products group division for just 7.3 times earnings.

But Kersh was desperate to do the deals, and Dunlap justified the price in his own mind by thinking that he could wring greater cost savings and efficiencies from Coleman than first thought. Indeed, Dunlap assured himself that he had gotten the better of the deal. Perelman's men had identified some $150 million in cost savings and supposed synergies that they factored into the price of the company. Morgan Stanley whittled the number down to half, providing a rationale to negotiate down the final price. Dunlap foolishly thought he had sandbagged Perelman because he and Kersh believed they could get $250 million to $300 million of cost out of Coleman.

Michael Price, the quintessential value investor, had his own doubts, but ultimately went along with the transactions because he remained an unshaken Dunlap believer. "I thought it was at the very, very upper end, but they were convinced it made sense," he said. "But it was not crazy. We paid too much, but we used our overpriced stock to get Coleman."

On February 27, in a meeting that stretched late into the afternoon on that Friday, Sunbeam's board of directors gathered for a special session at Morgan Stanley's New York offices at 1585 Broadway. Strong told the directors it was "an accretive deal," which in the language of investment banking meant that the payoff in additional earnings would be immediate, in the first year. By that logic, it was a no-brainer. The total price: $2.5 billion, some $1.8 billion of it in cash and stock, and more than $700 million in existing debt. Morgan proposed financing the transaction by issuing at least $500 million worth of bonds that could be converted into Sunbeam stock and through a $2 billion syndicated bank loan—both of which would generate massive fees for the investment banking firm.

With board approval in hand, the Morgan team worked over the weekend to complete their negotiations for the Lee companies. Sunbeam would pay $84 million in cash and $169 million in assumed debt for Signature Brands. The company also would pay $133 million in cash and $45 million of assumed debt for First Alert.

Dunlap was jubilant. For the scheduled announcement of the deals on Monday, March 2, he had flown to New York with his wife, Judy, and checked into the Palace Hotel. Kersh, Fannin, and investor relations chief Goudis gathered there as well. To celebrate, Dunlap invited all of them, including Fannin's wife and their son and daughter, to a banquet dinner the night before at Mr. K's, a posh Chinese restaurant at Lexington and Fifty-first.

They all walked down the block to the restaurant that Sunday evening and took a table in the main dining room. Dunlap was his exuberant self, at the center of attention, telling the same stories everyone had heard a number of times, from his exploits with Sir James to his days in Australia with Kerry Packer. Every tale was told loudly enough so that all the people in the restaurant looked up from their plates at the man who commanded notice.

Dunlap surmised that this had to be the first time that any corporation had acquired three public companies in a single day. Whether it was true or not didn't matter.

"Three in one day," he gloated. "Never been done before. A triple!"

Even now, when he was at his most upbeat, there was a nervous and edgy energy in the air. With Dunlap, everyone always walked a tightrope because the most innocent remark could send him into some odd and extended rage. Yet he was inviting both Kersh and Fannin to pepper him with questions in preparation for the next day's conferences before the analysts and the media. He made the exercise a little game, and when Dunlap delivered a particularly pithy remark, he happily congratulated himself for it.

"Pretty good, huh?" Dunlap told the table.

"Try something hard," he said with a laugh. "You can't stump me!"

On Monday Wall Street greeted the news with great enthusiasm. Sunbeam's stock soared $3.875 on March 2, closing at $45.625. Two days later it would hit a record high of $52 a share.

For a few days, at least, the euphoria provided Kersh and other executives a brief respite from their very real fears about Sunbeam's core business. Dunlap's mood changed for the better. Managers throughout the company recalculated the worth of their stock options. Michael Price and Ronald Perelman, two of the savviest investors on Wall Street, were beaming with confidence as well.

Meeting with Perelman at his New York conference room, Price proclaimed: "I wouldn't sell this stock short at sixty dollars a share!"

His ebullience was not shared by one of Perelman's men. Within days of the deal's completion, Jerry Levin exercised his 350,000 Coleman stock options and immediately ditched his position in the company for a tidy $7.4 million profit. "I sold my stock immediately because I didn't think that what Dunlap said would work," Levin maintained. He would be right.

Beneath the exuberance, a disaster was pending.

14

INDECENT DISCLOSURE

NO MATTER HOW HARD his managers were scrambling to keep things together in Florida, Albert Dunlap betrayed no mood of worry or crisis. Facing a crowd of potential investors in the sedate ballroom of New York's St. Regis Hotel on March 18, Dunlap turned in a vintage performance.

"We will become the P&G of our industry," he boomed. "We'll become stronger and stronger and our competition will become weaker."

The luncheon session was part of a three-day road show to interest investors in buying $500 million of zero-coupon convertible bonds to help finance Sunbeam's trio of acquisitions. He explained that the purchase of the three companies reflected the launch of his strategy to grow through acquisitions and consolidate the fragmented consumer products industry along the way.

A mere two weeks after announcing the deals, and with Ron Perelman now a major shareholder of Sunbeam, Dunlap was already attacking Coleman's prior leadership. "The previous management at Coleman said they completed a restructuring," he groused. "What they did doesn't begin to approach what I consider a restructuring. In fact, I believe that Coleman is very similar to the old Sunbeam. Too many factories, too many SKUs, and underperforming product lines and very weak management. Rest assured we'll fix all of that very quickly!"

208

As Dunlap wooed the St. Regis crowd, however, a couple of worried Morgan Stanley officials pulled general counsel David Fannin aside. Ruth Porat, a strong-willed career woman who is a managing director in equity capital markets, approached Fannin with Jim Stynes, who had helped to close the deals. Over the past two weeks, a team of Morgan people were doing the "due diligence" for this bond offering. Porat and her colleagues spoke with major retailer customers, including Wal-Mart and Kmart, Arthur Andersen auditors, and several Sunbeam operating executives, including Don Uzzi.

To her surprise, Porat discovered that Sunbeam's first quarter sales were not going very well. The issue had bubbled up during the due diligence process. It first arose in conversations between Arthur Andersen auditors and Davis Polk-Wardell lawyers who represented Morgan Stanley. Then it was passed on to Morgan's bankers. Porat and Alan Dean, a circumspect partner at Davis Polk, were in agreement that Sunbeam would have to publicly disclose that it was unlikely to meet Wall Street's estimates for the first quarter. A downturn in sales and profit wouldn't scuttle the bond offering, but if the company knew that sales were soft, that fact needed to be out in the open for buyers of the convertible bonds.

"Are you aware of how disappointing the sales are so far this quarter?" Porat asked Fannin.

"I know it started out slowly," he replied, "but January is always slow."

"Well," said Stynes, "we hear sales are running at about half of what they were last year. We think you're going to have to make a disclosure if you are going to close on these bonds."

Fannin told them he would look into it and quickly placed a call to controller Robert Gluck. Unable to find him, he informed Kersh of his conversation with the Morgan officials and then hurriedly left to see what he could find out on his own. After a brief stop at his Palace Hotel room to pick up an umbrella, he walked in the rain to outside counsel Finn Foggs office on Third Avenue and Fifty-fifth Street.

At Skadden, Arps, Slate, Meagher & Flom, Fogg's office on the forty-seventh floor looks like something out of an old movie. Tucked into the northeast corner of the building, it is filled with antique furniture and clutter. Papers are strewn everywhere, on the desk that once belonged to Fogg's father as well as the leather couch that lies along one wall. Like so many Dunlap associates, Fogg had known Dunlap for over a decade. He had advised him and Sir James Goldsmith on their hostile $23 billion takeover of BAT Industries in 1989. Though it failed, Dunlap kept throwing business to Fogg, hiring him at Scott Paper and Sunbeam.

Fogg, a New Englander who grew up in Augusta, Maine, had lawyering in his veins. His grandfather and father are attorneys, as is one of his sons. Fogg looked the part of a big-league M&A attorney as well: an avid cigar smoker, he wore tortoise-framed glasses, slightly unkempt silver-gray hair, and fuzzy sideburns.

After trying unsuccessfully to reach Uzzi in Delray Beach, the two lawyers located Deborah McDonald, director of corporate planning on Kersh's staff. By keeping track of sales and profits on a daily basis, McDonald had a front row seat on the company's worsening financials. On February 11, some five weeks earlier, she sat in a boardroom meeting with Dunlap and Rich Goudis to hear Don Uzzi provide a sobering account of the latest numbers. At the session, Uzzi told Dunlap that the quarter was shaping up as "sloppy," partly because Sunbeam's "customers were loaded." At the time, company documents showed, Wal-Mart had twenty weeks of Sunbeam stand mixers in inventory and thirty-one weeks of the company's bread makers. At K-Mart, it was worse. The retailer was loaded with seventy weeks of Sunbeam bread makers and eighty weeks of stand mixers and rotisseries. The company, warned Uzzi, was $39 million under its expected sales by February 11, with $29 million of the gap due to weaker revenues in the U.S. and $10 million due to lower overseas sales.

"How could this happen?" shouted Dunlap. "We're in the middle of a transaction. You've got to make the numbers!"

Uzzi said he also was launching a rebate program on blankets and a marketing campaign for outdoor grills, but things were not looking good. In fact, the executive told Dunlap, Sunbeam's sales in January were not much more than half of what the company had projected.

"The only way to close the shortfall is by doing another bill-and-hold," Uzzi said. "It's up to you to decide what to do."

Since then, McDonald had been writing frequent memos to Kersh about the company's continued turn for the worse. Unable to reach Kersh, who was tied up with the details of the acquisition and other matters, McDonald began to worry that the chief financial officer was purposely evading her so he could later claim not to have been informed about the company's deteriorating condition. In late February, she confided to Uzzi her fear that Kersh was "setting her up." So McDonald began keeping a careful record of her numerous attempts to reach him by voice mail, fax, and memo.

Now, on the telephone with Fannin on March 18, McDonald agreed to fax to New York a memo, detailing the numbers, account by account. There was no question that the year started out badly. In the first two months of the year, Sunbeam sold only $79 million of product, compared to $145 million in the same period a year earlier. The news could not have been a complete surprise. Every morning by 8:15, Fannin received, along with Dunlap, Kersh, and other top managers, daily sales "scorecards" that tracked domestic and international shipments and orders to date. Only a week earlier, during a telephone call, Kersh also had given Uzzi approval to do another bill-and-hold sale in the hopes of making the first quarter numbers. The sales picture was weakening so badly, however, that even another bill-and-hold wasn't going to close the gap.

At 4 P.M., Uzzi and McDonald were patched into a telephone conference call with Fannin, Fogg, Morgan's Porat, and Davis Polk's Dean. Surprisingly, the conversation focused entirely on sales and not earnings, which would have been adversely impacted anyway because of massive discounting. Uzzi carefully reviewed the document forwarded to the lawyers earlier in the day. It showed that Sunbeam had two estimates for first-quarter sales: a low forecast of $267 million and a more optimistic projection of $293 million, the latter of which was the mid-point of Wall Street's expectations. Through March 17, however, only $168.7 million of sales had been booked. With less than two weeks left in the quarter, Sunbeam had to generate $126 million of revenue to satisfy the Street. The single-page fax showed "potential orders" of only $86 million, including $14.8 million from Home Depot and $9.4 million from Wal-Mart.

Though conceding the company was behind, Uzzi said he would do everything possible to meet Wall Street's forecast. Some participants recalled that Uzzi expressed confidence that first-quarter sales would at least exceed the year-earlier revenue of $253.5 million. Uzzi later insisted he gave no such assurances.

"Well, will you make the numbers or not?" asked Porat.

"I can't guarantee that we'll make it," Uzzi recalls saying.

Uzzi said he hoped to close the sales gap by doing more sales of Sunbeam grills and running aggressive promotions on other Sunbeam products. Frequently, he explained, the company pushed a lot of product out in the final weeks of a quarter.

"Can you guarantee that Sunbeam will make the numbers?" she asked.

Uzzi said he refused to promise that it could be done, and he again described the plan.

"Well, we appreciate that you have a plan to get there, but obviously you aren't there now and there's a chance you could fall short," said Porat. "If we're going to price these bonds tomorrow, we have to make some kind of disclosure."

It was now clear to Fogg and Fannin, however, that the company needed to draft a statement that would be released the following morning. Their view was reaffirmed by Bill Strong, who called in from Morgan's San Francisco offices.

"Look," Strong said, "I can tell you that Morgan Stanley can't close on this deal unless we make some kind of disclosure. If you want me to, I'll call and tell Al."

"That would be a great idea," said Fogg, laughing, "but we really can't let you do that. We'll call him together."

When Fannin picked up the receiver to dial Dunlap at his room in the Palace Hotel, he believed this would be one of the most agonizing telephone calls he would ever have to make. He was sweating, and his heart didn't want to stay in his chest. He won a small reprieve when there was no answer. The Palace, where many of the waitresses, bellhops and doormen knew Dunlap as Mr. D., was his favorite Manhattan hotel. When the paperback version of his book had been released three months earlier, he had strolled through the hotel's lobby and corridors, handing out autographed copies to the employees.

Finally, around 7 P.M., Kersh called Fannin to tell him that he and Dunlap were having dinner at Giambelli's, an Italian restaurant Dunlap favored for the generous slices of hard round cheese the waiters brought to every table.

"Russ," Fannin said, "we're going to have to put out a press release."

"You've got to be kidding," Kersh responded. "We can't do that."

Fannin gave him a quick run-through of all the conference calls that day, and Kersh told him he would call back with Dunlap as soon as they returned to the hotel.

Around 8:30 P.M. Dunlap was back in his room and patched into a telephone call with a bevy of advisers, lawyers, and bankers all over New York. Strong was linked into the call from a private telephone booth at United Airlines' Red Carpet Club in San Francisco.

He took the lead in the conversation, explaining the problem and the need to issue a statement. Dunlap immediately protested.

"Al, you have to do it," said Strong.

"You're just trying to cover your ass," Dunlap shot back.

"Al, we're a small part of it. What's more important is *your* credibility. You have great credibility with Wall Street. You're as honest as the day is long. Al, this is a small price to pay for your credibility and integrity."

Dunlap kept screaming into the phone. He knew the announcement would tank Sunbeam stock and could even jeopardize the success of the debenture offering. It also wouldn't help his reputation as a turnaround master who had proclaimed victory only two months earlier. Dunlap held firm, even though he had been told by Uzzi just five weeks earlier that sales were plummeting, millions short and getting worse, and that customers had months of inventory that was holding up new orders. Dunlap continued to argue that he wasn't certain what the final numbers for the quarter would look like.

"Finn," asked Dunlap, "what do you think?"

"Al, I don't think you have any choice. You have to do it."

"I don't know," shouted Dunlap. "But the last time I heard, a quarter was three months long, not two months and two weeks. A quarter isn't over until it's over. Nobody knows what the numbers are going to be and I don't know. Don is telling me we're going to make it."

"Are you going to make it or not?" asked Strong.

"I can't predict the future. I don't know."

They argued some more, until even Dunlap seemed to grow tired of the fight.

"Do whatever you want to do," he yelled. "Fuck it. I'm going to bed."

Fannin remained at Skadden Arps, working with Fogg to draft the language for the press release. Once they crafted the three-paragraph announcement, they faxed it to Morgan Stanley and Davis Polk. While they waited for their replies, they ordered Chinese food from Chun Lee, a nearby takeout joint.

At 11 P.M., Uzzi, in bed at his home at the Woodfield Country Club in Boca Raton, was awakened by the telephone. It was Fannin, who read him the approved statement. Sales "may be lower than the range of Wall Street analysts' estimates for $285–$295 million, but net sales are expected to exceed 1997 first quarter net sales of $253.4 million." The shortfall "if any, would be due to changes in inventory management and order patterns at certain of the company's major retail customers." Sunbeam was still "highly confident" about the full-year sales outlook.

"David, this will beg more questions than it answers," said Uzzi. Indeed, it would.

EARLY THE NEXT DAY, March 19, the road show would travel to Boston, where Dunlap and Morgan Stanley officials would meet with more institutional investors, including Fidelity, Putnam, and Massachusetts Mutual. At New York's Palace Hotel, Fannin was waiting for an elevator that would take him to the lobby, where he was to meet Dunlap, Kersh and investor relations chief Rich Goudis. When the elevator doors opened, there was Dunlap, glowering alone in the corner.

"Fuck!" shouted Dunlap, as the doors closed.

They stood in silence as the elevator took them to the ground floor. Dunlap had not yet seen the release, which was in Fannin's briefcase. He refused to look at it in the lobby or in the car as they drove to the Teterboro, New Jersey, airport, where they boarded the private plane that would take them to Boston.

Being next to an angry Dunlap in a small corporate jet may be almost as uncomfortable as sitting in the electric chair. Near-legendary stories tell of executives who have been chewed out for the entire length of a flight. Lee Griffith, for example, had gotten his initiation from Dunlap on a flight from Philadelphia to Mobile, Alabama, that Griffith later described as "one of the longest rides he ever was on." For the entire trip Dunlap hammered him unmercifully with caustic questions and comments about the performance of Scott's sales staff.

Kersh and Fannin knew that this short hop to Boston would be filled with turbulence. Dunlap, already smoldering with anger, began his eruption shortly after Fannin handed him the release. Though he didn't say so, Fannin could still make minor changes on the copy if Dunlap demanded them. If not, all he had to do was call Skadden Arps, and the warning would be posted on the wire.

"I never should have let you guys talk me into this," Dunlap complained. He was now talking about 1998 being a transition year, one in which he would take new write-off charges with his acquisitions, just as he had done after joining Sunbeam in 1996.

"Goddamn it," he yelled, "if anybody in this plane talks about the old goddamn Sunbeam . . . fuck it. They can take the keys and fuckin' run the company themselves. I'm not going to do it. Ninety-eight is a throwaway year. A throwaway!"

They sat silently, Fannin directly across from Dunlap, Kersh behind him and next to Goudis. All sat stone-faced, glumly peering out of the plane's windows, trying to mentally shield themselves from the abuse. Over the twenty months that Fannin had now worked with Dunlap, he had developed the ability to tune the man out whenever he went on one of these extended tears. He had to keep enough of an ear, just in case he was dragged into conversation. But in his mind's eye, he would fix on an upcoming event that he and his wife, Lucille, would attend, transporting himself to a seat next to her at an opera or to the soft stretch of sandy beach outside his condo in Fort Lauderdale where they often walked hand-in-hand. Instead of letting Dunlap's words soak into him, he let them roll off. It was the only way he could survive.

As the news hit the market later that morning, Sunbeam stock began to sink. Bill Strong, who had taken the red-eye flight from San Francisco to Boston, knew as soon as he spotted Dunlap that he was still angry over it. Dunlap refused to shake Strong's extended hand and gave him the cold shoulder all day long. When Strong pleaded with him in the car that they had made the right decision to get the news out, Dunlap failed to acknowledge Strong's presence. He derisively told his colleagues that the only reason Strong came to Boston was to get a company-paid trip to visit his son, who was enrolled at the University of Massachusetts. It was not true, of course, but Dunlap persuaded himself of it.

The announcement had created a flurry of calls from worried analysts. During the road show luncheon in Boston, Rich Goudis fielded them on his cell phone, trying to reassure frenzied analysts with Dunlap's own comments. With his All-American good looks and charm, Goudis, thirty-six, had been one of the most gung-ho of Sunbeam survivors when Dunlap first arrived on the scene. But after gaining responsibility for investor relations in April 1997, he soon learned how difficult it could be to work closely with Dunlap. Goudis, who went to the University of Massachusetts on a wrestling scholarship, initially hit it off well with the CEO. They forged a kind of athlete-coach relationship. Dunlap would tell him to run a little faster and jump a little higher. And Goudis, who had already thrown all of himself into the job, would push himself a little more.

But he had been greatly disturbed by an incident that had been quietly covered up by the company only a few months ago. It involved a person he had hired into Sunbeam, someone who had a role in finance and analysis. Goudis had recruited this young woman directly from college when he was employed by another corporation. After arriving at Sunbeam in 1995, he hired her again. A tall and attractive woman, she was smart and savvy. She had an effusive personality that lit up a room. Dunlap had been tough on her, as he had been tough on most of his executives. Sunbeam managers heard him ridicule her as a "bitch" and a "pom-pom girl" and once told her that she was as dumb as the screwdriver she held in her hand one day as she was repairing her computer.

Late one afternoon, just before 6 P.M., Dunlap asked to speak with the young woman after a meeting in Kersh's office, where they had been discussing the potential firing of marketing chief Kevin McBride. What happened next she described in a "personal and confidential" memo she wrote the following day. "As we entered his office lobby, I noticed that Sean Thornton (Dunlap's bodyguard) was already gone, and the office lights were out. Al continued talking about Kevin McBride and his organization as he entered his dark office. I proceeded to follow him to the doorway (where the lobby light ended), and he continued into his office. He started speaking a little softer and continued his discussion from inside his office (near his couches). I continued discussing marketing talent . . . and partially entered his office so he could hear me and I could hear him. He then faced me and put his hands on my shoulders, arms, and back. He also leaned in for a kiss at this point. He pulled me closer. He then reached down and grabbed/rubbed my buttocks. I pulled away and he continued to discuss marketing management, the Christmas party, and the fourth quarter.

"At this point, I mentioned Ms. Judy Dunlap and a discussion we had at the party regarding the Humane Society and possibly opening a new center in Boca Raton under their names. (I was exiting the office at this time and Al was also exiting.) We were in his lobby and he faced me again, pulled me to him, and kissed me on the mouth. He also hugged me and grabbed/rubbed my buttocks again. I proceeded to walk out and he also was walking out, and Al grabbed my hand to walk me down the hallway . . . "

When a mailman spotted the two of them, Dunlap let go of her hand and smiled. Once the employee passed by, Dunlap grabbed her hand again. "Before he walked through the doors to the main lobby," she wrote, "he turned for a kiss and a hug, and grabbed me again. I then walked the other way towards his office. I was extremely shocked and embarrassed by this event and needed to talk with someone about it."

She rushed into Goudis's office, shut the door, and asked him to get off the telephone. Visibly shaken, she told him what happened and openly wondered, according to her memo, if Dunlap's unwanted sexual advances were caused by the day's strong rise in Sunbeam's stock. The shares ended the day up nearly $3.50, an increase of more than 8 percent. Dunlap, whose moods shifted with every peek at the Bloomberg terminal outside his office, was elated. Goudis apparently did not respond to her speculation, but told her he had never seen Dunlap behave that way with anyone else.

She went back to her office and telephoned her husband. While on that conversation, Goudis called her from his cell phone. He told her he had to leave the office because he was so shocked by what she told him. Both Goudis and her husband advised the young woman to immediately see Gary Mask, the current head of human resources.

Mask, who had worked with Dunlap before at other companies, professed to be just as surprised to hear of the incident as Goudis. But unlike her mentor, he advised her "to avoid Al at all costs and that if it happens again, I should tell Al it makes me uncomfortable," she wrote. "I also stated that I did not think I could work in this organization any more."

The detailed memo, written the next day, was given to Mask, who eventually helped to negotiate a deal with the employee. Under the arrangement, she left the company after signing a confidentiality agreement that awarded her a generous severance and prevented her from bringing legal action against either Dunlap or Sunbeam. When Mask confronted Dunlap with the charges, he quickly denied them. He said he was sad and hurt that she would accuse him of such inappropriate behavior.

If the allegations were all true, as many executives who knew the employee believed them to be, they would have been completely out of character for Dunlap. Unlike many powerful men, his eyes never wandered. His revulsion against his father's infidelities had kept him a faithful, if sometimes verbally abusive, husband. If anything, the accusations were more evidence that Dunlap was becoming unhinged.

When Goudis heard about the episode, he was enraged—and lost what little respect he had left for Dunlap. Over the nine months he had worked and traveled with the chief executive, he had seen him become increasingly disengaged from the business and more self-absorbed as Bill Strong failed to come up with a buyer for Sunbeam. The company's other executives and some of Dunlap's longtime associates saw the same behavioral change. All were seeing the man who had cleverly fashioned a folksy Horatio Alger persona for what he probably always was: a crude and coarse predator who believed the weak were his natural prey, a man who worshiped money more than God, and who measured his life's success only by his wealth. Dunlap was becoming, as one executive so plainly put it, uglier and uglier.

Dunlap had been involved in another bizarre incident in early February 1998 when a golfer on the Boca Raton Resort and Club course charged that Dunlap had assaulted him. According to the police complaint, Frank Schienberg hit his golf ball near the shore line of a small lake at the fourteenth hole of the course late in the afternoon on Sunday, February 1. As he and his wife, Marsha, strolled toward the lake, Schienberg saw Dunlap fish his ball out of the water with a metal golf ball retriever.

Schienberg approached Dunlap, whom he apparently did not know or recognize, and asked him if the ball was a Titleist, a professional ball that sells for $54 a dozen. Without saying a word, Dunlap casually looked at the ball in his hand and then heaved it into the deep area of the lake so it could not be recovered. When Schienberg asked why he threw away the ball, an angry Dunlap rushed at him wielding the retriever, pressed the metal bar against his throat, and forced the man to his knees.

"You don't know who I am," Dunlap told the astonished man. Then Dunlap hurried away with his wife, Judy.

Schienberg, who regularly winters in Florida, reported the incident to the police, who were able to identify Dunlap as a suspect with the help of the resort's employees. Dunlap denied that he assaulted Schienberg, but conceded he was out retrieving golf balls from the lake and refused to hand the man his golf ball. Instead, Dunlap said, he dropped the ball back where he found it and walked away as Schienberg shouted obscenities at him and tried to provoke him into a fight. In an effort to discredit Schienberg, Dunlap had Sunbeam pay for a private detective to investigate the man. In any case Schienberg failed to follow up on the charge and it was dropped. Why Dunlap would be fishing used golf balls out of water traps on a Sunday afternoon could not be explained.

But many of his colleagues had witnessed often unexplainable behavior by Dunlap over the years. Any executive who worked closely with him has seen more than his fair share of Dunlap tantrums. At the housewares show in Chicago in January, only a few weeks after the Dalberth incident, Dunlap repeatedly refused to answer reasonable questions from analyst Scott Graham of Oppenheimer at a breakfast investment conference. Graham simply wanted to know how the Asian economic crisis might affect Sunbeam's sales.

Dunlap dismissed the question, using one of his pet phrases, calling the query "a peanut at a gourmet dinner."

But it was a perfectly legitimate question, and Graham asked it again. When Rich Goudis finally attempted to respond, Dunlap placed his hand on Goudis's chest and said: "Rich, don't answer that question!

"I'm not going to answer that question anymore," shouted Dunlap. "You write whatever the hell you want. But if it's wrong, I'll come after you like a freight train. This meeting is over!"

Much to Goudis's embarrassment, Dunlap stormed out, leaving him and Uzzi in a room full of puzzled analysts. Dunlap was more interested in signing copies of his own newly updated paperback than answering legitimate questions about the company's operations.

A devout Catholic who proudly served as a Eucharistic minister at St. Jude's Church in Boca Raton, Goudis began to believe that Dunlap and Kersh were providing the Street with misleading information about the company's financial condition. He believed that when Sunbeam reported its fourth quarter numbers, it should have informed analysts that the sales figures included $35 million in bill-and-hold sales of grills. Kersh vetoed the suggestion. Goudis also believed the company should have revealed that it had sold $59 million in receivables to an outside firm in the fourth quarter. Receivables are the amount of money owed the company by its customers for merchandise, and several analysts had expressed concerned about the rising level of receivables on Sunbeam's balance sheet. Kersh disagreed that a disclosure was necessary when the company's financial figures were announced. The result was that sales were inflated by the massive discount program on barbecue grills, and the balance sheet looked better only because Kersh had sold off the company's most creditworthy receivables.

Goudis grew so uneasy with these accounting measures that he began to answer tough questions from analysts with a maneuver of his own that prevented him from telling an outright lie and yet still managed to allow him to save a job he no longer wanted. The next morning, in fact, he would interview for a new job at Rexall-Sundown, the Boca Raton–based maker of vitamins. Whenever the analysts asked him a question he felt he could not answer truthfully, he would precede his answer with the phrase "I talked to Al about that and this is what he is saying." It was the only way Goudis could sleep at night.

"Hey, I've got thirty seconds," he told one analyst after another, his cell phone to his ear. "What Al is telling people is that he can't say he's going to make it and he can't say he's not going to do it. The only reason we did this is because the lawyers made him do it." And then Goudis would try to get off the call and deal with another before facing a tougher grilling from any of the analysts desperate to ferret out the real story.

NO ONE, not even Goudis, could completely calm the Street's jitters. By day's end, when Sunbeam stock fell 9.4 percent to $45.375 on the New York Stock Exchange, Dunlap steadfastly refused to attend Morgan's New York dinner to celebrate the completion of the bond offering. Instead he sent Kersh and Fannin with instructions to convey his displeasure to the Morgan team.

Even worse, Dunlap lashed out at Strong in front of an institutional investor who asked why Sunbeam had issued the warning.

"Because these fuckin' bankers and their goddamn lawyers insisted we do it," he said, pointing his finger at Strong and his Morgan colleagues. "I put that out because the lawyers made me do it!"

That kind of bluster with an investor had worked before so Dunlap believed it would work again. He believed that the tougher you were, the more resolve you showed, the more likely it was that any challenger would be convinced of your rectitude. Ironically, he had employed the same strategy in Boston thirteen years earlier when he was on the road show to promote the initial public offering of Lily-Tulip. An official at Fidelity Investments questioned why it should buy the stock in a company that lacked a track record proving that a real turnaround had occurred.

"I don't give a damn if you buy stock," Dunlap roared as he grabbed his coat to leave the meeting. "And if you don't buy the stock, the hell with you!" His in-your-face performance ostensibly worked because Fidelity purchased a significant share of the public offering.

His latest outburst certainly didn't hurt the outcome of this debenture offering. It was a enormous success. Morgan had hoped to raise about $500 million. Investor demand, however, was so high that Sunbeam raised $750 million, and Strong believed he could have pulled in as much as $1 billion in the sale. Obviously there was no shortage of Dunlap believers in the marketplace, no shortage of investors who naively assumed that Dunlap could work magic where so many had failed.

Most of the Wall Street analysts who followed Sunbeam generally took the news in stride as well. None of them downgraded the stock, and several went out of their way to give an explanation for the warning that could have fallen out of Dunlap's own mouth. "Sunbeam is an earnings-driven industry consolidator," explained Graham of Oppenheimer. "I think investors should be looking at it for what they are trying to do long-term rather than worrying about them missing in an off-season quarter by a couple of cents a share."

In retrospect, Sunbeam's announcement that first-quarter sales would still exceed the year-earlier numbers and that it was still confident it could make its 1998 estimates was inadequate, given the utter chaos inside the company and the dreadful downfall to come. Phil Harlow, the Arthur Andersen partner in charge of the Sunbeam account, later expressed disappointment that he was not involved in the drafting of the release. If Harlow had seen the warning earlier, he told Fannin later, he might have been inclined to be far more cautious and far less "highly confident" about the full-year results.

AS ANGRY AND VOLATILE as Dunlap was the day before, he was apoplectic the next morning when he turned to page 33 of the March 20 *New York Post* and read the following headline: "Sunbeam's Cloudy Outlook: Chainsaw Al Warns on Profits."

"Just ten days after giving himself a huge raise in pay, Sunbeam Corp. CEO Al Dunlap admitted yesterday that the company's first quarter sales and profits would not meet analysts' expectations." The story attacked not only Dunlap's new pay package but also his ability to lead the company. "Dunlap's failings as a manager are becoming abundantly clear now, said analysts, since he can no longer eke out cost cuts and must turn his focus to boosting sales."

To say that Dunlap did not take the criticism well would be an understatement. Both Kersh and Fannin, standing in the lobby of the Palace that morning, had never seen him so angry and upset. The look on his face was cold, hard rage.

"Those fuckin' lawyers!" he screamed, tossing the newspaper at them. "I knew we shouldn't do this! You guys insisted. You guys are weak-kneed. It's not your ass that is on the line. I'm the one who is hanging out there. I'm the one taking all the abuse. I'm the one who's embarrassed by all this."

In the ornate lobby of the Palace, all heads turned. Even Dunlap's security guards couldn't hide their own embarrassment. Kersh and Fannin hung their heads. Dunlap seemed to be shouting without ever taking a single breath, preventing them from saying a word in defense, if they so dared.

"Come with me!" Dunlap commanded. They followed him through the lobby to the top step of the grand staircase in the Palace lobby, where Dunlap continued to berate them.

That is where the men were spotted by Thomas Hardy, a head-hunter with SpencerStuart who had arrived for a scheduled breakfast with them.

Hardy, a self-described washed-out WASP, admired Dunlap and knew him in a way that few did. It was Hardy who had gathered all the character and business references on Dunlap for the Scott Paper search. He had spoken directly with Sir James Goldsmith and Coopers' Donald Burnett and learned of the man's strengths and weaknesses from those who had known Dunlap throughout his entire career. He had worked with SpencerStuart chairman Thomas Neff in bringing Dunlap to Scott, and then lured a cadre of talented executives into the organization. Dunlap jokingly referred to the headhunters as his "Two Toms," or "Tom-Tom." Only a couple of weeks earlier Hardy had been engaged by Kersh and Fannin to find a chief operating officer for Sunbeam. At this 8 A.M. breakfast meeting the headhunter came armed with a list of sixty-eight possible candidates for the job.

Facing Dunlap's muscular back, Hardy could see Kersh and Fannin cowering before the executive. Just as Hardy began to climb the stairs and approach them, a bodyguard intervened with an outstretched arm. "Hey, you want to stay away for a few minutes," he was told.

They all eventually took a table on the brass rail of the Palace's restaurant off the main lobby. Dunlap was still seething with anger, his angry monologue far from finished.

"Goddamn lawyers!" Dunlap said. "I should have never listened to them. Unbelievable. I'll tell you what else is unbelievable, that Tom Neff wouldn't have the common courtesy to bless us with his presence. You can bet if your pal George Fisher [the chairman of Eastman Kodak] were in Manhattan for the day, he'd make the effort to at least say hello."

With Dunlap's face not much more than five inches from his own, Hardy sat and absorbed the harangue without blinking.

"What's he doing anyway?" Dunlap continued. "Playing golf with your corpucrat buddies? Tell me what they have done for their shareholders. And another thing, neither you or Neff called me when I went to Sunbeam. Not once. Not a peep out of either of you."

"Well," Hardy quipped, in an effort to lighten the conversation, "you gave all your work to Korn/Ferry."

Dunlap gave him a long, hard stare, seemed to count for five seconds in his head, and then went on again in a voice that was four times Hardy's decibel level.

"What? You guys too good to do house calls? We have to call you. Tell me why you should do anything for us. Name anybody good you've placed since Scott Paper that's worth a crap. And [don't name] any of your usual friggin' corpucrats. Come on. Name one."

Years earlier Dunlap and his mentor, Sir James Goldsmith, had coined the term "corpocracy," their term for a corporation that acted more like a bureaucracy. Since then Dunlap frequently used this made-up word to ridicule executives whom he thought behaved more like bureaucrats. Hardy tried to satisfy Dunlap's challenge to name one of his better placements.

"Chuck Berger," uttered the headhunter.

"Who's he?"

"He's the CEO of Scotts, the lawn fertilizer company."

"Never heard of him," replied Dunlap. "Come on. I hope you can do better than that. Let's see if this report has any corpucrats from no-name outfits. Jesus, it's been six to eight weeks since you've been screwing around with us."

Hardy, who had only gotten the assignment two weeks earlier, recognized that this would not be a productive meeting. Every time he brought up a candidate's name, Dunlap abruptly dismissed the person out of hand.

"He's with a shitty company," said Dunlap. "Next."

Nearly everyone in the restaurant could hear his voice. A European couple next to their table seemed shocked by Dunlap's remarks. Kersh and Fannin felt like crawling under the table and hiding.

Hoping to gain more consideration for some of his potentials, Hardy told Dunlap that Prudential Securities analyst Nick Heymann had thought the next candidate would move the stock price as soon as his name was announced.

"Oh fuck," Dunlap retorted, "what does he know?"

Not a single candidate on the list won even a hint of approval from him. At one time Kersh tried to save the name of one executive on Hardy's list by talking up the strengths of the person's corporation. It made no difference to Dunlap, who discarded the person like all the others. Hardy had never sat through as unproductive and as offensive a session. Kersh, worried that Hardy would resign the account, walked the stunned headhunter out of the hotel and down the street to reassure him that Dunlap's behavior had nothing to do with him.

When Kersh returned, another candidate for the job was already at the table. He had been recommended by Perelman, who had been searching for a president for Coleman. Gary Mask, Sunbeam's human resources chief, had already interviewed the man. They hoped he would click with Dunlap because he had been a Vietnam veteran. Instead Dunlap was just as dismissive with him as he had been with Hardy. "It was not an interview," recalls Fannin. "It was an attack. I felt sorry for him. It was so bad and so ugly."

When the candidate left, thunderstruck, Dunlap asked: "Who's got a cell phone?"

Kersh handed him one, and Dunlap quickly called Fogg at Skadden Arps. It was his time to get chewed out over the disclosure matter.

"Finn," he said, "I've worked with you for a lot of years. You and Jimmy [Goldsmith] and I go way back. Finn, you've never let me down before. But you've let me down now, and I expected better from a friend."

After the call, Kersh, Fannin, and Dunlap checked out of their rooms, took a limo to Teterboro airport, and boarded a private plane together back to Florida. The storm had blown out. Dunlap was quietly seething for most of the flight. So were Kersh and Fannin as they contemplated their futures. Kersh told Fannin that day was "as close as I have ever come to just telling Al to go fuck himself and walk out." He didn't. Neither did Fannin, who felt the same way. Arriving home drained and exhausted, Fannin seriously considered turning in his resignation.

If he quit now, however, he would get nothing of the big pay package he had just been granted. He also feared that Dunlap could be so vindictive that he might prevent him from getting another corporate job. He thought of going back to Louisville into private practice as a lawyer, but he really didn't want to do that. He wanted to stay in a corporate setting.

Unlike ex-Sunbeam executive Newt White, he didn't have "fuck you" money. He had a sizable mortgage on his condo, a daughter still in high school, and a large loan that he had taken out to buy Sunbeam stock on Dunlap's orders. "We felt trapped," said Lucille, his wife. "We needed that money to live on. I didn't know how to get him out."

This time, perhaps, Dunlap may have understood that he had crashed through the bounds of decency. In a gesture that could never excuse his patent cruelty, he gave both Kersh and Fannin unexpected gifts. A few days after their return to Florida, they each received a small bronze sculpture of a menacing cougar, poised to pounce off a tree limb. It was his peculiar way of offering an apology for his outlandish behavior, of saying he was sorry, something Dunlap probably could not bring himself to verbalize.

15
AN ANALYST'S CALL

AL DUNLAP WAS not only angry at his most trusted lieutenants and advisers for forcing him to do something that would hurt Sunbeam's stock. He was enraged at Donald Uzzi for letting him down, for failing to make the irrational first-quarter numbers that Dunlap had promised Wall Street.

"You didn't try hard enough," groused Dunlap a few days after Uzzi had refused to guarantee that Sunbeam could meet the Street's expectations. Uzzi assumed that Dunlap blamed him for the release, but his boss could just as easily have been referring to the company's weakening performance that forced the disclosure in the first place. Disenchanted, Uzzi didn't bother to ask what Dunlap meant by the comment.

By now, he had long known that his boss didn't really consider him part of his small inner circle. Though still technically on Dunlap's operating committee, Uzzi had been the odd man out for months. He was excluded from the acquisition discussions as well as the new rich employment contracts Dunlap arranged for himself, Kersh, and Fannin.

Uzzi was not alone in resenting all of them for the extra money they coaxed out of the board. Like everyone else, he had been working outrageous hours, trying to fulfill Dunlap's outrageous demands to make the numbers, no matter what. He resented those new contracts for himself, but also for his staff, whose own bonuses would be limited since they failed to meet Dunlap's expectations for 1997.

He had never worked for anyone who was as emotionally abusive or as irrational as Dunlap. Yet he put up with the maltreatment and remained at least outwardly a believer while quietly waging a guerrilla war against his boss. He didn't fire people when ordered to do so. He pushed back on many of the idiocies recommended by Coopers, from the closing of the Bay Springs wire plant to the moving of the McMinnville factory to Mexico. He decorated his office with classic Sunbeam appliances from the 1950s, a contrast to the pair of grotesque predator paintings that Dunlap had selected and placed in his office.

Yet some people under Uzzi viewed him as a Dunlap apostle. He had often passed down the brutal pressure to his subordinates, becoming more like Dunlap than he ever imagined possible. Uzzi had always been tough, but he had never been cruel. He believed that Dunlap created a poisoned environment that affected nearly everyone's behavior, including his own. Sometimes,, Uzzi began yelling at his people, just as Dunlap berated him. "I started to take a look at who I had become and said, 'I don't want to be like this. This is wrong.' The environment was so abusive, yet so fraught with the opportunity for success, that you became subverted by it. You got the stink of this guy on you from working with him."

Dunlap must have sensed Uzzi's doubts. Their working relationship began to deteriorate during the second half of 1997 as Uzzi tried to engage in serious discussions about the business, only to be rebuffed by Dunlap with a shout or a rant. Soon most of Uzzi's dealings were with Kersh. Early in the fourth quarter, Dunlap would unmercifully criticize Uzzi in front of his own staff.

Little by little, Dunlap began to box him out. Though he was the third-highest-ranking executive, Uzzi had never made a presentation before the board of directors, except to demonstrate the air and water products. By the third quarter of 1997, Dunlap no longer invited him to board meetings. Uzzi, however, made sure that he was always in the office when the board of directors was in town, hoping that a board member might seek him out. In the early days, director Charles Thayer would always wander through the halls to informally visit with the company's top executives. Since Dunlap had cast Thayer off the board, no one ever came by for a discussion. If someone did, Uzzi might have been tempted to complain. He might have told the directors what he told Dunlap in mid-January of 1998 before Sunbeam announced its 1997 results.

Then, Uzzi urged Dunlap to tell Wall Street that the year's 20 percent increase in sales was not "true year-to-year growth." He wanted Dunlap to explain that there was a difference between what was shipped and what was consumed by retailers. "Real growth" was more on the order of 12 percent, itself an impressive number in an industry where sales rose not much more than 3 percent a year. He wanted Dunlap to explain that the remaining sales growth was to build retail inventories to better balance seasonal sales and gain greater market share. "I kept pushing back trying to make my point," recalled Uzzi, "and he just yelled: 'You fuckin' guys! You've got to get off your dead asses.' Obviously we were moving stuff up to make the numbers. He wouldn't listen."

In February, as sales worsened because retailers were loaded with inventory they could not sell, Uzzi went to Dunlap's office to update his boss on the company's deteriorating condition. Dunlap wasn't there. His secretary informed Uzzi that the boss was out looking at yachts. The next day, he found Dunlap in his office, feet plopped on the desk, reading the Style section of *USA Today*. When Uzzi asked to speak with him, Dunlap roared, "I don't have time to see you now."

Dunlap's hasty dismissal angered the executive, who had increasingly viewed his disengaged boss as someone who used the corporate headquarters as a private clubhouse. Along with other executives, Uzzi had been in Dunlap's office for important business when the CEO invited his tailor inside and asked for help in picking through fabric swatches for a custom suit. Once, at an operating committee meeting, Dunlap popped into his office VCR a twenty-minute tape of Kenny Rogers's expansive estate in Georgia that Dunlap was considering buying. Another time, Uzzi found Dunlap and Kersh engaged in ordering guns from mail-order catalogs spread before them. On still another occasion, when Dunlap mused about purchasing a private plane for himself, he heard Kersh suggest that Dunlap should get Sunbeam to buy the plane. Dunlap could alter his employment contract, opined Kersh, so that the CEO could buy it from the company later at a cheaper, fixed price.

It galled Uzzi that Dunlap would sometimes arrive at 8 A.M. and, like a drill sergeant, make a quick inspection of headquarters to see who was in and who was out. Yet Dunlap often disappeared for two-hour lunches and periodically took the chauffeur-driven Mercedes to a beauty salon to have his graying hair dyed blond. While at work, Uzzi thought, Dunlap often focused on frivolous concerns. Once, for example, he insisted on filing a lawsuit against the landlord of Sunbeam's headquarters because another tenant posted a sign on the building. The litigation, which quickly became known as "the great sign war," was later settled out of court.

By January 1998, a disgusted Uzzi badly wanted out. He had become sick of doing Dunlap's bidding, having to fire people he did not believe should be fired. In that month, Uzzi believed the firings reached a new level of insanity. Shortly after the Christmas holidays, Dunlap ordered him to fire three ex-Scott Paper executives who were among the company's best executives: international vice president Dixon Thayer, general manager Bill Kirkpatrick, and international licensing director Ronald Fox. Dunlap wanted them out because he believed they failed to commit to the company by refusing to move their families to Florida. Yet Uzzi not only had to fire them; he also had to indulge in what he considered a sick routine with Dunlap, who insisted on hearing how each reacted to the news.

On the morning that Uzzi was to terminate Kirkpatrick, Dunlap telephoned him the moment he walked into the office to find out if he had already done it.

"No," replied Uzzi, "he's not in yet."

Some forty-five minutes later, with Kirkpatrick finally in Uzzi's office, the phone rang again. It was Dunlap, demanding to see Uzzi in person.

"So how did he react?" asked the CEO.

"Al, he's sitting in my office right now," said Uzzi. "I haven't had a conversation with him yet."

"Well, I want to know exactly how he reacts as soon as it's done," demanded Dunlap.

Later, Uzzi returned and Dunlap asked him if Kirkpatrick had given him a hard time.

"No," replied Uzzi, wanting only to cut the conversation short. "He took it very professionally. He asked how he could help with a transition."

Uzzi now began to think incessantly about his own transition out. He seriously considered walking, and his wife, Sally, urged him to do so. But Uzzi believed "the place would have collapsed" without him. After all, he was essentially running the day-to-day operations of the company. So Uzzi went to human resources chief Gary Mask and told him he no longer wanted to remain at Sunbeam.

"I don't want to stay here and be part of this," he said. "I'm willing to hang on until Al finds someone else, but I'm not going to hang around for six months for nothing." In exchange for working through a transition period, he wanted the vesting of his stock options accelerated.

Mask was supposed to talk to Kersh, who was supposed to talk to Dunlap. Somehow, the conversation never moved up the ladder. Kersh probably knew that Dunlap's reaction would not be positive. For months, Dunlap had been blaming Uzzi for the company's problems. He often compared him with Newt White, the hard-charging Scott Paper executive who walked out on Dunlap early. "If I saw Newt walking down the street, I'd cross and walk down the other side," Dunlap told associates. "But if Newt White were here, things would be different."

After the Morgan Stanley–imposed disclosure, Uzzi concluded that it was only a matter of days before he, too, would become another notch in Dunlap's downsizing belt. Of course, he was right. In anticipation of leaving, Uzzi hadn't replaced his secretary, who had been gone for several weeks. In early March, the company had engaged headhunter Hardy to find a new chief operating officer to replace him—even though Kersh had told Morgan Stanley during its due diligence review two weeks later that no management changes or departures were anticipated in the near future.

Uzzi, frustrated at his inability to get an answer on a transition deal, began to pressure Mask again for a more profitable exit. On March 29, Kersh called Uzzi to find out exactly what he had in mind.

"Look," he told Kersh, "I know I'm history. I know I'm the odd man out. Al doesn't like me, and I really don't need this. I could be out playing golf.

"I'm happy to provide some continuity while you do this, but I'm not going to do it just to collect my salary. If you guys want me to stay around until you bring in a replacement, I'll do it, but I want some compensation."

Kersh asked what he had in mind. Uzzi replied that perhaps the company could accelerate the vesting of a portion of his stock options. In exchange, he would stay for a six-month transition period. In the negotiating dance before he joined Sunbeam, Uzzi had fought hard for them, to the point of sparking a huge blowup between Dunlap and then human resources chief Wilson.

Uzzi had amassed an appreciable options' fortune worth nearly $6 million during his eighteen months of work. But only a third of his options were fully vested. If he quit or was fired by Dunlap for cause, he would be leaving nearly $4 million on the table.

When Kersh relayed Uzzi's message to his boss, Dunlap predictably exploded.

"Do you get a load of this shit?" he asked. "This fucking guy is giving me the ultimatum? Fire him! You go over there right now, and you tell him he can either fucking resign or he can get fired. It's his fucking choice."

As Dunlap thought a little more carefully about Uzzi, however, another idea popped into his head. The following day, April Fool's Day, all the company's general managers were scheduled to convene for an all-hands meeting in the boardroom at 10 A.M. Rather than fire Uzzi, Dunlap considered humiliating him in front of Sunbeam's top twenty to twenty-five people at the session. He openly relished the thought of tearing into the executive, ripping him apart to force his resignation.

"By the time I'm through with him at this meeting," Dunlap said, "he'll quit."

Fearful of the effect a public trashing of Uzzi would have on the management team, Mask and Fannin opposed the idea. Most of the company's managers were under tremendous strain and pressure. Many of them were engaged in the same review process that Uzzi had just concluded. They were evaluating whether they even wanted to stay at Sunbeam. Since the start of the new year, they had watched one top officer after another walk out the door for the last time. McBride, the marketing vice president and general manager of household products, was ousted in December. In early January it was Thayer, Fox, and Kirkpatrick. New products chief Paula Etchison quit in February. A public beating of Sunbeam's highest-ranking operating executive by Dunlap would only push more of them over the edge and out the door. Frankly, concluded Mask, Sunbeam couldn't afford to indulge Dunlap's wish to abuse Uzzi into leaving.

Kersh agreed, and Fannin put together the termination letter they would hand Uzzi the next morning. Though the executive's contract entitled him to written notice of "performance deficiencies" and thirty days to eliminate them before he could be fired for cause, Dunlap didn't want to wait.

At 8:30 A.M., on April 1, the two of them strolled down the hall to the other side of the building and walked into Uzzi's office.

"Look," said Kersh, "it's obvious that this hasn't worked."

"Does this mean I'm getting fired?"

"Well, you have a choice," replied Kersh. "Al says you can either resign, or we'll have to fire you."

It was hardly a surprise. "What's my severance package?"

"Don," said Fannin, "there isn't any package."

He gave Uzzi a termination letter signed by Dunlap. It did not mention even a day of additional pay.

"Essentially, this is it," said Fannin.

"Well, what am I supposed to live on?" asked Uzzi.

"It's over," said Kersh. "You can resign right now, or you're going to be fired."

"Well, I want to think about it," replied Uzzi.

"You need to let me know right now," Kersh said.

"I'm not going to decide that."

Uzzi, who had already packed up most of his office belongings, left the office. By the time Dunlap was addressing his managers later that morning, the marketing executive was headed for the golf course to play a round with some neighbors. In a later settlement, Uzzi was awarded the severance package which Dunlap denied him. But his vested stock options had become worthless by the time he was permitted to exercise them.

In the company's large conference room, Dunlap could not resist taking a few parting shots at his latest casualty. He blamed Uzzi for doing low-margin sales deals with retailers. He blamed him for not measuring up to his own expectations of performance.

"You have had leadership that has let you down and didn't perform for you," he told his assembled troops. "Shame on us for not dealing with it sooner. We've dealt with it now, and it's a new day. We're going to get the message out that you can't get the same old deals from Sunbeam."

THE PRESSURE WAS BUILDING, mostly because of the company's deteriorating performance. But it was also growing from an unlikely source within Sunbeam, a young, low-level employee in the company's internal audit department. Deidra DenDanto felt that nearly all her work at the company had been little more than a futile exercise. There was little, if any, follow-up to her recommendations. There were few satisfactory answers to the questions she posed about the company's aggressive sales activities. The trailer truck sales that she had challenged due to inadequate controls continued into the new year. Product returns, the focus of one of her earliest audit reports, had become an even larger problem. In one thirty-day period ending in mid-January of 1998, Sunbeam customers deducted $2.8 million from their invoices by returning nondefective products to the company. A study of returns in Canada alone showed that fully one-third of the merchandise sold in the country had been returned to Sunbeam in 1997. "There was no consequence to it," she said.

DenDanto was becoming so frustrated by her inability to change what she regarded as improper that she herself began to change, for the worse. She had long regarded herself as a high-spirited person with an effervescent personality. Now, increasingly tormented by what she saw at work, she had become, in the words of her fiancé, "an unhappy and jaded person, with nothing good to say." Her level of discontent had reached an explosive stage. One afternoon in late 1997, while in a car driven by a Sunbeam colleague, she began screaming a constant stream of profanities. With the windows up and the radio on, DenDanto and Roger Ross, a finance executive who worked for Robert Gluck, shouted every obscenity that came to their lips for at least two straight minutes, a peculiar release of their mounting tension. They burst into laughter when it was over, strangely embarrassed by their behavior but momentarily purged of the day's disappointments.

No amount of cursing, however, could relieve DenDanto's misgivings in early March of 1998.

It was while she was working on a computer project, helping to streamline the sales process, that DenDanto had a worrisome conversation with a Sunbeam customer service manager in Hattiesburg, Mississippi. The manager came to DenDanto with several questions on how to account for the bill-and-hold transactions that were then moving through the system. Did the credit terms start from the date of the delivery or from the date of sale? Some customers believed they didn't have to worry about credit terms until the goods were delivered to them. The service rep thought otherwise. "There was really no clarity to it," DenDanto said. "We would think payment was due in six months from the delivery to a warehouse in January. The customer would think the payment was due six months after they received the goods in June."

The confusion heightened her concern about the sales and made her feel as if her own integrity was being violated. "If you bathe in dirty water long enough," DenDanto said, "you get dirty." In a way that few low-level managers do, however, she felt an obligation to the company's shareholders as well. She wanted to put her frustrations on the record, to document her concerns for her boss and others.

In an extraordinary memo dated March 12, 1998, DenDanto took the first step toward that goal. In the document, she raised serious questions about the function of the internal audit department, the company's bill-and-hold transactions, and the accounting measures for them. She also expressed her growing frustration over her department's apparent inability to correct perceived misdeeds or mistakes at the company.

"It is with much disappointment that internal audit must again bring to management's attention the lack of prudent, ethical behavior being engaged in by this organization in order to 'make numbers' for the company. . . ," she wrote. DenDanto charged that some Sunbeam managers were engaged in sales activities that put shareholder assets at risk, and she complained "that no corrective action has been taken against people participating in these activities."

She maintained that Sunbeam's bill-and-hold sales were "clearly in violation of GAAP." She also recalled an incident in which a financial officer interrupted a computer systems meeting attended by numerous employees and outside consultants to ask for the documents to complete a bill-and-hold transaction. In DenDanto's view, the request "clearly sent the message that it is acceptable to violate company controls as long as it is to meet executive management goals."

The memo was intended to be addressed to Dunlap, Kersh, and Uzzi. She planned to copy it to Hartshorne and the board of directors. Before sending it, however, DenDanto wanted her boss to see it first. Though she was angered by what she saw, she also felt a sense of loyalty and obligation to Hartshorne, who, she thought, was "stonewalled" as often as she was. On March 12, at Sunbeam's plant in Hattiesburg, Mississippi, she called her boss aside in a hallway and handed him a copy of the two-page memo.

"I'm done," she said. "I'm so sick and tired of doing my job and having it mean nothing."

Hartshorne glanced at the document and quickly ushered her into an empty office reserved for visiting executives.

"You can't send this to the board," he said.

"Well, I'm very angry and this is what came from it," she said. "Tom, you're my boss. It's my responsibility to pass this to you. You do with it what you want."

She had first voiced her concerns about the bill-and-hold sales to Hartshorne in October 1997—three months before the board's audit committee knew of the transactions. Now, Hartshorne, who often told her he admired her integrity, dialed Kersh's phone number in Florida.

"Russ," he said, "I've got Deidra here with me. She's very upset."

"What?" Kersh asked.

Hartshorne, without mentioning the memo, explained DenDanto's concerns. Kersh attempted to reassure the upset auditor as she sat stiffly and silently in the sterile room, under the low hum of the office's fluorescent lights.

"There's nothing going on here," Kersh told her. "It's not what you're thinking. It may look worse than it is, but it will all become clear in a couple of months."

After Kersh hung up, Hartshorne again advised her against sending the memo. "Let's see what happens," said Hartshorne. "I'm sorry you're frustrated. But let's just wait."

DenDanto, not wanting to undermine her boss and reluctant to violate the chain of command, decided to keep the document in her laptop computer. But Kersh's words did little to comfort her. "I felt my voice was falling on deaf ears," she said later. "We were a token internal audit department. I believed the intention was that we do nothing."

ON APRIL 2, 1998, the day after Uzzi was fired and exactly two weeks after Dunlap reluctantly agreed to warn Wall Street that Sunbeam's sales would be lower than analysts expected, Finn Fogg and David Fannin were conferring again on issuing yet another statement. For one thing, Sunbeam had to announce Uzzi's termination because after Dunlap and Kersh, he was the company's most senior officer. His departure was important news to the company's investors. Fogg advised that Sunbeam could wait no longer than the end of the week to report Uzzi's firing.

For another, the company's first quarter results had fast deteriorated to the point where its previous warning clearly didn't go far enough. In fact, the warning now stood in complete contradiction to the latest facts. Bob Gluck, Sunbeam controller, glumly told Kersh and Fannin that the company's revenues would fall below its year-earlier first quarter. He told them Sunbeam would not even make a penny of profit in the first three months. Instead, it would report a sizable loss.

All the loading and channel stuffing in the previous year and the massive turnover in management ranks had conspired to slow sales. No amount of financial judgment calls—other than outright fraud—could prevent red ink from spilling onto Sunbeam's income statement. At least one top Sunbeam executive heard Dunlap urge the financial staff to somehow grind out a profit in the quarter. According to the senior executive, Dunlap stated that there "had to be a way for Gluck's finance people to find an operating profit. They weren't trying hard enough. I know that there are always enough 'judgment' matters to get there."

By driving hard to complete the Coleman acquisition in the first quarter, however, it might be possible to use a write-off or restructuring charge to conceal the seriousness of the downturn. Kersh managed to close the Coleman deal by March 30, a mere twenty working days after the acquisition was announced. That still was one day beyond the normal close of Sunbeam's first quarter. So Kersh solved the problem by changing Sunbeam's reporting dates, extending the first quarter by two days to March 31. He could justify the alteration by insisting—as Sunbeam later would—that the quarter was changed "to standardize the fiscal period-ends of Sunbeam and each of its recent acquisitions." Generally, though, an acquiring company does not conform to the reporting dates of a company it gobbles up. Instead an acquirer imposes its own standards and rules on the companies it buys.

By gaining two extra days in the quarter, Sunbeam was able to declare "one-time acquisition charges" due to Coleman. Just as importantly, Kersh would be able to tack on an additional $14.8 million of sales from Coleman and an extra $5 million from Sunbeam to somewhat cushion the severe decline in first quarter sales. Excluding the two days' worth of Coleman revenue, Sunbeam sales would have fallen 9.5 percent, well below the 3.6 percent decline the company eventually would report.

Sunbeam wasn't expecting to report any of these numbers until April 29 at the earliest. But because it was now clear that Sunbeam's figures would be far worse than expected, Fannin drafted yet another press release on April 2. He faxed a copy to Fogg at his Park Avenue apartment in New York and steeled himself for another confrontation with Dunlap. To save himself a long and hard struggle, Fannin told his boss that it was Skadden Arps that was insisting that the company issue the warning. Dunlap protested, but essentially resigned himself to the need to release the statement the following day. One idea was to send out two announcements. The first would report good news: that Sunbeam's cash offers for Signature Brands and First Alert were now completed. Then, after the stock market closed, Sunbeam would release the negative earnings report, along with that of Uzzi's termination.

Rich Goudis, who normally would help to draft the company's press releases, wasn't in the office. He had stopped by early in the morning before going to a doctor's appointment and then gone to Rexall-Sundown headquarters to formally accept a position as the vice president of finance. When he pulled out of the driveway near noon on a beautiful Florida day, he considered whether he should take a right and go home or take a left to Sunbeam headquarters on South Congress Avenue. Goudis turned his white Maxima right, deciding to spend the rest of his day with his wife and his family.

At 5 P.M. Fannin called to alert him to the press release strategy. "David," Goudis said, "you can't do that. This smacks of manipulation. You're going to send out a positive sign to the street that the deals are closed and then later on you're going to jam it the other way? You can't do this."

Fannin agreed. "You're absolutely right," he said. "Come in early tomorrow morning, and we'll review a different script."

That night Goudis lay awake in bed, thinking he should turn in his resignation first thing in the morning. He would take his two weeks' vacation and give no notice at all. "I don't really want to put up with this crap tomorrow," he thought.

ANDREW SHORE WAS fast asleep in on the downstairs couch of a friend's house in the Pacific Palisades section of Los Angeles when the phone rang at 4 A.M. It was R. T. Quinn, one of Shore's associate analysts back in New York, where the time was 7 A.M. Quinn, sitting at his desk in a cramped cubicle, had assumed Shore was staying at a hotel, and he hung up when he heard the unfamiliar voice of Shore's startled friend on the line. He thought he had the wrong number.

Quinn called Shore's wife, Dana, to verify the telephone number and soon discovered he had the right place. When the phone rang again, Shore knew it had to be R. T. The day before, after Shore had given a luncheon presentation to investors at PaineWebber's offices in San Francisco, he had accessed his voice mail box in New York and heard a mysterious message. "Did you hear Uzzi left?" the anonymous voice said. To no avail, Shore tried several times that afternoon to verify that information with Sunbeam, but no one would call him back.

Now R. T. was calling to tell him that he had discovered employee rumors on Internet Web sites suggesting that Uzzi was no longer at Sunbeam. It was important news because Uzzi was respected on the Street and brought credibility to Dunlap's shrinking management team. "But we didn't know if he was fired, if he resigned, or what," Quinn later reflected.

Shore and Quinn picked up another scrap of evidence when they discovered that the message on Rich Goudis's phone had been changed. In place of Goudis's voice, there was that of a woman saying, "For financial information, call Russell Kersh."

"Is this any big deal?" asked Quinn. "People change messages all the time. People leave all the time. You don't cut numbers just because people leave."

Shore immediately phoned Goudis at his home in Boca Raton. "I almost had a heart attack when I got him," recalls Shore.

"What are you doing at home?" he asked.

"I just resigned."

"Rich," Shore said, "I hear things are really, really bad. I hear the place is falling apart."

"You have to call the company," Goudis told him, refusing to say anything else.

"I hear Uzzi left," continued Shore, trying to bait Goudis into confirming at least that piece of information. "I hear the company is going to miss the numbers."

Goudis wouldn't budge, so Shore frantically dialed Kersh again and left him a terse message.

"Russ, I heard Uzzi got fired. If this is true, I'm downgrading the stock immediately." Kersh never called back. Another call to Dunlap elicited little more than a message from his secretary that he was in a meeting.

Unable to confirm Uzzi's departure and aware of Goudis's resignation, Shore admitted he didn't have much evidence to go on.

"It was more visceral," he told Quinn. "It just smells bad."

Besides, he had become increasingly troubled over the ongoing departure of many of the company's managers and executives. He decided to downgrade the stock.

"You have to have something," Quinn countered. "You don't even know if the earnings are going to be bad."

If Shore was mistaken, he knew that he probably would face Dunlap's wrath himself. The CEO was known not to shy away from belittling Wall Street analysts for the slightest slip or blunder. When Deepak Raj, a top-ranked analyst with Merrill Lynch, had incorrectly predicted that Sunbeam would slightly miss its second quarter sales number in 1997, Dunlap could not wait to hear from Raj. The moment the analyst was announced as the next questioner during a conference call, Dunlap screeched: "DEEPAK!!! Do you want to say you're sorry? You apologize? You got it wrong? Or all of the above."

"On what?" Raj replied in a perplexed voice.

"On your report you put out there, for godsake!" Dunlap roared. "You guys are following too many of those junk companies."

"I don't think so," Raj said softly.

"Ah, come on, go ahead," Dunlap goaded. "I think the bull went and got mad-cow disease."

Dunlap's rejoinder, a reference to Merrill Lynch's advertisements featuring a bull, drew a hearty laugh from everyone, including Shore, who did not relish Raj's awkward position. But Shore, who had been skeptical of Dunlap from the start, felt he had been positive on the stock long enough. From the very beginning he believed his clients could make money on Dunlap. He only had to understand when to get them out of the stock. Months earlier, when Shore saw and noted the deterioration of Sunbeam's balance sheet, he had held off from issuing a downgrade. "Al was still a persuasive demagogue," he said. "Balance sheets really don't lie, but stocks don't always react to them until six or nine months later. I spoke to so many investors during that time and was never able to read anything different from their body language. No one was ready to jump ship. They still believed the man."

Now, in his gut, Shore felt this was finally the time. "What we did know is that if Uzzi and Goudis were gone, it wasn't good, especially with all the other defections," Shore reasoned. "What it basically comes down to is this: if you wait until you have all the facts, almost always in investing you are too late."

He wasn't going to be too late on this one. Quinn, however, feared an investor backlash because Dunlap was still popular with clients.

"You realize what you're doing to me here, don't you?" Quinn pleaded.

With Shore on the West Coast, all the furor of a downgrade would fall on his young associate. Something always seemed to go wrong when Shore was traveling. Investors, including Shore's own clients, are likely to blame the messengers of bad news for their losses as much as they are likely to fault a company for its own mistakes. A downgrade that would cause stock prices to fall would hurt many PaineWebber clients who were invested in the stock. Quinn would catch all the flak.

"If we're wrong, we're going to be fired, but we have to do this," Shore said.

The analyst called PaineWebber's compliance department to issue the downgrade, explaining that he didn't have all the facts yet but was lowering his rating on Sunbeam from a buy to neutral based on little more than his gut. It wasn't necessary to downgrade the stock to a sell rating. Every investor with even the slightest familiarity with analyst research would interpret the downgrade as an outright sell.

At 7:50 A.M., Eastern Standard Time, Shore got on the squawk box—the term for the morning conference call that linked the analysts in New York with more than 5,000 stockbrokers around the world—

and stunned PaineWebber's sales force by announcing the downgrade. Shore could hear groans on the other end of the telephone call, and several people back in New York groused that he was making a mistake. Battalions of salesmen soon began phoning their clients—from the largest institutional shareholders to individuals who invest in the market through PaineWebber—to notify them of the change.

It had an electrifying effect. The moment news of Shore's decision finally hit the market at 9:09 A.M., Sunbeam stock began to plunge, falling $4 within minutes.

TWO HOURS EARLIER, Rich Goudis had driven his Maxima into the parking lot at the Sunbeam building—before anyone else had arrived. He returned his fax machine from home as well as his cell phone, leaving both on his desk. He also left a succinct letter of resignation on Kersh's desk, making copies for both Fannin and Gary Mask. It was a gracious letter, one that certainly disguised his disgust. "I have been very fortunate over the past several years to have worked in such a dramatic turnaround environment. It has been both a professionally and personally enriching experience."

Goudis was leaving the building when David Fannin pulled into the lot in his white Lexus.

"Hi, Rich," he said. "What's going on? Where were you yesterday?"

"Well," Goudis replied nervously, "that's why I wanted to see you. I want to say goodbye. I'm leaving the company."

"You're leaving? I'm very sorry to hear that."

"I've always had great respect for you, but I can't work with Al and Russ anymore."

It was not a good omen for the day. Fannin thought it was the worst possible time to leave. They were about to disclose news that would rock the stock market and draw hundreds of telephone calls from analysts, reporters, and investors on the same day their head of investor and media relations was quitting.

Fannin rushed up the stairs and straight to his office, where he found a note from Goudis on his desk. In a neat looping hand, Goudis had scribbled at the bottom of the letter: "I have enormous respect for you, but over the past few months, I have lost the passion to follow Al and Russ. Fortunately, a great opportunity found me and I look forward to taking all the knowledge of turnarounds and business to my next employer. Best of luck always, Rich."

Oh great, thought Fannin. He called Kersh at home, only to speak to his wife, Martha, who told him that Kersh was still in the shower. When he called back, Fannin gave him the bad news.

"Rich Goudis has resigned," he said.

"Oh shit!" replied Kersh. "What's that all about? Why is he doing it?"

"He's taken another job. He left notes for everybody."

"All right," he said, "I'll be in in a few minutes."

Dunlap strolled into the office around 8:15 A.M., his normal starting time, with his normal starting words.

"What's happening?" he asked Fannin.

"Well, for starters, Rich Goudis is gone. He quit."

"Goddamn it!" said Dunlap. "I don't understand this generation. Well, we'll deal with it."

Once Kersh arrived, Fannin and he went into Dunlap's office with a draft press release announcing still more disappointing news to Wall Street that Dunlap refused to read. The chief executive didn't want to have anything to do with it. Dunlap believed another release was suicidal.

"No one should be looking at the current results," Dunlap said. "They should be looking at the potential of the combined companies." Shifting the blame to others, as he often did, Dunlap added, "Look, we were all let down and misled by Uzzi. Now they want to take a situation and make it worse.

"I let you guys talk me into this once before," he said. "Shame on me. I never should have allowed you to talk me into it the first time. I'm not going to do it again. If you're going to do this, get yourself a new boy. I'm out of here! You tell Morgan Stanley and Skadden that if that's what they want to do, they can just get themselves a new boy."

Soon after the stock market opened at 9 A.M., Sunbeam shares began to crater and the telephone calls came into headquarters with the ferocity of a violent thunderstorm. Goudis's secretary kept running back and forth between the offices with messages. "What do I tell them about Rich?" she asked. "Who's going to talk to them?"

Kersh soon discovered that the stock's tumble was caused by analyst Andrew Shore.

"That son of a bitch," shouted Dunlap when he found out.

UNABLE TO CANCEL his marketing calls that morning, Shore was driving a rented car on a California freeway to a 7:30 A.M. breakfast meeting in Pasadena. When he tapped into his voice mail box with a cell phone at 6:49 A.M., it was already jammed with thirty caustic and bitter messages. Most of the callers, including some of PaineWebber's own salespeople, wanted him fired.

As Shore clicked through the messages, he was horrified by their content.

"What do you mean you did it from your gut?" asked one money manager. "What do you really know? You have no information. I can't believe it!"

"What a stupid, irresponsible call!" screamed another caller. "You should be fired for that!"

"I can't believe you have been in the business this long," moaned an anonymous person.

Quinn, meantime, sat at his cluttered desk in a small office off the Avenue of the Americas in New York, inundated with scathing calls.

"You must be the one who did it!" shouted one caller into the receiver.

"Actually, I'm not solely responsible," Quinn responded, trying to fend off the complaints.

The telephone call Quinn lived in constant fear of receiving that morning was the one from Dunlap himself. He knew how abusive the executive could become, and he dreaded the idea of a tongue-lashing from him, even if it could only be delivered through more than 1,000 miles of telephone cable.

"It was a nightmare," Quinn says. "I was pretty scared because I was waiting for that call from Al Dunlap. I did not want to take that one."

Anticipating this reaction, Shore had tried to convince his boss that he should cancel his appointments for the day and simply stay by a telephone at his friend's house to defuse the anger from many of his clients. But his boss never imagined that the downgrade on a relatively small company, whose total market value was only $3 billion, would cause such a stir.

Compared to some of the other companies he covered, like Procter & Gamble, Sunbeam was, as Shore put it, "like an R&D experience at P&G. It would be a test market company." But Dunlap's loud persona had greatly magnified the company's importance in the market. "Dunlap had made the whole thing larger than life," thought Quinn. "So not many people around here realized what the reaction would be like."

Without any official word yet from Sunbeam itself, Shore and Quinn worried that they might have made one of the biggest mistakes in their careers.

FANNIN WAS IN his office, typing some final changes into the press release, when Kersh rushed in.

"Al wants to see us," he said.

The two scrambled into Dunlap's office. In the face of Shore's downgrade and the stock's freefall, Dunlap had become resigned to the fact that they would have to put out the press release. But he was looking for ways to get some favorable news into it.

Since Uzzi's firing, Lee Griffith, the ex-Scottie who was vice president of sales, had been lobbying for Uzzi's job. Eager to put some positive spin on the bad news they were about to make public, Dunlap decided to promote Griffith to president of Sunbeam's household products division. He overlooked the fact that Griffith was just as involved, if not more so than Uzzi, in the rampant discounting to retailers that Dunlap knew about and approved.

"Well," said Dunlap, "Lee wants the job. Let's just give it to him."

Reaching Griffith on the telephone in California at a sales meeting, Dunlap told him: "After careful deliberation, we're going to make you president of the household products division."

"Yes, sir," responded Griffith. "I'm excited by the challenge."

Fannin prominently positioned the news in the release, scrambling to get it out on the business wire at 11:01 A.M. Shortly afterward, at Dunlap's insistence, the company's chief lawyer left headquarters in the middle of the meltdown to negotiate Dunlap's personal dispute with the Boca Raton Resort and Club. Dunlap was bitterly angry when he discovered that the club paid a $2,500 settlement to the man who alleged that Dunlap attacked him on the golf course in February. If that person's complaint was worth $2,500, Dunlap insisted that he should get $2.5 million. So as Sunbeam stock kept tumbling and the telephones rang off their hooks, Dunlap demanded that Fannin still go to his scheduled luncheon appointment to bargain on his behalf. At least one person benefited from the turmoil that day: the club agreed to pay Dunlap $25,000 to go away.

BACK IN NEW YORK, at PaineWebber's offices, Quinn read the statement Sunbeam put out and shouted a cheer of delight. The company said it expected to show a loss for the first quarter on sales that would be 5 percent below the year-earlier period. The company reported that Uzzi had been terminated, and that Griffith had been named to the new job.

"Our first quarter started slowly this year after an excellent holiday season," Dunlap was quoted as saying in the release. "However, we fully expected our grill sales, especially reorder business late in the quarter, to meet a level which was not realized. Grill reorder business can be difficult to forecast, as the demand may come late in the first quarter or in the second quarter. In addition, we believe retailers are continuing to manage down their inventories, although retail sales reports are encouraging. We were offered opportunities to sell additional product at margins which we felt were unacceptable, and we rejected that business. We felt it was more important to preserve the integrity of our brands and not to sacrifice the future of our business for short-term results . . . "

Not much later, Shore called into New York.

"R. T., what's going on?" he asked.

"Did you hear the news?"

"What news?" asked Shore.

"It's on the tape. They're missing their numbers."

A broad smile crossed Shore's face. "My heart had fallen into my bowels," recalls Shore. "The news made it come back into my chest. I felt the most amazing sense of relief." And when Quinn read him Dunlap's line about not wanting to sacrifice the future for short-term results, Shore laughed aloud. Dunlap, he knew, had been doing nothing except running the company for the short-term from the first day he arrived.

Within minutes the angry messages were replaced by congratulatory notes. When Shore's secretary read him some of them, he felt relieved.

"Great call!"

"Sorry about comment."

"Amazing job."

"It really felt good," conceded Shore.

Later in the afternoon, after arriving for a scheduled appointment with the portfolio manager of Arco Investments in downtown Los Angeles, he was congratulated and thanked for getting the fund out of their Sunbeam position that day. At Arco, Shore and portfolio manager Susan Perkins interrupted their meeting to listen in to Dunlap's conference call with analysts on a speaker phone.

Dunlap was not his usual easygoing self. Reading a prepared statement, he stumbled over the words in his script and sounded stilted and wary. He insisted that the market had overreacted to the news that Sunbeam would post a loss in the quarter. "I used to be called shortsighted," he quipped, "but some of this shortsightedness is lunacy." Dunlap claimed the loss Sunbeam expected had "nothing to do with ongoing operations" but led the analysts to believe it would result from one-time charges for compensation and costs associated with the company's acquisitions. "We haven't closed all of our quarter," he said. "We haven't tabulated everything yet . . . We're erring on the side of being supercautious because we've got acquisitions and financing, and we're being cautious."

Shore was hoping to grill Dunlap on the call, but couldn't get a question through the operator. By the time the market closed at 4 P.M., Sunbeam stock had become the most active on the New York Stock Exchange, plunging by 24.6 percent, to $34.375.

Shore's Wall Street colleagues generally followed his lead. William Steele of Buckingham Research advised his clients to bail out of the stock after the company's official statement. Three days later, Constance M. Maneaty of Bear Stearns & Co., R. Scott Graham of CIBC Oppenheimer Corp., and even Lisa Fontenelli of Goldman Sachs & Co., Dunlap's favorite analyst, issued their downgrades. It was Fontenelli who fawningly engaged in idle prattle with the CEO in private and in public. After Dunlap missed Sunbeam's 1997 fourth-quarter earnings forecasts, a surprise that sent the stock down 9.5 percent, she gleefully congratulated him and agreed that he was "awesome." "Al," she said with unabashed devotion, "you did a great job, and we actually look forward to you doing it again." Now even Fontenelli abandoned the stock.

Surprisingly, though, Dunlap still had a couple of believers: Nicholas P. Heymann of Prudential Securities and Justin C. Maurer of McDonald & Co. Heymann was the more influential of the two. A former auditor for General Electric Co., he was best known for his encyclopedic knowledge of the GE empire. His research reports on Jack Welch and GE were book-length tomes that explored every detail of the company's operations and management. Heymann began following Sunbeam shares in early 1996, when he was a little-known analyst at NatWest Securities Corp.

On Al Dunlap, he was an unabashed cheerleader. Even in early February, after Sunbeam's disappointing fourth-quarter results and just before things began to fall apart, he was strongly urging investors to buy the company's shares. Heymann cheered Dunlap's acquisitions and even his big, fat contract. "Al Dunlap put investors' fears to rest once and for all by signing a new three-year contract which is heavily stock-oriented," he wrote in a March 12 report reiterating his buy rating on the stock. "This should prove to investors that Al Dunlap will continue to create tremendous value for shareholders . . . "

They were words that Heymann should already have been regretting. Instead he held firm in his belief that Dunlap could work his way out of the mess. That afternoon, when Dunlap retreated to his office to work the phones for support, Heymann was among the first he called.

FOR KERSH, Sunbeam's keeper of the numbers, it had to be one of the most turbulent days of his professional career. It could not have eased his worries when Deidra DenDanto came into his office late in the afternoon to say goodbye. Disenchanted by the company's accounting practices, she had quit her internal auditing job. Earlier in the week, she had gone to the general counsel's office to get the names and home addresses of the outside board members, with the intent of sending her March 12 memo to them.

As DenDanto entered Kersh's doorway, he said, "I hear you're leaving us. Where are you going?"

"Nowhere," she replied, wanting to emphasize the point that she was quitting in disgust.

"What do you mean?" asked Kersh.

"I'm leaving because I don't agree with some of the business practices here," she said boldly. "Executive management isn't committed to the long-term viability of the organization. I don't want to participate in what's going on here."

Kersh grew ashen. "He looked at me with his jaw dropping," DenDanto recalled later.

She extended her hand, and he took it numbly.

"Thank you for the roller-coaster ride," she said, walking out.

It was, to put it mildly, not a good day at headquarters.

Sunbeam was in total chaos.

16

"EXCUSE ME, I'M NOT A COOK!"

THE DAY AFTER Easter Sunday, Al Dunlap was sitting in a dentist's chair in Philadelphia as his orthodontist attended to his bridge work. It was a routine visit, paid for by the company, for the self-proclaimed friend of shareholders. It was apparently just one of the perks in his contract, a benefit under which Sunbeam paid for first-class airfare for both Dunlap and his wife, along with limo charges and a stay at the Philadelphia Four Seasons.

Yet, on this Monday, April 13, as the dentist worked on Dunlap's oversize teeth, Dunlap had to be more obsessed with his public rather than his physical image. For as the bad news continued to seep out of Sunbeam, the media had turned on Dunlap with a vengeance. The man who customarily received rave reviews, even a celebrity-style profile in *People* magazine, was now taking a horrendous beating.

Dunlap, who thought of himself as a media master, badly needed help. After failing to meet Wall Street's profit expectations in the fourth quarter and disclosing that Sunbeam would post a loss for the first three months of 1998, Dunlap had lost virtually all his credibility with the journalists and the analysts who followed the company.

Troubled by the disapproving coverage of his client, Morgan Stanley's Bill Strong called a prominent New York communications

250

boutique for guidance. Strong had steered clients to Sard Verbinnen & Co. ever since the firm had been launched six years earlier by George Sard and Paul Verbinnen, a pair of young, ambitious men who viewed public relations not as publicity but as a strategy to shape image and credibility. Along with Kekst & Co. and Robinson & Co., it was one of only three or four specialist boutiques savvy in financial PR. Sard Verbinnen often worked behind the scenes with investment bankers and attorneys on high-stakes financial maneuvers and takeover battles.

Strong thought the firm might assist in developing a strategy and tactics to help Dunlap win back investor confidence. To Strong's surprise, however, Sard was somewhat reluctant. The world of public relations was a small one, and the word on the street was that Dunlap was a difficult, if not impossible, client to please. Within the past sixteen months, he had either fired or quit the two largest public relations firms in the business. After getting some unfavorable press early in his tenure at Sunbeam, Dunlap had fired Burson-Marsteller's Peter Judice, a veteran PR man who had gotten Dunlap more news coverage than any executive in America with the exception of Microsoft's Bill Gates. He then hired Hill & Knowlton, which assigned former top business editor Geoffrey Smith to Dunlap. But after one negative story in *Barron's*, Dunlap demanded that Smith be taken off his account. Hill & Knowlton helped to handle Sunbeam's announcement of its three acquisitions in early March, but had since resigned the business.

"This guy has really got himself in trouble here," Strong told Sard. "He badly needs some good advice to restore his credibility."

The day after Dunlap was having his teeth cared for in Philadelphia, he and Fannin were in Sard Verbinnen's conference room on 630 Third Avenue, bringing a team of PR specialists through the events of the past couple of months. Sard and Verbinnen, thought Fannin, did not appear eager to accept Dunlap as a client.

"Why are you so reluctant here?" Dunlap asked, surprised that anyone might not want his business.

"You've got a reputation for not listening, and frankly, we're concerned about that," said Sard.

Dunlap, however, turned out to be unexpectedly reasonable, and Sard agreed to help him with his next presentation when the CEO would announce first quarter earnings later in April. The PR advisers thought it would be disastrous to put out bad numbers without a detailed plan to regain the Street's trust. So they counseled Fannin and Dunlap to delay the reporting of the financial results until a strategy could be articulated to Wall Street.

Dunlap told them that Coopers & Lybrand had already been engaged in a crash project to come up with a plan to integrate the three new acquisitions into Sunbeam. Don Burnett, the Coopers consultant and Dunlap friend, was expecting to complete his study by mid-May. Sunbeam's annual shareholders' meeting had already been set for May 12, so Dunlap's presentation needed to be done before then, possibly on May 11.

"What would be your media strategy until then?" asked Dunlap.

"Radio silence," replied Sard. "Go dark. Stay focused on the presentation. If people buy it, the media will start to take care of itself over time."

Dunlap wasn't so sure. He separated the media into two camps: friendlies, who wrote uncritical, if sometimes fawning articles on him, and enemies, whose stories almost always had an unfavorable bent. Among the journalists he favored were Glenn Collins, a gifted writer at the *New York Times* who had reported glowingly about his efforts at both Scott Paper and Sunbeam, and Patricia Sellers, a *Fortune* magazine journalist who had penned an especially upbeat story on him only four months earlier.

Dunlap particularly favored the broadcast media because he felt they were less likely to "edit" his remarks. He could handle tough questions as long as he had the chance to dominate and control the conversation. Dunlap especially liked Neil Cavuto, an anchor for CNBC in New York, who had once told Dunlap on the air that he was "a very magnetic guy," someone who lights "up a room when you get into it," and Lou Dobbs, the cherubic anchor and product of CNN's *Moneyline News Hour*.

"You are going to get some bad press," Sard advised Dunlap and Fannin. "You've got to stop focusing on that. You can't turn the press until you turn the Street. You've got to underpromise and over-deliver."

That certainly made sense to Fannin, who agreed. But Dunlap said he had been contacted by *Fortune*'s Sellers and was inclined to give her an exclusive when they were ready to announce the recovery plan. Counseled against doing the interview by Sard, Dunlap still insisted that it would be okay. "Oh no," Dunlap said, "Patty Sellers is my friend. I can talk to her."

"Don't do it," Sard told him. "You're going to get killed, regardless of what she wrote in the past. In fact, largely because of what she wrote in the past, she's going to have to go after you."

The only time Dunlap seemed a bit perturbed was when Sard noted that Dunlap had to restore his credibility. Dunlap could not accept that he had lost it. "He was pretty much in denial," recalls Fannin. "He refused to accept that his credibility was diminished."

Dunlap and Fannin left the two-hour meeting that day with a new firm to help Sunbeam put a bit more gloss on things.

DONALD BURNETT, Dunlap's long-time consultant and adviser, meanwhile was working on getting a handle on the company's new acquisitions. Kersh was spending virtually the entire month at Coleman's Wichita, Kansas, headquarters assessing the largest of the three new companies. He showed up in Kansas with an armed body-guard who sat outside his office, much to the discomfort of the employees. An army of Coopers & Lybrand consultants combed through the plants and headquarters of the three companies, inter-viewing executives and managers, gathering headcounts at every facil-ity and details on every product. Burnett's team worked swiftly. With Burnett and fellow partner Andrew Molenar orchestrating the effort, some ten consultants were initially assigned to the project.

They had begun the work on March 9 in three separate teams. By the end of March they had interviewed nearly 160 managers in eleven different locations. In just eighteen working days, Burnett already was recommending the closure of seven plants and the possible closing, sale, or consolidation of thirteen other manufacturing sites. Burnett urged Dunlap to consider ditching Coleman's $30 million spa busi-ness, its $20 million furniture operation, and nearly its entire Powermate line of air compressors, air tools, and pressure washers, a business that did over $90 million in annual sales.

Much of the presentation was based on the hurried and superficial analysis. Coopers's review of Coleman's main Wichita plant, a massive facility with 1.2 million square feet, was condensed into four bullet points, occupying a third of a page. The consultants estimated that the plant used less than 40 percent of its capacity and noted that it had "very high" hourly labor costs of $20 per hour in wages and benefits.

Even though its review of Sunbeam's product lines had not yet begun, Burnett told Dunlap to consider closing the company's new, modern plant in Hattiesburg in favor of an outsourcing strategy for appliances. The team still had to visit the European and Asian operations of Coleman, complete its interviews with managers, and ponder the "synergistic benefits" that it would suggest in a final and more thorough report by May 4.

On April 16, as Burnett's team was frantically racing to complete its consulting work, Sunbeam's board of directors met via telephone. For almost all the directors, it was a deeply disturbing meeting. Dunlap, who had generally been on his best behavior before his directors, was angry and profane. He blamed everyone but himself for the company's problems, for the fall of the stock, and for the departure of key executives.

"Fuckin' Uzzi," shouted Dunlap, who used the ousted executive as a scapegoat. "He said he would make the numbers, and he didn't. He made stupid deals, stupid fuckin' deals. Goddamn it! We had to get rid of him . . .

"Goudis was just horrible timing. He got a job at Rexall. He left . . .

"And Coleman is a lot worse than people said it was. It's crap. Just crap. It's a mess. The Coopers people are out there now."

Dunlap explained that he would hold another board meeting on May 6 to roll out the Coopers plan to integrate the new acquisitions and to provide more detail on the first quarter numbers and expectations for the rest of the year. "What we'd like to do is get you all back to New York for the analysts' meeting on May 11," said Dunlap. "Then we'll all go down to Florida together for the shareholders' meeting the next day."

Nearly three weeks later, on Wednesday, May 6, Sunbeam's directors gathered again at 11 A.M. around a large round table in a high-tech conference room at Coopers & Lybrand's New York offices on the Avenue of the Americas. The room was packed with as many as thirty people, including Finn Fogg and Rich Easton from Skadden Arps, Bill Strong from Morgan Stanley, and a platoon of Coopers consultants headed by Burnett and partner Frank Pringle.

From the start, Dunlap was edgy. Director Faith Whittlesey, who lived and worked in New York, had come through the door fifteen minutes late. Dunlap was not pleased.

"Don't ever be late again," he lectured. "This is not the first time and this is an important board meeting. Members of the board, it's your responsibility to get here on time. Come to town the night before if you know there's going to be fog in Boston. There's always fog in Boston. Just get here the night before. There are lots of hotel rooms in New York City. For you to take our time like this is not right."

Once through with the reprimand, Dunlap focused most of the meeting on the report that Burnett and his team had turned in only two days before. Burnett's cost-cutting recommendations had become the Dunlap growth plan. It was, thought some of the company's managers, just another indication of Dunlap's detachment from the business. Rather than use the consultants' views as one of many inputs into his decision making, as most CEOs would, Dunlap let the consultants' report become the de facto plan.

Reading from a thirty-six-page script, Dunlap tried to reassure the board with an upbeat pep talk. "I want to first make it clear that we view the health of the combined company as extremely sound, our strategies are intact, and we foresee an excellent future for Sunbeam," he said.

Then the West Point graduate employed an elementary metaphor, one more appropriate for a grammar school classroom, to describe his new strategy. "Rebuilding and repositioning the combined company involves what I have described as a three-legged stool. Each leg is vitally important, and without any one of the legs, the stool will topple. We feel that we have a plan today that will provide you the assurance as a board of directors that this stool is solid and will withstand whatever we face in the future."

Of his three legs—the right organization, cost structure, and plans to grow the business—one was much longer than the other two. It was, predictably, Chainsaw Al's forte: slashing and burning. No part of Dunlap's presentation was rendered more enthusiastically than Burnett's plan to cut costs. Dunlap said he would jettison at least four businesses, including Coleman's backpack, spa, and compressor operations as well as the camping equipment maker's plant in Lyon, France. Morgan Stanley, Dunlap assured the board, had told him he could expect to get between $250 million and $350 million by selling these businesses.

In all, Dunlap said, he would eliminate 6,430 employees and close

75 out of 120 facilities. Some 2,330 people in the acquired companies would lose their jobs outright. Another 1,300 would be transferred from the Sunbeam payroll when their businesses were sold. By closing two more Sunbeam plants in Mexico City and Acuna in Mexico, Dunlap would gain another 2,800 layoffs.

"Just look at our headquarters savings in terms of personnel and occupancy costs," Dunlap said, with fervor. "We are going from 1,020 employees at the current separate headquarters to around 250 at our new consolidated worldwide headquarters in Boca Raton. Square footage shrinks from 360,000 square feet to 123,000 occupied at our new building."

Dunlap figured he would save $250 million annually by the staff and facility reductions and by sourcing more product from outside vendors. "We will realize some $50 million in labor costs annually . . . and this is just in the acquired companies. We anticipate additional total savings from the outsourcing strategy and the closure of Mexico City and Acuna at over $50 million annually. A portion of this represents labor efficiencies by reducing some 2,800 workers from those two facilities in Mexico.

"As I have always said, if you cannot complete a restructuring in twelve months, you cannot do it. We will complete this restructuring by the end of May, 1999, within the twelve-month period from now."

Not once did Dunlap speak about his plans to deal with the massive disruptions those plans would cause. Not once did he speak about how he planned to retain the most talented people in the acquired organizations and gain their loyalty and commitment as he chainsawed through their friends and colleagues. Not once did he talk about how he would assure product quality or uninterrupted customer deliveries while undergoing Burnett's drastic cost-cutting strategy. "You just gotta get those costs out," Kersh told the board. "You've got to drive down and get them out."

Dunlap let Kersh deliver the worst news to the board. He told them Sunbeam would report a loss of $44.6 million in net income for the first quarter of the year, a loss of 52 cents per share. The sales for the quarter would be $244.3 million, a 3.6 percent decline, when Sunbeam had been expecting to approach $300 million. The sales number, moreover, included an extra $20 million in sales that Kersh was able to get into the quarter by extending the reporting period by two days. This time, at least, Dunlap assumed some responsibility for the declining sales and earnings, though he still pointed a finger at Uzzi and the weather.

"It was bad judgment," Dunlap said. "It will never happen again. I took my eye off the ball. I was running around on these acquisitions. I shouldn't have left Uzzi in charge of operations . . .

"I can't believe I'm doing this," Dunlap said. "I always said I never would, but it was the weather. It was El Niño. People don't think of buying grills during a storm."

For the second quarter, Kersh said, the company would swing back into the black, with net income of $8.1 million, or 7 cents per share, only a third of the earnings it had reported for the same period a year earlier. Finally, for all of 1998, a year in which Dunlap had promised the Street that Sunbeam would earn $2 a share, Kersh was now forecasting the company would make $1.04 a share, or a net income of $108.5 million.

As sobering as some of the projections were, they seemed remarkably optimistic given the company's problems, the huge debt load of more than $2 billion it now carried, and the tasks ahead to integrate three new companies into an organization that already was in total chaos. Dunlap's numbers to support a recovery, moreover, were based on many assumptions that were naive, if not inane. The Coopers team, for example, believed the combined companies could gain $40 million in sales through "synergies." Some of the "synergistic" ideas the consultants proposed were desperately comical in their leaps of faith. Coopers suggested, for example, that the company could get an extra $5 million in sales by taking an Oster meat grinder, slapping a Coleman label on it, and selling the device as a portable meat grinder for hunters—as if they would grind up deer meat in a forest before taking it home. They thought they could get an extra $10 million in sales of heating pads simply by selling them to sporting goods shops that took Coleman product. Never mind that there are rarely electrical outlets to power heating pads in tents.

Langerman, worried whether Dunlap's aggressive targets could be achieved, asked some tough questions about the numbers and the assumptions behind them.

Throughout the session Dunlap seemed strained and tense. Only a few days before, *Forbes* magazine had published a highly negative story on him and the company by one of its savviest financial journalists, Matthew Schifrin. Tipped off by a short-seller of Sunbeam stock, the inquisitive Schifrin acquired a copy of the company's 10K statement filed with the Securities & Exchange Commission on March 6. In the voluminous document, Sunbeam had finally disclosed—at controller Gluck's urging—the bill-and-hold sales of grills that inflated the company's fourth quarter results as well as the $59 million in accounts receivable Kersh sold to raise cash. The story openly accused Dunlap of accounting gimmickry and predicted more "hocus pocus" by him to divert further attention from the company's deteriorating operating results. "This time," concluded Schifrin, "it's not only the employees who got a taste of Al's chainsaw. The shareholders and debenture holders are likely to shed a lot more blood before this is over."

THE SOURCE WHO tipped off Schifrin was Meyer A. Berman, a shrewd and uncommon investor who had befriended the journalist years earlier when Berman owned a small brokerage firm in Great Neck, New York. The Brooklyn-born investor was a short-seller of some repute, having placed his very first bet nearly six decades ago when as an eight-year-old he wagered friends that they could not hit his marble with theirs from across a city street. If they could, he would give them 100 marbles. If not, they had to pony up their own stash. In recent years the crusty and outspoken Berman had relocated to Boca Raton, where he opened a brokerage office in Mizner Park, not much further than a mile and one-half from Dunlap's home. Mostly, though, Berman traded his own money by intuition and homework.

He had a habit of going to Liberty's, a well-stocked bookstore, every night before returning to his apartment. While browsing the bookshelves on a Saturday evening, Berman was abruptly approached by a man in a silk tan jacket.

"Did you buy my book?" Dunlap asked him.

Berman recognized the man instantly. He had first seen Dunlap on television in a debate in which he stoutly defended massive layoffs and maintained that shareholders were management's only constituency. Juxtaposed against Aaron Feuerstein, a grandfatherly entrepreneur who owned Malden Mills, the maker of Polartec fabric, Dunlap cast a cruel contrast in the debate. Feuerstein had won fame for keeping 1,400 workers on his payroll after the company's plant had burned down in Lawrence, Massachusetts. "What right do I have to destroy a major city just to get a few more dollars in the bank that I won't spend before I die?" he said.

Dunlap, mocking the mill owner's position, was forceful in asserting that business had no social responsibility to keep people on a payroll merely to help them and a community. Berman took an immediate dislike to him. "I said to myself then, 'What an animal this Dunlap is.' He was what he was. He hurt a lot of people."

The television debate sparked an interest, and Berman began to closely watch Dunlap's career, read his press, sift through all the Scott Paper and Sunbeam financial documents, and stay alert to every change in Sunbeam's stock price. Berman became convinced that Dunlap was an opportunist, someone who fooled Wall Street time and time again. He also thought that at Sunbeam, Dunlap wouldn't get away with it.

Berman began to bet against the stock by shorting it. On the Street, short-sellers like Berman are a mysterious bunch of risky gamblers who often dish gossip and tips to make money. A short-seller makes a calculated wager that a particular stock will go down in value in the near future. To sell short, an investor borrows shares from a broker, paying interest on the stock. When the shares fall, you buy them and then give them back to your broker, pocketing the difference between the borrowed price of the shares and their lower value.

The quick, dazzling rise in Sunbeam's stock under Dunlap attracted a swarm of short-sellers to the company. Two months after Dunlap became CEO, the number of Sunbeam shares sold short jumped by 50 percent, to 7.4 million by mid-September 1996. That was when the stock was only $24 a share. Even Paul Kazarian's former partners, one-time general counsel Michael Lederman and chief financial officer Robert Setrakian, had shorted the stock during Dunlap's tenure.

So many shorts were betting against Dunlap that Michael Price went public in warning them they were making a huge mistake. "These people who have been shorting Sunbeam are crazy," Price told *Barron's* in an interview in mid-1997 when the stock was at $37 a share. "I feel very good about everything that Al Dunlap is doing at that company. I'm saying to the disbelievers, 'Be careful, be careful.' The upside could be huge."

At the bookstore Dunlap, who had no idea who Berman was, poked the man who was clearly a "disbeliever."

"Did you buy my book?" he asked again.

"I don't buy cookbooks," Berman replied.

"I'm not a cook!" Dunlap said in a frosty tone.

"Yes, you are. You are one of the great cooks of all time."

Dunlap apparently failed to understand what Berman was really saying to him.

"Excuse me," he insisted again, "I'm not a cook. Don't you know who I am?"

"No," Berman quipped again, "you're a cook. Aren't you a cook?"

Frustrated, Dunlap finally said, "I'm going to buy you my book, autograph it, and give it to you for free, damn it."

Dunlap picked up a hardback copy of *Mean Business*, rushed over to the cash register, scribbled his name on a blank page in the book, and eventually tossed it at Berman, who thanked him for the "cookbook" and walked off as Dunlap shrugged his shoulders. Berman brought it home to his apartment and threw it in the garbage. "To think that I wanted his autograph," reflected the short-seller. "He didn't know me from a hole in the wall. But his ego was so large."

Keeping tabs on every Sunbeam filing with the SEC, Berman was among the first to notice in April the footnotes in the 10K on the bill-and-hold transactions and "early buy" program on grills. The disclosures, he believed, showed that Sunbeam had sacrificed margins and future revenues to artificially pump up sales and earnings in 1997. Berman had plenty of reason to tip off Schifrin. A negative article in *Forbes* would more widely circulate the bad news, causing Sunbeam stock to tumble further. That, in turn, would make short-seller Berman an even larger bundle of profit. When he finally cashed in his chips, he had made so much money that he considered sending Dunlap a case or two of champagne. Berman, however, resisted the temptation. But when he bumped into Dunlap weeks later at a black-tie function in Boca, he put his arms around Dunlap and told him, "I love you." "He didn't know who I was," laughed Berman, who did not introduce himself. "He didn't remember me, but I had made a lot of money off of him."

WHEN MICHAEL PRICE read Schifrin's story, alarm bells began to sound in the investor's head. He had seen Dunlap overreact in Perelman's home. He had handed him a new, huge contract before any downturn was ever in the cards. And now the company and the stock were in deep trouble. But it was Schifrin's story that began to shed some light on exactly what had happened. "I had a sense that with the Coleman deal the stock would be volatile because we were issuing a lot of stock," Price said. "You've got Ron Perelman there; you've paid a high price, and you're going to have an extraordinary charge. I first started getting nervous due to the *Forbes* piece. To me, the first sign of trouble was the inventory situation."

Price, who can often make himself scarce to reporters, actually telephoned Schifrin shortly after reading the journalist's brief story.

"If you're right," Price told him, "it looks like fraud."

Schifrin said that virtually every fact in the story came straight from the company's own documents filed with the SEC. Price then confided to the reporter that he had told Dunlap to stay quiet and start producing. Dunlap did not seem to know of the conversation between Price and a journalist on his enemies' list, but the unsolicited telephone call confirmed in Schifrin's mind Price's own concern over his investment and the man he had put in charge of it.

At the board session, Dunlap did not hide his feelings about the article. "It is bullshit and garbage!" Dunlap yelled.

He said he spoke with *Forbes* publisher Jeff Cunningham about the story. Dunlap claimed that Cunningham agreed it was "a sloppy piece of journalism." "*Forbes* is coming apart," contended Dunlap, who then began to refute the story's contents.

"Al, I've been with you for twenty-three years, and I've got to say what is happening is so unfair," said Burnett, his longtime friend and ally. "I just have to say it. When I see what they're doing to you, it just makes me mad."

Dunlap seemed restless, uneasy. "He wasn't quite himself," recalled Elson. "He was down, very down. He was angry, irascible, extremely moody, and he would swear. I ascribed it to the pressures of the acquisitions. I was a little worried about him."

So was Langerman, who frankly worried about how the Sunbeam disaster was reflecting on him. From the start he had functioned as Price's eyes and ears on the investment, through the Kazarian,

Schipke, and now Dunlap eras—all of them filled with some degree of chaos, turmoil, and disappointment. Would this latest disaster cause Price to pass him over as the new chief executive of Mutual Shares when his boss would quit later in the year? He was the chief operating officer of the fund and was widely perceived to be the front-runner for the top job. But with Sunbeam becoming a debacle, anything was certainly possible.

The cautious lawyer was sensitive to that possibility. After Price had mentioned only two of his five lieutenants—Ray Garea and Larry Sondike—in a recent *Wall Street Journal* interview, Langerman admitted that he called his boss to find out if he should read something into the omission of the others, especially himself. Price assured him he should not.

As the board was breaking up and leaving the conference room, Dunlap turned to Langerman.

"Well what did you think of the presentation?" he asked.

"I'll be honest with you, Al," Langerman replied. "My biggest fear is that somebody will try to bait you and he'll succeed."

"I can't believe you would say that to me," snapped Dunlap. "Don't you think that I know how to give a public speech? How many times do you think I've given a speech? Russ, how many times have I given a public speech? Have I ever blown up, Russ?"

"No, Al," Russ said obediently.

"Look, we can wrap this up by the end of the day if you want. I'll get my lawyer here and we can wrap this up."

"Al, what are you talking about?" asked a stunned Langerman.

"Well, if you're not happy, and you want me to go, I'll get my lawyer down here and by 5 o'clock, we'll be done. I'll be out of here."

Langerman assured Dunlap that he did not want him to leave, but he stored the incident away, something else to make him fret a little more. They walked to another conference room at Coopers where Dunlap made the same presentation before Michael Price.

Like Langerman, Price thought Dunlap's game plan was highly aggressive, and he wasn't sure that Dunlap could achieve the numbers he so confidently gave him. It was the *Forbes* story, however, that disturbed him more than anything else, prompting a pointed question that Price would recall months later.

"Al," he asked, "is Wal-Mart or Sunbeam running the inventory risk on the unshipped grills?"

Dunlap didn't waver in his answer. "They own them," he said abruptly. "We don't."

17

"I'LL COME BACK AT YOU TWICE AS HARD"

THOUGH DUNLAP WAS in a struggle for survival, his credibility on Wall Street and his public image in the media severely injured, he failed to grasp the urgency of the moment. He viewed the upcoming analyst presentation not as a do-or-die effort to restore his credibility, but rather as something of a "coming out party," as one of his top executives put it. Dunlap, disengaged and detached for months, could not come to grips with the ugly reality he now faced. To many around him, he seemed to be preoccupied not by the problems of the business but by his own image. Few egos were more fragile than Dunlap's and more insatiably demanding.

His new public relations firm had worked frantically to help craft the presentation. They had spent most of the weekend before the Monday presentation rehearsing Dunlap, Kersh, and two other executives who would also play key roles in the effort. They did mock interviews, with aggressive, hostile questions to prepare Dunlap for the worst. They insisted that at least one of the executives directly address the bill-and-hold issue. The Sunday afternoon before the presentation, Dunlap and his colleagues even went over to the Equitable building on Fifty-first

Street and Seventh Avenue, where the presentation would be held, for a complete run-through with slides.

The next morning, when Dunlap left the Palace Hotel on his way to Sard's office and the Equitable's Tower Room on the fiftieth floor, he had two worries: PaineWebber analyst Andrew Shore and *Forbes* magazine writer Matthew Schifrin. He didn't want either of them to get through the door.

Schifrin didn't show up, but Shore slipped through with his assistant, R. T. Quinn, without signing the register at the front desk. Since Shore had downgraded Sunbeam's stock over five weeks earlier, he had been called and asked for a private briefing by Jerry Levin, a key lieutenant to Ronald Perelman. He also had a couple of telephone conversations with Peter Langerman, Price's right-hand man and key liaison on the Sunbeam investment.

Levin's interest in Sunbeam was natural. Many of the executive's friends were either still employed at Coleman or had already jumped ship. Perelman, his boss, was becoming increasingly worried about his new investment in Sunbeam stock. Since he sold Coleman to Dunlap, the value of Perelman's holdings in Sunbeam had fallen by hundreds of millions. A recent *Wall Street Journal* story, quoting unnamed sources, had expressed the view that Perelman was not happy. Shore had gotten to know Levin by covering Revlon, where Levin had been CEO before moving to Coleman. Levin and his staff were anxious to learn what Shore was hearing from his retail and other sources about Sunbeam.

"The place is going to fall apart," Shore told them at a meeting on April 9. "This company is not turning around."

Shore said Sunbeam was giving outrageous discounts to retailers who already were stuffed with inventory. Management defections at Coleman were widespread, making it more difficult for Dunlap to gain quick control over its operations.

Curious about Levin's keen interest, he asked: "Do you want Dunlap's job?"

"I'm not so sure I want it," Levin told him. "So don't lobby for me."

In the aftermath of his downgrade, Shore had called Langerman to explain why he did it and to give him the same information he had gathered from retailers and fed to Levin. Langerman welcomed the call, though he said up front, "Given my situation, I have to do a lot more listening than talking." Shore also wanted to ensure that his decision to downgrade Sunbeam, a decision that cost Price's Mutual Shares a good deal of money, wouldn't destroy any business between Shore's PaineWebber and Price and Langerman's Mutual Shares. "Hopefully, this is above that," Shore said. "This is just one analyst, speaking his voice."

On this Monday, May 11, however, Shore intended to speak his voice again. He was eager to get the microphone to challenge Dunlap, sick of hearing too many easy questions lobbed like softballs from analysts who should know better. "I thought the world should finally call this guy's bluff," said Shore. "I was tired of all the Q&A being composed of featherweight questions. It was now time to ask him really difficult questions and hold him accountable. I couldn't wait to confront him."

Though Shore was passionate about his work, it was rare for him to be so emotionally exorcised about a chief executive officer. Over the years CEOs of the companies he covered sometimes grew angry over what he said and wrote. Hicks Waldron, the former chairman of Avon Products Inc., once became enraged over a quote he gave a magazine journalist. "When Hicks gets up to shave in the morning," Shore said, "what he sees is the $2 dividend." Waldron, who promised shareholders he would never cut Avon's dividend payout, was angry because Shore insisted he would have to. He eventually did. Incensed about Shore's opinions on Alberto-Culver, the head of the shampoo company once penned a letter of complaint to PaineWebber Chairman Donald Marrin. But never before in his sixteen-year career as a Wall Street analyst had Shore developed as tempestuous a relationship with a chief executive officer as he had with Dunlap.

Yet when Dunlap sauntered on stage, before some 200 Wall Street analysts and major investors, Shore could not believe what he saw. The executive was wearing what appeared to be sunglasses inside the conference room. "Why does he need to wear dark glasses?" thought Shore. "He couldn't face anyone, just like he had to hide behind his smile. It was pretty damn rude."

At the podium Dunlap was forceful and even somewhat contrite. He promised Wall Street the company would earn $1 a share that year and $2 in 1999. He told them that Sunbeam would make only 5 to 10 cents per share in the second quarter of the year, a huge drop from the

21 cents a share in the year-earlier period when the company was half its current size.

"My senior management team and I were off making acquisitions," Dunlap explained. "And we took our eye off the ball. I was working on the acquisitions and I left the marketing guy in charge of operations. Big mistake . . . Unfortunately, the marketing guy I left in charge signed off on some stupid low-margin deals without our knowledge. We learned in time about a couple of stupid deals, ridiculously low margin, and we rejected them. But too many had already gone through, much too many."

Dunlap's story was less than complete. The investment bankers kept him as far away as possible from the negotiations for the deals because they feared he would screw them up. Uzzi, as operations chief, was no more responsible for any "stupid deals" than Dunlap himself. Uzzi, like everyone else at Sunbeam, was reacting to the brutal pressure placed on him to deliver unrealistic goals and targets set by Dunlap. The executive who bore the greatest responsibility for those "stupid deals," as Dunlap characterized them, was Lee Griffith, then the vice president of sales, who Dunlap promoted on the spur of the moment. But Dunlap looked for a scapegoat and publicly made one out of Don Uzzi.

Kersh followed Dunlap, and Griffith followed Kersh. Griffith delivered his segment with the panache of a Baptist preacher. He tried to explain away the bill-and-hold transactions, calling them "simply a convenience for our key customers. They want it, we sit down and talk about it. Again, it's a standard practice. The customer commits irrevocably to the purchase and we store the product for them in a segregated warehouse. It's their product. They own it. We deliver it to them when they need it."

Shore waited patiently as the presentation wore on, occasionally making a snide remark heard by some of the directors seated in the row in front of him. When Dunlap claimed that Sunbeam would make $1 a share for the year, Shore hurriedly scribbled on the company's handout of projections: "No Fucking Way!"

Sitting next to his boss, R. T. Quinn was pumping pure adrenaline. "My heart was racing so fast," he recalled. "I knew Andrew's questions were going to be confrontational because we had gone through what he wanted to do. I was so nervous." One of the questions Shore hoped to ask was about Dunlap's compensation. He planned to ask if Dunlap would emulate Lee Iacocca, the once-celebrated CEO of Chrysler Corp., who in 1979 agreed to work for a buck a year. He knew the question would rattle the tightfisted Dunlap.

After another analyst asked if Dunlap's $1 profit forecast for the year included asset sales, Shore was finally given the microphone.

"Al, earlier you mentioned that a lot of the problems were your doing, or you take responsibility. Are you willing to give back your bonus and work for a dollar this year?"

Dunlap shot him a chilling stare.

"No," Dunlap boomed, "I am not willing to give back my bonus and work for a dollar this year, Andrew Shore."

"Why is that?" Shore asked.

"Excuse me?"

"Why is that?" challenged Shore.

"Why is what?" Dunlap said.

"You say you're going to take responsibility. Why wouldn't you do that?"

"That's a vintage Andrew Shore question. I accomplished what I accomplished last year. It was a tremendous turnaround. I also was the person who led the three acquisitions. And we have acquired three great companies. And we have put together a great strategy, and I'm quite sorry if you don't like that, Andrew. That is your problem, not our problem, not the shareholders' problem. This was an outstanding program of sales, of international growth, and what has happened has happened."

Dunlap then recognized another analyst's question, but his cold blue eyes kept darting back toward Shore in a brutish scowl. Langerman's worse fears about a Dunlap explosion were beginning to materialize. Dunlap was visibly rattled and enraged. If a glare could kill, Shore would have been atomized.

Even as he fielded some two dozen questions from analysts scattered all over the room, Dunlap's head kept turning to Shore. What he didn't yet realize was that his public relations advisers had made a strategic error in failing to control the microphone. Instead, a conference center employee handed the mike to anyone in the audience who wanted to ask a question. When Shore got up again, he was given the microphone, to Dunlap's shock and chagrin.

"Wait a minute," said Dunlap, hoping to get the mike out of Shore's hand. It was too late.

"Al, I reread your book this weekend and you made numerous references in the book about putting together a great management team. My simple question is: what happened to the last great management team of the old Sunbeam?"

"Andrew," Dunlap roared, "we've got a lot of people here today who want to constructively find out what's happening with the company.

"Andrew, please, you've asked your question. Andrew! Andrew! Andrew, it's time to be quiet! We've all read your reports, which I think any thinking person finds unbelievably biased, unbelievably slanted. Every other analyst, whether they agree or disagree, we respect them.

"We have put together a team, Andrew. You write whatever you want to write, and those people that follow you, let it be. But you have been anything but objective. Your attitudes have been quite colored, and we think we know why. But so be it. Let's get on with constructive meaningful questions that should be conducted in a meeting like this."

As Dunlap scanned the room for another analyst, he quipped, "I'm glad you like the book. I'm glad you can read."

"I'm only trying to—" said Shore.

"Andrew! Andrew, if you want to speak to me after the meeting, please do that. We have a lot of professionals in the room. I'll be here after the meeting, and I'll be delighted to talk to you. Go on, please.

"Don't be disruptive, Andrew. That's disrespectful of your colleagues."

The exchange finally over, Dunlap had clearly lost his cool. Shore was steaming too.

He leaned forward toward Michael Price, who was sitting directly in front of him, and said, "You oughta fire Dunlap!" Price, who had been quietly watching the exchange, seemed stunned by the analyst's comment. Dunlap, meantime, was quietly seething because Price had not yet gotten up to give his prearranged statement of support. Growing tired of waiting for it, Dunlap asked Price if he wanted to say something.

Price reluctantly stood.

"That was a tremendous presentation," he said in a barely audible voice. Price then abruptly sat down. Dunlap, expecting far more than four words of support, stewed on stage. But Price could not muster the will to provide much more than a favorable sentence spoken into his sleeve. He felt it was management's presentation, not his own, and he harbored quite a few doubts over the game plan and the turn of events. "I was in the phase of scratching my head, asking myself 'What's going on here?'" he recalled. "The Wall Street thing had turned. He alienated the banks and a number of investors. And then you add up the *Forbes* or whatever negative stories and it gets to be, 'What's going on?'"

Afterward, as Shore was walking out of the conference room, Dunlap rushed up from behind and grabbed him by the left shoulder.

"You son of a bitch," he snarled in Shore's ear. "If you want to come after me, I'll come back at you twice as hard."

"Okay," replied Shore, shaken by the frosty look on Dunlap's face and the hate in his voice.

"You should be objective," shouted Dunlap.

"That's the problem, Al. I wasn't for too long."

IN A BREAKOUT ROOM behind the stage, meantime, *Fortune* reporter Patricia Sellers was interviewing Michael Price, who did not want to be interviewed, for an exclusive story Dunlap had been told not to invite. It was only at Dunlap's insistence that the investor agreed to sit briefly with the journalist.

"Look," Price told her, "this is an interesting stock at $25. It's down in an up market. The company's got a great mix of products. It has two guys who control 30 percent of the shares."

The reporter kept pressing Price, asking how actively involved he and Perelman were at Sunbeam. Not satisfied with Price's answer that he was not active day-to-day, Sellers pressed ahead, asking if he would intervene if things went further south. "We're not going to sit around and let Al wreck the company," Price finally said in frustration. "We're paying a lot of attention."

Back at his suite in the Palace Hotel, Dunlap flicked on the television set to check on the market's reaction to his speech. The news wasn't good, even though Dunlap was certain the presentation would put air in the company's stock. Sunbeam was down two more dollars in a strong market.

"That's okay," he told Sellers, who was in the room with him for the "exclusive interview" Dunlap gave her. "It'll come back."

This time, Sellers's questions were tougher than they had been five months ago when she wrote what Dunlap himself called a "puff piece." After Sunbeam was literally falling apart in the fourth quarter, Sellers wrote that the company's "increasing revenues apparently reflect deeper improvements." The three-page article, appearing in the January 12 issue of *Fortune*, ran under the headline: "Can Chainsaw Al Really Be a Builder?" Sellers's story answered the question in the affirmative.

Dunlap was convinced she would give him another "puff piece" at a time he most needed it. Nearly everyone else around Dunlap knew otherwise. "Why couldn't he figure out that she was desperate to get the interview to resurrect her own standing?" Fannin wondered.

During the interview in Dunlap's hotel room, Sellers asked if the chief operating officer the company was now seeking might be his replacement before his three-year contract ran out.

"Am I afraid of losing my job?" Dunlap bellowed, repeating the reporter's question. "Get goddamn serious!"

By the time Dunlap was driven by limo to Teterboro airport in New Jersey to meet a chartered plane to fly back to Florida, Sunbeam stock had fallen 7.4 percent. Even a Chainsaw Al announcement of job cuts, 6,400 of them, wasn't enough to appease Wall Street this time.

Three of the directors—Kristol, Elson, and Rutter—were late. After the Equitable presentation, they were driven to Kristol's offices for an audit committee meeting. A lengthy discussion of bill-and-hold sales ensued, during which Arthur Andersen's Philip Harlow again insisted that he had "thoroughly reviewed these transactions and that they were appropriately recorded by the company," according to minutes of the session. The directors, betraying their uneasiness with the issues, insisted that the audit committee be advised of any future bill-and-hold programs implemented by management.

At the session, internal audit director Thomas Hartshorne failed to mention that internal auditor Deidra DenDanto had handed him a memo alleging that the bill-and-hold sales were "clearly in violation of GAAP." He didn't tell the board members that DenDanto complained about "the lack of prudent, ethical behavior" by Sunbeam managers "to make numbers" or that she believed these actions put shareholders' assets at risk. Hartshorne also failed to inform the directors that DenDanto was so troubled by these issues that she had resigned in disgust only one month ago.

DenDanto had decided against sending her memo to the board. "I opted not to do so because of how it would reflect on my career," she said later.

The meeting went longer than expected because of the extended discussion over bill-and-hold, and then their cab got lost on its way to Teterboro airport.

"He can't get too upset," joked Elson, sitting in the back seat. "We have three directors in this car and that's enough to terminate him."

Whittlesey was already at the airport, waiting on the tarmac with Dunlap, Kersh, and Fannin. Langerman was coming down later on a commercial flight.

"Shore has a problem with me, and I have a problem with him," Dunlap explained to his directors. "I wanted to be clear that it was him for those who were listening and this was personal and had nothing to do with business."

When they landed, Judy Dunlap was waiting for her husband at the airport. The directors left for the Boca Raton Hilton, where the annual shareholders' meeting would be held the next morning.

In the ballroom, some 150 investors in Sunbeam showed up to hear pretty much the same speech Dunlap delivered on May 6 in the Coopers conference room before his directors and the day before in the Equitable building in New York before the analysts. Remarkably, Dunlap faced a group of shareholders and employees that still seemed to believe in him. Dunlap joked that his death would put dozens of reporters out of work, which, he surmised, might not be a bad thing because all the papers wrote about were the jobs he cut.

Frank Feraco, Sunbeam's new chief of its outdoor leisure division, delivered a pep talk that, in the written words of a local reporter, "would have made Knute Rockne seem nonchalant by comparison." Feraco said he was lured to the company because of his admiration for Dunlap, whom he equated with Jack Welch of General Electric. Sunbeam, Feraco claimed, was about to write a business story for the ages. "They will write about this company and will say, five or six years from now, how the hell did they do it?"

Dunlap's directors, kept in the dark about the company's turmoil, still stood firmly behind him. "We're enthusiastic about the job he's done," Whittlesey told a reporter for the *Palm Beach Business Review*. "We have great confidence in him," Elson added. "The company is in sound shape to move forward." Agreed Kristol: "The problem with sales isn't going to happen again."

One of the few shareholders to ask a question was a medium-built man with gray hair in his mid-sixties. Arthur Jacowitz, an insurance salesman from Miami, looked inoffensive enough to be handed a microphone. Jacowitz, who had been dabbling in the stock market for twenty years, first bought Sunbeam shares shortly after reading that Dunlap had invested $3 million of his own money in the stock. He sold at a tidy profit, only to watch the stock move higher, until buying into Sunbeam a second time at $37 a share. To his chagrin, however, it had since fallen to $25 not long after Dunlap was given his new rich compensation package.

He asked, like Shore the day before, if Dunlap would consider a pay cut. Jacowitz thought a voluntary cut in pay would send a strong message to the stock market and Sunbeam investors that Dunlap believed in the company's future. No, he would not, Dunlap quickly replied. "Buying stock is not like buying Treasury certificates," he lectured. "It goes up. It goes down . . . I fully intend to make a great deal of money."

The remark won Dunlap applause, and when the meeting was over, many of the Sunbeam employees and shareholders who packed the room gave him a standing ovation. "It was almost like a revival meeting," recalled Elson. "He was in top form. He seemed to have the fire in the belly again. He was back."

BUT THE STOCK WASN'T. Not only did it fail to recover or stabilize, it kept tumbling downward. Jacowitz dumped his small investment of 1,000 shares, losing about $12,000. Other investors followed suit. Dunlap concluded the analysts and the shareholders just didn't get it. They failed to understand the savings he would be able to wring out of the acquisitions. Instead of focusing his attention on the business and its problems, Dunlap was convinced he needed to go on the campaign trail to talk up the stock. He wanted to go on television, where, he believed, he had more control over the process.

"I took your advice, and it was a mistake for me," he told Sard, who had urged him to duck all media interviews. "I ran a media empire in Australia. I know how to deal with the media, and I'm really good on television."

When the Sellers story came out on June 8, it proved Sard right. Not only was the piece highly skeptical, it also contained the quote from Price, which only enraged Dunlap.

In a telephone call to Price, Dunlap groused that the investor failed to speak up at the May 11 meeting.

"And what did you mean by that remark in *Fortune?*" Dunlap asked.

"Look," Price told him, "it was taken out of context. But yes, I made the remark. I also said you had done a good job."

Dunlap got Price to agree to issue a statement. Grudgingly, Price complied, with a four-paragraph press release blasting the article and its author. "The article completely mischaracterizes my views on Sunbeam and Al Dunlap," Price was quoted as saying in the statement. "We have been and remain completely supportive of Al Dunlap, and the *Fortune* reporter missed that essential message in trying to convey the erroneous impression that we are not supportive of Al and Sunbeam. She cannot possibly have been listening to anything I said to have come away with the false impression that we want to replace Al Dunlap. He is an outstanding executive and Sunbeam is fortunate to have him."

Yet even the statement, which sounded as if Dunlap himself had drafted it instead of Price, failed to placate him. He thought Price took longer than he should have to produce it, and he believed that Price didn't get the press release into the hands of enough reporters and investors. Dunlap didn't know it for sure, but he was right.

18
"TOO RICH AND FAMOUS"

ONLY TWENTY-FOUR DAYS after wooing Wall Street with a promising portrayal of Sunbeam's future, Lee Griffith sheepishly walked into Dunlap's conference room armed with a stack of handouts and more bad news. The chamber was a quiet and cozy place, just off Dunlap's office, with a table that matched the one in the boardroom. A pair of predator paintings practically leaped off the walls, which were papered with a shroud of overlapping light gray squares.

On Thursday, June 4, Dunlap, Kersh, and Fannin gathered informally in this space to hear Griffith deliver an update on the company's second quarter business. Griffith filled out a well-tailored suit, stretching the seams of the blue oxford button-down shirts he usually wore. He was a strong, broad-shouldered man, an old linebacker from Auburn University who could still hit a golf ball a mile. When he greeted you, your hand easily disappeared in his. But his years were beginning to show. Griffith unsuccessfully covered his baldness by combing long strands of dark hair over the top of his head. He wore his half-moon spectacles halfway down his nose and peered over them to take in a full room.

Dunlap liked him because he was almost always optimistic and exuberant. Throughout his career, he was always considered the consummate salesman, a spirited cheerleader who was especially adept at rallying the troops. The Sunbeam salesmen nicknamed him "the coach" because he was forever employing hackneyed sports metaphors to psych them up. "Lee is a rah-rah type of guy, a super salesman," said Jerry Ballas, a Scott Paper executive who knew him. In another day Griffith would have been a Bible-thumping nostrum peddler at the back end of a horse-drawn wagon.

Despite the massive turnover throughout the company, Griffith managed to keep the sales staff relatively intact through 1997. He was generally well liked by many of Sunbeam's salesmen, who sometimes worried that Griffith might die from the demands imposed on him by Dunlap and Kersh. It was because he wore the anxiety and pressure wherever he went. After one particularly grueling meeting with Dunlap, Griffith slumped with sagging shoulders through the office door, his face pale and puffy, his eyes sunken. "That man is going to have a heart attack," said Denise Valek, Dunlap's secretary.

What he was not known for was strategic thinking. Griffith, his colleagues confided, was something of an empty suit. He was not the executive you would call on to devise an insightful strategy, author a clever marketing plan, or create a sophisticated sales program. Like Dunlap and many of his recruits, Griffith failed to comprehend the dynamics of a slow-growth, mature industry in which consumers bought one blender or toaster every seven years. On one occasion, he suggested that Sunbeam dispatch trailer trucks loaded with electric can openers to Kmart parking lots for weekend sales. It didn't occur to him that it would be impossible to move 4,000 can openers from a trailer truck over two days in a Kmart parking lot. The buyer rebuffed the idea with a smirk and a laugh. (The company did, in fact, later run more than two dozen trailer truck sales to eke out more revenue.) Essentially Griffith was a sales guy who had been effectively slapping backs for more than three decades. He was, after all, the man whom Dunlap promoted with little more thought than to get something positive into a press release that overflowed with adverse news.

On June 4 Griffith's message was stark. Visibly tense and nervous, he told Dunlap that the company was facing an $80.9 million shortfall in revenues for the quarter. The retailers and distributors, he said, were "loaded" with Sunbeam merchandise and were struggling to manage their inventories. He said the company's new products, so highly touted by Dunlap in the past, had performed below expectations. He said the company had "lost momentum" as a result of voluntary recalls of outdoor grills, problems in integrating the new acquisitions, and the shift in strategy to being an industry consolidator from simply planning to sell the business.

A memo given to Dunlap and Kersh from Griffith showed that every single category of business, including every major brand, would fail to meet the company's second quarter objectives. Sunbeam's core appliance business, Griffith predicted, would fall short by $16.1 million in the United States alone, reaching $45.0 million instead of the company's $61.1 million objective. Despite the "due diligence" by Morgan Stanley on the newly acquired Mr. Coffee business, its revenues were expected to miss the budget by $5.3 million, with estimated sales of $39.5 million rather than the anticipated $44.8 million. All told, Griffith's household business alone showed a $38.1 million gap in the United States, with another $7 million shortfall overseas.

Griffith estimated that Sunbeam's grill business would fail to hit its second-quarter $88.1 million target by $12.1 million— a figure that grossly underestimated the gap because retailers were crammed with merchandise they could not sell. The mainstream Coleman business in the United States, the memo showed, would miss the budget by $10.1 million, with estimated U.S. sales of $152.8 million versus the budgeted $162.9 million. Ironically, the brand least affected was one that Dunlap told Wall Street he was planning to sell. Eastpak, the Coleman unit that sold leisure backpacks, was expected to miss its $20.4 million revenue objective by $200,000. The U.S. outdoor business, Griffith reported, would likely suffer a $26 million shortfall against a $328.9 million objective.

Griffith said he thought the gap could be narrowed to $60 million, but he did not propose or detail any plans or programs to reduce the shortfall. This was disastrous news. If second quarter sales were off by at least $60 million, the shortfall would completely wipe out the 5 to 10 cents per share profit Dunlap had promised Wall Street only a few weeks earlier. In all probability, in fact, a shortfall of that magnitude also would force Sunbeam into the red for the second quarter in a row. Dunlap and Kersh were facing the likelihood of having to go back to Wall Street again to make yet another disclosure of bad news. If so, it would be the fourth consecutive time, dating back to the missed fourth quarter of 1997, that Dunlap would surprise the investment community. It was unlikely that Wall Street would be forgiving.

Remarkably, however, Dunlap seemed resigned to Griffith's report. There was no explosive tantrum, not even a sharply worded demand to make the numbers. He and Kersh wore their stone masks as they listened to the sober news, even when they perused Griffith's handouts that openly addressed the channel stuffing that Dunlap had so indignantly denied in public. In those documents, Griffith reported that Kmart had an "inventory load" of fifteen to twenty weeks, and Costco ten to twelve weeks. Gross sales of Sunbeam appliances in the United States alone, he predicted, would fall by 25.7 percent in the second quarter.

In this same conference room, less than four months earlier in late January, Don Uzzi had tried to explain that the loading of customers in 1997 was hurting first quarter sales. Uzzi said only 12 percent of the company's 20 percent rise in sales in 1997 had been "consumed." The remaining 8 percent was already backing up and hurting sales, he explained. Dunlap went ballistic and stormed out of the meeting, angry that something he was denying publicly was being acknowledged by his top operating executive as a major problem. Once Dunlap had left, Uzzi began pleading with Fannin, who also was in the meeting. "David," he said, "you need to understand what I'm saying. These are the facts. This is why it is what it is."

Now, with problems worsening, Dunlap appeared oddly quiescent. Griffith knew that Dunlap was not acting his confident, bombastic self anyway. Earlier in the week, he and Frank Feraco, the new hire from Kohler who was in charge of Sunbeam's outdoor business, had flown to Seattle to visit Costco, a major customer. Before they departed from Fort Lauderdale, Feraco had told Dunlap that "if we make the numbers this quarter, you better give us the Congressional Medal of Honor." They had just gotten off the airplane when they heard their names paged on the airport's public address system. It was Dunlap.

Feraco spoke to him first.

"I need to know a couple of things," Dunlap said oddly. "Frank, do you have faith in this company?"

"Yes," Feraco responded. There was a slight pause and then Dunlap asked another question.

"Do you have faith in me?"

"Yep," he said.

"Okay, I just want to make sure. Is Lee there?"

Feraco handed the receiver to Griffith, and Dunlap repeated the same two questions and then hung up.

"We have a problem," Feraco informed Griffith. "When a guy with his ego who has turned around eight companies in a row calls up and asks questions like that he has a definite problem with his confidence. That means we have a problem, too."

IN ANY CASE, Griffith's presentation was hardly a surprise. Over a period of months, Dunlap and Kersh had regularly been hearing bad news. In a memo dated May 1, 1998, the general manager of Sunbeam's core appliance business had nothing but wretched information to deliver. Debra Kelly-Ennis was relatively new to Sunbeam, having joined in early 1998 from Gerber Foods, where she had been senior vice president of marketing. She was one of a new wave of recruits (42 executives were hired in the first quarter of 1998 alone) replacing many of the executives and managers Kersh had ordered Uzzi to fire. A trim blond who wore vibrant red lipstick, Kelly-Ennis had an MBA from the University of Houston, and had begun her career in sales at RJR-Nabisco. Like most of the new recruits, she was somewhat naive about the condition of the company and what it was like to work for a Dunlap.

Her memo—issued directly to Kersh only five days before Dunlap and Kersh painted a rather favorable view of the future to the board of directors—openly addressed the company's channel stuffing and "loading" of customers. She reported that Wal-Mart, which preferred four weeks of inventory on hand, was loaded with 23.61 weeks of Sunbeam appliances, the result of overly aggressive sales efforts designed to artificially inflate the company's 1997 results. Wal-Mart had 19.61 weeks of inventory it didn't need, valued at $8.9 million. Sunbeam would have to stop all shipments of appliances to its most important customer for nearly five full months before inventory levels would get back to normal. Sunbeam loaded Kmart with 16.45 weeks of excess inventory, valued at $4.8 million. The company loaded Target, another major customer, with 6.27 weeks of unneeded inventory worth $3.2 million. Other retailers were sitting on an additional $6 million of excess inventory.

Kelly-Ennis's numbers, moreover, included neither the massive inventory buildup in Sunbeam's overseas appliance business nor the excess grill-business inventory that had been fueled by so many buy-and-hold deals. In many cases, retailer inventory of grills, much of it still held in Sunbeam's leased warehouses, was even worse. Her assessment also didn't cover all of Coleman's lost sales due to Dunlap's bungling of the acquisition, which had prompted the instantaneous departure of many of its best people.

The overhang obviously would prove devastating to 1998 sales. What was just as troublesome, however, was that all the dealmaking, the heavy discounting of merchandise, the extension of credit terms, the guaranteed sales, and the sales by consignment had changed the expectations of Sunbeam's customers. If the company was so willing to bargain in 1997, its customers would hold out for the same kinds of wanton deal-making in 1998. Sunbeam's competitors, moreover, were forced to respond to Dunlap's moves by cutting more aggressive deals to move their products. In the high-margin clipper business, for example, one competitor was trying to buy at cost all the Sunbeam inventory carried by a major customer and then replace it with its own merchandise. The rival then planned to dump the goods on the market at enormous discounts as a tactical move to damage Sunbeam's pricing. It was going to be extremely difficult for the company's sales force to wean its customers off those foolish deals made with Dunlap's knowledge and consent. It also was going to be tougher to fight off angry competitors who were beginning to launch fierce offensives against Sunbeam.

While these issues greatly threatened the company's 1998 business, Kelly-Ennis seemed even more concerned with Dunlap's starvation of Sunbeam's product-development function. Wrote Kelly-Ennis: "Because we failed as a company in 1997 to place enough emphasis on new product development, we have had to take $16 million of forecasted revenues and $6.4 million of margin off the table for 1998. This represents an additional 6 percent of very profitable revenue growth for our appliance business."

She wasn't very optimistic about the newly acquired Mr. Coffee business either. Besides forecasting that it would eliminate Sunbeam's $5 million in coffeemaker sales, she believed the basic Mr. Coffee brand would lose another $12 million in revenues for the year.

NOW, A MONTH LATER, Kelly-Ennis's boss, Lee Griffith, was giving an abbreviated version of the same facts. Sunbeam would not only fail to meet its sales targets for the quarter, it was very possible that previously booked sales would flow back into the company, forcing it to subtract revenue and profit. There were massive defections among the sales staff who had become disenchanted with all the game-playing. As many as twenty-five out of roughly thirty people in sales had quit since Dunlap came aboard, many of them within the last four months. Many of the independent reps who sold Sunbeam merchandise had become disenfranchised as well because the company was slow in paying them their earned commissions. Not one of the new products introduced under Dunlap could even remotely be described as a blockbuster. Many of them lost money.

All, however, was not apparently lost. Among the handouts Griffith gave his boss and Kersh was one labeled "1998 BIG IDEAS." Under that heading, the coach proposed two major objectives. The first was a no-brainer in a Dunlap company, while the second was so obvious after the acquisition of three companies that it was worthless.

The handout read:

"Cancel all National Advertising."

"Focus on Integration Issues."

There were no new and bold product introductions, no innovative marketing campaigns, not even a proposal to tap into the burgeoning Internet boom in a way that might boost sales or transform distribution.

At any other company, Griffith's recommendation would have been an astounding admission that he really had no idea how to manage his way out of the mess. But at a Dunlap-led concern, cutting costs was always a big idea, if not the only idea. If you were the human resources chief, you slashed the training budget. If you were head of product development, you trashed the R&D expenses. If you were in manufacturing, you axed all the maintenance work. And if you were in marketing, you eliminated advertising. In short, you cut off every expense without an expeditious payback, every investment related to a company's ability to compete in the long-term.

Griffith's "big idea" was a striking contrast to the speech he had given to Wall Street analysts and Sunbeam investors less than a month earlier. In New York he was proselytizing about "pull and push programs" to leverage Sunbeam's brands and drive consumer demand. "Ladies and gentlemen," he intoned on May 11, "this is the new face of Sunbeam." The room then went dark and up on an immense screen Griffith showed them one television commercial after another for the failed water product, electric blankets and throws, mixers, blenders, and grills. He showed seven TV commercials in all, giving the impression that Sunbeam was prepared to heavily invest in the equity of its "power brands."

Now Griffith's "big idea" was dumping all national advertising to save money when Sunbeam hardly spent much on advertising anyway.

Even Chainsaw seemed unimpressed.

"You guys deal with it," he said dismissively as he rose to leave the room. "I'm too rich and famous to have to put up with this."

19
"YOU WANT TO QUIT?"

JUST AFTER LUNCH on Saturday, June 6, Russ Kersh and David Fannin were driving over to Dunlap's house. In the car with them was a leading candidate, sent down by headhunter Tom Hardy, for the chief operating officer job. Kersh and Fannin had met the executive at the company's headquarters in Delray Beach in the morning, spent a pleasant lunch with him, and now were ferrying him to Boca Raton to meet their boss.

The candidate, a top executive at Philip Morris, thought everything was going smoothly until he stepped out of the warm Florida weather and into Dunlap's cool, air-conditioned home. From the start, Dunlap seemed preoccupied and distant. He welcomed the man into his home, fetched him a soda, and then excused himself, taking Kersh and Fannin with him. Dunlap nervously escorted the two executives into his master bedroom suite, a room soundproofed with padded walls. The men stood around the king-size bed as Dunlap angrily showed them a copy of the latest *Barron's*, the financial weekly newspaper.

It was already turned to page 17. Under the title "Dangerous Games," the two-page story was a devastating piece of financial analysis by *Barron's* reporter Jonathan R. Laing. The story, which quoted only a single source by name, analyst Andrew Shore, delved deeply into the company's accounting methods. Laing's conclusion: Virtually all the earnings from Dunlap's self-proclaimed turnaround year of 1997 were manufactured through accounting gimmickry.

"Sunbeam's financials under Dunlap look like an exercise in high-energy physics, in which time and space seem to fuse and bend," wrote Laing. "They are a veritable cloud chamber. Income and costs move almost imperceptibly back and forth between the income statement and the balance sheet like charged ions, whose vapor trail has long since dissipated by the end of any quarter, when results are reported."

Dunlap was livid. "This is scurrilous," he said. "We've got to do something about it. I know all about the First Amendment. I used to run a media empire. There has to be a way to deal with this situation."

Fannin hurriedly scanned the article and determined its seriousness. It was a highly detailed examination of Sunbeam's financial numbers that also predicted that Dunlap's days at the company were numbered. Kersh was just as upset as Dunlap, who oddly thought that someone—perhaps Price or Perelman, or maybe even both of them—were out to get him and hurt the company. He told Fannin and Kersh that he suspected *Barron's* rushed the story out earlier than intended to undermine the company's efforts to obtain a $2 billion loan package from a syndication of banks to help pay for recent acquisitions. On Tuesday morning, Dunlap was supposed to make his pitch to a room full of bankers at the Waldorf-Astoria Hotel in New York.

First there had been the story in the *Journal* about Perelman being upset with the fall in the value of his new investment in Sunbeam. Then there had been the *Forbes* story, quickly followed by a couple of shareholder lawsuits and a wrap-up on them in the *New York Times*. Now this piece in *Barron's*, by far the most damaging and authoritative of them all.

"I really see a conspiracy here," whispered Dunlap. "Price isn't being supportive. I don't think that quote in the *Fortune* story was unintentional. If they want to get rid of me, I'm ready to go. If they are not going to be supportive, I'm going to be out of here."

While the three top executives conferred in Dunlap's bedroom, the candidate sat patiently in the living room of the house. Dunlap later went out to speak with the man. But on this day, the visiting executive didn't get a tour. He didn't get a sandwich prepared by Dunlap's wife. He got only the bum's rush. When he called Hardy to report back, he told the headhunter that Dunlap had displayed little interest in him.

He was certain he wouldn't get the job. He was right, but for the wrong reason.

THE *BARRON'S* STORY did not appear out of nowhere. Dunlap had heard that Laing, who had written about him unfavorably before, was poking around. Gluck wrongly suspected that Deidra DenDanto, the former internal auditor, was the source. Officially the company refused to cooperate on the story. Laing was a hard-hitting reporter with a reputation for doing what Dunlap would call a "hatchet job," and Dunlap was already beginning to feel like chopped meat.

After the candidate left Dunlap's house, Sunbeam's three top executives sat around the kitchen table with the article.

"Russ, you go through this item by item," Dunlap commanded. "Take me through this and explain these issues to me."

Fannin sat in uncomfortable silence as Kersh carefully went through the story.

Laing reported that Sunbeam booked sales and profits before products were shipped and payment received from the retailers.

"Well, that's not true," Kersh complained.

He then gave an explanation to rebut the charge, and Fannin jotted down the response on a yellow legal pad as Dunlap paced the kitchen floor. Kersh claimed the bill-and-hold transactions were for seasonal products where customers requested storage of inventory on their behalf at third-party warehouses. There was a clear transfer of title to the customer, he maintained, and it all met generally accepted accounting principles (GAAP). Besides, Kersh said, recognizing sales before payment is received is normal business practice. That's why companies have accounts receivable.

Dunlap listened intently. He was not ranting and raving. He seemed oddly calm and introspective, even a bit melancholy.

"Russ," he asked at one point, "it's not true, right?"

"Al, there are explanations for all of this," replied Kersh. "We'll go through it all and deal with it."

Laing reported that Sunbeam wrote down to zero some $90 million of its inventory in 1996, then sold the goods at 50 cents on the dollar, sometimes more, and put that money into net income in 1997. Laing charged that as much as a third of the company's income for 1997 came as a result of this writedown and sale.

Kersh claimed no profits were recorded on the disposal of the inventory.

Laing also reported that Sunbeam prepaid everything it could in 1996, from advertising and packaging costs to insurance premiums and inventory expenses, so that it would not have to expense those costs in 1997. The *Barron's* reporter alleged that this practice alone contributed as much as $15 million to net income in 1997.

Kersh, however, insisted that all the spending in the fourth quarter of 1996 was for work performed in that quarter.

"Well," said Dunlap, "I'm going to be in New York on Tuesday, and I want to get the board together. We're going to talk about all of this, and we're going to get Arthur Andersen there."

Fannin would have to arrange for a place for the board to meet, contact all the directors, fax them the story, link up with the company's public relations firm in New York for a public response, and ponder the uncertain future of his deeply troubled company. He had left his condo for work that Saturday morning in an upbeat mood. Fannin was anxious to meet the COO candidate whose background credentials were highly impressive. He had been optimistic that the company was getting close to landing a person who could implement the strategy outlined by Dunlap on May 11.

As Fannin drove home, down Interstate 95 from Boca to Fort Lauderdale, he was downhearted and exhausted. It seemed that nearly every time his spirits would be bolstered by some positive development, something new would pop up to steal away his optimism. What next? he wondered.

Fannin shuffled through the door of his sixteenth-floor apartment with a gloomy face. "What's really sad," he told his wife, "is we have this article with all these accusations in it, and the fact of the matter is, Al doesn't have a clue in the world about any of it. Whether it's true or not."

PETER LANGERMAN found the story in the mailbox outside his home in Short Hills, New Jersey, that Saturday morning. Initially he thought many of the article's charges had already appeared elsewhere. *Forbes* had written about the company's bill-and-hold practices. It was publicly disclosed by the company, and it was reviewed in some detail by the board and its audit committee. The *Wall Street Journal* had reported instances of "inventory stuffing" during 1997, in which Sunbeam either sent more goods than had been ordered by customers or shipped goods even after an order had been canceled. Several Wall Street analysts, including Shore, had expressed worries about such things as rising receivables and inventories in their reports. Steele of Buckingham Research had even downgraded the stock in mid-1997 over some of these same accounting issues.

As a former certified public accountant, Langerman also believed that some of the practices that the article described in highly negative terms were in accordance with accounting standards. Many companies that took massive restructuring charges, for example, often put more money aside in reserves than was needed to cover the costs of employee layoffs and plant closings. Those extra reserves would later be used to offset expenses, a move that would artificially inflate profits. It was a game that nearly every company that ever declared a write-off played.

Still, Langerman saw the story as an awful indictment of the company and its accounting practices. It was a much more damaging story than any of the other articles that had appeared in recent months in *Forbes*, *Fortune*, and the *New York Times*, all of which lacked the detail and analysis that Laing brought to his piece. Langerman was nervous about the impact the article would have on Sunbeam's already depressed stock price. So was his boss, Michael Price, who was struck by the remarkable detail in the story. "It almost made me feel they had a lot of inside poop," he said. "It set off alarm bells. Everybody was nervous." When Langerman received a call from Fannin that evening, he felt some reassurance in the fact that at least Dunlap wanted to immediately respond to the story at a special board meeting on Tuesday afternoon.

CHARLES ELSON, Sunbeam's youngest director, was at New York's La Guardia Airport on Sunday afternoon, waiting for a flight back to Tampa, Florida. The law professor was in a cheerful mood. He and his wife had spent the weekend in the city so they could attend a brunch on Great Neck, Long Island, with Elson's brother and his future bride and mother-in-law. An essay he had written on CEO succession and stock ownership had appeared in the *Sunday New York Times*.

The plane was delayed until 7 P.M., so Elson called home to listen to his voice mail messages. There was an urgent call from Fannin on the machine.

"Call me immediately," Fannin said ominously.

Elson, in a private phone booth at the U.S. Air Club, quickly dialed Fannin's home.

"What's going on?" he asked.

"There's an article that appeared in *Barron's* on Sunbeam, and I think you need to get it right away," Fannin said. "We're going to have a meeting to discuss it on Tuesday."

"Why?"

"It's bad," Fannin replied. "Go and get it."

Elson rushed to the nearest newsstand and saw the issue. On its front cover, over the *Barron's* logo, were the words: "Checking Up on Chainsaw Al: Did Sunbeam Really Earn a Profit in '97?"

Elson plopped down $3 for the issue and brought it back with him to the U.S. Air Club.

"Oh, my God!" he said after reading the story. "This is horrible."

Before he went back to the phone booth, he gave the paper to his wife. "Why don't you read this and tell me what you think?" he asked her.

Elson first called Fannin, and then Dunlap. He wanted to know exactly what happened, why it happened, and what the company's official reaction to the story would be. In the twenty months that Elson had served on Sunbeam's board, the man once denigrated as a Dunlap "lap dog" had in fact become a conscientious and informed director. As an academic who studied, wrote, and taught issues of corporate governance, he considered it an honor and a privilege to serve on the board of a public corporation. From the beginning, Elson was determined to make the most of it.

He did not conceal his admiration for Dunlap, yet he didn't hesitate to question and challenge him either. He arranged to tour Sunbeam factories to glimpse firsthand how the products were made and to collect information from the field on Dunlap's boardroom assertions. Whenever he ventured into a retail store, he always checked the counter space devoted to Sunbeam products. On at least one occasion he even persuaded a customer to purchase a Sunbeam iron over a competitor's product.

The article unnerved him. Dunlap, he knew, was easily the most difficult person he had ever met. But he was not, Elson thought, someone who played fast and loose with the numbers. "This was not a guy who was going to walk on the edge," he said later. "Was he tough and mean? Yes. Engaging in fraudulent conduct? No. That just wasn't his personality. My instinct was to not believe it. We had a clean bill of health from Arthur Andersen. I wondered where the hell was this coming from?"

When he reached Dunlap, the CEO was livid.

"Is any of it true?" Elson asked him flatly.

"No," Dunlap barked. "It's absolutely false. It's crap. I've had people here all day yesterday going over it. We're going to have a meeting on Tuesday. We're going to refute every line. It's utterly false. This is terribly damaging. We should sue them, goddamn it, or demand a retraction."

On the plane ride back, however, Elson could not stop rereading the article. Something is wrong, he thought.

"Something is going on here," he told his wife, Aimee. "I'm worried about him. He's been in a state lately. I don't know what is going on. Maybe it's a piling effect from all the criticism he's taken in the press. Whatever it is, we've got to get to the bottom of it."

FOR MUCH OF that Sunday Fannin and his wife faxed the article out to the other directors, to Bill Rutter, the local banker who chaired the company's audit committee; to Faith Whittlesey, the former ambassador to Switzerland who lived in New York; and to Howard Kristol, Dunlap's longtime personal attorney, who received it at his Scarsdale, New York, home. Kristol agreed to hold the board meeting Tuesday afternoon at his law firm's offices in Rockefeller Center.

Fannin also spoke with Sard in New York about the range of alternative responses, from issuing a press release to considering a libel suit against *Barron's*. By Monday morning, however, there was no more talk of legal action. Instead, Sard and one of his assistants, Maureen Bailey, helped to draft a written statement for immediate release. They were still advising Dunlap not to speak directly to reporters, who would only want to ask him about the *Barron's* article.

With help from controller Bob Gluck, who had been closeted in his office at headquarters all weekend with the article, the company assembled a detailed rebuttal. Surprisingly, however, no one really seemed to have a good grip on the facts. When pressed for further explanation to rebut an assertion in the article, Gluck's answer often would be slightly different from his first response. It did not inspire much confidence and certainly wouldn't hold up to direct questioning by reporters.

For now a strong, less-than-specific rejoinder attacking the veracity of the story would have to do. Then, at the Tuesday board session, the directors could weigh other options to more fully respond. The press release, put on the wires early Monday, blasted Laing and *Barron's* without rebutting any of the specific charges in the story. "I know that I am a controversial figure, but for a Dow Jones publication to impugn my integrity and that of our management, our board and its audit committee, and to suggest that Sunbeam has committed fraud—with absolutely no factual support for its outrageous accusations—is beyond the bounds of any standard of journalistic ethics," Dunlap said in the statement.

With the release out, Dunlap seemed reasonably calm and civilized before boarding a plane with Kersh for New York. But once they landed, Dunlap had worked himself into a frenzy. He became convinced that the "radio silence" media strategy, the plan to decline all interviews with reporters, was only ruining his reputation. In the face of all the negative news, Dunlap believed he had to go on the attack himself to tell his side of the story in person.

"The media strategy isn't working," Dunlap argued to his PR advisers. "We've got to tell our side of the story. We're getting killed. They're beating the shit out of me. We're taking the punches, and I'm not a guy who takes punches. People who believe in me are wondering if something is wrong because I'm not responding, and I'm not defending myself. I've got to get out there."

When Dunlap did get out, at the Waldorf-Astoria meeting on Tuesday morning, he encountered universal skepticism from bankers and institutional investors. Sunbeam stock had dropped again, losing 5.7 percent of its value on Monday. It was now down to $20.625, some 60 percent below its March peak. Dunlap was not at his best, even displaying a bit of gallows humor.

"If I ever get hit by a truck, sixty-eight reporters will lose their jobs, and some days it actually seems like a pretty good option," he quipped again.

The bankers grilled him over the company's results and the *Barron's* article, and Dunlap sharply rebuked the questioning from potential investors. Some participants said they were not satisfied by Dunlap's responses. Others were put off by his swagger, particularly at a time when there were so many unanswered questions. He spent more time in self-promotion, expounding on what he considered his glory days at Lily-Tulip, Scott, and other firms, rather than dwell on what he termed the current "hiccup" at Sunbeam. "I'm happy to match my record with that of anyone who's ever done a restructuring anywhere," he boasted. At least one banker considered it "tacky" that Dunlap was handing out autographed copies of his book before the meeting. It was not a very good start to convince the banking community to pony up $2 billion in financing.

WHEN DUNLAP WALKED past the massive bronze statue of Atlas Bearing the Heavens outside Rockefeller Center's international building on Fifth Avenue, he must have felt a little like Atlas himself. Beaten and battered by the media and investors, Dunlap bore the weight of the world on his shoulders that afternoon.

Upstairs, in a sparse eleventh-floor conference room with beige fabric wallpaper, the directors sat around a sixteen-foot-long rectangular table, waiting for him and Kersh to arrive. Only Rutter, who was still in Florida, was not present. They would have to patch him into the meeting by telephone. Skadden Arps attorneys Finn Fogg and Rich Easton were already there. So were Fannin and Gluck, as well as Phil Harlow, the somber Arthur Andersen partner who oversaw the Sunbeam account. George Sard and Maureen Bailey had just arrived.

Dunlap seemed strangely subdued and quiet. He calmly told them the story was nonsense. "There is no truth to it."

"Okay," said Langerman, "let's just go down the specifics. Let's address each point."

Gluck then began to rebut the article's charges. The young controller calmly ticked off each allegation and then served up the company's official response, with Kersh and Harlow filling in some details. The directors appeared satisfied that the article was riddled with inaccuracies and misstatements. Then Dunlap took charge.

"Members of the audit committee, are you satisfied that you have done your job?" asked Dunlap in a loud voice, referring to Gluck's explanations.

Kristol and Elson nodded. Over the speaker phone Rutter responded with a yes.

"Partner from Arthur Andersen, are you satisfied that you've done your job?"

Harlow had the dull appearance and personality of a classic accountant. He was a trim man, with closely cropped silver hair, in his late fifties. He always dressed in conservative suits and spoke in a monotone voice, with no obvious sense of humor.

"Yes," he said soberly.

"Do you stand by those numbers? They are your numbers."

"Yes," Harlow said again.

Some of the people in the room, however, noticed that the accountant's body language was at odds with his continued support. He seemed tense and uneasy with the directness of Dunlap's interrogation.

"Is there anything that makes you uncomfortable?" Dunlap asked again.

Harlow paused momentarily and then raised the issue of bill-and-hold sales.

"While bill-and-hold can be appropriate in certain circumstances," he said, "it's not something—"

Dunlap did not allow Harlow to finish the thought.

"Do you stand behind the published statements?" Dunlap barked. "Is bill-and-hold considered an acceptable practice in the industry?"

"Yes," agreed Harlow, who had signed off on the company's audit.

"This is standard industry practice," insisted Dunlap.

The discussion began to drift over what action they should take to respond to the article. The outside directors concluded that it served no purpose to prolong a pissing match between the company and *Barron's*. They directed Sard and Bailey to draw up a more detailed response that could be sent to shareholders in letter format.

Suddenly Elson popped the question.

"So how's the second quarter going?" he asked.

"Russ, you handle that," Dunlap said.

"Sales are a little soft," Kersh said soberly.

"Well, do you think you're going to make the numbers?" Elson asked.

"It's going to be tough," Kersh said.

"What does that mean?" asked Langerman.

Dunlap, growing visibly angry, interrupted the exchange.

"Look, I trust Russ with my life," he said. "You have to understand. This is a transition year. You've got to stop worrying about specific numbers. You can't hold me to a quarter."

"Yeah," said Elson, "but you told the world you were going to make 5 cents this quarter."

Dunlap, annoyed at the questioning, turned to Kersh.

"Russ, should I tell them now?"

"No," he replied, "later."

"Let's just deal with it now."

"No," Kersh said again.

Dunlap began to complain about the attacks on him and the company, prompting Bailey to note that the only way to stop the negative coverage was by posting good results.

Dunlap savagely attacked her, shocking everyone in the room.

"You don't know a goddamn thing about results!" he shouted. "You don't have to worry about the analysts. Why are people questioning me? I've done nine turnarounds . . . "

His rant finished, Dunlap said he and Kersh wanted to discuss something privately with the board. The bevy of advisers got up out of the brown swivel chairs and filed out of the room. Over the next twenty minutes, Dunlap told the board that either he needed their unconditional support or he and Kersh were prepared to go.

"Look," he said, "I'm knocking myself out and busting my ass and I don't feel you're supportive. I don't think all these articles would be coming out like this unless somebody is behind it."

Dunlap told them he suspected that Perelman was engaged in a conspiracy to drive down the company's stock so he could buy Sunbeam on the cheap. He suggested that if Price really backed him, he would buy out Perelman's $280 million stake.

"We can't fight a battle on two fronts," said Dunlap. "Either we get the support we should have or Russ and I are prepared to go . . . Just pay us."

The board was stunned. "Al, we don't know what you're talking about," retorted Rutter. "We're supportive of both of you."

"Either back me and Russ or we'll be happy to take our money and go."

"But Al, no one has ever suggested that we want you to leave," Rutter added.

"Perelman is behind all of this," Dunlap shouted, "and he sold me a piece of crap. It's crap. Coleman is a mess. You can't believe what a mess this place is. You guys ought to get together to buy him out."

"Al, I haven't heard anything from Perelman," Langerman said.

Dunlap's face grew flushed with anger as he stared directly at Langerman. "I know," he said. "I'm a rich guy and I talk to other rich guys, and I know. Look, you guys didn't support me at the analysts' meeting, and then there was the thing with *Fortune*. And why are you talking to Andrew Shore? That son of a bitch is going around telling people he has Mutual's ear. Either you do something, or Russ and I are ready to settle up."

"Look, Al, Michael doesn't feel that way at all," said Langerman.

Kersh, his head hung low, sat at the end of the table in silence. He seemed visibly distraught, ready to break down in tears.

"Al," said Langerman, "let me address the Andrew Shore question. I think I did take a call from Andrew Shore. I listened to what he said. I'd rather know what people are saying. I never said I supported him or his views. I just listened to what he had to say.

"Al, what do you expect us to do? What do you want us to do? We're here. Mike came out with his statement of support for you."

Dunlap wasn't appeased. "And why didn't the press release come out quicker?" he shot back. "It was supposed to come out in the morning and it was delayed. Why did you guys only put it out on the Dow Jones wire?"

Langerman explained a clerical error briefly held things up, but that he and Price were completely behind him.

"Al, what do you want us to do?" asked Kristol in frustration.

"We're behind you," assured Whittlesey. "Let's dig in our heels here. Things are tougher than expected, but we have a good plan. We're with you."

It was as if Dunlap could not hear her or anyone else. "If you really want me and Russ to go, then let's settle up the contract and we'll go," Dunlap insisted. "I have a document in my briefcase that we can go over and get it done."

"Now wait a minute," Kristol responded. "Al, are you saying you want to quit?"

"If we're not going to get the support we need," Dunlap repeated, "we're out of here!"

He told the directors to think it over and get back to him. He would be leaving for London on Saturday to give a speech and promote his book. Kersh was planning to take some vacation time in Ohio with his in-laws.

"Well," Dunlap said, "we'll talk to you. Let us know."

And he marched out of the conference room, through the reception area, and out the double glass doors to the elevator bank. Kersh and Fannin, the board secretary, followed.

FANNIN WAS JUST as confounded as the board by Dunlap's behavior. Now, after the meeting, he would have preferred nothing more than to walk down the block, past St. Patrick's Cathedral, straight to the Palace Hotel and into his room. He wanted badly to be alone. After all he had been through with Dunlap, he was near the breaking point.

Instead, not knowing how to get out of it, he accompanied his boss and Kersh to dinner.

"Do you think they got it?" asked Kersh. "I don't think they did. I don't think they got it at all."

"Well, I want to make changes on the board," said Dunlap. "I want to get rid of some of those people. The first one is Howard."

It was surely a strange remark from someone who clearly wanted out. Yet Dunlap seemed agitated enough that perhaps getting rid of a few directors would satisfy some sense of vengeance in him. Dunlap's irritation soon gave way to his usual blustery self. He told more Sir James stories. He compared himself to Bill Parcells, the coach of the New York Jets. "I get a winner wherever I go," Dunlap said, unwilling and unable to acknowledge that his team was in utter disarray.

From Fannin's vantage point as the odd man out, it was an unpleasant dinner. Dunlap prattled on, Kersh sulked, and he sat quietly, wanting the dinner to end before it started, regretting that he had agreed to go. Fannin had little appetite that evening, but at least he wouldn't have to travel back to Florida with Dunlap. His boss was taking an early flight the next morning, and he had to stay in town for a couple of business meetings, including a session with Sard to follow up on the response to the *Barron's* story. Kersh, meantime, was flying out in the morning for the ten-day vacation with his family in Ohio. After the meal, Fannin went directly to bed.

WHEN DUNLAP STORMED out of the board meeting, the four outside directors sat incredulous and quiet for what seemed like a couple of minutes. Kristol, the small, owlish attorney whose shoulders were bent over in a perpetual slump, broke the silence. Of all of them, he had known Dunlap the longest. For more than twenty years he had served as his private attorney. He had drafted the lush employment contracts that brought Dunlap to Sir James Goldsmith, to Kerry Packer, to Scott Paper, and to Sunbeam.

"That is complete bullshit," he blurted out. "Just bullshit."

"I agree," said Elson. "I agree with Howard completely. Al didn't answer my question."

Some of the directors already were up, gathering their coats, ready to leave. But now they settled back into the brown swivel chairs to talk about the bizarre scene they had just witnessed.

"I don't know about you, but what I'm clearly hearing is that Al and Russ want out," said Kristol.

He was personally outraged by the thought that they wanted to skip and run after the board had handed both of them huge contracts. He regarded the alternatives Dunlap posed as disingenuous. The directors could not prevent the media from running critical stories. They could not muzzle Wall Street analysts either. And they weren't about to buy out Dunlap and Kersh when there was no one to take their places. As a litigator who immersed himself in detail, Kristol wasn't as comforted by the rebuttal to the *Barron's* article as some of the other directors. He noticed that many of the story's assertions were left unchallenged by Gluck or Kersh.

"Something is terribly wrong," said Langerman. "We've got a big problem. Big problem. We did the acquisitions. We did the contract. We have an aggressive plan. Things begin to unravel a bit, and Al should be here saying, 'I know there are nay-sayers out there, but we have a sound plan and we're going to deliver.' Instead what I heard was someone saying, 'I don't want to do this anymore. I don't have the confidence to do it anymore. And I'm looking for someone else to be responsible for what is going on here. I'm looking for a way out.'"

Whittlesey was just as shocked. "Al's emotionally distraught," she said. "He's coming unglued." She told her fellow board members that the bad publicity was getting to Dunlap, that perhaps he didn't really want to quit. He was just upset. Some people were able to take unbearable criticism. Others weren't.

They sat there wrestling with questions to which they could not readily find answers.

"Does he have the will to continue in the job?"

"How sound are the profit forecasts he made less than a month ago?"

"What if he and Kersh resign? Where would that leave the company? Who would replace them?"

"What will Michael Price think?"

Before leaving the conference room, the directors exchanged personal phone numbers so they could stay in close touch over the week. Langerman, who as a Russian studies major at Yale University had once entertained the idea of becoming a spy for the CIA, agreed to dig more deeply into the company and question other Sunbeam executives.

WHEN THE MEETING finally broke up around 8 P.M., Elson was so distraught that he spent the next three hours aimlessly wandering the streets of Manhattan. "I was devastated," he said. "I just felt like my stomach was in my mouth. I felt queasy and uneasy. I needed fresh air to clear out my head."

Elson walked up and down Fifth Avenue, over to Madison and Park and Third Avenue. He covered much of midtown and some of the East Side. At a pay phone on Lexington and Sixty-third Street, he dialed his wife in Tampa using an MCI card. Elson dejectedly told her what had transpired that afternoon.

"I think this may be the end," he said. "I'm not sure what we'll do next, but I think it's over for Al. This could mean the beginning of a very difficult time."

Elson said he was going to walk a little more and that he would call again when he returned to his room at the University Club.

"It might be late," he warned.

"Well, be careful," his wife told him.

And he kept walking, wondering why Dunlap had ducked his question.

The moment Dunlap had dismissed his perfectly legitimate question on Sunbeam's sales and profits, Elson knew it was over. He knew the board would probably have to fire Dunlap, but only needed more facts to do it. Dunlap often eluded questions he did not want to answer, but never in the boardroom, where Elson found him candid and open. And clearly Dunlap wanted out—but completely characteristically, he wanted to be paid to leave, no matter what shape the company was in.

When Elson first gained his seat on the board, he had joked to friends that as an academic who studied governance, he now would play guinea pig for some of his own theories. As he walked the dark New York City streets, Elson thought how true that had become. It made him remarkably sad to think about the prospect. For as much as Elson had helped Dunlap, introducing him to the governance crowd, talking him up in the media, getting him on the board of trustees at the all-black Talladega College in Alabama, and writing a letter of support of him for the Horatio Alger award he failed to win, Dunlap also helped Elson. By championing the academic's most heartfelt belief, stock ownership by directors, Dunlap helped to make it common practice for board members to be paid in stock. And by putting Elson on his board, the same board that Elson nominated for the Wharton School's board of the year award, he had lent the professor far more prominence in the governance field.

By midnight, still walking and thinking, Elson found himself in front of Carnegie Deli at Fifty-fifth Street and Seventh Avenue. He stopped for a pastrami on rye, slathered it in mustard, and ate the sandwich at a small table in the restaurant. It was dry and stale, just like the day.

20
A MATTER OF CONSCIENCE

DAVID FANNIN HAD just about had it. He had been the first executive at Sunbeam to work directly for Al Dunlap. He had earned his quick favor by cobbling together the employment contract for Kersh over a weekend so that Kersh could be at Dunlap's side on his very first day. Unlike many of his colleagues, Fannin had cheered the new CEO's arrival. After years of turmoil and indecision, he thought Sunbeam would be led by a decisive, no-nonsense leader. Something would finally happen.

Like everyone else at Sunbeam, however, Fannin wasn't so sure he would be a part of it. He assumed he would be shown the door within days of Dunlap's arrival. Instead he thrived in the new hotly competitive culture Dunlap wrought. Fannin, who arrived at Sunbeam in the aftermath of Paul Kazarian's ouster in 1993, gained a promotion to executive vice president and a spot on Dunlap's operating committee. Of the company's top dozen senior executives, he became the only survivor, someone who viewed himself as a "moderating influence" on his mercurial boss.

Those first months under Dunlap were among the most gratifying of his career. Though he sometimes had misgivings about some of Dunlap's decisions, Fannin had become as caught up as anyone in the excitement of moving the company forward. He initially believed that Dunlap brought a new resolve to Sunbeam. Dunlap populated the

299

management ranks with new, highly driven talent. He shuttered plants that should have been closed years ago. He launched new products that quickly found their way onto retail shelves. And nearly everything Dunlap did attracted widespread attention.

Yet it did not take long for Fannin to realize that Dunlap was the most capricious and egotistical hothead he had ever encountered. Fannin's wife, Lucille, sensed that her husband would undergo great adversity from the start. After she sat next to Dunlap at a get-acquainted dinner, the CEO kept turning up in her dreams for weeks. They were all nightmares.

Still, she could never truly know what it was like to have Al Dunlap as your boss. Fannin endured Dunlap's profane and irrational harangues in sick horror for nearly two years. He heard the blaring voice thunder with insane intensity too many times. It was a voice that never seemed to stop, not even to breathe, as it unleashed bitter and painful torture on people who were only trying to help Dunlap succeed: Kersh, himself, Fogg, Strong, Burnett, Uzzi, anyone who ever got near him.

How Fannin ever thought it would work was beyond him now. It's true, they were both self-made men. Like Dunlap, Fannin grew up without inheriting either advantage or privilege. He was the son of a strict Baptist steelworker in a tiny backwoods town, Catlettsburg in eastern Kentucky, population 4,000. A precocious boy and straight-A student, Fannin spent countless hours in the nearby Ashland library, reading entire sets of encyclopedias from cover to cover. Even as a youngster, raised on *Perry Mason*, he discovered that the law greatly appealed to him. It was a profession that involved two of his great passions: reading and speaking. So he eventually found his way into law school and partner status at Wyatt Tarrant & Combs, Louisville's premier blue-chip firm. It was a place that taught the country boy not only how to be a lawyer but also how to become a gentleman.

All the same, Dunlap and Fannin were virtual opposites. Dunlap was fond of money, dogs, and his wife, in that order. His greatest devotion seemed to be to his ego. He was not well-read or well-bred. He lacked even the slightest interest in art, music, or culture. Fannin, on the other hand, had a passion for opera, good books, and lingering walks on the beach with Lucille. He had fallen in love with opera at the age of twelve when he first heard *Turandot* broadcast from the Met via a radio station in Charleston. Weaned on Puccini, Fannin had graduated to the greater complexities of Wagner. He devoured the great Greek classics in college, studied literature at Oxford in England, and now he rushed to read the latest novels. He played Cole Porter tunes on the grand piano in his living room.

If his interests were a study in contrast with Dunlap's, so was his demeanor and personality. Fannin was as mild and unruffled as Dunlap was volatile. He was, frankly, the kind of man whom Dunlap would have singled out for mistreatment at West Point. When Fannin was drafted into the army in 1969, he struggled through basic training and managed a soft landing in the Signal Corps at a NATO base in Holland, as far away from 'Nam as possible.

As Fannin knew full well, Dunlap had not changed much over the years. Even as a handsomely rewarded member of Dunlap's inner circle, the genteel Kentucky lawyer had become increasingly disillusioned by what he saw at Sunbeam. Many times, in fact, he considered quitting. "But it was like being in an abusive relationship," he said. "You just didn't know how to get out of it."

ON WEDNESDAY MORNING, shortly after getting out of bed in his elegantly appointed room at the Palace, Fannin finally took the first step. Though he had kept silent at the previous day's board meeting, he was greatly disturbed by what he saw and heard. Only five days earlier, Fannin had been with Dunlap and Kersh when household products chief Lee Griffith said he hoped to narrow an $80.9 million shortfall in the second quarter to $60 million. So when he heard Kersh tell the board that sales were a little soft, Fannin was shocked. That answer didn't begin to capture the size of the gap. Only a month ago, Dunlap and Kersh had told the board Sunbeam would post sales of $700 million for the quarter. Now they were staring at a 9 percent to 12 percent shortfall that made it doubtful that Dunlap could turn in a profitable quarter as he had promised Wall Street and his board.

Fannin felt he had to tell Langerman. He dialed the Mutual Shares office in Short Hills, New Jersey, and got Michael Price's deputy on the line. Initially he wanted to gauge Langerman's reaction to the meeting.

"The directors met after you guys left last night," Langerman said. "Everybody is worried this thing is not getting better. We're worried about Al because he's showing all the signs of someone who is out of it."

"Well," said Fannin, "you need to know that Russ was not forth-coming yesterday in response to that question on sales."

He then informed him of the Delray Beach meeting. "It's not a good situation," said Fannin, "and you need to be aware of that."

If Langerman was shocked, his voice betrayed no hint of it. He had had his own considerable doubts about Dunlap since early May. He had listened to Andrew Shore's warning that Sunbeam was doing everything it could, including massive discounts and extended credit terms, to coax retailers into taking more merchandise. And later that afternoon, Langerman said, he was going to meet with some of Perelman's men who were worried about the worsening condition of Coleman.

"We're pretty well convinced that Al and Russ want to quit," Langerman said. "We've concluded that's okay with us, but Faith isn't quite sure."

Langerman said that Perelman's associates had identified a potential Dunlap successor, former Duracell CEO Bob Kidder, who might be available.

"If Al is going to go right away," said Langerman, "we have to find someone to run the company. Let me call you at home tonight."

Before going off to his appointments, Fannin stopped by St. Patrick's Cathedral, where Dunlap often visited during his New York trips to light a candle. The general counsel walked down one of the long, marble aisles, picked out a quiet and unoccupied pew, and prayed for strength.

FOR PETER LANGERMAN, it was déjà vu all over again. Five and one-half years earlier, he had been on the telephone for hours with another of Sunbeam's chief legal officers. That time, it was Michael Lederman, Kazarian's general counsel, who was telling him that Paul Kazarian had lost the support of many of the company's top execu-tives. And just like the Dunlap crisis, the Kazarian blowup seemed to come from nowhere. Only five months before Langerman fired Kazarian, the company had successfully gone public and the stock had moved higher. Now, only three months after Sunbeam stock had hit its $52 peak, Langerman found himself in secret conversations with

Fannin, the man who had succeeded Lederman as the company's general counsel.

Ever since he first got involved with the company, going on its board of directors in 1990, there had been far too many ugly surprises. Langerman had no doubt that Dunlap wanted out. He also knew that financially the company was in worse shape than he had thought. But what most troubled him now was what he did not know. Andrew Shore had alerted him to Sunbeam's shortsighted deals with retailers. The Perelman camp were concerned about Coleman's condition since the acquisition. He wondered what other surprises were still out there, waiting to be discovered. How bad could it get?

Langerman gained a little more insight when he went into Manhattan that day to MacAndrews & Forbes Georgian brick townhouse headquarters on the Upper East Side. In light of Dunlap's belief that Perelman was engaged in a conspiracy to take over the company, Langerman was especially sensitive about the visit. Though it had been scheduled before the board meeting, he did not let any of his fellow directors know about it. He also had no intention of letting Perelman know that the board might possibly oust Dunlap in the near future.

What he heard in the townhouse surprised him. Jerry Levin, the former CEO of Coleman, and Howard Gittis, Perelman's right-hand man, told him that the company's employees, customers, and competitors said that Coleman was a mess.

"Look, we don't know if this stuff is right or wrong," said Gittis. "All we know is what people are telling us. You guys better look into this."

Levin said he had volunteered to assist Kersh in the transition, but Kersh did not want his help. Ever since his last day at Coleman on March 2, Levin said he had been getting phone calls from former Coleman colleagues and other business associates who told him one horror story after another. Typically, the phone calls began with the phrase, "You won't believe what happened today." Then an executive would recount the latest firing or resignation, or some quirky idea that Kersh or a Coopers consultant was trying out on the executive team. Kersh, for example, wanted to immediately impose a no-return policy on Coleman products with Wal-Mart and Home Depot, a decision that Levin believed would damage relations with two of its most important retailers. On another occasion, Coleman's advertising agency called Levin because Kersh wouldn't return its phone calls.

Levin's former colleagues told him that Kersh and Dunlap were calling him a "moron" and an "idiot" because of some of the decisions he made at Coleman.

Dunlap and Kersh, Levin said, had fired many of Coleman's best executives. Many more had already quit rather than work with Dunlap, while still more were on the verge of getting out. The departures not only affected the senior management of the company, they eroded the management ranks at least three levels deep.

"No one is running the place," Levin concluded. "Coleman is going to hell in a hand basket."

The spring of every year had always been the crucial selling season for outdoor gear, but the mass defections of Coleman staff had severely hurt its ability to move inventory into retail stores.

"Everything is in paralysis," Gittis told Langerman. "They're going to blow the entire selling season." He said Coleman had lost a major camping equipment sale to Kmart after the salesman who arranged the deal quit and no one else followed through. "We don't want to see the business getting destroyed," said Gittis. "Some of those employees had been with us for ten years. They love the company and the products. They live it. These people are in tears about what is happening to the company."

To Langerman, it was another affirmation that Dunlap had lost control of the company.

That evening, not long after Fannin had arrived home, he got a call from Langerman.

"We're thinking that this is probably about over," he said. "What do you think the reaction will be if Al were gone?"

"Well, I can do some looking into it," Fannin replied. "Because things are so tense and difficult, I think most people would see it as a positive. But let me talk to some others."

Langerman also told him about Perelman's concerns and asked Fannin to discreetly check around to see if he could gain additional confirmation about the company's financial condition.

Fannin agreed.

WHEN DUNLAP RETURNED to Florida the day after his board meeting, he spent most of his time cooped up in his dimly lit office. Kersh was out, on vacation. Fannin was still in New York. Over the next three days, he needed to work on his London speech, approve a letter to shareholders that would rebut the *Barron's* article, and try to marshal some support from Wall Street and his investors.

On Wednesday Dunlap took a call from Whittlesey, who was worried that all the bad press was overwhelming him. As someone who had worked in the Reagan Administration, she knew firsthand how a media assault could damage a person's willingness to fight on. Some leaders can rise to the occasion. Others simply cave in. When he worked for Sir James, it was Goldsmith who had endured the attack, not Dunlap. At Scott, his coverage had been remarkably positive as it had been in his early days at Sunbeam. Until now Dunlap had never had to endure a consistent stream of bad publicity. Whittlesey worried that the attack had posed a dangerous distraction.

Unaware of what Fannin had told Langerman, Whittlesey was hoping to cheer Dunlap up and help him cope with his bad press.

Dunlap groused again about the negative coverage and his fears that Perelman was behind it.

"Al, the higher you go, the more people are going to be out there trying to tear you down," she said. "If it's not Perelman, it will be somebody else."

He agreed, recalling that Goldsmith once told him that "when you accomplish great things in life, leave it to others to cast dirt on you. Consider it a compliment. Never give up and never give in." But his voice conveyed little conviction.

"You've got to dig in and do the job," she told him. "Don't even read the press accounts. You can't bail out."

They had an agreeable conversation but, as she later told her fellow directors, Whittlesey could hear in Dunlap's weary voice that he was suffering terribly.

"You ought to call Howard," she said. But Dunlap said he would only speak to Kristol if the lawyer called him. Kristol refused.

Failing to reach Elson that afternoon, Dunlap finally connected with him early Wednesday evening.

"So what did the board think?" Dunlap asked. "How was I?"

Elson was circumspect, not wanting to tell him the reaction in the boardroom.

"You were okay," he said. "But I'm worried about you, Al. I think you're losing your perspective. Maybe you need some time off."

"Well, it's been very tough," Dunlap said.

"You're going to Europe. Just take a day and drive through the country or something."

"Maybe I will," Dunlap said sadly.

It was an awkward exchange. Dunlap sounded empty and hollow. Elson couldn't tell him the truth.

ON WALL STREET only a single supporter remained: Nick Heymann of Prudential Securities. He had jumped on the bandwagon early, recommending the stock on the day Dunlap was named CEO. Although every other analyst had now downgraded Sunbeam, Heymann stayed on the bandwagon, hopeful that the market had overreacted to the bad news.

He had been an analyst for fifteen years, starting with Drexel Burnham Lambert just after gaining his MBA from Dartmouth College in 1983. Over those years he had seen the market react irrationally to all kinds of information, negative and positive. And in Sunbeam he was not a disinterested observer. Unlike Shore, Heymann had invested a sizable amount of his personal money in Sunbeam stock, at one point owning outright more than 10,000 shares.

Heymann covers seventeen companies for Prudential, from Boeing to Whirlpool, and he typically owns stock in the companies that he recommends to investors. "Right or wrong, I have a tendency to ride through the ups and down," he says. With Sunbeam he was on a roller-coaster that was into an extended plunge. So were many of his clients because Heymann had introduced Dunlap to as many as 200 of them.

Although the May 11 presentation failed to win Dunlap a single upgrade from the analysts, Heymann was boldly optimistic that the company's problems were already behind it. He discounted the Shore-incited acrimonious exchange because Dunlap and Kersh had told him that Shore was on a vendetta because Sunbeam did not give PaineWebber any investment banking business. After the May 11 show, he believed that Dunlap was so keen on underpromising and overdelivering that the company's forecasted earnings for 1998 "wouldn't be missed if a comet hit retail sales tomorrow."

Sticking with his buy rating on the stock, Heymann predicted that Sunbeam shares would rebound to the mid-$30s or more over the next six to twelve months. "In our opinion," Heymann wrote, "this stock is not about to enter Death Valley. Instead, Sunbeam's shares are now looking for a chance to move to higher ground . . . There is unlikely to be any additional negative news with which to burden shareholders."

While giving such buoyant appraisals publicly, Heymann was more quietly counseling Dunlap on how the CEO could restore his credibility. A week before the May 11 meeting in New York, the analyst sent Dunlap a highly detailed memo with sixteen suggestions to make his presentation a success with the Street. Among other things, Heymann advised Dunlap to enlist Michael Price's public support at the meeting. He also passed along some scuttlebutt that two top executives from General Electric Co., David Cote and Steve Sideta, who respectively were chief executive and chief financial officer of GE Appliances, might entertain offers to join Sunbeam.

"You either pull it off very well and all the new investors we have had you phone recently buy into the stock, or you fail to convince people and the stock continues to languish," wrote Heymann. "I know everyone at SOC [Sunbeam's ticker symbol] has been working overtime to get things turned around. You and your team are more than up to the challenge . . . you'll just write another chapter on how to win for shareholders!"

After the publication of the *Barron's* article, Heymann began urging Dunlap to mount a media offensive by issuing a point-by-point rebuttal of the *Barron's* story and going on television and radio to press his case. "You should be proactive," the analyst wrote Dunlap on June 12, a day after speaking to him on the phone. "Using the press to get the message out is a mandate because of your lack of close coverage in the investment community."

In remaining loyal to Dunlap, Heymann had put himself out on a long, embarrassing limb. He was dispensing advice as if he were on Dunlap's payroll in hopes that Sunbeam stock might stabilize and finally rise as he had forecast. In his most recent fax to Dunlap, the analyst had begun to sound somewhat desperate. "We are currently at a very critical juncture," he wrote. "You must issue your release today regarding the *Barron's* article. In all honesty, waiting only means you have more issues and misrepresentations to deal with. You simply don't have the time to wait any longer . . . "

Heymann even conceded that he felt like Dunlap's "outsourced investor relations department." "I like to work with upstanding and honorable companies and managements, and love to win. But I simply can't do it all by myself. I can't dedicate 50 percent of my time to SOC alone. We need access to and assistance from someone at your company who can help answer the endless questions I am besieged with on a daily basis."

Heymann signed off by scrawling: "Hang in there & let's beat this, Al!"

THROUGHOUT THURSDAY, June 11, Fannin remained in close contact with Langerman. He told him that human resources chief Gary Mask confirmed his own opinion that Dunlap's exit would be greeted favorably by most employees. Careful not to suggest that the board might oust the boss, Fannin told Mask that Dunlap might be thinking of quitting.

Fannin and Langerman spoke so often that day that the general counsel was becoming paranoid that Dunlap or Kersh might walk in on him during one of their telephone conversations. At one point Fannin left the building to call the director from the cell phone in his car.

"We are going to have a meeting of the outside directors," Langerman told him. "I want you to be there on the phone or in person to give your sense of the state of things and to tell the board what you think the reaction would be to Al's departure."

Fannin agreed. The meeting was set for Saturday at 8 A.M. in Kristol's offices in New York. Langerman also asked if he could get confirmation of what Perelman's deputies and Shore had told him about the hurtful deals the sales staff had been making to inflate the top line. "Any light you can shed on that would be helpful," he said.

DAVID FANNIN WAS not the only player on Dunlap's team who had become disaffected by what he saw and heard. Frank Feraco, easily Dunlap's most important hire since his early months at Sunbeam, had been on the job for only five weeks. Already, however, he realized that he had made a tragic mistake, perhaps the worst of his twenty-nine-year career in business. Lured by a corpulent option package and a Dunlap pledge to make him rich, Feraco violated one of rules that had long guided his unblemished years in business. He took a job for no reason other than the money.

He arrived eager and guileless the week before the May 11 presentations as president of the outdoor business, the division with all the newly acquired Coleman products as well as Sunbeam's grills. On that day in New York he ventured out onto the roof of the Equitable building to take in the grand view of a city he loved. Looking northeast to the Bronx, he could glimpse the tops of the tenement buildings where he had been born and raised by Italian immigrant parents who worked in the city's garment industry. His mother, who had raised four sons and worked as a seamstress, would be proud of him now, he thought. If things turned out well at Sunbeam, he figured he would never have to work again. When Dunlap joined him on the roof, Feraco's eyes ventured west across the Hudson River.

"Aren't you from Hoboken?" asked Feraco, pointing to the tiny skyline of the city.

"Yep, I'm from there, and sometimes I wish I never left there," replied Dunlap.

Feraco could appreciate the strain Dunlap had been under. He knew full well the pressures business imposed. Like his boss, he was a self-made man who never had the benefit of an Ivy League education or family connections. He went to a state university on an athletic scholarship, earning extra change during the summers by working in the post office and a funeral home.

Everything he'd achieved, he'd achieved on his own. He'd climbed upward through the sales route at Mobil Oil, Merrill Lynch, and finally Emerson Electric, where over a sixteen-year period he rose from a district sales manager based in Westchester, New York, to senior vice president of sales and marketing of the company's Skil power tools division. He joined Sunbeam from Kohler Co., the bathroom fixture giant, where he had been president of a $1.7 billion division.

Feraco physically resembled New York Yankees manager Joe Torre and had, in fact, excelled at the game of baseball. He played four years of varsity ball, setting up behind the plate as a gritty catcher for the University of Rhode Island team. He earned the nickname "Mongoose" for his agile and grizzled play as a linebacker for the varsity football squad. He was built hard and tough, and he stayed that way by running thirty miles a week and lifting weights into his early fifties.

As soon as Feraco went on the road to visit Sunbeam's customers, he discovered immediate trouble. At Wal-Mart headquarters, a buyer told him the retailer would soon have to deal with the oversized inventory of Sunbeam product. The buyer told Feraco that Sunbeam would have to accept the return of the merchandise or deeply discount it so Wal-Mart could sell it at bargain prices.

Alarmed by what he heard on his customer visits and at Coleman's former headquarters in Wichita, Feraco asked Kersh on several occasions for an updated profit-and-loss statement on his business. Kersh, however, refused to supply him with the numbers.

"Don't worry about it," Kersh told him. "Just go out and generate some business."

Why one of the two highest operating executives in the company couldn't get a P&L for his own business perplexed and worried him. His concerns grew daily. On Monday, June 8, in a telephone conference call, a finance official urged Feraco to go out and cut some deals.

"Why don't you do what we've always done," she said. "Just go out and extend some dating and do some business."

"We can't do that anymore," Feraco replied. "Wal-Mart has warehouses filled with our stuff. So do Home Depot and Kmart."

Even if he wanted to extend credit terms or discount product, it was too late in the season to do it. Virtually all grill sales to retailers were completed for the season.

"It's the wrong time to do that," Feraco added.

"So what?" she responded. "Do it anyway."

After the conversation, Feraco confronted Alan W. Lefevre, the chief financial officer of the household products division. A tall, thin man with a boyish face in a perpetual smile, he wore starched white shirts and often pulled on the belt around his trim waist. Widely known as "Little Al" to distinguish him from Dunlap, Lefevre was aware of what Sunbeam was doing in the field. It was Lefevre and his lieutenants who had to approve the terms of every sale before an order was entered into the system. Sunbeam's salesmen knew him well because he was often on the other end of the telephone encouraging them to jam customers with merchandise.

"What the hell is going on here?" Feraco asked.

"Look, this has been going on for every quarter for the last two years," Lefevre admitted.

"This is bullshit, and this is going to stop right now," Feraco insisted. "Al, we have a problem. I was born in the Bronx, I'm a street kid, and I know this is bullshit. I'm not going to waste my time and ruin my career for a bunch of guys who don't care about us."

Two days later, on Wednesday, he walked into Dunlap's office and asked him for a P&L for the business. Big Al's reply was the same as Kersh's days earlier.

"Why do you need that?" asked Dunlap.

"I want to know were we stand," Feraco replied.

"That's a bunch of crap. Just go and do your job," Dunlap ordered.

Feraco left the office and immediately called his wife, Joan, on her cell phone. She was out with a real estate agent, looking for a new home to move the family from Lake Forest, Illinois, to Florida.

"Stop the presses," he told her. "Don't buy anything."

It didn't surprise her. Shortly after Feraco joined the company, they had gone to Dunlap's home for dinner. Before the meal, Dunlap gave his new executive an extensive tour of the house. Everywhere, it seemed, there were lions. The gate outside Dunlap's home was decorated with the crest of a lion. There were lions in the tiled floor as well as a mosaic of a lion at the bottom of Dunlap's swimming pool. When Feraco asked him the significance of it, Dunlap said it was his family crest. Driving to their hotel after dinner, Feraco told the story to his wife, a trained psychologist.

"He's from Hoboken, New Jersey!" marveled Feraco. "How the hell can he have a family crest?"

"Frank," she replied, "this guy is the most egocentric maniac I have ever met in my life. I hope we didn't make a mistake here."

Now, with Dunlap's indignant refusal to give him a P&L, Feraco concluded that he had indeed made a serious mistake. It did not take him long to size up the game he had unwittingly entered. The channel stuffing "was a smoke screen to get the company sold," Feraco believed. "I can't even begin to tell you how much pressure was there. Al had a very immature approach to business. He believed that if you banged on the table enough, screamed at enough people, you would scare them into what you wanted. Al coerced the staff of people there. He said, 'If you stick with me, we'll ride this stock up and everyone will make a ton of money.'"

Feraco's professional and personal life was guided by a set of ethics and values instilled by hardworking parents and plain common sense.

If Dunlap and Kersh wanted him to play games with the numbers, he was painfully ill-suited for the job. For Feraco this was a matter of conscience and survival. He decided to do something he had never done before: write what he confided was a "cover-your-ass" memo that made clear the deeply troubled nature of the business and the need to disclose the news to Wall Street. He was scheduled to meet with the Street's analysts the following week on Monday, and he wasn't about to misinform them about the company's condition.

On Thursday, June 11, Feraco sat in his office with Lefevre and drafted the one-page memo. He wrote that the company was facing a $200 million shortfall for the second quarter, more than double what Griffith predicted only a week earlier. There would be no profit in the quarter, Feraco wrote, and there was no way to make up the gap. Feraco said he didn't think he was misreading the numbers, but because he lacked a P&L, he was giving Dunlap the facts as he saw them. The harsh facts were, he wrote, that the company didn't have the orders in the system to make the numbers promised Wall Street. Feraco added that the magnitude of the shortfall placed the entire year in jeopardy. He urged Dunlap to immediately communicate the news to Wall Street.

To ensure that the contents of the memo could not be suppressed, Feraco sent copies to many of the company's top executives. Besides Dunlap and Kersh, the document went to controller Bob Gluck, treasurer Ron Richter, Lefevre, and Karen Clark, the chief finance officer for Feraco's division. In all, eight top executives received the memo.

After writing the memo Feraco left the office for the Fort Lauderdale airport. He had to fly to California to attend the funeral of a friend over the upcoming weekend. Before boarding the plane, however, he telephoned Griffith, who agreed to put his signature on the memo as well.

"Lee, you have a family," Feraco told him. "I have a family. This has to stop."

Griffith confided to Feraco that he didn't feel comfortable stuffing the channels. Griffith's lower estimate of the shortfall on June 4 was simply a more optimistic assessment of the company's situation.

"Well, you better just pull in your horns and stop doing it," Feraco advised. "They can't shoot you. They might fire you, but they can't shoot you. I'm not going to do it."

Feraco then boarded his plane to go west, disappointed that he would not be there to witness Dunlap's reaction to his memo.

THE NEXT DAY, Friday, Fannin still hadn't spoken to the person who was privy to all the ins and outs of Sunbeam's finances: Bob Gluck, who had delivered the rebuttal of the *Barron's* article before the board on Tuesday. As corporate controller, he was the second highest-ranking financial officer in the company after Kersh. He was the day-to-day guardian of Sunbeam's financial records. Every number in the company had to pass through him, as well as every deal and every transaction that affected either the balance sheet or the income statement.

Fannin walked into Gluck's office, closed the door, and told him that at the request of the board of directors, he was there to ask questions about the state of the company's financial condition. The usually reserved accountant's response surprised him. Terribly frustrated and upset, Gluck apparently felt the need to unburden himself. Like Fannin, he had worked tirelessly in an impossible environment under an exacting and abusive boss. He greatly regretted his involvement in approving transactions that only had short-term benefit in boosting sales and long-term dire consequences.

As the business began to unravel in the fourth quarter, he was under especially brutal pressure to push the envelope of generally accepted accounting principles. If Kersh was, as he so contentedly pointed out, the company's single biggest profit center, it was because Gluck allowed Dunlap's friend to run roughshod over him.

"We tried to do things in accordance with GAAP, but everything had been pushed to the limit," Gluck said, near tears. "There were things I should have stood up and said no to. I should have just said, 'No, you can't do this. You can't book it that way.'"

Gluck detailed examples in which the sales staff scrambled to make their numbers any way they could. In at least one instance, Gluck told Fannin, the company had sold to a distributor who provided Sunbeam products to a regional retail chain while selling merchandise to the same chain direct. The distributor obviously had no chance of selling to the retailer and would have to return the goods to Sunbeam. In the interim, however, the company booked the sale and the profit.

To increase sales, Sunbeam cut lots of deals in which product was heavily discounted and credit terms were extended, and it also began to guarantee sales, allowing distributors and retailers to return merchandise without penalty or freight charges if they could not sell it. Gluck told Fannin that the *Barron's* article he had so thoroughly refuted at the board meeting three days ago was accurate in particular respects that had not been addressed at the meeting, especially in regard to guaranteed sales. Sunbeam had rented warehouse space in several locations around the country to receive and store returned goods. A massive 1-million-square-foot facility near Tulsa, Oklahoma, once used to build World War II bombers, had been leased by Sunbeam in the spring and filled with an entire season's supply of barbecue grills at what was now the height of the summer grill-selling season.

Fannin could certainly empathize with Gluck. He had experienced similar pressure directly from Dunlap, and he had seen the CEO terrorize virtually every executive and outside adviser with whom he had come into contact. When he left Gluck's office, all that Fannin wanted to do was get out. He told Dunlap he was going to leave the office early for a meeting in Fort Lauderdale. Of course, all he would be "meeting" was an airplane en route to New York for the session Langerman had called for Saturday morning.

Fannin was driving south on I–95 to Fort Lauderdale to catch his 4:30 P.M. flight when his car phone rang.

"Hold on for Mr. Dunlap," said Denise Valek, his secretary.

For a terrifying instant, Fannin imagined that Dunlap knew what he was about to do. He thought of picking up the phone, saying, "Hello, hello," and hitting the off button, anything not to speak with his boss. But suddenly Dunlap's thundering voice was reverberating in his Lexus.

"I have Finn Fogg on the other line," boomed Dunlap. He was trying to put together a three-way call to discuss the *Barron's* story yet again.

"Oh God," thought Fannin. "Now what?"

Dunlap, of course, did not know that his general counsel would be having dinner with Fogg and Rich Easton only a few hours later in New York. Fortunately Dunlap was completely inept when it came to anything involving technology. He couldn't make the telephone connection.

Fannin breathed a deep sigh of relief. "I'll call Finn," he said, and then hung up.

Later, over a meal at the Mark Hotel, where Delaware-based Easton preferred to stay when in New York, the three lawyers got a laugh out of Fannin's scare. They discussed what was likely to be a meeting of high drama on Saturday and wondered how it would all turn out. Fannin told the Skadden Arps attorneys that Sunbeam was in complete turmoil and that Dunlap had lost the ability to lead the company.

"If the board doesn't get rid of Al, I have to go," he said.

"Look, you're doing the right thing," counseled Fogg. "This has got to be tough, but you're doing what's right."

ROUGHLY SIXTEEN BLOCKS south, at a side table at Ben Benson's steak house on Fifty-first Street, Charles Elson and Howard Kristol were sadly musing over their very different relationships with the man they expected to cast out of office the next day. "It was like a wake the night before the funeral," recalled Elson. "We both were morose because we knew the story was going to have a very unhappy ending."

Over sirloin steaks and hash browns, they commiserated about the one thing that linked every friend that Al Dunlap has ever had: the compulsion to defend him. The two attorneys, like every other Dunlap acquaintance, had withstood endless questions from colleagues and friends who could never fathom how they could have befriended such an egotist and bully. Elson had got it from fellow professors and many involved in the governance movement. For years Kristol had heard it from the partners in his law firm. If you were an acquaintance or a friend of Al Dunlap's you were forever defending him from people who, it turned out, knew him better than you.

They shared stories of how they first met Dunlap. It was four years ago that Elson had lunched with him at Scott Paper's expansive Philadelphia corporate headquarters, where the offices were so empty and quiet that it seemed as if the building had been struck by a neutron bomb. It was just that Dunlap, of course, had fired most of the people who had once worked there. Kristol, who is just a week younger than Dunlap, recalled taking him on as a client in 1983 before he landed his first CEO job at Lily-Tulip Inc. Kristol helped to draft his contract for the move, a pact that made Dunlap a millionaire.

They laughed about how Dunlap had obliged each director to buy dozens of copies of *Mean Business*. Elson assigned the book to graduate students in his corporate governance classes. Kristol purchased several boxes of the book, thinking he would hand them out to clients for free. His partners were appalled at the idea because the book only confirmed their negative view of the man. Nearly two years later, boxes filled with the books were still stacked in Kristol's office. Since their Tuesday meeting with Dunlap, they had independently flipped through the pages of *Mean Business* again, only to conclude that Dunlap had violated many of the tenets in his own book.

"His own book is a damning indictment of everything he has done in the past few weeks," marveled Elson, between sips of a martini. Kristol nodded agreement.

Dunlap's first rule was to get the right management team. Yet nearly everyone he had hired at Sunbeam had quit or had been fired. Other than Kersh and Fannin, his "dream team" was a shambles. Rule two was to pinch pennies. Yet he had just fought hard for a lush contract that forced Sunbeam to take a $31 million write-off in the first quarter of the year. Rule three was to know what business you're in and to focus on it like a laser. But Dunlap, they agreed, seemed disengaged, and hardly focused at all on the core business.

Kristol left early, bundling up against a torrential downpour, to catch a train to his Scarsdale home. As Elson sat, finishing up the few bits of hash browns left on the table, he thought how ironic the turn of events had become. Elson and his fellow directors were about to hold Dunlap accountable for his often-expressed view that a board should get rid of a CEO if he can't turn around the business in twelve months. "If we fired him tomorrow," he thought, "we would be following Al's own advice."

21
WHAT GOES AROUND, COMES' AROUND

ANGRY THUNDERSTORMS drenched New York on early Saturday morning. The rain fell like bullets from a brooding sky. It was as if the gods of Wall Street were outraged that Sunbeam's outside directors would dare meet secretly behind the broad back of Albert Dunlap.

On this June 13 the board members made their way through the wet and empty streets to Rockefeller Center, only to find the main entrance of the international building closed. To get inside they had to scurry to the back entrance, near the center's skating rink. After winning the approval of a sleepy guard just beyond the back doors, they ventured toward the elevators that would carry them to the tenth floor and the offices of Howard Kristol's law firm.

The directors met promptly at 8 A.M. in the same beige-walled conference room they had occupied only four days earlier. A box of Krispy Kreme donuts served as a quick and sugary breakfast. Sunbeam's outside attorneys, Fogg and Easton, were already there as well. Rutter, the local banker who chaired Sunbeam's audit committee, was patched in by conference phone from Captiva Island, Florida, where he was on a

317

family vacation. Peter Langerman, who had been on the Sunbeam board longer than any of them, spoke first.

"As you know," he said solemnly, "we've been talking for the last few days about our grave concerns over the company and the meeting with Al and Russ last Tuesday. I've asked David to come and give us his views on the state of things. He's willing to do that even though he is obviously putting himself at great risk. I've assured him that whatever the outcome, the board would provide him some degree of economic protection."

Fannin had spent most of Thursday evening in his den, typing up prepared remarks for this session on his computer. He had reviewed those notes in his hotel room just before going to bed the previous night. He updated his comments by scribbling in the margins pieces of his conversation with Gluck. But as he faced the outside directors, Fannin barely relied on the notes.

"The day-to-day atmosphere at the company has really deteriorated," he told them. "Al is no longer in touch with the business and what's going on at the company. I've had conversations with Kersh in which Kersh said he thought the only chance the company had long-term was to get someone else in. Even someone as loyal to him as Kersh is saying that 'it isn't going to work with Al around.' Al isn't talking to people. He has cut himself off."

The drama of his presentation was only heightened by the quiver in his voice and a persistent twitch in his face, a quirk that had become particularly bothersome as the stress from working with Dunlap mounted.

He told the directors about the meeting at which Griffith said he hoped to narrow the more than $80 million gap in second quarter sales to $60 million, only a few days before Kersh said that sales were merely soft and Dunlap cut off all further discussion on the numbers. There was no way that Sunbeam was going to meet the second quarter promises that Dunlap had made to the board and Wall Street only a month ago. It would be his third missed quarter of earnings in a row.

"The numbers aren't soft," said Fannin. "They are horrible. We're far below the sales numbers."

Fannin's news put into perspective Dunlap's odd behavior only a few days earlier, and it outraged his friends in the boardroom. They were incensed by the prospect that Dunlap and Kersh knew the company was in trouble and simply wanted to skip and run, and even worse, get the board to agree to some sort of severance deal so they could pick up still more money while leaving them to clean up the mess.

"They were looking for a way out," said Langerman. "They were giving us the bait the other day, hoping that we would take it. That would have let them off. Al could say, 'Everything was wonderful. I did my best. I succeeded and this board decided it didn't want me.' He just isn't prepared to be responsible."

Like Elson and Kristol, Langerman also had read Dunlap's book again and brought it with him to the board meeting.

"You know," he said, "Al had a lot of good ideas. If you could get through all the ego stuff, there was a basic and sound business philosophy in that book. But he lost it. He didn't subscribe to it anymore."

For Whittlesey the last straw was Dunlap's decision to go off and promote his book while the company was in the midst of a crisis. To her, it demonstrated the extent to which Dunlap was disengaged from his job of running the business.

"I can't believe he's going to London," she told her fellow board members. "If there is a crisis, you cancel. You don't go off to London on a book tour. And Russ is on vacation?"

What Whittlesey didn't know would have shocked her all the more: Dunlap had been telling some executives that he now considered himself Sir James Goldsmith. "What I need at Sunbeam," he said, "is an Al Dunlap."

What the board now needed was someone to take his place. The directors could speed up the ongoing search for a chief operating officer or possibly upgrade it to an attempt to find a new chief executive. There was still the possibility that the ex–Duracell CEO Kidder might be interested in the job or that they could recontact the COO candidate from Philip Morris who had turned down the job. Maybe he would be interested in it now if he were named chief executive. For the immediate future, however, the directors agreed that Langerman would serve as chairman and oversee the company's three operating executives: Lee Griffith, Frank Feraco, and Franz Schmidt.

By 10 A.M. the outside directors all concluded that Dunlap had to go. But he would probably be leaving his house before 3 P.M. to catch his flight to London. It didn't leave much time to get it done.

Kristol suggested waiting until Thursday when Dunlap returned. He felt it was unfair to embarrass Dunlap just as he was promoting his book in England. But there also were some pragmatic concerns. Having a few extra days would give the board a little more time to legally prepare for the firing, to consider who would eventually succeed Dunlap, and to communicate the news inside and outside the company.

Fannin was aghast, gripped by panic and dread.

"I cannot work for that man another day," he said, his voice wobbly with emotion. "I can't do it."

"Don't go into the office," advised one director. "Just call in sick on Monday."

"He'll call me. He'll know that this meeting took place. I just can't do it. I cannot work for that man another day," said Fannin. "I will not talk to him again. I will not have him yell at me again."

Fannin broke down and abruptly left the room. He went outside to pace the hallway and regain his composure. After a sleepless night and nearly two years of work under Dunlap, he was utterly depleted. It had taken Fannin every ounce of energy to come to this meeting and tell a board largely composed of Dunlap's pals that they should fire their friend. Even the thought of another hour under Dunlap seemed an intolerable burden.

"Well, my mind is made up," said Elson. "He's got to go, and I think we've got to let him go today. We made a decision. Once you do that, you can't wait. You've got to get him out of there."

Elson then related a family story to make the point.

"My dad once had an employee who was stealing from him," Elson related. "He called my grandfather up because he didn't know what to do. My grandfather said, 'Well, what's the problem?'

"My father told him, 'He's getting kickbacks from suppliers, but he's very valuable and I don't know who could fill his shoes.'

"My grandfather said, 'Well, that's a tough problem. But what would happen if he were to die tomorrow? What if he dropped dead?'

"And my father said, 'I'd move this person over here and this person over there.'

"'The hospital just called,' my grandfather said. 'He's dead! Fire him!'"

"His point was that once you make up your mind, as difficult as it is, you have to move ahead. We have to get rid of him. We've got to do it now," said Elson.

The heads around the table nodded favorably.

"It probably isn't going to accomplish a lot to wait," agreed Langerman. "Let's do it now."

But the directors still were in a quandary. Sunbeam's corporate bylaws allowed only the chairman of the board, Dunlap in this case, to call a board meeting. Every director, including Kersh, also had to have twenty-four hours' notice. The only way around these restrictions, explained attorney Easton, was to get both Dunlap and Kersh on the phone and to immediately call the meeting to order. If they didn't object, the session would be under way, and the board could then fire him.

If Dunlap hung up or Kersh couldn't be reached, the board would have to delay the firing. If Dunlap had even an inkling that the board was about to fire him, all he had to do was make Kersh unavailable. The board then would have to wait at least another day to take action.

Inspired by Fannin's emotional appeal, however, the board pressed ahead. Langerman tried in vain to reach Tom Hardy of SpencerStuart to see if the chief operating officer search could be accelerated. Elson began calling Hardy's colleague, Dennis Carey, but could not find him either. Sandwiches were ordered as Skadden Arps lawyer Fogg began scripting the words for the directors' eventual phone call with Dunlap. The one-page script outlined parts for Fannin and three directors, with most of the words to be read by Langerman. Fogg so hurriedly drafted the accompanying formal resolutions to oust Dunlap that he failed to spell Dunlap's name correctly. Though he had worked with Dunlap for many years and his firm had billed his companies millions, he typed up the statements referring to Dunlap as "Dunlop."

Langerman finally decided to call Kersh first, get him on the line, and then try to patch in Dunlap. But when he called Kersh's in-laws in Ohio, they told him that Kersh was at an amusement park with his children. They didn't know exactly when he would return, but thought he might return shortly. Langerman called again later, only to get a busy signal.

Dunlap had, of course, left open the door for a meeting. When he and Kersh stormed out of the previous session, he had told them to consider his request and get back to him.

"I'll call Al, and we'll just try to get Russ on the phone."

Langerman easily reached Dunlap and told him he was in a room with other directors and they had been discussing what Dunlap had said earlier in the week. He told him it would be helpful to speak to both him and Kersh at the same time.

"I'll call Russ right now," Dunlap said. "Call me back in ten or fifteen minutes."

The tension in the room mounted.

WHILE THE DIRECTORS were deliberating Dunlap's fate, he had spent much of the morning on the telephone with Lee Griffith, Frank Feraco, and his public relations advisers in New York. Before leaving for London that afternoon at 3 P.M., Dunlap hoped to finalize a letter to shareholders on the *Barron's* article as well as the speech he planned to deliver in England. Unaware of the secret meeting of directors, he was frantically trying to reach both Fannin and Fogg to patch them into a conference call with Sard and Bailey. While Dunlap was on the phone going through the details of his speech and letter with Sard, his wife, Judy, was calling Fannin's home. Fannin's wife and daughter let the phone ring and ring that morning, knowing from caller ID that it was Dunlap.

At one point, while Dunlap was still on the line with Bailey, Langerman was conferring with Sard about the best way to handle the announcement if Dunlap were fired. Only five minutes after concluding their discussions with Dunlap, Sard and Bailey received a telephone call from Fannin. He had first called them at 7 A.M. before leaving his hotel room to inform the public relations advisors that the board was secretly meeting in New York. Fannin said then they might be needed later in the day. Now he asked them to come to Kristol's offices as soon as possible. "The board," he said, "is expecting to fire Al at 2 P.M."

Dunlap apparently did not receive Feraco's memo until early Saturday morning. When he did, he quickly became incensed. Feraco finally heard from Dunlap at 7 A.M. at his hotel in Newport Beach, California. Dunlap and Kersh had been in an extended rant with Griffith for nearly half an hour over the memo by the time Feraco joined the conference call.

"We don't understand why you and Lee can't make these numbers," snapped Dunlap. "Russ," asked Dunlap, "how can this be?"

"There's no way it can be that much," claimed Kersh. "That's an exaggeration. It's closer to $70 million. If these guys get out and get their sales people in gear, we wouldn't have this problem."

"I want you to retract the memo," insisted Dunlap, before lighting into Feraco and Griffith with a stream of ugly invective.

"Fuck you," said Feraco. "I'm not going to retract something I believe to be true. Unless you can disprove it, I'm not going to get up in front of the analysts and tell them we're going to make the numbers."

Irate, Dunlap began shouting so loudly that Feraco was able to hold the phone an arm's length from his body and still hear his boss scream profanities at him. Feraco had worked for some hard-driving personalities in the past, including Emerson Electric's Chuck Knight, who had a reputation as a tough and demanding taskmaster. But Feraco had never been subjected to as vicious an attack as the one Dunlap had unleashed.

"You guys have to get out!" Dunlap boomed. "It's your responsibility to make the numbers!"

When the phone went dead after twenty minutes or so, Feraco immediately dialed Griffith.

"Lee," he said, "I've been making numbers for twenty-seven years, in recessions and in good times, and this is the first time in my life I've ever told anyone I couldn't make a number."

Feraco believed that Dunlap wanted both him and Griffith to do anything to reach the projections his boss had made to the Street. "It was obvious that they wanted me to do something I shouldn't do to make the number," he said later. "But they were careful enough not to say that. He was screaming and shouting."

His advice to Griffith in sunny Florida: "Go play golf," Feraco said. Both of them were unaware that the company's outside directors had already decided to fire their boss.

BACK IN NEW YORK, Sard and Bailey were unable to get a cab in the torrential rain. They walked thirty blocks north to get to the meeting, and arrived soaked to the bone just before 2 P.M. Fannin took them aside to fill them in on what had transpired.

Director Rutter was patched in first, then Dunlap, and finally Kersh at about 2:20, just thirty or forty minutes before Dunlap was to leave his home for the drive to Miami Airport for a 4 P.M. flight to London.

"Do we have Al, Russ, and Bill on the phone?" Fannin said, reading every word, even an elementary greeting, from the script. "Good, all of the directors being present in person or by telephone, this meeting of the board of directors of Sunbeam Corp. is duly convened. Peter, I believe you would like to speak first."

"Al," Langerman slowly read, "the outside directors have considered the options you presented to us last Tuesday and have decided that your departure from the company is necessary. Here is what we propose:

"1. You be removed from all positions with the company and its subsidiaries effective immediately. You may continue to serve as a director of Sunbeam, unless you choose to resign from that position."

Everyone in the room was waiting for an explosion to occur, but Langerman gathered speed as he read and didn't allow a pause for interruption. Dunlap was stunned into silence anyway.

"2. The board names a new chairman of the board and we expand our ongoing search to encompass a search for your successor.

"3. Then, our lawyers talk to your lawyer about our respective rights and obligations with respect to your contract.

"Do I hear a motion," asked Langerman.

"I move the adoption of the following resolutions," said Elson.

But Elson could not bring himself to read the statements that would lead to his friend's ouster. "It felt too cruel," he recalls. "We had gone back a long way, and I just couldn't do it."

So Fannin read the formal resolutions, and as soon as Langerman asked for a second, Whittlesey read her bit part on the script.

"I second the motion," she said.

Before Dunlap or Kersh could utter a word, Langerman then said, "All in favor."

All the directors in the room said yea.

"All opposed."

There was silence.

"The resolutions have been duly adopted," read Langerman. "Al, who would you like our lawyers to call to discuss your contract?"

"I think I'm entitled to an explanation," said Dunlap calmly. "And what about Russ. We came in as a package."

Langerman told him to have his lawyer contact Fogg.

"Russ, what are you going to do?" asked Dunlap. "What about Russ?"

Kersh, whom everyone assumed would quit in a sign of solidarity with his friend and mentor, remained silent.

"Just have your lawyer contact our lawyer," said Langerman finally.

The phone hookup went dead. Dunlap was gone and fired. There was a sense of relief among the directors, who thought it would have been so much more difficult to fire him in person. The mood in the room was quiet and sober. With Fogg's help, Langerman was putting together a list of all the key executives the board would have to contact to tell them the news. Fannin called his associate and general counsel Janet Kelly to secure Dunlap's office. She arranged for a locksmith to change the locks on Dunlap's office and for a security guard to prevent him from entering the headquarters building.

Langerman called Phil Harlow of Arthur Andersen to ask if there was any information the board should know now that it had dismissed Dunlap. Once again he stood firmly behind his audit of the company's numbers. It was when the board reached Griffith that it began to gain the sense that things were even worse than Fannin imagined. Griffith said he had been on the phone that morning with Feraco and Dunlap. Instead of a $60 million shortfall in the quarter's revenues, Griffith said it looked more like $100 million. He and Feraco had concluded that there was no way to make up the shortfall.

As the afternoon wore on, the news began only to worsen. The sales gap grew larger, eventually hitting the $200 million mark predicted by Feraco in his memo. But the biggest jolt occurred when Langerman reached treasurer Ronald R. Richter. Richter had only joined Sunbeam in March from ABN AMRO N.A. Bank in Chicago and had filled in as head of investor relations when Goudis resigned. As treasurer he obviously was in a key finance job and could shed still more light on the company's true financial condition. The shortfall in sales, thought Richter, could pose problems with Sunbeam's creditors. During the conversation he began to mention the word "covenants" (requirements imposed by a lender to protect its loans). It immediately set off panic in the boardroom.

"We might not make the covenants," Richter said.

"I can't believe this," said Langerman. "We could default."

"What do you mean?" asked Elson.

"If these sales numbers are right, we could be in default," added Langerman.

"What do we do?"

"Bankruptcy," said Langerman.

The boardroom fell quiet. Everyone in the room now realized they weren't simply dealing with another down quarter. The company was teetering on the verge of bankruptcy. It was possible, Richter conceded, that Sunbeam could be in technical default of its loan agreements.

"We've got two weeks to go, and this is where we need to be," Richter said. He explained that within two weeks, the company's banks could call in the $1.7 billion loan if Sunbeam failed to hit a certain ratio of pretax earnings to its debt. It looked highly unlikely that Sunbeam would pass the test.

Ever since Kazarian had taken the company out of bankruptcy, Sunbeam had never had a cash problem. Indeed, it had a pristine balance sheet with little debt on the books. But Dunlap's acquisitions had forced the company to go heavily into hock. Sunbeam had to earn about $150 million a year just to meet the interest payments on that debt.

When Langerman later reached controller Bob Gluck, another explosion went off.

"What are we using for cash these days?" asked Fogg.

"What?" asked Gluck.

"What are we using for cash?"

"Well, there's the revolver," replied the controller.

Another shock coursed through the room.

Langerman, standing by the credenza for the speaker-phone conversation, quickly slumped into the nearest chair—in total horror.

"You are meeting the payroll with revolving credit?" asked Fogg, incredulous.

It was a profound revelation. Dunlap, the man who thought himself the best chief executive in America, had driven the company into the ground. In the service of his own ego and greed, he had laid off thousands of people, closed dozens of facilities, made impossible demands on countless survivors—yet he still could not get the company to earn a true and healthy profit, even in the short term. For all his personal quirks and failures, Kazarian had done that and more. Even Schipke, whose leadership qualities were legitimately questioned, had never turned in a loss or taken a write-off.

"You know," said Langerman, "this is a big problem, bigger than we thought this morning. It's becoming more and more clear to me that the operating people we have in place might be able to handle it, but it's not the best solution."

Elson and Kristol agreed. "I don't know if Jerry Levin is available," said Langerman. "I don't know if he wants to do it. But maybe we should call Ron Perelman and his people to see if they would help."

It seemed a good idea, anyway. Perelman was the company's second-largest shareholder. He and his men clearly were upset about the deterioration of Coleman under Dunlap. And as Fogg put it, "It's better to have a camel inside the tent pissing out than one pissing in." So Langerman called the twenty-four-hour switchboard at McAndrews & Forbes headquarters where he had met with Levin and Gittis three days before. He left a message informing Perelman that Dunlap had been fired and asked whether Levin might be willing to help out. He invited him to a meeting the next morning at the offices of Skadden Arps and hoped for the best.

The directors had started their day with what they assumed was a leadership problem. As the hours went on they realized it was far more severe than that. The company was beset with all kinds of operational and balance sheet problems. Dunlap's Sunbeam could not pay its remaining employees without tapping into a credit line. Within weeks it would likely be in technical default on its loans, a prospect that could force the company into bankruptcy. Dunlap's early portrayal of Sunbeam as a "basket case" was finally accurate, only he was responsible for the mess.

22

"I SCREWED THE POOCH!"

JERRY W. LEVIN AND his wife, Carol, had left their Upper East Side apartment in Manhattan early on Saturday afternoon to catch a 4:55 P.M. flight to Minneapolis. They were traveling there for the weekend to attend a friend's party that Saturday night. But Northwest Airlines kept postponing the La Guardia Airport flight, so the Levins began to kill some time by stopping to shop at Bloomingdale's and a few other New York stores.

As the delay stretched into the early evening, they cancelled the trip, deciding instead to catch an early movie. But just as they were stepping out of a car on the Upper East Side, Levin's cell phone rang. Carol Levin had become accustomed to unexpected calls like these that interrupted the normal routines and simple pleasures of life. After all, her husband worked for Ronald Perelman.

On the phone this time was Gittis.

"Langerman just called to say the board fired Dunlap," he said abruptly. "They might want to borrow you to be CEO."

"What the hell does that mean?" asked Levin.

"I don't know, but we're going to meet with them tomorrow morning. Can you make it?"

"Fine," said Levin, anxious to get inside the movie theater to see comedian Steve Martin in *The Spanish Prisoner*.

A longtime aide to Perelman, Levin wasn't sure he wanted the job.

In the nine years since leaving Pillsbury Corp. to work for Perelman, he had confronted some of the most interesting challenges of his career. Levin had been CEO of Perelman's most visible conquest, the cosmetics giant Revlon, for five years. When Coleman was near bankruptcy Levin had been dispatched to the company's Wichita, Kansas, headquarters to clean up the mess.

It was one strange trip, moving from the glamour world of cosmetics and fashion models in New York to the rather prosaic world of sleeping bags and camping lanterns in Wichita. In his year at the helm of Coleman, Levin made some progress toward a turnaround but much more work had to be done when the company was sold to Dunlap. Levin watched in surprise and anger as Dunlap undid many of the positive changes he had made at Coleman. Still, he was somewhat reluctant to go back and take on not only his old company but also the larger problems of Sunbeam. He and his wife were already building a retirement home in Tucson, Arizona, and planned to split their time between their New York apartment, which once belonged to Richard Nixon, and Arizona. What Perelman thought of all this, Levin didn't yet know.

Gittis's telephone call to him was made before Gittis could contact his boss. As an observant Jew, Perelman did not conduct business from Friday sundown until Saturday sundown. Armed with Langerman's news, Gittis rushed about, making the phone calls to get a team of people together to meet with Sunbeam's board on Sunday morning. He had changed his plans for Saturday evening, eventually arranging to meet with his boss around 10 P.M. at Nick & Toni's, an East Hampton eatery known for its open-hearth wood oven, its Mediterranean fare, and the rich and famous who often occupy its tables.

Gittis spotted the bald-headed Perelman immediately, and the two quickly exchanged whispers in the crowded restaurant, until Perelman left a companion at his table and followed Gittis outside. In the parking lot, Perelman expressed surprise at the board's decision and agreed with Gittis that it was important to meet the board.

"We've got a large investment here," he told him. "We've got to do whatever is necessary to save this thing."

When the platoon of Perelman's men showed up at the offices of Skadden Arps, they swaggered into a conference room as if they were walking off a page in *Bonfire of the Vanities*. Toting large, fat cigars, dressed in their Palm Beach best, they brought a cool, tough, and jaunty attitude into the conference room. They also brought with them decades of street-smart business acumen.

The five men formed the powerful brain trust that ran Perelman's empire of companies. Howard Gittis, sixty-four, had been the billionaire's earliest adviser, his right-hand man who ran day-to-day operations. Donald Drapin, a scrappy preeminent takeover lawyer, functioned as the in-house merchant banker and strategist. It was Drapin who helped plot Perelman's hostile takeover of Revlon in 1985. Paul E. Shapiro, fifty-seven, a veteran lawyer, had accompanied Levin to Coleman as general counsel. Barry Schwartz, yet another attorney, served as general counsel of MacAndrews & Forbes.

They didn't enter the room as much as fill it up.

"I gotta hand it to you," Gittis quipped to the directors, between puffs on a Don Diego cigar. "It took a lot of balls to knock off someone as mean as Chainsaw."

"Hey Finn," called the balding Drapin, " I hear your son is making partner at Cravath. Good boy. Congratulations!"

"So you need some leadership, huh?" quipped Gittis. "Well, Ronnie's not happy. He's lost a lot of money. But let's see what we can do."

After brief introductions, they settled around the table and Levin delivered a strikingly informed overview of the company's problems and what needed to be done about them. Fairly detailed reports from Perelman loyalists at Coleman kept him up to date on at least that part of the business which accounted for 40 percent of Sunbeam's revenues. His forty-five-minute presentation, delivered coolly and rationally without the bombast and bluster of a Dunlap, impressed the directors.

Levin agreed to fly down to Florida immediately with other Perelman associates and take control of the situation. In exchange for his services, however, Perelman wanted two seats on the board of directors: one for Levin and one for Gittis. Perelman's lieutenants left the room so that Langerman, Elson, and Kristol could discuss it.

Frankly, they could hardly refuse the offer. Fearful of being in technical default by the end of June, the board members realized that the company could easily spiral out of control. It could not afford the time to wine and dine a handful of candidates, a process that could take months. Sunbeam sorely needed someone immediately who could convey confidence to the Street and who also could confront at least some familiar territory. Levin, having run nearly half of the company, already knew a good many of its warts.

"Here's a guy who could come in, hit the ground running, and stabilize things," Langerman told his fellow board members. At the very least, that would give them more time to find a long-term replacement, or if things worked out, Levin could hold the job longer. It also would serve another purpose: to align the interests of Sunbeam's two largest shareholders.

Kristol, though, worried that shareholders and others would think that Perelman had taken over the company. With two board seats and a management team loyal to him, Perelman would have significant control over Sunbeam and its operations. To balance that control, Kristol suggested that Price have two board seats as well.

The directors agreed, and Levin, Shapiro, Langerman, and Fannin left at 3 P.M. to fly down to Delray Beach headquarters immediately. During the thirty-minute ride to the airport, Levin worked the cell phone like a frenzied stockbroker making cold calls. Trying to reassemble his old Coleman team, he telephoned at least eight former executives, asking each of them to call their people in turn and recruit them back to the company. After all, twenty-seven of the top thirty jobs at Coleman were now empty in the middle of the company's most important selling season.

"Al is gone," Levin said, over and over again. "Meet me on Monday morning in Florida. We'll work out all the details later. Pass the message on."

One former Coleman executive was in his car, on his way to St. Louis to start a new job. Levin asked him to turn around and come back to the company. He declined.

"It was a long ride to the airport," recalled Levin nearly a year later. "But during the course of that ride, we hired back most of the Coleman people."

That evening, Levin met with Sunbeam's top executives. He told them he was "declaring amnesty" for everyone who agreed to promptly inform him of problems and past mistakes.

"If you feel you were part of something that wasn't right," Levin said, "come in and tell me now. I'll be in a forgiving mood. In a few weeks, I'll be far less forgiving to get negative news."

On Monday morning, his new recruits began to report into headquarters. A finance team quickly began to take apart the company's financials. Within a few days, Levin realized the company would probably have to restate its financials. His finance group would work fourteen to sixteen hours a day, six days a week, for the next nine months, to get control over the numbers.

The changes could not be made official until the full board gathered on Tuesday in a telephonic meeting. Dunlap and Kersh, still directors because they could only be thrown off by shareholder vote, were on the call. They limited their vocabulary to just two words: "here" and "abstain." Otherwise Dunlap and Kersh sat mute as the directors voted Levin the new chief executive, installed Gittis and Levin as Perelman's representatives on the board, and named Lawrence Sondike, a key Price associate, a director. Until early August, when Dunlap and Kersh resigned their board seats, they attended every meeting by telephone, as if maintaining a strange vigil over the company's affairs. Not once, however, did they utter a single word other than "here" and "abstain."

They were there to hear how one crisis after another crashed onto the new management team. A day after Levin officially took charge the SEC launched an investigation into the company. A week after that Arthur Andersen withdrew its unqualified audit of Sunbeam's books. By the end of June Sunbeam was in default of its loan covenants and Levin had to negotiate an extension with the banks. By early August the board's audit committee announced that it would have to restate Sunbeam's financial results for Dunlap's entire reign as chief executive. The committee, headed by Kristol, came to that conclusion after hiring Deloitte & Touche to help Andersen review all of Dunlap's financial statements. The New York Stock Exchange also wanted to throw Sunbeam off its exchange because the company failed to meet its minimum performance standards.

As if all these problems weren't enough, Levin and his new recruits found themselves digging into the company's affairs amid a pile of lawsuits from angry investors and bond holders. By year's end, at least fourteen different lawsuits were filed against the company, its top executives and directors, including a pair by Sunbeam's insurance carriers who wanted out of the liability policies they had underwritten to protect the company's executives and directors.

IN THE WAKE OF Dunlap's dismissal, the man with the oversized ego suffered the worst comedown possible. Rarely does anyone express joy at another's misfortune, but Dunlap's ouster evinced unrestrained glee from almost all quarters. Former employees who had been victims of his legendary chainsaw nearly danced in the streets of Coshatta, Louisiana, where Dunlap had shuttered a Sunbeam plant. Fellow chief executives believed his demise a welcome relief. "He is the logical extreme of an executive who has no values, no honor, no loyalty, and no ethics," said David M. Friedson, CEO of Windmere-Durable Holdings Inc., a Sunbeam competitor. He made the remark in an interview published by *Business Week*.

Even the long-estranged members of Dunlap's own family seemed ebullient. Upon hearing the news of his father's sacking on CNBC at 6:20 A.M. in Seattle, Troy Dunlap chortled. "I laughed like hell," he said. "I'm glad he fell on his ass. I told him Sunbeam would be his Dunkirk." Dunlap's sister, Denise, his only sibling, heard the news from a friend in New Jersey where she still lived. Her only thought: "He got exactly what he deserved."

After getting the ax, Dunlap canceled his trip to London as well as a calendar filled with activity and holed up in his home in Boca Raton. For once he refused all interviews and contact with anyone in the media. At home, he sank into a deep funk, admitting that he felt "personally, financially, and professionally devastated." Through his New York lawyer he pressed the board to award him severance pay.

Dunlap did not resurface until a month later, after Arthur Andersen no longer stood by its audit of Dunlap's numbers and the SEC had issued subpoenas in its investigation of his tenure at Sunbeam. Eager to restore his credibility, he went on a brief and sometimes teary media campaign in early July. He went to dinner at Rush Limbaugh's home in Florida, an occasion that prompted the conservative radio personality to go on the air and promote Dunlap's see-no-evil, hear-no-evil defense. Still distrustful of the general media, Dunlap gave just two public interviews, one to the *Wall Street Journal* and the other to his favorite broadcaster, Lou Dobbs of CNN's *Moneyline*.

On the day he sauntered onto the *Moneyline* set in CNN's New York studios, Sunbeam stock had fallen to $10 a share, $42 below its peak a mere four months earlier. It had not yet reached its floor, a low of under $5 a share. The July 8 interview saw him in a feisty and combative mood, a wide and frightening grin imprinted on his face, even as Dobbs threw him hard-ball questions. He wore his trademark blue shirt with a white collar, a red tie with white polka dots, a dark blue pinstriped suit, and a Florida tan.

It was yet another vintage Dunlap performance.

"Al," Dobbs began, "it's good to see you, but I know this has got to be tough. You have shareholder lawsuits against you. You have been fired from your job, and the press has had a field day. As one analyst put it today, 'It's fun to kick Al Dunlap when he's down.' How do you feel right now?"

Dunlap, his hands clasping his knees, was perched forward on the edge of his blue chair, as if he were readying himself for an attack.

"Well, first, Lou, I passionately believed in Sunbeam," he said firmly. "I believed that we had accomplished the first phase of the turnaround. I believed we positioned ourselves for the future. I believed the acquisitions we made would work out well. But remember, these were all very troubled companies . . . And by the way I was only there ten weeks from the time we acquired these companies and no one would have done it in ten weeks. What happened was the basic Sunbeam ran into some marketing problems, and some of the new products were delayed because of the new technology and, on top of that, Coleman proved to be a far greater challenge than even we had realized."

A few questions later, Dunlap complained that his own losses on Sunbeam stock had been "horrific."

"What do you say to the shareholders who were in that stock counting on Al Dunlap to perform as he had before and look down today and see a $10 stock?"

Pointing a finger at the broadcaster, Dunlap said, "I feel great empathy for them. But Lou, I never sold a share myself," he added, bringing his hands to his chest. "I never exerted [exercised] an option," he said, mistakenly using the word. "Now if I didn't believe in the future of the company, I would have sold shares like every CEO. I would have exerted options. I could have taken a great deal of money off the table. I also, Lou, signed a new three-year contract at the pinnacle of my career. So obviously I was committed to doing the job, or I wouldn't have signed. I had a lot of other opportunities at that point in time."

"You signed an extremely lucrative contract," Dobbs interrupted. "Did you have a sense of how much trouble you were in at that point?"

"What I believe, Lou, is that these acquisitions could be made to work. I believed we could put together a great strategy and turn-around. The contract I signed was very heavily incentivized with stock. So obviously if I didn't believe in the ability to do this, I wouldn't have accepted a contract that was so heavily incentivized with stock."

"Heavily incentivized with stock," Dobbs repeated. "You haven't sold any. All of that to your merit in this incentive-based world. But at the same time, the current management of Sunbeam says they cannot rely upon the accounting results. The SEC is investigating. You have shareholder lawsuits against you and many of them are very serious lawsuits. What in the world are you going to do?"

Dunlap again flashed his oversize choppers, his face for a moment tense, a washboard of lines on his forehead and his eyebrows furrowed. "Let me address that, Lou," he said. "I am outraged that people say they can't believe the numbers. As I sit here tonight I absolutely believe those numbers. We had outside auditors, and I had no relationship with them. We had three outside directors on the audit committee. I had no involvement with audits. I relied on them. I relied on the general counsel who was on the operating committee and attended the audit meetings [and the] outside counsel. I relied on these people. I have no reason not to believe the numbers. You can't have it both ways."

"You are known as a fighter," said Dobbs. "You are known as being one tough son of a gun. Were you walking into that boardroom, your final meeting, with your resignation in hand or were you surprised that you were fired?"

"It was a two-phased board meeting," answered Dunlap. "The first phase . . . I wanted absolute certainty from the people responsible for the numbers that they were good because I was being pilloried. I got that. In the second phase of the meeting, I said, 'Listen, I've become a lightning rod for criticism. If you want a different type of executive, that's fine. You can get a different type. Just honor my contract because last year when I had a lot of opportunities I honored the contract' and I said, 'If you want someone else beyond the contract you can do it.' I'm just a human being. I was unbelievably frustrated."

"Are you still claiming your severance package?" asked Dobbs.

"Of course. Of course. I honored my contract."

"Now that," Dobbs said, "that's the Al Dunlap I know."

Dunlap's smile grew as wide as the span of the George Washington Bridge. "Thanks a lot, Lou," he said.

"What's your next step?"

"My next step is to clear my good name," Dunlap boomed. "You know, for three weeks to four weeks, I've been an absolute punching bag. It's like going duck hunting. It's a lot of fun to go duck hunting, I guess, but once the ducks start shooting back, it's not fun anymore. I'm not going to be a punching bag, anymore. I'm going to come out [and] restore my good name. I believe passionately in this company. I believed in the numbers. I never sold stock. I committed to a new contract."

Watching the interview in an airport lounge in Philadelphia, Elson stared incredulously at Dunlap's image on the screen. When the segment was over, a stranger next to him said, "God, what a jerk!"

"You better believe it," replied Elson, who walked off to catch a plane.

Dunlap later lobbied the *New York Times*, hoping that one of its reporters could be convinced to tell his side of the story just before Sunbeam restated the company's numbers. But he offered no new details beyond the lengthy statement he had released months earlier. The *Times* passed.

But his most telling comment came not in his interviews with either the *Journal* or Lou Dobbs or his dinner with Rush Limbaugh. It came in an aside to a friend shortly after his firing. Without explanation he sadly confided: "I screwed the pooch."

From the General Patton of management, it was an appropriate military phrase. It meant that he had blundered, a rare, albeit private admission that he had failed miserably. During the greatest bull market in the history of the Stock Exchange, the longest economic expansion in U.S. history, the self-proclaimed friend of shareholders had lost hundreds of millions of investor dollars at a consumer products company when consumer spending reached record highs.

PERHAPS THE MOST unsympathetic victim of Dunlap's deceit was Michael Price. For years the mutual fund maven had been milking Sunbeam for every penny of profit. Through the early years Kazarian fought with him over Price's attempts to gain short-term advantage or profit. Although Price assured Roger Schipke that he wanted to build the company for the long haul, Schipke said he quickly discovered otherwise when Price began ditching his stock and forced the CEO through a disruptive and failed auction for the company.

Indifferent to Dunlap's reputation for massive disruption and wholesale cutbacks, Price helped to recruit him to Sunbeam and then quickly became one of his most vocal cheerleaders. He so admired the chief executive that he had placed his picture near the computer on his trading desk. He unabashedly sang Dunlap's praises over and over. Even as the company was in total chaos, Price handed Dunlap one of the most outrageous compensation packages ever granted to a chief executive. Few people were slathered with more egg on their face from Dunlap's fall than Price. Few were as thoroughly humiliated. Measuring the loss from Sunbeam's peak to its nadir, Price's investment in the company fell by nearly $850 million, to just $81.1 million.

The company's disastrous decline not only hurt his reputation as a savvy stock picker, it also severely damaged the performance of his mutual funds in what became his final year as chief of the Mutual Series group. Sunbeam took a full two to three percentage points of performance off the funds at a time when they could least afford it. In a year that saw the stocks in the S&P 500 rise by 26.7 percent, Price's largest single fund, Mutual Shares, returned a mere 0.45 percent, far less than an old-fashioned savings account.

All mutual funds based on value investing are typically out of favor when stock market performance is dominated by big company growth stocks and technology concerns. Yet Price's largest fund performed so miserably in the year that Sunbeam collapsed that it trailed by nearly a full percentage point the average returns for similar value funds run by rivals. With performance that dismal and Price anxious to leave, the investors in his four big funds made net withdrawals of $4 billion in 1998, the largest one-year defection ever.

For the supposed master of value investing, it was the worst possible comedown. Price chose to limp off stage, turning over his job as CEO to Langerman on November 1, at the lowest point of Price's career. His choice of the cautious lawyer as his successor surprised observers, who viewed Langerman as more responsible than any other lieutenant for the Sunbeam debacle. It was Langerman, after all, who directly oversaw the investment from the beginning. He was the most knowledgeable director on the board during Dunlap's tenure, the one who should have known by experience and instinct that Dunlap's goals were not merely aggressive but rather destructive and ruinous in a mundane, slow-growth industry. Yet, in the aftermath of Dunlap's dismissal Langerman embarrassingly maintained that Sunbeam was "fundamentally better" than when Dunlap had taken over. Not surprisingly, Price did not put the key investment decisions of his funds in Langerman's hands. Instead he named another associate, Rob Friedman, as chief investment officer, to handle that more important role.

Still, Price had to shoulder a good deal of the blame himself. Just as Dunlap had violated many of the basic tenets he had advocated in *Mean Business,* Price had disregarded the teachings of his mentor, Max Heine, by holding on to Sunbeam when it rose to over $35 a share. Price believed the stock's true value was less than $35 when Dunlap made the acquisitions, far below the $53 peak it hit a few days after the deals were announced. In value investing, an investor buys when a stock falls below the company's intrinsic value and sells when a stock rises above that level. For most of Dunlap's tenure at Sunbeam, the stock had traded well above the company's true worth. Price's absolute belief in Dunlap and his own lust for greater profit, however, blinded him from selling at least a part of his stake. The investor dubbed "The Scariest S.O.B. on Wall Street" also claimed that he worried about Dunlap's reaction to a sale. "Al would have said, 'You don't have any confidence in me. I'm leaving,'" reflected Price. In retrospect, Price concedes he probably should have sold 5 to 10 million of the more than 17.5 million shares Mutual funds owned. "At some point, Sunbeam was no longer a value stock," he said. "We should have gotten out of it earlier."

Few know the psychology of investing better than Price, even if he occasionally fell victim to it. It was not unlike a gambler's greed in a casino. Once the gambler wins, he does not believe he can lose. The more he wins, the more he plays, even in the face of insurmountable odds against him. And when he begins to lose, he always believes that he can win it back. As Sunbeam stock went higher, Price thought he would ride it higher still, even when he knew it was trading at levels as unrealistic as Dunlap's assumptions about the business.

Yet Price now assigns some of his own misplaced euphoria in Dunlap on the Street's shortcomings. "Wall Street should blame itself for some of the debacle because Wall Street gets the needle in its arm about expectations and then sets itself up for disappointment," he said. "Wall Street gets so aggressive with estimates and expectations. After the news of the Coleman deal, Shore wrote it up as a buy. It was already so fully priced at $50, yet Wall Street gets crazy with what can happen on the upside. Sunbeam never should have been $12 the day we hired Al. It never should have been $40 or $50. When you get characters like an Al, you tend to get very aggressive projections, and then Wall Street cries when the thing comes down, but it really should be blaming itself. Wall Street is to blame." Never mind that Dunlap set those expectations and failed to meet them. Never mind that two of the sharpest investors of the era—Michael Price and Ronald Perelman—were made fools by a loudmouth.

Through the downfall that made victims of so many, Price belatedly learned a valuable lesson. "I've always believed that at Mutual," he observed, "we were pretty good stock pickers but we're not really control players. Sunbeam reinforced my belief that we are not control players. If you're a control player, you've got to be able to work closely with management. I think we can be good directors, but when it comes to finding management and being close with them, it's very tough. People like Kohlberg, Kravis, and Roberts are set up for that. We don't have the network of operating management like they do. That's what you basically need."

If Sunbeam's descent wasn't enough of a comeuppance for Price, he was further humbled by a deal that the *New York Observer* likened to "legalized extortion" by Ron Perelman. Soon after Levin took control of Sunbeam, Perelman threatened to withdraw his management troops and file a lawsuit against the company because the value of his Sunbeam shares had fallen by 65 percent. To head off that prospect, the board gave Perelman warrants in mid-August to buy 23 million shares of Sunbeam stock for $7 a share. While the agreement normally would require the consent of shareholders, Sunbeam gained an exception from the New York Stock Exchange on the grounds that seeking approval would jeopardize the company's ability to survive.

A special committee of the board struck the deal with Perelman, but as always, Price was active in the background, suggesting to Langerman how it might be structured. "The board had guns to its head," Price explained. "Perelman was one gun. The banks were another. All of this would have been litigated, and I think litigation is a huge waste so you tend to avoid it at any cost. I'm a believer in moving things along and not getting stuck in the sand."

It was, nonetheless, another embarrassment for Price. For every $1 increase in Sunbeam stock beyond the warrant price, Perelman now stood to make an extra $23 million. If Levin could make Sunbeam a $20 stock again, Perelman's opportunistic gambit would be worth nearly $300 million. The warrant deal boosted Perelman's interest in the company to more than 28 percent, surpassing Price's stake.

THE DAY ANDREW SHORE discovered that Dunlap had been fired was the happiest day of his life after his marriage and the birth of his child. Dunlap's ouster was not only confirmation that Shore's skepticism had been well founded from the start, it also gave him a sense of satisfaction to know that someone who caused great harm to so many people had finally gotten the ax.

Shore's glee in Dunlap's unraveling showed little restraint. His associate, R. T. Quinn, laughed that Dunlap obviously left out of his book the chapter on cutting R&D to zero. "Yeah," chuckled Shore, "he also forgot the chapter on product innovation." To friends, the analyst joked that Dunlap would probably wind up in Australia. "That's where they sent all the criminals years ago," he laughed. He told others that when Dunlap dies, the only people who would likely show up for his burial were his wife and two dogs. "And the dogs would probably be there only because they wanted food."

The black humor, however, also gave way to outright fear. Shore might have hastened Dunlap's dismissal but he didn't cause it. Nonetheless, the executive's stern warning to him on May 11, when Dunlap called him a son of a bitch and growled that he would come back at Shore "twice as hard," echoed in his head as Dunlap lost his job and his reputation.

"Andrew, please be careful," his mother pleaded with him. "Please be careful. He's a very powerful man."

His mother's admonition played on him. Less than two weeks after Dunlap's firing, Shore's wife left him a frantic message. The new home they were building had caught fire. As he drove out to the site in Armonk, New York, all he could think about was whether Dunlap had done it. "All I heard in my head was: 'You're going to come after me?

I'm going to come after you twice as hard.'" When he reached the property, he found his new home a pile of smoking timbers. It was burned to the ground. The first thing he asked the police was whether they suspected foul play. It turned out that the fire was accidental, caused by a plumber's mishap.

Aside from the jokes and the fears, Shore had to acknowledge that he had played a role in the Dunlap mythmaking as well. Despite his early skepticism, he had urged clients to buy Sunbeam shares again and again for nearly eighteen months. Even while growing increasingly concerned about the company's rising receivables and inventory levels, he had maintained a buy rating on the stock.

How could he explain his often positive reports through much of those eighteen months? "Al was like morphine," Shore said. "He was a drug. It was the drug of instant gratification and profit. Who better than Al to provide that? It felt good, and it numbed the pain. We all created him. We knew he was going to make money for investors. The only question was when to get out. It was a gamblers' mentality. We were seduced by the possibility of big wins. We wish we could change it. We wish we could change the pressure for short-term earnings, for quarterly performance. But we can't."

In the meantime the analyst put aside his personal skepticism over Dunlap and even his concerns for the victims of those Dunlap-inspired profits. "When I wear my suit and tie," he said, "I have to forget that he laid off 6,000 people who have to go home one night and tell their wives and children they no longer have a job. But a company is more than just the products. It's about the people who create and sell those products. And when morale turns south in an organization, it's one of the single greatest destabilizing forces in nature. Can you honestly believe that the guy can come in that quickly and make an honest assessment that 6,000 people had to go?"

Dunlap, Shore realized, proved that any executive in America or the world can produce one great year. "You could stop spending money so there is no marketing, no advertising, no R&D," Shore said. "You could sell product at half cost. You could fire half the people. But real business lasts more than 360-odd days. Al didn't just cut costs. He pulled out the fat and the muscle, the tissue, the plasma, the neurons, and even the skeletal structure out of organizations. The truth is, Al pulled the life out of companies."

In some small way, perhaps, that is why Shore so rejoiced in Dunlap's termination. He bitterly resented his own role in helping Dunlap craft his own myths about being an extraordinary turnaround artist, about being interested in nothing but creating shareholder value. It bothered Shore greatly that in sitting in his skyscraper office in New York, helping Dunlap trumpet his false triumphs, he bore some responsibility for all the people who became Dunlap's victims in the hinterlands of America.

After watching Dunlap's interview with Lou Dobbs, Shore's father telephoned his son.

"But why was he smiling so much?" he asked, mystified.

"Dad," Shore responded, "he was smiling to hide his tears, to keep from crying."

IF SUNBEAM WAS one of Shore's finest hours as an analyst, it was a debacle for his rival at Prudential Securities. Nick Heymann's unwavering faith in Dunlap caused the worst stock pick of his career. "You almost have to work at trying to be that wrong on a stock," said one rival analyst. Heymann did not downgrade his buy rating to a hold until June 25, ten days after Dunlap's firing was made public. By then the stock had fallen to $12.25 a share, the closing price on the day before Dunlap was named CEO. "It was the biggest mistake I ever made in my career," he conceded. "This is the only time we lost a lot of money for investors, and I care about every investor who loses a dollar on my advice."

His advice cost clients plenty, probably tens of millions of dollars. Heymann personally lost some $640,000 on his own investment in Sunbeam. The collapse also exacted a severe toll on his personal appearance as well. Heymann, a Type-A personality fortified by gulps of Mountain Dew and Surge, gained twenty-five pounds and averaged three hours of sleep a night in the year that Sunbeam fell apart. He also drew the wrath of dozens of clients and investors who wrote furious letters to the chairman of Prudential. Many of them wondered why Heymann failed to see what nearly every other analyst on the Street did more than two months earlier when they abandoned the stock. They groused that Heymann, who took pride in doing prodigious amounts of research on his companies, hadn't done his homework on Sunbeam.

Fearful of lawsuits from investors eager to recover their losses,

Prudential's lawyers required Heymann to reconstruct what went wrong. The humbled analyst spent weeks in June and July trying to unravel Sunbeam's game-playing and to gather evidence to show he was not errant in doing his "due diligence" on the company. Heymann went out and interviewed former executives, distributors, and retailers. He documented every contact he ever had with Dunlap. "It was as if I was shipwrecked 1,000 miles from shore and had to swim back," Heymann said.

The bill-and-hold transactions didn't raise a red flag for him because as an auditor at General Electric Co. in the early eighties, Heymann had been familiar with the practice. He had run across it at GE's seasonal housewares business. He now regretted discounting the Shore and Dunlap exchange at the May 11 presentation. "Andrew obviously felt it in his gut really strongly," Heymann said. "He had a lot of reasons to think this guy was a major scam. In hindsight, Andrew had a lot better smell than I did. I should have been a better judge of character."

Yet, he said, his ongoing telephone calls to retailers did not uncover excess Sunbeam inventory at stores, a key reason that Heymann failed to lose his enthusiasm for the stock. The analyst later discovered, however, that the reason some retailers weren't stuck with inventory was that they shipped it back at Sunbeam's cost to six warehouses that were quietly leased by the company. In the meantime, however, Sunbeam booked the sale and profit on the shipped product, figuring it could camouflage the later credits against the accounts when it declared huge restructuring charges for the acquisitions. "It was playing float," he said. "Instead of cutting checks, you cut invoices. I'm not a criminologist, but it was a fairly elaborate scheme to make it look real because the inventory wasn't out of whack at Sunbeam's Mississippi warehouse."

Once his own investigation was complete, Prudential's lawyers took all of Heymann's files, including his computer disks. SEC investigators interviewed him several times and collected much of his research from the company's legal counsel. "What I had to come to grips with was that if somebody was going to misrepresent the fundamentals to the SEC, why would they tell anything different to me," he said.

After Dunlap's firing, Heymann spoke with the chief executive at least a couple of times. But his contacts yielded no new insights. "He was thick-skinned about it all," Heymann said. "My gut tells me that Al had a finger on what was going on. When we first took him out to clients, he brought five loose-leaf binders with him that contained every detail on the company. He went from someone who could tell you how much gas they used in trucks to someone who said the numbers weren't his problem. It doesn't add up."

After issuing his hold rating on June 25, Heymann began to short the stock in the teens, allowing him to recover about a third of the $640,000 he had originally lost on Sunbeam shares. "There was no reason to get mad at being hoodwinked. I just tried to get even." He further downgraded Sunbeam to a sell on August 10, raising the possibility that Sunbeam's creditors could force the company into a Chapter 11 bankruptcy. It was only the second time in his career that he had rated a stock that low. His second downgrade sent Sunbeam shares skidding another 11.1 percent to just $6 a share.

Like many observers, he's not optimistic that Levin can avoid a bankruptcy proceeding. Heymann's betting that Perelman's men will get the banks to write down 50 percent of Sunbeam's debt and then file for Chapter 11, a prospect that would allow Perelman to pick up a tax credit of $300 million on his losses. Under bankruptcy protection, the company could dispose of all the shareholder lawsuits and then launch a reorganization under which Perelman could buy a large chunk of Sunbeam's convertible debentures that were trading for 12 cents on the dollar in early March. Under the reorganization, thought Heymann, Perelman could squeeze the banks for another haircut, reducing the debt load to a quarter of Sunbeam's current total and come out with control. To be sure, it is not a shareholder-friendly scenario.

"Given the loss and the magnitude of what happened," Heymann said, "it was an out-of-body experience for me. You take your scalp and march around with it and then you're done. It's the same way when you win. They remember you for a day and then it's on to the next one."

AT SUNBEAM, Levin worked feverishly to restore calm and order. On his first day at headquarters, he had all of Dunlap's predator paintings taken down and put in storage. He recast the top management team, bringing aboard a number of Perelman loyalists and associates from Coleman and Revlon. Indeed, the composition of the new team was as much an indictment of Dunlap's leadership as nearly every action Levin took in his first year as CEO. Of the top thirty-five executives in mid-August 1998, only four had been at Sunbeam for more than six months.

Fannin, his energy and will spent, left the company. So did Dunlap's two chief operating executives: Lee Griffith, the former Scottie, and Frank Feraco, who had only joined Sunbeam in May but left in September for a better job at Textron Inc. Gluck, named acting chief financial officer when Kersh was fired, also eventually resigned.

Levin and his team quickly found that Dunlap had overproduced goods, heavily discounted product, extended credit terms, and burdened retailers with too much inventory in an effort to boost short-term profits. Levin believed too that Dunlap had gone too far in centralizing management in the hands of a small group at headquarters. "The business has been pushed too hard and stretched too far," he told employees. It was virtually the same comment that had been made by the chief financial officer of Kimberly-Clark shortly after its acquisition of Scott Paper Co.

In what amounted to a clear repudiation of Dunlap and his consulting pal Burnett, Levin reversed many of the decisions announced on May 11 to cut back on people and plants. On the job less than three months, Levin decided to keep open four of the eight plants Dunlap had intended to shutter, delay the closing of another facility, and retain two businesses that were slated to be sold. Instead of cutting 6,400 jobs, Levin planned to trim just 2,300 employees. "The plants are being kept open to ensure a high level of quality and customer service, as well as a consistency of supply," he said.

It took, however, nearly four months for auditors to unravel the "ditty bag" complications of the company's accounting under Dunlap and Kersh. The review, made public October 20, proved what so many Dunlap skeptics had long suspected. Dunlap's so-called turnaround of Sunbeam in 1997 was little more than a manufactured illusion based on improper accounting moves. Instead of the $109.4 million net income Dunlap reported in 1997, the company's restated net was just $38.3 million—less than Sunbeam made under any one of Kazarian or Schipke's full years.

Auditors from Deloitte & Touche and Arthur Andersen concluded that Dunlap had overstated Sunbeam's loss for 1996, vastly exaggerated profits for 1997, and understated the magnitude of its first quarter loss in 1998. For certain periods, the accountants found that Kersh and Gluck incorrectly recognized revenue on Sunbeam's bill-and-hold program and guaranteed sales transactions, and that they had failed to account or incorrectly recorded allowances for sales returns, co-op advertising, customer deductions, and reserves against product liability and warranty expenses.

The auditors reversed $29 million of bill-and-hold sales for the fourth quarter of 1997 and instead recorded those sales in the first quarter of 1998 as the shipments were made. Another $33 million of bill-and-hold sales originally booked as sales in the first quarter of 1998 were nixed and moved to subsequent periods when products had been shipped. The accountants also reversed $36 million worth of guaranteed and consignment sales made by Sunbeam in 1997, a change that took $17 million off of the company's pretax profits. The *Wall Street Journal* characterized Dunlap's "turnaround" as a "mirage."

Dunlap's crippling impact on the company didn't end with the restatement, however. Throughout 1998 and 1999 Levin continued to work off excess inventory built up by Dunlap and his management team. For the full year, Sunbeam's losses totaled $898 million, a sum that wiped out all the net income the company had made under both Kazarian and Schipke for five years. Dunlap had so grossly overpaid for First Alert that Levin had to take the unusual step of writing off $63 million of the $186 million purchase price—the gap between the value of the company's assets and what Dunlap paid for the smoke detector maker. The new Sunbeam was so heavily leveraged that its total debt of $2.3 billion was nearly five times its shareholder equity. Just the interest payments on that debt cost Sunbeam $131 million in 1998, up from just $11 million a year earlier. A full year after Dunlap's departure, the company still struggled to earn a profit, while the stock was mired in its own bear market, trading at between $5 and $7 a share. Sunbeam also remained in default of its loan agreements.

Nonetheless, in the year of Sunbeam's collapse, when Dunlap was on the payroll for only six months, he was paid an extraordinary $26.9 million, including $13.7 million to reimburse his income tax bill on company stock and other benefits. Still, he wanted more.

He filed an arbitration claim, seeking $5.3 million in severance pay,

$58,000 worth of accrued vacation, and $150,000 in benefits. He sought to have his stock options repriced at $7 a share. And he sued the company for dragging its feet in reimbursing him for more than $1.4 million in legal and accounting fees racked up in defending himself in lawsuits that alleged securities fraud. A judge ruled in his favor this past June.

SOME OF THE COMPANY'S board members, angry over Sunbeam's decline under their watch, vowed not to pay Dunlap a cent. They had joined the board at Dunlap's invitation, ponied up their own money to buy Sunbeam stock, and agreed to be paid not in cash but only in company shares. Their friend had betrayed their trust and caused them to suffer huge personal losses. Charles Elson and Howard Kristol, for example, each bought 6,000 shares of Sunbeam stock. For Elson, this was not an inconsequential investment. He had more equity tied up in Sunbeam than he had in his residence.

In the three months between Sunbeam's stock price high and Dunlap's dismissal, Elson and Kristol saw their net worths plummet by more than $315,000 each. Faith Whittlesey lost nearly $200,000. William Rutter's loss totaled $120,000. Langerman's fund took the biggest hit, of course, dropping in value by $614 million. The board's quick decision to fire Dunlap, thought some commentators, was evidence that stock ownership by directors was an important motivator. "The governance lesson is that an equity-holding board works," reflected Elson. "It was not a long, agonizing process. We did what a board had to do."

Left unsaid, however, was why the board failed to realize until it was too late that Dunlap's "turnaround" was little more than a "mirage." Sunbeam's directors wondered how they could have been in the dark over the extent of the company's problems. "We didn't even get an anonymous call from any of the executives," said a baffled Elson. He and his fellow directors overlooked the fact that their friendship with Dunlap silenced many inside the company who might have otherwise come forward. With the sole exception of Langerman, whose fund benefited greatly from Sunbeam's perceived success, the directors were hand-picked by Dunlap. He stacked the board with friends and associates, controlled the flow of information to them, and ran the company like an imperial potentate. There were no CEOs on the board other than Dunlap. In fact, none of the directors had any significant experience in business operations. The board met only five times in 1997, and its audit committee held only two meetings.

To company insiders, blowing a whistle in a boardroom filled with Dunlap's friends may have seemed far too risky, far too likely to fall on deaf ears. "The board was Al's," explained Rich Goudis, the company's former vice-president of investor relations. "Unless you could mount a group of people to raise objection, you knew you would get shot. You had a high-profile CEO who had great strength and power. If you got blackballed, it would have been over. So you feared for your career and your family."

With the exception of Fannin, however, none of Dunlap's top executives tried to notify the board. None made an anonymous phone call nor sent an unsigned note to a single director, even after being fired and having little to lose. Their silence, motivated by a mixture of fear, self-interest, and possibly complicity, kept the extent of Sunbeam's deterioration concealed from the board.

That makes the governance lesson of Sunbeam more complex. If the board was composed of outsiders who were not Dunlap's friends, it could have reacted more slowly to the crisis. It's possible that other board members might have wanted more time for deliberation and debate. Oddly enough, Sunbeam's directors quickly ousted Dunlap *precisely* because they were his friends. Their sense of betrayal and outrage ran deep—both emotionally and financially—due to the personal relationships they forged with him and the stock ownership he demanded.

FOR THE THOUSANDS of employees and managers touched by Dunlap's chainsaw, it has been a mixed blessing. James Clegg, Sunbeam's chief operating officer and Dunlap's earliest casualty, has been unable to find another job in corporate America. He started a small business in Mexico, where he owns a sugar cane plantation. His friend and ex-Sunbeam household products president, Richard L. Boynton, used his stock option gains to purchase a water sprinkler company in New Hampshire. He recently sold the outfit and is now vice president of sales and marketing for M. F. Blouin. Many of the executives, including Donald R. Uzzi, Lee Griffith, and Dixon Thayer, collected their severance packages and do a bit of consulting work.

Still others found new and productive work lives elsewhere. After a stint as a consultant, manufacturing chief Ronald L. Newcomb became vice president of operations for the Stanley Works in New Britain, Connecticut. James Wilson, ex-vice president of human resources, quickly found a similar job at Lennox Inc. in New Jersey. David Fannin found new work as general counsel of Office Depot Inc. in Florida. New products chief Paula Etchison was seeking capital to launch her own company in the Chicago area. Internal auditor Deidra DenDanto landed a job as a consultant in New York.

In Bay Springs, Mississippi, many of the older employees who lost their Sunbeam jobs simply retired. Most of the younger workers found positions paying slightly less money at other nearby plants. In McMinnville, Sunbeam still employs about 400 people, including Marsha Dunlap, who continues to work a production line. Her friend Charlotte Redman had been unemployed for more than a year before landing a job at a denim factory, where she washes and presses blue jeans. Sunbeam's Mexico City plant, meantime, was closed down. The retail clipper business was moved to the company's factory in Acuna, Mexico.

After clipper boss William Kirkpatrick was fired on Jan. 7, 1998, he drove home to the Philadelphia area in one eighteen-hour push to find a "Welcome Home Dad!" sign put up in the driveway by his eight-year-old daughter. In Kirkpatrick's first year off, he played 65 rounds of golf, rode his Harley Sportster motorcycle 2,000 miles, and read 200 books, from *Tuesdays with Morrie* to *L.A. Confidential.* Kirkpatrick, who rid his closet of all business suits "except two for funerals and weddings," spends some time consulting. Generally, though, he is living off the gains he collected from his Scott Paper and Sunbeam stock option and severance packages. "When Sunbeam stock hit fifty dollars a share, I genuflected and blessed Al every minute of the day," he says. "Al Dunlap has improved the wealth of my family."

Few of the Sunbeam executives inherited by new CEO Levin survived for long. Controller Robert J. Gluck stayed with the company through the new audit that led to the restatement. Friends said he sat dumbfounded through the process as auditors from Arthur Andersen, with Deloitte & Touche at their side, disapproved many of the accounting transactions Andersen had previously okayed. Gluck resigned and was later named executive vice president of finance and administration for Dycom Industries, Inc., a telecom construction concern in Palm Beach Gardens, Florida. He abruptly left Dycom, however, in December 1998, the same month in which his appointment was publicly announced.

One survivor under Levin was "Little Al" Lefevre, the financial officer under Griffith who had approved many of the guaranteed and consignment sales that were later challenged and reversed by auditors. Lefevre, in fact, won a promotion to senior vice president of finance for Sunbeam's household products group. His advocates argued that although his signature was required to permit many suspect sales, he did not approve the subsequent accounting treatment for them.

Before their dismissal, Dunlap and Kersh had been planning to move Sunbeam into new corporate headquarters in Boca Raton, their hometown. The plans, discovered Levin, were for Dunlap and a few allies to be isolated in a separate building from everyone else at Sunbeam. Dunlap's office suite was to contain one room for his dogs and another for his bodyguard.

Neither Dunlap nor Kersh has found a job, though both have spoken to headhunters in the hope of landing new positions. Some of the caretakers of the golf course at the Boca Raton Resort and Club report seeing Dunlap wandering around the links with a bag, retrieving stray golf balls. The local police department has not received any new complaints involving Dunlap.

EPILOGUE

My success has everything to do with being a poor kid
who was always being put down. Making my way in the
world became a matter of self-respect for me, of a kid
trying to prove he was worth something.

—*Albert Dunlap*

ALONG THE WAY, the businessman who described himself as a
"nothing kid" from Hoboken, New Jersey, worked for and with some
of the world's most intriguing tycoons and financiers. He made and he
lost hundreds of millions of dollars for investors. He captivated many
on Wall Street and Main Street. He captured headlines around the
globe.

But it was a kind of Dennis Rodman wealth and fame. Albert
Dunlap was a peculiar business eccentric whose life nearly stumbled
into farce. His celebrity was based less on achievement than his eager
willingness to say and do the offensive and the outrageous. He gloried
in making millions at the expense of tens of thousands of people he so
easily discarded. He brashly congratulated himself as an executive who
was peerless while publicly attacking more accomplished chieftains at
other corporations. He insisted that the sole purpose of a business was
to make a cash register ring. "If you're not interested in making
money," he brusquely advised, "go into the clergy, go into academia,
go into the rotary."

Somehow, Al Dunlap forgot the watchwords drilled into him and
every West Point cadet: duty, honor, country. They were words that

should have applied not only to the military, but also to an enriched and meaningful life. They were standards that Dunlap should have carried with him from the grand military academy perched above the Hudson. He did not.

Dunlap succeeded in accumulating wealth not because he was a good manager or leader, not because he could build or grow a business. He succeeded for a time, at least, because he did things that authentic leaders, guided by a set of values and morals, would refuse to do. They didn't cut corners, debase employees before their peers, enrich themselves at the expense of others, or forfeit the long term for a few months of outsize results.

None of that seemed to matter to Wall Street, where greed has never gone out of style. Chainsaw Al was a creation of the Street and its ceaseless lust for profit at any cost. He came of age when the market routinely rewarded layoffs with lofty stock prices. The more people tossed out in the street, the higher stock values went. Dunlap, the quintessential corporate hit man, appealed to Wall Street's desire for slaughter, for fast money, for the illusions of a speedy turnaround that pumped up the price of a stock. So in the giddy exuberance of the longest bull market on record, Chainsaw was embraced by the Street and its cutthroat investors and deal makers, people like Michael Price, Michael Steinhardt, and Ronald Perelman, not to mention those highly regarded advocates of shareholder value George Soros, Robert A. G. Monks, and Nell Minow.

They should have known better. True leaders are not ambitious for themselves. They are ambitious for their companies. True leaders do not impose unrealistic demands on people. True leaders demonstrate compassion and respect for those who devote their professional lives to an organization. True leaders believe in shared sacrifice. They invest for the long term because they believe there will be a long term. They understand that public corporations do have social responsibilities not only to serve their shareholders but to serve their employees as well as their customers. They have an obligation to produce well-built, long-lasting, useful products.

These were not mere ideals, with little value in a vastly altered business world that now placed investors over employees and communities. They were attributes that attracted talented and committed people to business organizations; they were attributes that, in fact, rewarded "patient capital," the new term for shareholders who weren't as caught up in the game for instant returns. For the tension between creating shareholder value and tending to other constituencies is often a false dichotomy. Building shareholder wealth for the long term often means doing things that don't produce an immediate return.

Yet, even after Dunlap's fall, some observers still considered him a capable if limited "one trick pony." According to this theory he was a manager adept at savagely cutting costs but not building or maintaining organizations. They were wrong. Dunlap did not know how to cut fat without destroying muscle. He did not know how to remove a diseased organ without killing a heart. Al Dunlap was little more than an opportunist, an impostor who merely cloaked himself as a friend of the investor, as a creator of shareholder wealth. When Dunlap headed a company, no wealth was more important than his own. No constituency was more important than himself.

He fell victim to a disease common to every Greek tragedy or Shakespearean drama: hubris. He became seduced by the all-too-flattering media reports, even by his own book, which propagated the myth that he was some modern-day Horatio Alger figure who made it big. "The klieg lights, the book, the speeches became him," mused one board member and friend from Sunbeam. "It's the old sin of pride. It's vanity. He became more concerned about his image and his speeches than the company."

His ego refused to allow him to accept responsibility for the havoc he wreaked. For after misleading his board of directors and Sunbeam's shareholders and leaving the company a shambles, Dunlap still possessed the temerity to demand severance pay. No less shocking, he insisted that the board reprice his stock options so that he would not be penalized by the plummet in the shares his blunders and misdeeds produced. In doing so, there was what some might regard as a delicious irony to his demise. The man who spent most of his life ridiculing stakeholders was now a stakeholder himself, a disgruntled employee demanding severance the shareholders did not want to pay.

And why should they? Al Dunlap sucked the very life and soul out of companies and people. He stole dignity, purpose, and sense out of organizations and replaced those ideals with fear, intimidation, and pirates' wages. In the service of a quick buck, he imposed brutal pressure on honest people, placing their careers, incomes, health insurance, and pensions at stake. He made impossible, irrational demands that were ruinous to the long-term prosperity of companies. The leadership style he practiced was inconsistent with good business, thoughtful management, a strong economy, even a civilized society.

Some would say that assessment is too harsh. The apologists would argue that at one time, at least, Dunlap was a competent general manager for a tough or dirty job—as long as someone hovered over him ready and able to say "no." Sir James Goldsmith performed that function for years. So did the Australian media magnate Kerry Packer. It was only when Dunlap landed his job at Scott Paper Co. that he was finally responsible to no one but himself. He got lucky, not in turning around the company but in riding the upswing in the paper industry's economic cycle. If Kimberly-Clark had refused to buy Scott, the Dunlap story would have ended there, most likely, in disaster.

Instead he wrote himself a new chapter. Of course he would have preferred to do that at a General Motors or a Westinghouse, companies more befitting his ego. But the offers that he hoped would come his way failed to materialize and so he ended up at Sunbeam, with ever higher expectations of himself and the people around him. "Al was like a guy walking a tightrope," a Sunbeam director suggested. "As he gained more confidence, he made more daring gestures. At Sunbeam, reality finally collided with his expectations."

Dunlap began to overpromise and overreach. One longtime friend who watched Dunlap's unraveling from afar compared him to a drug addict. Once dependent on drugs, an addict would stop at nothing to score. He would rob, cheat, even kill, to shoot or snort a high back into his body. "That's Al Dunlap at Sunbeam," he says. "He had made all these promises, and Al Dunlap not only lives up to his promises, he exceeds them. So he had to do whatever it took to make good on what he promised Wall Street."

At Sunbeam, he eluded all the safeguards of a public corporation: a well-meaning board of directors, independent, outside auditors, and an army of honest and talented executives. Every system depends on people, people who will say no even when faced with the threat of losing a job or a business. Dunlap worked so hard at creating fear, dependence, and guilt that no one dared to defy him—until it was too late. It is a lesson no one should ever forget.

AUTHOR'S NOTE

If he were on fire, I wouldn't piss on him.

—Albert Dunlap on the author

I WAS NEVER one of Albert J. Dunlap's favorite journalists. There were plenty of reporters and writers who had won his favor over the years. Not me. As a senior writer at *Business Week* magazine, I first encountered the executive in late 1995 shortly after he had reached agreement that Kimberly-Clark Corp. would buy Scott Paper Co. I had watched his widely celebrated "turnaround" of the stodgy paper producer from the sidelines, growing increasingly skeptical as Dunlap became ever more boastful.

My subsequent cover story, "The Shredder," wasn't one that Dunlap would paste in his scrapbook. It reported that Dunlap was an opportunist who simply prettied up the company for a quick sale. He cut muscle along with the fat, sacrificed the long-term future of a once-great company and its people for a quick buck, and took credit for the achievements and hard work of others. Though he claimed a turn-around and too many journalists believed him, Scott had lost market share in all three of its major product areas during Dunlap's tenure. He and his executives reaped tens of millions in gains while thousands of employees lost their jobs and their livelihoods.

My interest in Dunlap did not fade when he landed at Sunbeam Corp. in July 1996, or when his vainglorious *Mean Business* was published in September of that year. When he took over at Sunbeam, I wrote a "memo to Al" that urged him to be a builder instead of an

355

asset stripper. When he wrote of the importance of his family in his book, I wrote a revealing article on his past that, among other things, reported that he did not even attend the funerals of his mother and father. All told, I have written five *Business Week* stories, including two cover-length features, on the executive in less than three years.

That coverage set the stage for the book in your hands. Despite repeated efforts to reach Dunlap, he and his handlers declined every request for cooperation. So did Dunlap's longtime associate, former Sunbeam vice chairman and chief financial officer Russell A. Kersh. However, more than 250 other executives, directors, advisers, and Dunlap acquaintances helped me provide what is essentially the non-fiction version of *Mean Business*. I am greatly indebted to them, especially those who displayed a great deal of courage by going on the record.

Thanks to their cooperation I have managed to reconstruct numerous scenes and extensive dialogue. In some cases sources actually wrote out line-by-line accounts of conversations as they remembered them. In piecing together dialogue I have attempted to interview as many participants as possible to gain the corroboration necessary to make the scenes as accurate as memory might allow. In some instances I interviewed as many as eight of ten people involved in a single discussion. I thank them for their patience and their indulgence.

The same is true of my family and friends. An undertaking like this requires loved ones willing to endure and tolerate obsessions and sacrifices. There were long periods of time when I virtually disappeared for days and weeks into the work of reporting and writing. At other times, even when I seemed present, I often was absorbed in the complexities of the book. I thank my wife, Sharon, and my wonderful children, Jonathan, Katie, and Sarah, for their love, for their understanding, and for their tolerance.

I also want to thank my editor at HarperCollins, David Conti, and my long-time agent Martha Millard. Conti, who edited my previous book, *Informed Consent,* at McGraw-Hill, was an enthusiastic supporter of this book from the start. So were Adrian Zackheim and Lisa Berkowitz at HarperCollins. Millard, who has been my agent since my first book was published fourteen years ago, intuitively knows when I need nudging and thankfully is not shy about poking and prodding me when I need it.

I especially want to thank my editors and colleagues at *Business Week* magazine, my professional home for more than a dozen years. I have been fortunate to work under one of the most influential editors of our time, Stephen B. Shepard, who has set extremely high standards for general excellence, accuracy, and fairness. I am indebted to him for granting me a leave of absence to focus exclusively on this book and for his continued faith and trust in me. I'd also like to thank Sarah Bartlett, Mark Morrison, Mark Vamos, and Bruce Nussbaum for their steady encouragement and support. My manuscript was much improved thanks to the comments and suggestions of several *Business Week* colleagues, especially Hardy Green, Jennifer Reingold, and David Leonhardt. Mark Vamos, who is now at *Smart Money,* also helped me polish a rough draft. He edited my first cover story on Dunlap and challenged me to rethink the article in a way that made it far more insightful, even if it did not endear me to Al.

When Dunlap was lobbying the *New York Times* for favorable coverage in late 1998, he told reporter Dana Canedy exactly what he thought of me. "If he were on fire, I wouldn't piss on him," Dunlap quipped. His public relations advisers complained that my past coverage of Dunlap was unfair and critical. I would agree with the latter, but not the former. I have made every effort to give Dunlap's side of the story, in every magazine article I have written about him and in this book. That is also why I have reprinted, in their entirety, the statements released by Dunlap and Kersh on July 9, 1998, in an appendix to the book. The truth, however, is not flattering to either of them.

APPENDIX

THE FOLLOWING STATEMENTS, drafted with the help of their lawyers, were released on July 9, 1998, as Albert J. Dunlap and Russell A. Kersh attempted to counter media coverage of their dismissal from Sunbeam Corp.

Dunlap Statement

"I believed in the future of Sunbeam and was confident that I would be able to turn it around.

"If I wasn't confident, I wouldn't have signed a three-year contract at the board's request in February. In fact, earlier this year I was approached to run other companies, but because I had a contract I didn't entertain those approaches. In February, the board asked me to sign a longer-term contract to assure that I would stay during the period when Sunbeam would be acquiring other companies and integrating them into Sunbeam. It is because I believed in the strategy and was confident I could make the strategy work that I entered into a three-year contract.

"I personally bought stock at my own expense and also received stock in compensation. I have never sold a single share or exercised an option, even at the top. My interests are identical with the interests of other Sunbeam shareholders, and like them since spring the value of my Sunbeam holdings has declined dramatically. I continue to own 1.491 million shares of Sunbeam. I have never sold a single share.

"I had turned Sunbeam's cost structure and operations around in a year. We positioned ourselves in the marketplace as a lean and strong company. 1998 is a transition year in which we bought some very powerful brands that resided in companies that were poorly run, requiring a further turnaround of the new companies and integration with Sunbeam.

"This spring we embarked on a growth strategy, the key to which was an equivalent turnaround of Coleman and [the] other two acquired companies.

"This second-phase turnaround was only just beginning. While I remain confident that I would have been able to turn the acquisitions around and integrate them with Sunbeam, Coleman's problems were even greater than we anticipated. Still, I am confident the strategy would have worked and that 1999 would have been a great year for Sunbeam.

"Sunbeam is still a work in progress, and only time will tell whether the strategy will work. I never got the chance to find out, being dismissed only 10 weeks after the acquisitions closed.

"I had no reason to doubt the accuracy of any financial statement Sunbeam made while I was CEO, and I have no reason to do so now.

"As CEO, I was expected to maintain an arm's length distance from the day-to-day operations of the audit committee and of the auditors, and I have maintained that distance throughout my tenure at Sunbeam. This is common at most large companies.

"At Sunbeam, I relied on the lawyers, audit committee, and auditors to do what they are expert at doing. I had no reason not to rely on them. My instructions to them were unambiguous and were repeated often: I wanted the truth and the facts; I couldn't manage the company without good information. Above all, I wanted accurate information and an honest assessment of our operations. This was my consistent style at every company I have run.

"The audit committee of independent directors and our general counsel were fully apprised of all financials and expressed comfort with them. David Fannin, who is executive vice president, general counsel and corporate secretary, was inextricably involved in preparation and review of all financial statements. He attended operating committee and audit committee meetings. He now expresses surprise, but did not express any concern to me when I was CEO. I understand that he has made certain statements implying that I had early knowledge of the deterioration of our business, but I had none beyond what I've publicly disclosed. I find his conduct now totally offensive.

"The audit committee of three independent directors—Charles Elson, Howard Kristol, and William Rutter—and our external auditor at Arthur Andersen reviewed all of our financials and expressed confidence in them. The audit committee is now expressing doubts they never expressed to me or to the board. I am shocked that they are shocked because I relied on them and they never expressed doubts to me.

"I never attended an audit committee meeting, did not direct preparation of the financial statements, did not have a personal relationship with our auditor, and did not direct any audit. Arthur Andersen was the company's auditor when I arrived at Sunbeam. Although I have long-standing relations with another auditing firm, I did not suggest replacing Arthur Andersen because they knew the company well and such a recommendation is within the purview of the audit committee.

"My instructions to all financial people at all times were to act always in ways that were morally and legally responsible and that met our fiduciary duty to shareholders. Our financial people were instructed that if there was a question of judgment, the question should be worked out with the auditors. I did not direct any particular interpretation of accounting principles.

"Sunbeam did indeed engage in certain 'bill-and-hold' transactions. But such transactions were proper under accepted accounting principles, and were done primarily for seasonal products where the customer requested storage of the purchased inventory on their behalf at third party warehouses.

"Recognizing a sale before payment is received is a normal business practice for every company—i.e., 'accounts receivable.' There is absolutely nothing improper about this practice.

"There was a clear transfer of title, risk of loss, etc., to the customer, the inventory was properly segregated, and all revenue recognition criteria under generally accepted accounting principles (GAAP) were met.

"At the June 9 board of directors meeting, the Arthur Andersen partner reaffirmed the appropriateness of this practice, and confirmed that the auditors had spoken to customers to confirm their understanding of the arrangements, which were consistent with ours.

"I directed that all sales be final, a policy that I consistently communicated and that was well-known throughout the company. The sales were genuine and all the merchandise was shipped in due course.

"Sunbeam was hit by an unfortunate convergence of two negative factors, the combination of which had an unexpected adverse effect on the financial performance of the company in the second quarter:

"a) We had some serious Sunbeam problems. As a company with seasonal product lines, we were hurt by the unduly warm winter and a wet spring that caused a lag in the sale of seasonal items such as electric blankets and grills. This was coupled by an unsuccessful marketing plan for grills and some problems with new products.

"b) Coleman, which we acquired on March 28, was in much worse shape than we expected. Sales were much worse than we thought, and we were trying to hire people to fill important management positions. As a result, the integration and turnaround of Coleman and the other recent acquisitions was taking longer than we expected.

"Sunbeam certainly isn't the only company to have very disappointing sales and earnings in the first two quarters of this year.

"We knew that the first quarter would be disappointing in March and promptly told investors what we knew. Problems continued into the spring.

"At the June 9 board meeting I told the board that this would be a difficult quarter that would fall short of expectations; that we should see 1998 as a transition year but that 1999 would be a great year. I also told them that I would keep them posted on our sales as I received information.

"It was only on Saturday, June 13, that I received a memorandum from Lee Griffith, president of household products, and Frank Feraco, president of outdoor leisure, informing me that the gap in sales had widened substantially in the quarter and laying out a plan to overcome the gap. The Coleman shortfall was a significant part of this gap. This was the first I had heard about the magnitude of the sales shortfall. I was dismissed about an hour later.

"I can't say whether the audit committee knew of this information earlier than I did, although they were in direct contact with operations.

"As CEO, I am ultimately responsible for the financial performance of the corporation, and I accept responsibility for Sunbeam's poor performance over the past two quarters.

"If the board chose to dismiss me because the company did not meet our projections, the board has that right. In my book I wrote, and I continue to believe, 'Directors are responsible for seeing that a company has proper management in place. They should monitor management to ensure it does what it is supposed to do. If not, the directors should take corrective action.'

"In this spirit, and aware of recent negative coverage suggesting problems at Sunbeam, at the June 9 board meeting I told the board that I needed their full support; that if I didn't have their full support they could pay me under the terms of my contract and dismiss me. At that meeting, the board unanimously expressed its support.

"Four days later, out of my presence, it appears that the board changed its mind. While I believe that their decision was ill-advised, and while the company is bound, in good faith, to honor my contract, I have no alternative but to accept their decision.

"Sunbeam is a work in progress, and only time will tell how the strategy will work. What I object to is dismissal on terms that are a clear violation of an unambiguous employment contract.

"I object to the suggestion that I had lost confidence in the company or in my ability to turn around the new company plus recently acquired companies. At the June 9 board meeting I reacted the way any normal human being would react who was being criticized relentlessly by outside parties for the poor performance of his company—I got frustrated.

"I object to the suggestion that sales or accounting practices at Sunbeam are suspect. The board cannot have it both ways: It cannot accept the findings of the audit committee and outside auditors and recognize that I maintained an appropriate arm's length distance from the audit committee and auditor, but suggest that I somehow was directly responsible for the accounting of 1997 numbers."

Kersh Statement

"There have been many press accounts quoting people within Sunbeam and its board suggesting that I and Al Dunlap withheld information from the board about Sunbeam's deteriorating sales position and otherwise engaged in questionable accounting practices.

"These suggestions are completely without merit and are contrary to the track record I and Al Dunlap have built at other companies where we worked.

"Al Dunlap's instructions to me, and my instructions to those who reported to Al and to me were very clear: We wanted the truth and the facts; we couldn't manage the company without good information. Above all I wanted accurate information and an honest assessment of our operations.

"Al's instructions to me at all times were to act always in ways that were morally and legally responsible and that met our fiduciary duty to shareholders, and I did. I instructed the same of those who reported to me.

"Al and I expected those who reported numbers to us to be factual and candid, and not to withhold negative information. Similarly, we shared negative information with the board, and disclosed it publicly, as it was known.

"With respect to the June 9 board meeting, I told the board at that meeting that sales continued to be soft. At the time we were still waiting for specifics from the field on what to expect in the quarter. Some days after the meeting, Al Dunlap received a memo from Lee Griffith, president of household products, and Frank Feraco, president of outdoor leisure, informing us that the sales gap had widened substantially in the quarter. This was the first we had heard about the magnitude of the sales shortfall. Al was dismissed about an hour later, and I was dismissed soon thereafter. I did not even see the memo until after I was dismissed."

NOTES & SOURCES

CHAPTER 1: MEAN BUSINESS
Page

1   *One by one*: Author's interviews with James Clegg, Richard Boynton, Rob Johnson, David Fannin, Paul O'Hara, James Wilson, Spencer Volk, and Charles Thayer.

3   *Survivors*: Author's interviews with Jerry Ballas, William Kirkpatrick, Dixon Thayer, Fannin, and Wilson.

3   *"Yeah, Al, I understand"*: Author's interview with Wilson.

4   *Roger Schipke was a quiet, unassuming man*: Author's interviews with Fannin, O'Hara, Wilson, Clegg, Boynton, Johnson, and Robert W. Schwinger.

5   *"He actually thought"*: Author's interview with Clegg.

5   *"It was like a dog barking"*: Author's interview with Boynton.

5   *Based on the presentation*: Author's interviews with Thayer and Fannin.

6   *"O'Hara is dead"*: Author's interview with Boynton.

8   *"It was shocking"*: Author's interview with Cynthia Clegg.

8   *Not content to simply fire him*: Author's interview with Fannin.

9   *The very next day*: Sunbeam press release dated July 24, 1996.

9   *The most unusual part*: Author's interviews with Wilson and over a dozen ousted Sunbeam executives.

CHAPTER 2: "I SO LOVE THEM"
Page

10   *The day after:* Author's interview with Andrew Shore.

10   *In the 1990s:* Joseph Nocera, "Who Really Moves the Market?," *Fortune,* Oct. 27, 1997, pp. 90–110. Also, author's interviews with several Wall Street analysts.

10   *Not all that long ago:* Ibid, p. 92.

11   *"This is like the Lakers signing Shaquille O'Neal.":* James R. Hagerty and Martha Brannigan, "Inside Sunbeam, Raindrops Mar Dunlap's Parade," *The Wall Street Journal,* p. B1. Also, author's interviews with Nicholas P. Heymann and William H. Steele.

11   *On a typical day:* Albert J. Dunlap with Bob Andelman, *Mean Business: How I Save Bad Companies and Make Good Companies Great* (New York: Simon & Schuster, 1996), p. 275.

11   *Shore simply didn't believe:* Author's interview with Shore.

11   *Schneider had become:* Institutional Investor, 1996.

12   *"Al Dunlap is the perfect . . . ":* Joann S. Lublin and Martha Brannigan, "Sunbeam Names Albert Dunlap as Chief, Betting He Can Pull Off a Turnaround," *The Wall Street Journal,* July 19, 1996, p. B2.

13   *Dunlap told the analysts:* Robert Frank, "Sunbeam's New CEO Begins to Revamp Management, Plans to Prune Products," *The Wall Street Journal,* July 25, 1996, p. A4.

14   *Shore wasn't impressed:* Ibid.

14   *But Shore held firm:* Andrew Shore, with Hari Chandra, "Let the games begin," PaineWebber research report, SOC0731 AS, July 31, 1996.

14   *Dunlap didn't suffer fools:* Author's interview with Wilson and Fannin.

15   *On October 3:* Author's interview with Shore and Chandra.

15   *Less than a week:* E.S. Browning and Eleena De Lisser, "Is It Time Yet To Cash Out of Sunbeam?," *The Wall Street Journal,* Sept. 27, 1996, p. C1–C2.

16   *After meeting with potential investors:* Dunlap, with Andelman, *Mean Business,* pp. 246–247.

17   *At night, the dogs:* Julie Waresh, "Cutting through the Bull with Al Dunlap," *The Palm Beach Post,* Inside Business, Oct. 20, 1997, pp. 18–23.

17   *When he and Judy:* Dunlap, with Andelman, *Mean Business,* p. 6.

18   *In his will:* Author's interview with confidential source.

18   The very next day: Shore, with Chandra and R.T. Quinn, "Dunlap 'means business,'" PaineWebber research report, Oct. 11, 1996.

CHAPTER 3: "STRIP ME NAKED!"
Page
20   *From the start*: Author's interviews with Al Dunlap for *Business Week*. John A. Byrne, "The Making of a Corporate Tough Guy," *Business Week*, Jan. 15, 1996, p. 61.

21   *After four years*: Dunlap, with Andelman, *Mean Business*, pp. 114–116.

21   *Meyer grew fond of Dunlap*: Author's interviews with Walter Gold and Charles Elson.

22   *The executives and managers*: Author's interviews with confidential sources.

22   *He cast himself*: Allen R. Myerson, "If I Were Playing Tiddlywinks with an 8-Year-Old, I'd Hate to Lose . . . ," *Georgia Trend*, January, 1986, pp. 50–54.

22   *His success at Lily*: Allan Sloan, TK, *Forbes*, Dec. 17, 1984, pp. 134–150.

23   *On the surface*: John Jay, "Goldsmith Rides Again," *The Sunday Times*, March 12, 1989. Also, author's interviews with confidential sources.

23   *"Strip me naked . . ."*: Patty Shillington, "Rambo in Pinstripes," *The Miami Herald*, June 5, 1995, p. 12.

24   *Of Goldsmith*: Author's interviews with Dunlap for *Business Week*.

24   *It was only with*: Author's interviews with confidential sources.

24   *His path to fame*: John A. Byrne, with Joseph Weber, "The Shredder: Chainsaw Al Dunlap pulled off a stunning turnaround at Scott Paper . . . Or did he?," *Business Week*, Jan. 15, 1996, pp. 56–61.

25   *But tough competition*: Author's interviews with Gary Roubos, Richard K. Lockridge, Dixon Thayer, Morgan Hunter, Frederick Christianson, Robert M. Dragone, John Butler, Greg Winfield, William Kirkpatrick, Jerry Ballas, Theodore R. Ramstad, and confidential sources.

25   *The only caution*: Author's interviews with Thomas Neff and Thomas Hardy.

26   *Within two months*: Byrne, with Weber, "The Shredder."

26   *"I got rid of nine . . . ,"*: Author's interview with Dunlap.

26   *In fact, Dunlap*: Author's interviews with confidential sources.

27   *"What he did was . . . ,"*: Author's interview with Ballas.

28   *To push more product*: Author's interview with Ballas and confidential sources.

28   *The human sacrifices*: Author's interviews with Donald L. Langham and Emory Michael Cole.

30   *Jerry Michael Chambless*: Author's interview with Jerry and Marty Chambless.

30   *Dunlap insisted*: Author's interviews with Dunlap.

31   *It was not as if*: Author's interview with Peter Judice.

31   *Dunlap had, of course*: Donna Rosato, "Analysts: Scott Paper is on a roll," *USA Today*, Oct. 11, 1994, p. 3B.

32   *Kimberly's red-faced CEO*: Stephanie Anderson Forest, "Pulp Fiction at Kimberly-Clark," *Business Week*, Feb. 23, 1998, pp. 90–91.

32   *Going into the merger*: Author's interview with Ballas and confidential sources.

33   *Once out of Scott*: Author's interviews with Neff, Hardy, and Gerard Roche.

34   *It was on an airplane*: Author's interview with Shimon Topor.

34   *Topor's session*: Author's interview with Peter Langerman.

35   *But it was Price*: Dunlap, with Andelman, *Mean Business*, p. 274.

35   *The investor had briefly met*: Author's interview with Michael Price.

36   *The deal Price eventually*: Sunbeam Corp. proxy statement, 1996.

36   *On July 18*: Author's interviews with Langerman, James Clegg, Richard Boynton, David Fannin, James Wilson, Charles Thayer, Richard Ravitch.

CHAPTER 4: PIRATES AND TRIBES
Page
38   *The Sunbeam Corp.*: Carleen Madigan, "Al Dunlap at Sunbeam," Harvard Business School case study, April 8, 1999, pp. 1–17.

38   *Like the country itself*: Sina Dubovoj, "Sunbeam-Oster Co., Inc.," Corporate Histories, pp. 484–486.

39   *Under the portly*: William C. Symonds, "Big Trouble at Allegheny: Lavish Perks, Poor Investments—And a Board That Let It Happen," *Business Week*, Aug. 11, 1986, pp. 56–61.

40   *It took nearly two years*: Author's interviews with Michael Lederman, Robert Setrakian, Marty Nussbaum, Charles Davidson, and confidential sources.

40   *After the Kazarian battle*: Author's interview with Roger Schipke.

41   *Executives huddled*: Author's interviews with Fannin, Wilson, and Goudis.

42   *Everyone toiled at a horrendous pace*: Author's interviews with Ronald L. Newcomb, Donald R. Uzzi, Newton White.

42   *No one was more trustworthy*: Dunlap, with Andelman, Mean Business, pp. 36–37.

43   *One Sunbeam consultant*: Author's interviews with William E. Frank, Jr., and Robert Beatty.

43   *If not for Dunlap*: Author's interview with confidential source.

43   *Though Kersh would never defy*: Author's interview with confidential source.

43   *It was certainly the allure*: Author's interview with Newt White.

44   *When Dunlap called him*: Author's interview with Dixon Thayer, Rick Brenner, and Greg Winfield.

45   *Only six days*: Author's interview with David Fannin.

46   *Dunlap cheerfully volunteered*: Author's interview with Dunlap for *Business Week*.

47   *"My philosophy is to err . . . "*: Dunlap, with Andelman, Mean Business, p. 174.

47   *For someone who had made a career*: Author's interviews with James Wilson, Donald Uzzi.

47   *No one in the company*: Author's interview with Richard Boynton.

49   *By early August*: Author's interviews with Fannin, Wilson, White, Boynton, and Michael Beauregard.

49   *On August 7:* Author's interviews with Beauregard, Boynton, Wilson, Paula Etchison, Ilya Frumpkin, and confidential sources.

51   *Rob Johnson*: Author's interview with Johnson.

52   *To the delight*: Author's interview with confidential sources.

52   *Still, he had more immediate worries*: Sharyn Bernard, "Sunbeam in for a Pruning," *HFN, The Weekly Newspaper for the Home Furnishing Network*, July 29, 1996, p. 1; and Ray Allegrezza and Sharyn Bernard, "Sunbeam Show of Strength: Outdoor President Reassures Buyers," *HFN*, Aug. 19, 1996, p. 31.

52   *Dunlap's arrival*: Ibid.

53   *It was not an idle question*: Author's interview with Johnson.

CHAPTER 5: ANOTHER DOWNSIZING
Page

56   *The true architect*: Author's interviews with Scott and Sunbeam executives and confidential sources.

56   *Burnett began working*: Dunlap, with Andelman, *Mean Business*, pp. 155–166.

57   *Burnett knew the rules*: Ibid, p. 157.

57   *By the Friday of his first week*: Glenn Collins, "For a Struggling Sunbeam Shock Therapy: Chainsaw Al Is Back for More," *The New York Times*, Aug. 11, 1996, cover Sunday business section.

58   *While Burnett's people*: Author's interviews with David Fannin and Rich Goudis.

58   *From the earliest point*: Author's interview with confidential sources.

58   *Price went further*: Author's interviews with Michael Price, Peter Langerman, and Raymond Troubh.

59   *Intent on shaping the board*: Author's interview with Richard Ravitch.

60   *Finally, in early April*: Author's interviews with Fannin and Charles Thayer.

60   *Dunlap, meantime, had begun to stack*: Author's interviews with Howard Kristol.

60   *To replace Ravitch*: Author's interviews with Faith Whittlesey.

61   *In Thayer's place*: Author's interview with William Rutter.

61   *Of all Sunbeam's new directors*: Author's interview with Charles Elson.

62   *Delighted by the market's reaction*: Glenn Collins, "Scott Paper to Pay Directors in Stock," *The New York Times*, Aug. 31, 1994; and "Scott Paper Co. to Pay Outside Directors in Stock," *The Wall Street Journal*, Aug. 31, 1994, p. B3.

63   *When panel member*: Author's interviews with John Nash, Nell Minow, and Elson.

63   *After panel member Barbara Franklin*: Author's interview with Elson.

65   *Elson hung up*: Joann S. Lublin, "Sunbeam's Chief Picks Holder Activist and Close Friend as Outside Director," *The Wall Street Journal*, Sept. 26, 1996, p. B1.

65   *On Wall Street*: Ron Scherer, "Towns Dread Job Cuts But Investors Applaud The Role of 'Chainsaw,'" *The Christian Science Monitor*, Nov. 8,

1966, p. 1–4; and, Glenn Collins, "Sunbeam's New Chief Is Expected to Disclose Cuts Today," *The New York Times*, Nov. 12, 1996.

66   *On November 12*: Author's interviews with Elson, Thayer, Langerman, and Kristol.

66   *The cutbacks Dunlap proposed*: Robert Frank and Joann S. Lublin, "Dunlap's Ax Falls—6,000 Times—At Sunbeam," *The Wall Street Journal*, Nov. 13, 1996, pp. B1-B12.

67   *"It wasn't a question . . . "*: Ibid.

68   *Within days*: Author's interview with Wilson.

68   *Contrary to what Dunlap*: Author's interview with White and confidential sources.

CHAPTER 6: COPING WITH THE AL DUNLAPS
Page

70   *"One of the main things . . . "*: Hedrick Smith, "Running with the Bulls," Surviving the Bottom Line, Public Broadcasting System special, 1997. This television documentary, available on video, is a superb examination of how changes on Wall Street have put new pressures on corporate management.

70   *"Those jobs were gone anyway . . . "*: "Enter Dunlap, Ax in Hand," *Fortune*, Dec. 9, 1996, p. 83.

71   *Only a year before*: Andrew E. Serwer, "The Scariest SOB on Wall Street," *Fortune*, Dec. 9, 1996, pp. 71–88.

72   *Al Dunlap's most important benefactor*: Author's interview with Michael Price.

73   *Price's father*: Alyssa A. Lappen, "True Value: Mutual Shares' Michael Price has made millions for himself and his clients by buying value. But as his funds grow, will performance suffer?," *Institutional Investor*, Nov. 1994, p. 109.

73   *A gentle and humble man*: Jeffrey M. Laderman, "Finding the Bucks Buried in Corporate Debris," *Business Week*, July 9, 1984, p. 92.

73   *To Heine, Price became the son*: Peter J. Tanous, *Investment Gurus*, (New York: Simon & Schuster, 1997), pp. 33–52.

74   *The opportunity*: Author's interview with Charles Davidson

76   *Price's differing philosophy*: "The Heine/Price Legacy," *Mutual Funds Online*, www.mfmag.com, November, 1966, cover story.

76   *The Sunbeam deal*: Author's interview with Price.

76   *Impressed by Kazarian's analysis:* Author's interviews with Michael Lederman, Robert Setrakian, Price, Langerman, and confidential sources.

78   *For the next few months:* Hilary Rosenberg, *The Vulture Investors* (New York: HarperBusiness, 1992), pp. 162–230. Author Rosenberg provides an insightful and highly detailed account of the Allegheny deal.

79   *They didn't have to convince Price:* Ibid, p. 179.

79   *As Price put it:* Ibid, p. 187.

79   *It was a role:* Author's interview with Lederman.

81   *"There was money . . . ":* Author's interview with James Clegg.

82   *Kazarian, however, was a tough:* Author's interviews with Clegg, Richard Boynton, Earle Maxwell, Robert Schwinger, Rob Johnson, Lederman, Setrakian, and confidential sources.

83   *Kazarian's behavior:* Ron Suskind and Suzanne Alexander, "Out of Control: Fired Sunbeam Chief Harangued and Hazed Employees, They Say; Kazarian Called 'Mad Genius' But Autocratic, Erratic, Insensitive to Women," *The Wall Street Journal*, Jan. 14, 1993, pp. 1, A6. Geoffrey Smith, "How to Lose Friends and Influence No One," *Business Week*, Jan. 25, 1993, p. 42.

83   *Though he had studied:* Author's interview with Langerman and confidential sources.

84   *The board:* Robert W. Lear and Boris Yavitz, "America's Best and Worst Boards," *Chief Executive*, April, 1994, pp. 32–39.

84   *"It went well . . . ":* Author's interview with Price.

84   *Kazarian, however, may simply:* Author's interviews with Lederman, Setrakian, and confidential sources.

85   *"Paul was brilliant . . . ":* Author's interview with Roderick Hills.

85   *After the initial flurry:* Susan Beck, "Framed? How Deposed Sunbeam-Oster CEO Paul Kazarian Was Set Up By His General Counsel and By a Not So 'Independent' Investigation," *The American Lawyer*, May, 1993, p. 41.

85   *What emerged from the court:* Suskind, Ibid; and Suskind, "Price Sought Carter Hawley Data, Memo Says," *The Wall Street Journal*, July 16, 1993, p. C1.

86   *Still in mid-1993:* Ron Suskind, "Delicate Situation: Mutual Fund Boss Has Brokerage-Firm Link That Interests the SEC: Michael Price Buys Big Stakes But Says He's Careful Not to Misuse Information," *The Wall Street Journal*, June 9, 1993, p. A1.

86   *Only a year earlier:* Michele Galen and Laura Zinn, "The SEC Trails a Value-Hunter," *Business Week,* June 1, 1992, p. 30.

87   *The bizarre battle:* Author's interviews with Charles Thayer, David Fannin, and Roger Schipke.

87   *Reached at Ryland:* Author's interview with Schipke.

88   *To his dismay:* Interview with Schipke.

88   *"He wasn't a kid . . . ":* Interview with Wilson.

89   *But Davidson:* Interview with Davidson.

90   *As the company's problems worsened:* Interviews with Clegg, Boynton, O'Hara, and Thayer.

91   *These were not near-misses:* Numbers based on internal company documents.

91   *Van Orden, Hills, and Thayer:* Interviews with confidential sources.

CHAPTER 7: RAMBO
Page

93   *On a bright, temperate day:* Interview with David Fannin.

93   *The only prop:* Interview with Andrew Itkoff.

93   *Dunlap later regretted:* Waresh, "Cutting through the bull with Al Dunlap," pp. 18–23.

94   *Early one Monday morning:* Interview with James Wilson.

96   *"Hi Scum Bag,":* Letter dated Aug. 11, 1996, written by Virginia Egan Dale. Interview with Dale.

96   *Since Dunlap joined Sunbeam:* Fred R. Bleakley, "Here's One Solution: Hire a Few Ex-Employees as Security Guards," *The Wall Street Journal,* Feb. 19, 1997, p. B1.

96   *Dunlap had learned:* Dunlap, with Andelman, *Mean Business,* p. 119.

96   *Sean Thornton:* Confidential interviews.

97   *But Dunlap was no:* Interview with Denise Dunlap.

97   *Until Dunlap turned eleven:* Louis Lavelle, "Boy Next Door to 'Rambo in Pinstripes,'" *The Sunday Record,* Nov. 10, 1996, p. 1-A16. Lavelle profile of Dunlap was the most in-depth piece ever written on the executive's background. The enterprising reporter was the first to reveal the details of Dunlap's divorce. Also, Byrne, "Who Is the Real 'Chainsaw Al?'." *Business Week,* Dec. 2, 1996, pp. 40–41.

98 *Even as a youth*: Author's interview with Andrew Kmetz.

98 *After he graduated*: Author's interview with Dunlap for *Business Week*.

99 *Up against stiffer competition*: Author's interviews with Ken Sindora and Philip A. Tripician.

99 *Soon after graduating:* Don Sider, "The Terminator," *People*, Nov. 25, 1996, pp. 77–80.

99 *Slender and tall*: Author's interview with the former Gwyn R. Donnelly.

100 *Almost from the start*: Gwyn B. Dunlap vs. Albert J. Dunlap, Superior Court of New Jersey, Chancery Division, Union County, civil action, complaint, filed in 1965. All of the specific incidents leading to Dunlap's divorce are taken from this court document. In a statement dated Nov. 20, 1996, provided to the author, Dunlap stated: "I think the fact that I have been happily married to my loving wife, Judy, for the past 29 years speaks volumes about the ridiculous allegations contained in the divorce papers of that time."

104 *The judge, however, found Dunlap guilty*: Gwyn B. Dunlap vs. Albert J. Dunlap, Superior Court of New Jersey, Chancery Division, Union County, civil action, judgment for divorce, by Judge William Fillmore Wood, Nov. 25, 1966.

104 *He eventually met his next wife*: Author's interview with Dunlap.

105 *Dunlap hoped to marry*: Waresh, "Cutting through the bull with Al Dunlap," p. 23.

105 *She also understood*: Smith, "Running with the Bulls," PBS special, 1997.

105 *If his new wife*: Author's interviews with Donnelly and Troy Dunlap.

106 *By the late 1980s*: Author's interview with Denise Dunlap. In a statement dated Nov. 20, 1996, provided to the author, Dunlap said: "My sister and I have had a strained relationship for many years. She has been and is prone to making up stories about me that are baseless or exaggerated. Despite that, I have supported her many times over the years, both financially and careerwise, but my efforts were never appreciated. Her claims about my relationship with my parents are unfounded. I loved them very much and helped them a great deal. I am deeply pained and saddened by her latest comments."

107 *His only family seemed*: Author's interviews with confidential sources.

108 *Indeed. In early November*: Author's interview with Fannin.

CHAPTER 8: THE BLANKET WITH A BRAIN
Page
110 *Coopers' Don Burnett*: Author's interview with Donald R. Uzzi.

110 *Wal-Mart:* Joann S. Lublin and Oscar Suris, "'Chainsaw Al' Now Aspires to Be 'Al the Builder,'" *The Wall Street Journal*, April 19, 1997, pp. B1–B10.

110 *Much of the turmoil:* Author's interview with Dixon Thayer.

111 *After the meeting:* Author's interview with James Wilson.

112 *When a new marketing:* Jonathan R. Laing, "High Noon at Sunbeam," *Barron's*, June 16, 1997, p. 29. Investigative reporter Laing wrote the first highly detailed story critical of Dunlap's reign at Sunbeam.

112 *Among other things:* Author's interviews with Uzzi, Wilson, David Fannin, and confidential sources.

115 *Dunlap's office:* Jacqueline Bueno, "On the Prowl," The Wall Street Journal, Sept. 24, 1997.

116 *"I just love predators . . . ":* Laing, "High Noon at Sunbeam," *Barron's*, p. 29.

116 *Displaying his own:* Author's interview with Uzzi, Fannin, and Wilson.

117 *Though the loss of those jobs:* Ron Scherer, "Towns Dread Job Cuts But Investors Applaud The Role of 'Chainsaw,'" *The Christian Science Monitor*, Nov. 8, 1966, p. 1–4.

117 *In an era of Wal-Marts:* Author's interview with John Few.

118 *Dominated by teetotaling:* Author's interview with Earle Maxwell.

120 *The mayor of Bay Springs:* Author's interview with Jerry Evon Smith.

120 *Dunlap was not only closing:* Author's interviews with confidential sources.

122 *It was, thought general counsel:* Author's interview with Fannin.

122 *Later Newcomb would admit:* Author's interview with Ronald Newcomb.

122 *The news that Dunlap:* Author's interview with Cherrie Mae Gammage.

123 *Some saw it:* Author's interview with Jack Montgomery.

124 *Like Gammage, Paul:* Author's interview with Paul Strickland.

CHAPTER 9: A QUIET REBELLION
Page
127 *Once the New Year:* Author's interviews with James Wilson, Ronald Newcomb, Mark A. Bohling, John Davenport, and others.

128 *One of the tearful:* Author's interview with Charlotte Redmon.

128 *Marsha Dunlap*: Author's interview with Marsha Dunlap.

129 *It was a classic niche*: Author's interviews with James Clegg, William Kirkpatrick, and confidential sources.

130 *Don Burnett's freshly minted*: Author's interview with Bohling.

131 *At 7 A.M. the next morning*: Author's interview with Robert Terhune.

131 *"It was a good business . . . "*: Smith, "Running with the Bulls," *Surviving the Bottom Line*, PBS special, 1997.

133 *Among other things*: Author's interview with Davenport.

134 *In January*: Author's interview with Donald R. Uzzi.

134 *Bohling never would have guessed it*: Author's interview with Kirkpatrick.

CHAPTER 10: THE SECRET ROOM
Page
141 *When analyst Andrew Shore*: Author's interviews with Andrew Shore and R. T. Quinn.

141 *At Scott Paper*: Byrne, with Weber, "The Shredder," pp. 56–61.

142 *To counter the image*: Patricia Sellers, "Can Chainsaw Be a Builder?," *Fortune*, Jan. 12, 1998, pp. 118–120.

143 The new air and water: Author's interviews with Paula Etchison, Susan Robertson, and Rich Seligson.

145 *Yet whenever anyone dared*: Author's interview with David Fannin.

146 *Meantime, as the team*: "Inside our Best Ideas," NatWest Securities, April, 1997.

147 *In the water filtration*: Andrew Shore, with Hari Chandra and R.T. Quinn, "Did Al show his hand too soon," PaineWebber research report, February, 6, 1998, SOC0206 AS, pp. 7–8.

148 *Uzzi believed*: Author's interview with Donald R. Uzzi.

150 *On October 8*: Waresh, "Cutting through the bull with Al Dunlap," pp. 18–23.

152 *Yet in the immediate aftermath*: Andrew Shore, with Hari Chandra and R.T. Quinn, "Beaming in on Phase III; upgrade to buy," PaineWebber research report, October 29, 1997, SOC1029 AS, pp. 1–11.

CHAPTER 11: THE DITTY BAG
Page

154 *"No matter what happened . . . ":* Author's interview with Ronald Newcomb.

154 *In Dunlap's presence:* Author's interview with confidential source.

154 *"In a meeting with Al . . . ":* Author's interview with William Kirkpatrick.

155 *The payoff would come:* Author's interview with James Wilson and company documents.

156 *After ordering his staff:* Author's interview with Donald R. Uzzi.

157 *"They would say . . . ":* Author's interview with Dixon Thayer.

158 *"We gave customers . . . ":* Author's interview with confidential source.

159 *Technical analysts:* Author's interview with William H. Steele. Later in the year, Howard Schilit, known as a forensic analyst who runs the Center for Financial Research & Analysis, also questioned the quality of Sunbeam earnings.

161 *Bill-and-hold sales are not standard:* Securities & Exchange Commission, Exchange Act Release No. 1787, June 26, 1981; SEC, Accounting and Auditing Enforcement Release No. 108, Aug. 5, 1986.

161 *The concept of doing:* Author's interviews with confidential sources.

162 *He had been hired:* Author's interview with Michael Lederman.

162 *"I'm not going to . . . ":* Author's interview with Thayer.

163 *It wasn't until three months later:* Author's interviews with Charles Elson, Howard Kristol, and confidential sources.

163 *Shortly into the discussion:* Minutes of a meeting of the Audit Committee of the Board of Directors of Sunbeam Corp., Jan. 26, 1998.

163 *Harlow said the transactions:* Ibid.

167 *In the often esoteric:* Author's interviews with confidential sources.

167 *Throughout the 1997 year:* Sunbeam Corp. amended Form 10K for 1997, which contains restated financial statements for 1996 and 1997, filed Nov. 12, 1998. Also, restatement conference call with Sunbeam CEO Jerry W. Levin on Oct. 20, 1998.

168 *Only days before the close:* Author's interviews with confidential sources.

168 *One customer returned:* Sunbeam internal documents.

169 *In doing the audit:* Author's interviews with confidential sources.

CHAPTER 12: "DON'T YOU THINK I'M A BARGAIN?"
Page

171 *"I want the management . . . "*: Brenda Buttner, "Under the Hood: Talking Stocks and Strategies with Michael Price," *TheStreet.com*, Nov. 13, 1997.

172 *"You gotta love Sunbeam . . . "*: Ibid.

172 *It was as if Price*: Michael F. Price, *Introduction to The Interpretation of Financial Statements*, (New York: HarperBusiness, 1998).

173 *As he delivered*: Author's interview with Nell Minow.

173 *There were links*: Author's interview with Robert A.G. Monks.

176 *As turnaround specialists go*: Author's interview with Robert S. Miller.

179 *Two weeks after the trip*: Jeff Bailey and Greg Jaffe, "When 'Chainsaw Al' Puts Pen to Paper, It Can Be a Massacre," *The Wall Street Journal*, Dec. 22, 1997, p. 1.

180 *Unbeknownst to Miller:* Author's interviews with Peter Langerman, Charles Elson, and confidential sources.

180 *When his only son*: Author's interview with the former Gwyn R. Donnelly.

180 *In 1997, he donated*: Author's interview with confidential sources.'

181 *"That guy buys a huge stake . . . "*: Buttner, "Under the Hood: Talking Stocks and Strategies with Michael Price."

182 *Price agreed to double*: Author's interview with Michael Price and Sunbeam proxy statement.

182 *Everyone on the board*: Author's interview with Charles Elson and confidential sources.

183 *"Goddamn it. . . ."*: Ibid.

185 *The deal was roundly criticized*: Graef "Bud" Crystal, "Rambo In Pinstripes! Give Us A Break!," *The Crystal Report*, March 12, 1998, pp. 1–3; also Dana Canedy, "Did Sunbeam go too far to keep Dunlap in its corner office?," *The New York Times*, March 18, 1998, p. D6.

185 *"Can you talk a little . . . "*: Wall Street conference call, March 2, 1998.

CHAPTER 13: "A TRIPLE!"
Page

187 *All of Dunlap's hopes*: Author's interviews with confidential sources.

187 *After being described*: Bryan Burrough and John Helyar, *Barbarians at the Gate* (New York: HarperCollins, 1991), pp. 195–197.

188 *Most of the Goldsmith*: Dunlap, with Andelman, *Mean Business*, pp. 71–72.

188 *Davis not only assumed*: Author's interviews with confidential sources.

190 *Though it would take*: Oscar Suris and Joann S. Lublin, "Sunbeam CEO Dunlap Explores Sales of Company or Launching Acquisition," *The Wall Street Journal*, April 7, 1997, p. B2. Also, Jacqueline Bueno, "Sunbeam to Study Takeover or Sale," *The Wall Street Journal*, Oct. 24, 1997, pp. A3, A6.

193 *When Whitwam came on the line*: Author's interview with David Fannin.

194 *When asked, a director*: Author's interview with Roger Schipke.

195 *Earlier in the year, news reports surfaced*: Dan Dorfman, "Coleman Seen Following Marvel as Perelman's Next Disaster," *Finanical World*, March 18, 1997, p. 14.

195 *Indeed, Perelman had chided*: Author's interview with Jerry W. Levin.

195 *All of investment banker Davis's*: Author's interview with Howard Gittis, Michael Price, and confidential sources.

197 *For the big rendezvous*: Author's interview with Fannin.

202 *"It was a good deal . . . "*: Author's interview with Levin.

202 *"Our favorite company"*: Kathryn M. Welling, "Price Conscious," *Barron's*, February 16, 1998, p. 30.

203 *As the negotiations moved*: Author's interview with Charles Elson.

205 *On February 27*: Author's interviews with confidential sources.

205 *Dunlap was jubilant*: Author's interview with Fannin.

206 *On Monday, Wall Street*: Dana Canedy, "Three Acquisitions by Sunbeam in Separate Deals," *The New York Times*, March 3, 1998, pp. D1, D6.

206 *Meeting with Perelman*: Author's interview with Gittis.

CHAPTER 14: INDECENT DISCLOSURE
Page

208 *No matter how hard*: Copy of speech by Al Dunlap.

209 *As Dunlap wooed*: Author's interview with David Fannin.

209 *At Skadden, Arps, Slate*: Author's interview with Finn Fogg.

210 *By keeping track*: Author's interview with Donald R. Uzzi and internal company documents.

210 *"How could this happen . . . "*: Author's interview with confidential sources.

211 *Now, on the telephone*: Author's interviews with Fannin and Uzzi.

212 *Their view was reaffirmed*: Author's interview with confidential sources.

212 *The Palace*: Dana Canedy, "Sunbeam Dances with Mr. D: Is Albert Dunlap Saving the Comany or Setting a Sale?," *The New York Times*, Dec. 23, 1997, p. D1.

213 *Dunlap kept screaming*. Author's interviews with Fannin and confidential sources.

215 *As the news hit*: Dana Canedy, "A Big Sales Gain for Sunbeam Proves Costly to Investors," *The New York Times*, May 7, 1998, pp. D1, D12.

216 *The announcement had created*: Author's interview with Rich Goudis.

216 *Late one afternoon*: Memo obtained by the author from a source other than the person who wrote the memo.

218 *Under the arrangement*: Author's interview with confidential sources.

218 *Dunlap had been involved*: Aggravated battery report filed with the Boca Raton Police Dept., Incident No. 9800007520, Feb. 1, 1998. Also, supplement report by Officer G.T. Kosova, filed on same day.

219 *But many of his colleagues*: Author's interviews with Donald R. Uzzi, Rich Goudis, and Andrew Shore.

221 *No one, not even*: Dana Canedy, Sunbeam's Stock Falls 9.4% on Lower Projections for Revenue," *The New York Times*, March 20, 1998, p. D2.

221 *Even worse*: Author's interviews with confidential sources.

221 *That kind of bluster*: Dunlap, with Andelman, *Mean Business*, p. 258.

222 *"Sunbeam is an earnings-driven . . . "*: Canedy, "Sunbeam's Stock Falls 9.4% on Lower Projections for Revenue," p. D2.

222 *In retrospect*: Author's interview with Fannin.

222 *As angry and volatile*: "Sunbeam's Cloudy Outlook: Chainsaw Al Warns on Profits," *The New York Post*, March 20, 1998.

223 *That is where*: Author's interview with Thomas Hardy.

225 *When Kersh returned*: Author's interview with Fannin.

CHAPTER 15: AN ANALYST'S CALL

Page

227 *"You didn't try hard enough . . . "*: Author's interview with Donald R. Uzzi.

232 *When Kersh relayed*: Author's interview with David Fannin.

233 *"Look," said Kersh*: Author's interviews with Uzzi and Fannin.

234 *But it was also growing*: Author's interview with Deidra DenDanto and confidential sources.

237 *All the loading*: Author's interviews with confidential sources.

238 *By gaining two extra days*: Andrew Shore, with Hari Chandra and R.T. Quinn, "Blame it on the reign," PaineWebber research report, SOC0528, May 28, 1998, pp. 5–6.

238 *Rich Goudis, who normally*: Author's interviews with Rich Goudis and Fannin.

239 *Andrew Shore was fast asleep*: Author's interviews with Andrew Shore and R.T. Quinn.

242 *Two hours earlier*: Author's interview with Goudis and Fannin.

244 *Unable to cancel*: Author's interviews with Shore and Quinn.

245 *Fannin was in his office*: Author's interview with Fannin.

245 *At least one person*: Author's interview with confidential sources.

246 *Back in New York*: Author's interviews with Shore and Quinn.

247 *He insisted that the market*: Dana Canedy, "A Warning by Sunbeam Stuns Wall St., Revenue Forecast Sends Stock Plummeting 24%," *The New York Times*, April 4, 1998, pp. D1-D14.

247 *Shore's Wall Street colleagues*: Various research reports.

247 *Surprisingly, though, Dunlap*: Author's interview with Nicholas P. Heymann.

248 *For Kersh*: Author's interview with DenDanto.

CHAPTER 16: "EXCUSE ME, I'M NOT A COOK!"
Page
250 *The day after Easter Sunday*: Author's interview with confidential sources.

251 *Within the past sixteen months*: Author's interview with Peter Judice, Geoffrey Smith, and confidential sources. Also, "Hill & Knowlton and Sunbeam to Split," *The New York Times*, May 8, 1998, p. D18.

253 *Donald Burnett*: Author's interviews with confidential sources.

255 *Reading from a thirty-six page*: Internal company documents.

256 *Dunlap let Kersh deliver*: Ibid.

257   *Some of the "synergistic" ideas*: Ibid.

257   *Only a few days before*: Matthew Schifrin, "The Unkindest Cuts," *Forbes*, May 4, 1998, p. 44. Schifrin was the first journalist to report on Sunbeam's bill-and-hold sales. He also was the first to express skepticism that Dunlap could turn around Sunbeam. (See "Chainsaw Al to the Rescue?," *Forbes*, Aug. 26, 1996, p. 42.)

258   *The source who tipped off*: Author's interviews with Matthew Schifrin and Meyer A. Berman.

261   *When Michael Price read*: Author's interviews with Michael Price and Schifrin.

261   *At the board session*: Author's interviews with confidential sources.

261   *Dunlap seemed restless*: Author's interviews with Charles Elson and Peter Langerman.

262   *Like Langerman, Price thought*: Author's interview with Price.

CHAPTER 17: "I'LL COME BACK AT YOU TWICE AS HARD"
Page

264   *Though Dunlap was in a struggle*: Author's interviews with confidential sources.

265   *Perelman, his boss, was becoming*: Martha Brannigan, "For Perelman, Sunbeam Stake Turns a Bit Pale," *The Wall Street Journal*, June 4, 1998, p. C1.

265   *Shore had gotten to know*: Author's interview with Andrew Shore.

267   *"My senior management team . . . "*: Albert Dunlap speech before Wall Street analysts, May 11, 1998.

267   *Sitting next to his boss:* Author's interview with R.T. Quinn.

268   *After another analyst asked*: The dialogue between Dunlap and Shore is taken verbatim from a tape of the May 11th analyst presentation.

270   *Afterward, as Shore was walking out*: Author's interview with Shore and Quinn.

270   *In a breakout room*: Author's interviews with confidential sources.

270   *"Look," Price told her*: Patricia Sellers, "Sunbeam Investors Draw Their Knives: Exit for Chainsaw?," *Fortune*, June 8, 1998, pp. 30–31.

271   *"Am I afraid of losing my job?"*: Ibid.

271   *Three of the directors*: Author's interview with Charles Elson.

271 *A lengthy discussion*: Audit Committee meeting minutes dated May 11, 1998.

271 *At the session*: Author's interviews with directors.

272 *In the ballroom*: David Sedore, "Sunbeam Stands by Its Man," *The Palm Beach Daily Business Review,* May 14, 1998, p. A1.

273 *One of the few shareholders*: Author's interview with Arthur Jacowitz.

273 *But the stock wasn't*: Dana Canedy, "Amid Big Losses, Sunbeam Plans To Cut 6,400 Jobs and 8 Plants," *The New York Times,* May 12, 1998, pp. D1, D12.

273 *"I took your advice . . . "*: Author's interviews with confidential sources.

CHAPTER 18: "TOO RICH AND FAMOUS"
Page
275 *Only twenty-four days after wooing Wall Street*: Author's interviews with confidential sources and internal company documents.

275 *Throughout his career*: Author's interviews with Jerry Ballas, Dixon Thayer, William Kirkpatrick, and confidential sources.

277 *A memo given to Dunlap*: Internal company documents.

278 *Remarkably, however, Dunlap seemed resigned*: Author's interview with David Fannin.

278 *Before they departed*: Author's interview with Frank Feraco.

279 *In any case*: Internal company documents.

282 *Even Chainsaw seemed unimpressed*: Author's interviews with confidential sources.

CHAPTER 19: "YOU WANT TO QUIT?"
Page
283 *Just after lunch*: Author's interview with David Fannin.

283 *It was already turned*: Jonathan R. Laing, "Dangerous Games," *Barron's,* June 8, 1998, pp. 17–18.

284 *Dunlap was livid.* Author's interview with Fannin.

284 *Then, there had been*: Dana Canedy, "A Big Sales Gain for Sunbeam Proves Costly to Investors," *The New York Times,* May 7, 1998, pp. D1, D12.

284 *"I really see a conspiracy . . . "*: Author's interview with Fannin.

286 *Peter Langerman found the story*: Author's interview with Peter Langerman.

287   *Charles Elson*: Author's interview with Charles Elson.

289   *For much of that Sunday*: Author's interview with Fannin.

290   *"I know that I am a controversial figure . . . "*: "Sunbeam Corp. Responds to Barron's Article," company press release, June 8, 1998.

290   *When Dunlap did get out*: David Weidner, "Rough Welcome from Bankers for Sunbeam CEO Pitching $2B Loan," *The American Banker,* June 11, 1998, p. 29.

291   *Upstairs, in a sparse*: Author's interviews with confidential sources.

295   *Fannin was just as confounded*: Author's interview with Fannin.

296   *When Dunlap stormed out*: Author's interviews with confidential sources.

297   *When the meeting finally*: Author's interview with Elson.

CHAPTER 20: A MATTER OF CONSCIENCE
Page
299   *David Fannin had just about*: Author's interview with David Fannin.

300   *Fannin's wife*: Author's interview with Lucille Fannin.

302   *For Peter Langerman, it was*: Author's interview with Peter Langerman.

303   *What he heard*: Author's interviews with Howard Gittis, Jerry Levin, and Langerman.

304   *That evening*: Author's interview with Fannin.

304   *When Dunlap returned*: Author's interviews with confidential sources.

306   *On Wall Street, only a single*: Author's interview with Nicholas Heymann.

307   *A week before the May 11 meeting*: Memo to Al Dunlap from Nick Heymann, Re: Critical Issues for May 11th Meeting with Investment Community, dated May 4, 1998.

307   *"You either pull it off . . . "*: Ibid.

307   *After the publication*: Memo to Al Dunlap from Nick Heymann and Larry Feiler, Re: Follow-up Thoughts from Our Phone Call 6/12/98, dated June 12, 1998.

307   *"We are currently at . . . "*: Ibid.

308   *David Fannin was not*: Author's interview with Frank Feraco.

313   *The next day*: Author's interview with Fannin.

315   *Roughly sixteen blocks south*: Author's interviews with Charles Elson and Howard Kristol.

CHAPTER 21: WHAT GOES AROUND, COMES AROUND
Page
317   *The directors met promptly*: Author's interview with confidential sources.

317   *Rutter, the local banker*: Author's interview with William Rutter.

318   *Fannin had spent*: Author's interview with David Fannin.

320   *"Well, my mind is made up . . . "*: Author's interview with Charles Elson.

322   *While the directors were deliberating*: Author's interview with Frank Feraco.

323   *Back in New York*: Author's interviews with confidential sources.

324   *"Do we have Al . . . "*: From script prepared by outside counsel for directors.

324   *But Elson could not*: Author's interview with Elson.

CHAPTER 22: "I SCREWED THE POOCH!"
Page
328   *Jerry W. Levin:* Author's interview with Jerry Levin and Howard Gittis.

329   *When the platoon*: Author's interview with confidential sources.

331   The directors agreed: Author's interview with Levin.

333   *"He is the logical extreme . . . "*: Author's interview with David M. Friedson.

333   *Even the long-estranged members*: Author's interviews with Troy Dunlap and Denise Dunlap.

333   *At home, he sank*: Martha Brannigan and Ellen Joan Pollock, "Dunlap Offers Tears and a Defense," *The Wall Street Journal*, July 9, 1998, pp. B1.

333   *On the day he sauntered*: Dunlap's quotations are taken from a videotape of the Moneyline show.

336   *Watching the interview*: Author's interview with Charles Elson.

336   *But his most telling comment*: Author's interview with confidential source.

337   *Sunbeam took a full*: Jeffrey M. Laderman, "Michael Price's Retirement: What It Means," *Business Week Online*, July 29, 1998.

337 *Price chose to limp off stage*: Allan Sloan, "Price Cuts and Runs: A Star Manager Bails Out of His Sagging Mutual Funds. But Maybe You Shouldn't," *Newsweek*, Aug. 10, 1998, p. 69.

338 *Yet, in the aftermath*: Sallie L. Gaines, "Sun Sets on 'Chainsaw Al'," *The Chicago Tribune*, June 16, 1998, p. 1.

338 *Price believed the stock's true value*: Author's interview with Michael Price.

339 *If Sunbeam's descent*: Christopher Byron, "Ron Perelman, Wall Street Stickup Man," *The New York Observer*, Aug. 24, 1998, pp. 1–19.

340 *The day Andrew Shore*: Author's interview with Andrew Shore and R.T. Quinn.

342 *If Sunbeam was one of Shore's*: Author's interview with Nicholas Heymann.

344 *At Sunbeam, Levin*: Author's interview with Levin.

345 *It took, however, nearly four months*: "Sunbeam to Restate Financial Results: Discloses Adjustments for 1996, 1997 and First Quarter of 1998," company press release, dated Oct. 20, 1998.

346 *The Wall Street Journal*: Martha Brannigan, "Sunbeam Audit Finds a Mirage, No Turnaround," *The Wall Street Journal*, Oct. 20, 1998, p. A3.

346 *Dunlap's crippling impact*: Author's interview with Levin.

347 *Some of the company's*: John A. Byrne, "At Least Chainsaw Al Knew How to Hire a Board," *Business Week*, June 29, 1998, p. 40.

348 *For the thousands*: Author's interviews with various named sources.

349 *After clipper boss*: Author's interview with William Kirkpatrick.

350 *Before their dismissal*: Author's interview with Levin.

APPENDIX:
Page

359 "Albert J. Dunlap Affirms He Had No Reason to Doubt Accuracy of Sunbeam Financial Statements," July 9, 1998, press release issued by Clark & Weinstock, New York.

363 "Statement of Russ Kersh on Sunbeam," July 9, 1998, press release issued by Clark & Weinstock, New York.

INDEX